EXCLUSIONS

EXCLUSIONS

PRACTICING PREJUDICE
IN FRENCH LAW AND
MEDICINE, 1920–1945

JULIE FETTE

CORNELL UNIVERSITY PRESS
Ithaca and London

First published 2012 by Cornell University Press

Printed in the United States of America

Library of Congress Cataloging-in-Publication Data

Fette, Julie, 1967–
    Exclusions : practicing prejudice in French law and medicine, 1920–1945 / Julie Fette.
        p. cm.
    Includes bibliographical references and index.
    ISBN 978-0-8014-5021-1 (cloth : alk. paper)
    1. Lawyers—France—History—20th century.
    2. Physicians—France—History—20th century.
    3. Professions—Social aspects—France—History—
20th century.   4. Discrimination in employment—France—
History—20th century.   I. Title.
KJV172.F48   2012
344.4401'133—dc23   2011038589

Cloth printing   10 9 8 7 6 5 4 3 2 1

For Talia Mae

Contents

 # ACKNOWLEDGMENTS

Many people have helped me with this book. Herrick Chapman at New York University and Gérard Noiriel at the École des hautes études en sciences sociales have been invaluable mentors since its inception. Herrick Chapman incarnates the ideal role model: honest, committed, and passionate about rigorous scholarship. It is impossible to take stock of the ways in which he has fostered my academic growth. I am grateful for his generosity of spirit. Gérard Noiriel has been a great inspiration. He has taught me to ask hard questions of history, and to have the courage to propose unconventional answers. I also sincerely thank Vicki Caron, whose enthusiasm and magnanimity compete with her vast expertise in the subject matter of this book.

I have been lucky to be in the regular company of scholars whom I admire. So many of them have contributed valuable suggestions, beginning in the early phases of my research, especially Eric Fassin, Nancy Green, Shanny Peer, Jacques Revel, Martin Schain, and Patrick Weil. Still others have spent time discussing ideas with me at various stages: Christian Baudelot, J. D. Bindenagel, Christophe Charle, Donna Evleth, Catherine Fillon, Sarah Fishman, Christoph Irmscher, Jonathan Judaken, Sara Kimble, Francine Muel-Dreyfus, Christophe Prochasson, Denis Provencher, Victor Rodwin, Clifford Rosenberg, Henry Rousso, Judith Schneider, Willa Silverman, the late Nicholas Wahl, and Robert Zaretsky. Their exchanges with me have had lasting impact.

Several archivists and librarians aided my research: Stéphanie Méchine and David Peyceré at the archives of the Académie de Paris, Régis Rivet at the library of the École de médecine in Paris, Ségolène Barbiche and Bernard Vuillet at the Archives nationales, Yves Ozanam of the library of the Ordre des avocats in Paris, Vincent Tuchais at the Archives de Paris, Aliette Wintrebert at the Ordre des médecins, and Sandi Edwards at Fondren Library of Rice University.

I am very grateful to several institutions for intellectual and financial support. First and foremost is the Institute of French Studies at New York University, that special hub of intellectual discovery, my first academic home. I greatly appreciate the support given by NYU's Graduate School of Arts and Science for a MacCracken Fellowship and a Dean's Dissertation Fellowship, by the French government for a Bourse Chateaubriand, and by the University of North Carolina, Chapel Hill's Institut français de Washington for a Gilbert Chinard Fellowship. My three home institutions throughout the course of the later phases of my writing, Mount Holyoke College, the University of Maryland Baltimore County, and Rice University, have all offered grants for follow-up research. At Rice, I am particularly grateful for a Faculty Research Fellowship from the Humanities Research Center as well as steady support from the Department of French Studies and the School of Humanities.

I thank the publishers of the following chapters and articles, portions of which appear in this book: "The Apology Moment: Vichy Memories in 1990s France," in *Taking Wrongs Seriously: Apologies and Reconciliation,* ed. Elazar Barkan and Alexander Karn, 259–285, copyright 2006 by the Board of Trustees of the Leland Stanford Jr. University, all rights reserved, used with the permission of Stanford University Press, www.sup.org; "Pride and Prejudice in the Professions: Women Doctors and Lawyers in Third Republic France," *Journal of Women's History* 19, no. 3: 60–86, published and copyright 2007 by The Johns Hopkins University Press; "Xenophobia in the Professions: From the Third Republic to the Fifth," *Contemporary French Civilization* 21, no. 2 (2007): 9–38; "Apology and the Past in Contemporary France," *French Politics, Culture and Society* 26, no. 2 (2008): 78–113; and "Apologizing for Vichy in Contemporary France," in *Historical Justice in International Perspective: How Societies are Trying to Right the Wrongs of the Past,* ed. Manfred Berg and Bernd Schaefer, 135–163, copyright 2009 by the German Historical Institute, reprinted with the permission of Cambridge University Press.

People are what make the institutions matter, and the colleagues I have met in each university have influenced my work in many ways. At Rice University, I thank José Aranda, Bernard Aresu, Jean-Joseph Goux, Deborah Harter, Deborah Nelson-Campbell, and Philip Wood in the Department of French Studies. In addition, my gratitude goes to Carl Caldwell, Nana Last, Caroline Levander, Nanxiu Qian, and Lora Wildenthal for their penetrating comments, quick answers, indefatigable encouragement, and friendship. Many thanks also to Leticia Gonzales, Bill Klemm, and Theresa Grasso Munisteri for their support, as well as to undergraduate student Nga Yin Lau for her research assistance under the auspices of the Humanities Research Center.

I have enormous admiration for the people at Cornell University Press. Working with John Ackerman has been a pleasure, and I also thank Susan Specter, the manuscript readers, and all others who have been so professional and so kind.

I am profoundly grateful to my family and friends for having shared this journey with me with patience and enthusiasm. I thank all of them, too many to mention here, for supporting this endeavor over the years. Fellow IFS travelers have remained true: Scott Gunther, Mary Lewis, Claire Kerisel Miquel, William Poulin-Deltour, John Savage, and Sylvie Waskiewicz. I also thank Susan Claffy for standing by me daily in Houston. And I would be nowhere without the faithfulness of my three sisters.

Two very special people have been instrumental in the production of this book. Marie Benedict, stalwart editor and devoted friend, never ceased to amaze me with her inspiration, tirelessness, and humor. And Carolen Amarante comforted and fortified me through moments of darkness with her unwavering support. I am indebted to both, and this book would not have come to be without either of them.

Finally, this book is dedicated to a shining star, a precious gift: Talia Mae Cohen-Fette, my daughter. May her world be freer of exclusions.

 EXCLUSIONS

Introduction

In France between the two World Wars, lawyers and doctors complained that their professions were overcrowded, especially, they claimed, with foreigners and naturalized citizens. Activists rallied their fellow professionals to form a social movement and lobbied for state intervention to exclude undesirable competitors from the professions. These lobbying efforts were successful. New legislation in the 1930s banned naturalized French citizens from careers in law and medicine for up to ten years after they had attained French nationality. This was extraordinary: interest groups persuaded legislators to create a second-class level of citizenship in France. French lawyers and doctors continued their protectionist mobilization throughout the late 1930s, which culminated during the Vichy regime with another historical precedent: legislation imposing a 2 percent quota on Jews in both professions. Through the Law Order and the Medical Order (organizational structures that regulated the professions) during Vichy, it was lawyers and doctors themselves who evaluated their colleagues who were of foreign origin or Jewish and designated them for exclusion.

Three motivations explain this exclusionary movement: prejudice, economic protectionism, and a less obvious third instinct, professional identity-formation. In the 1920s and 1930s, medicine and law were both in the midst of a difficult transition from Old Regime corporatist orders based on honor and tradition to republican *professions libérales* based on meritocracy and professionalization, which made the arrival in their ranks of new social categories such as foreigners, naturalized citizens, women, and lower classes particularly threatening. By designating certain social groups as undesirable, lawyers and doctors sought to bolster the solidarity of their corps and enhance their homogeneity and prestige.

The socioeconomic stresses of the interwar period, particularly those of the 1930s, exacerbated lawyers' and doctors' anxieties about their status. Taken together, the economic depression, increasing competition among professionals, educational democratization, and an influx of educated immigrants and refugees contributed to fears of downward mobility and loss of distinction. Anti-Semitism was yet another factor in the middle-class lobbying for economic protection in France from the mid-1930s to the mid-1940s. Nevertheless, these interwar developments were part of a pattern that extended over a much longer period. Professionalization, protectionism, and xenophobia all predated the Great War and would remain prevalent themes in law and medicine after 1945. Although most of Vichy's discriminatory laws were repealed with the establishment of the Fourth Republic, the legislative restrictions on the right of naturalized French citizens to practice law and medicine remained in force until the late 1970s. This book, therefore, begins with a chapter on the origins of professional exclusion in the nineteenth century, when the foundations were laid for xenophobic surges in the interwar period, and ends with two chapters on the Vichy era, when professional xenophobia and anti-Semitism reached a historical paroxysm.

Lawyers and doctors were not the only interest groups to agitate and lobby for protections against foreigners during the 1920s and 1930s in France. Shopkeepers, artisans, and manual laborers, as well as dentists, midwives, veterinarians, and engineers banded into separate pressure groups, initiated press campaigns backed by inflated statistics on competition, scapegoated foreigners, engaged in strikes and demonstrations, lobbied politicians, and succeeded in various ways in reducing foreigners' participation in their fields.[1] The anti-foreigner movement within the liberal professions had unique characteristics, but it was part of a broader French drive for nationalistic protectionism.[2]

Focused on the elite fields of law and medicine within the complex setting of interwar and Vichy France, this book explores the intersections of xenophobia, economic self-defense, and professionalization. Lawyers and doctors represented a powerful force in French society, exercising their will in the educational, professional, and political domains. Standing at the crossroads of knowledge and power, lawyers and doctors offer a compelling perspective on discrimination.[3] They had long been dominant forces in French society: they ran the hospitals and the courts; they doubled as university professors; they were the most highly represented occupational groups in parliament and government during the Third Republic; they administered justice and public health for the nation. Not only did their status enable them to achieve their professional protectionist goals but their social and political influence was also crucial in spreading xenophobic attitudes and rendering them socially acceptable in France. Lawyers and doctors played a critical role in constructing representations of "others" and erecting barriers against them.

I analyze the motivations and strategies of lawyers, doctors, and students as a social movement "from below," in which outspoken individuals rallied colleagues to their cause, corporatist groups formulated exclusion into an official professional platform, and influential leaders guided legislative initiatives successfully into law. To grasp this veritable social movement—ultimately as a form of public opinion—I have grounded my research in sources emanating from doctors, lawyers, and students themselves and from the groups that represented them. At the Bibliothèque inter-universitaire de médecine (BIUM) at the University of Paris Medical School, I examined journals of medical student associations, medical school annals, student guides, medical dissertations, and monthly publications of medical unions from across France. At the Bibliothèque de l'Ordre des avocats du barreau de Paris, I garnered equivalent material for the legal profession. Complementary legal research was effectuated at the University of Paris Law School's Bibliothèque Cujas for law student association publications as well as parliamentary debates. At the Archives du Rectorat de l'Académie de Paris, I consulted materials concerning the university: journals of student associations, student tracts and petitions, correspondence among university personnel, police reports of political activity in the Latin Quarter, deans' reports to the rector, and reports on "intellectual unemployment" published by the Bureau universitaire de statistique. The Archives nationales provided a mass of critical sources from state organs. Notably, I was able to consult the Vichy-era archives of the Medical Order recently deposited in the contemporary division in Fontainebleau. Finally, memoirs and autobiographies of doctors and lawyers were consulted at the Bibliothèque nationale.

How well did professional organizations represent the opinions, desires, and concerns of doctors and lawyers? Approximately 80 percent of doctors were members of a medical union represented by the Confédération des syndicats médicaux français in 1930, and the Association nationale des avocats counted as members about half of all lawyers in the 1930s. If these organizations' representation of lawyers and doctors was imperfect, their influence in political circles was clear. When state actors wished to gauge public opinion in medicine and law, they consulted directly with these groups, and in many cases faithfully satisfied their demands. The French government gave the Confédération an advisory role in assessing naturalization candidates in medical fields. The petition from one dominant legal association, the Union des jeunes avocats, was adopted verbatim as the text of the legislation that banned new French citizens from entering the bar within ten years of their naturalization.

★ ★ ★

The seven chapters of the book proceed both chronologically and thematically. The medical and legal professions are examined together in chapter 1, where I trace professional transformations in law and medicine from the French Revolution to the early twentieth century, with a focus on battles over occupational turf. The forging of scientific, professionalized legal and medical fields, debates on conditions of access for practitioners, strategies to monopolize the health care and legal markets, and attempts to restrict certain categories of people from the practice of medicine and law are all related histories, and histories of *longue durée*. As part of the educated bourgeoisie, lawyers and doctors shared a self-image as natural representatives of the Third Republic, yet their notion of status was often at variance with the republicanism of the French Revolution. As a result of the democratization of education, the 1890s witnessed exclusionary flare-ups among lawyers and doctors that foreshadowed their interwar eruption.

Chapters 2 and 3 examine the movement to protect the medical profession between the wars. Two pieces of legislation in 1933 and 1935 instituted major restrictions on access to careers in medicine, requiring practicing doctors to have French nationality and a *diplôme d'état*. Detectable in the 1920s, anti-foreigner sentiment gradually intensified into an exclusionary frenzy by the end of the 1930s. The criterion of nationality was central to the protectionism in French medicine between the wars, but in chapter 3 I argue that classism and sexism were also prevalent in corporatist discourse and action. Fear of downward mobility was one factor that created a general climate of resentment against various kinds of competitors, regardless of national origins. Doctors targeted reputedly ill-prepared secondary students in an attempt to raise the intellectual standards of the profession. Proposals challenging women's right to access stemmed from fear that the traditional medical identity based on male honor codes was being undermined. Through quality-control measures, turf battles among practitioners, and the promotion of "masculine" values, the medical corps devised strategies unrelated to xenophobia to craft a distinctive professional identity. At stake ultimately was the profession's status in a meritocratic republic.

The structure of the law bar gave lawyers a critical edge over doctors in the quest for control over professional membership and identity-formation. Forced by legislation to accept women lawyers, the law bars nonetheless maintained authority over their membership and polished their image as an elite club. Chapter 4 reveals how lawyers worked to increase their profession's exclusivity by invigorating educational requirements and marginalizing competitors who were not members of the bar, such as legal consultants. Restrictions on naturalized citizens in the legal profession are the subject of chapter 5. Lawyers had long been insulated by a corporatist barrier unavailable to doctors, and gained further protections in 1934 when the French parliament legislated a ten-year assimilation period before naturalized citizens could practice law.

Members of the Chamber of Deputies, many of whom were lawyers, rationalized this precedent-setting restriction by equating law practice with public service. Whereas doctors led a feverish and public mobilization against foreigners and naturalized citizens, lawyers succeeded through quiet influence peddling. The exclusionary legislation was much more severe for naturalized lawyers than for naturalized doctors. The retroactive application of the discriminatory law stands out as particularly significant, coming as it did from legal professionals in a democratic regime.

After the "phony war," the Occupation, and the collapse of the Third Republic, the legal and medical professions continued to pursue their agendas of exclusion, which fell on fertile ground under the Vichy regime. In late summer 1940, legislation was adopted expelling French persons born of a foreign father from the professions, and in 1941 the Vichy government passed laws imposing a quota of 2 percent on Jews allowed to practice law or medicine. At least two thousand people were deprived of their livelihoods as a result of these exclusions. Paying close attention to professionals' decisions as to which of their colleagues to exclude or exempt from the discriminatory measures, chapters 6 and 7 offer a case study of the French public's embrace of Vichy's National Revolution and reveal the place of anti-Semitism in the broad, long-term structure of these exclusionary patterns.

Much of Vichy's discriminatory legislation was repealed immediately after the war, yet restrictions on naturalized citizens' rights to practice law and medicine remained in force until the late 1970s. The conclusion analyzes the rupture with the past provoked by President Jacques Chirac's public recognition in 1995 of the French state's role in the Holocaust, whereby French lawyers and doctors officially apologized for the parts their institutions played in implementing anti-Semitic legislation during the Vichy era. Given the limits of public apology and the problematic notion of collective responsibility, such professional turns at the end of the twentieth century demonstrate the necessity of analyzing protectionism, identity formation, and exclusion together.

 CHAPTER 1

The Nineteenth-Century Origins of Exclusion in the Professions

The nineteenth century was a period of major change for both doctors and lawyers. The medical and legal fields were disputed turf on which several types of practitioners battled for clientele. To gain a monopoly, doctors tried to diminish the influence of other healers. Lawyers were not as intent on eliminating other legal practitioners but instead concentrated their battles for professional dominance in a few strategic areas of legal practice that they deemed most prestigious, while leaving the rest to others. Despite the differences between medicine and law, the same processes of professionalization were at work throughout the century: developing qualifications, diminishing the number of competitors, defining areas of expertise, increasing legitimacy and prestige, in short, building a professional identity. Owing to a combination of forces, both groups emerged from the nineteenth century as the primary practitioners of their profession.

Within the two professions, responses to change were significantly different. Although the legal profession did not unionize like doctors, a movement of reform from within the law bars began at the end of the century. Both professions were well represented by colleagues in parliament and government during the new republican regime, and they used those connections to their professional benefit. The dynamic between state control and corporatist defense was continually negotiated into the twentieth century. The Third Republic's policy of educational democratization was especially responsible for the turn-of-the-century growth in the numbers of university students, in medicine and law as in all disciplines. In turn, new categories of young people began to demand access to the professions by the 1890s. A "plethora" of doctors was considered a major problem facing the profession. Lawyers, who controlled the number of law bar members, complained less of overcrowding than about the "quality" of the new social classes entering their field. Both professions, to a differing extent, tried to limit the entry into their ranks of foreigners and women, who symbolized a modern threat to the professions' very identity. The xenophobic protectionist initiatives in the interwar years cannot be understood unless we examine this nineteenth-century context. By 1914, professionalization, unionism, political representation, and educational democratization had together created a complex politics of exclusion that would have a significant bearing on the post–World War I period.

The Medical Field in the Nineteenth Century

Under the Old Regime, official medicine was inconsistently organized around private corporations, taught by various types of educational institutions, and governed by royal edicts. Throughout the eighteenth century, the state gradually increased its authority over the standardization of medical practice, but the medical corporations still held real control over who was allowed to practice medicine in each jurisdiction. Conditions of access varied according to locality, but in general they required doctors to be male, Catholic, French citizens,[1] and possessors of a degree from a French medical school.[2]

With its rejection of corporatism, the French Revolution changed this traditional organization of the medical field. For several years after the Revolutionary abolition of privileges, access to the medical profession was left entirely open. Then, in 1803, Napoleon passed a law to redress the excesses of deregulation without returning to a system of corporatist privilege. This law regulated official medical practice until the end of the nineteenth century. Its most significant immediate effect was to shift the authority over granting the right to practice medicine from the dissolved medical corporations to the medical schools, that is to say, into the hands of the state. In addition, surgeons and doctors were merged into one profession with standardized educational training, and professional licensing was provided by three state-controlled medical faculties (Paris, Montpellier, and Strasbourg). The 1803 medical reform also allowed Protestants, Jews, and foreigners to earn medical doctorates and to practice medicine in France. For doctors with foreign diplomas, the state granted special authorization to practice in France on a case-by-case basis.

Another major change was the creation of a new official category of practitioner in an attempt to improve health care in the French countryside. Health officers (*officiers de santé*) were intended to provide medical coverage throughout rural areas where doctors and pharmacists were in short supply. Health officers were restricted to the department in which they had passed their license exams, were not permitted to perform major surgical procedures, and were expected to charge low fees for the poor. This *officiat,* with its reduced educational costs and limited requirements, offered a medical occupation to young rural men unable to afford the long years of study for a degree in medicine leading to a career as a doctor (*médecin*).

Although the 1803 law governed the official practice of medicine, the health care field in nineteenth-century France remained heavily populated with other practitioners who fell outside the boundaries it prescribed. In fact, the great majority of medical care was provided by folk healers who had neither formal training nor a license to practice. These healers, who held great sway with the population and essentially dominated the medical terrain, included nuns and priests; unregulated technicians of paramedical specialties such as the bonesetter, orthopedist, podiatrist, and dentist; various types of popular healers pejoratively described by doctors as *empiriques* (referring to pre–scientific-theory medicine) or *charlatans* such as the *matrone* (an untrained but experienced midwife, quite common since licensed midwives were rare in remote areas), masseur, herbalist, urine analyst; and all of the quack healers or *médecins marrons* such as the sorcerer, mystic, hypnotist, witch, magician, fortune-teller, and hypnotist. Many folk healers were stable and well-known neighbors in local communities, but some traveled around the countryside either independently or following fairs. The female contingent in all of the paramedical categories probably numbered well over half of all folk healers.[3]

There were few sharply defined barriers among the various practitioners, and most healers practiced a combination of science and parascience. Many specialists of one kind of folk medicine did not hesitate to perform medical acts outside their established domain. For instance, bonesetters provided massage therapy for clients, and hypnotists prescribed special potions. Even among recognized practitioners, the boundaries between specialties were not clear-cut: midwives were called upon not just for birthing but for all female ailments; veterinarians helped humans as well as animals; and pharmacists determined their own prescriptions for clients. Many health officers were as experienced and knowledgeable as doctors, and in some instances it was only the inability to understand Latin that set them apart. Doctors sometimes overstepped their own professional boundaries, either by poaching on the terrain of pharmacists in providing drugs to patients from their personal stash, or by performing rites and prescribing potions that were considered "charlatanesque" at the time, well outside the biological remedies taught in the medical schools. One historian has asserted that during times of economic crisis, doctors resorted to all kinds of empirical techniques in order to survive, suggesting that the supply of healing practices was driven by demand, which during the nineteenth century was greatest for folk medicine.[4]

As one might expect of the nineteenth-century French economy characterized by pluriactivity, many healers had other nonmedical occupations. Folk healers were often first and foremost shopkeepers or grocers who practiced treatment on the side.[5] Doctors were also known to have other professions entirely, most commonly as landowners, especially in rural areas where medical honoraria rarely provided sufficient revenue.[6] Doctors themselves were an extremely heterogeneous group. A vast hierarchy of competence, experience, and status separated the hospital chief, faculty professor, or member of the Académie de médecine[7] at the top of the ladder from the simple country doctor, who generally had much more in common with local popular healers than with Parisian medical school professors.

Doctors' Quest for Monopoly

Throughout the nineteenth century, medical doctors pursued a variety of strategies to gain dominance over other healers and a monopoly over health care practice in France. Sometimes doctors made demands on the state for protection; at other times, doctors were in conflict with state interests. They opposed social welfare programs, which they perceived as a threat to their livelihood and professional independence. At the same time, they lobbied the state for regulation and enforcement of unlicensed folk healers.[8] In their quest for monopoly, doctors portrayed the general population not as informed medical consumers making independent choices but as innocent victims of quacks. Yet folk medicine remained so widely accepted that doctors' cries to eliminate or punish popular healers through state regulations usually fell on deaf ears. (In one town, the mayor himself was a part-time folk healer.) Doctors most hated the itinerant *charlatan,* accused of perpetrating the worst medical errors on the gullible populace while avoiding the consequences through their ceaseless mobility. The local population was more trusting of neighborly healers than roving miracle workers, but nonetheless turned to the itinerants in times of desperation. Because itinerant healers came from unknown places and practiced exotic rites in strange tongues, doctors' hatred of them can be understood as a historical precursor to their protectionist mobilization against foreign doctors in the 1930s. The notions of "foreigner" and "charlatan" were often coupled in interwar medical discourse.[9]

Doctors also led a public relations campaign to spread belief in the superiority of scientific medicine. They lobbied the government to abolish the health officers entirely, and they reinvigorated a long-lasting campaign for legislation against fraudulent self-representation as a doctor (*l'usurpation du titre de médecin*). Many doctors believed that the best way to regulate some paramedical practices was to formalize their courses of study and to professionalize their practice, and they thus argued for the institutionalization of degree programs for dentists, opticians, and orthopedists.

Despite these campaigns to gain a professional monopoly, however, there was also evidence of peaceful coexistence, even cooperation, between doctors and various healers. Caregiving nuns, for example, as both church representatives and women, inspired the confidence of the people. They charged no fees, and their counsel was taken as God-given. As the historian Jacques Léonard claimed, "Obeying these venerable virgins almost constituted an act of piety."[10] When faced with complicated cases, a sister would send her patients to a preferred doctor, who often instructed her in hygienic techniques. Given the great influence nuns held in their local communities, this kind of relationship was beneficial to doctors: it kept rival physicians out of the area, introduced doctors into the homes of many more families than they might have entered on their own, and exposed the rural populace to modern medicine.[11] In practice, doctors accepted other healers who relieved them of performing menial tasks like soothing fevers, especially at great distances for little remuneration. And of course midwives were necessary co-workers.[12] In this way, despite a noisy contingent of the medical profession that militated relentlessly against *charlatans* well into the twentieth century, many doctors lived amiably side by side with other healers.

Competition from other healers was not the only factor seen as a challenge to doctors' market share in medicine. Some doctors perceived of burgeoning welfare reform in the second half of the nineteenth century as a threat to their occupational security. As major social developments such as public schooling, the press, the railroad system, military service, and the rural exodus served to unify Frenchmen into a common experience, the right to free health care became a political issue.[13] Increased demand for scientific medical care paralleled the improving capacity of medicine to heal, and it was accompanied by the widespread belief that the state should provide such care to its citizens. Different systems of social health insurance began to appear as early as the 1840s, such as health offices, town dispensaries, and registries of doctors paid by municipalities for care of the indigent. The growth of mutual aid societies, which organized health care for workers in particular trades by hiring doctors at reduced rates to treat their members, was an especially important trend in the late nineteenth century. More than 15,500 such societies had been founded by 1902.[14] The Free Medical Assistance Act (Assistance médicale gratuite, AMG) of 1893, which guaranteed free medical care to the indigent, standardized and made permanent both the trend in state welfare and the state's role in regulating medicine. For example, the fee schedules in these programs were set by the government, not by doctors. Physicians battled bitterly with the state to lower income eligibility in these insurance programs. Whereas medical welfare was undoubtedly good for the French populace, some doctors claimed that it was not good for them. They were forced to choose between joining the staff of a mutual aid society (while accepting reduced fees and forfeiting the traditional patient-doctor relationship) or continuing to practice independently but losing their clientele to the free services.[15]

Why did French doctors not only fail to pioneer medical welfare but also vigorously resist the trend? Indeed more than fifty years of welfare initiatives from the nineteenth into the twentieth century emanated consistently from politicians, not doctors. Understandably, doctors viewed welfare as a burden placed solely on their shoulders by the state. Although doctors carefully cultivated the image of their profession as honorable and charitable work, such an identity broke down when they were required to provide their usual services for less remuneration. The growing role of the state in medical welfare reduced their social prestige (sullying their hands with care of the poor; taking orders from the state) and squeezed many doctors who were already financially strapped. Because of these developments, combined with intense competition from paramedical practitioners and a perceived oversupply of doctors, the medical profession experienced considerable anxiety at the end of the nineteenth century.

La Pléthore: Too Many Doctors?

The democratization of medical studies in France was another issue that pitted doctors against state policies. In the second half of the nineteenth century, as democratic reforms opened access to higher education to ever greater numbers of students, professional strategies shifted from denigration of non-doctor competitors to denunciation of a supposed "plethora" of doctors. Jacques Léonard has remarked, "Nearly all doctors at the turn of the century, holding forth on their profession, would put into service the ancient myth of overcrowding."[16] The growth in the number of medical practitioners, however, was moderate and was justified by several social factors.

New medical schools were founded in Nancy in 1872, in Lille in 1875, and in Lyon and Bordeaux in 1877–78. Their creation coincided with two larger aims of the young republican regime: democratization of education and decentralization from Paris.[17] Under the Third Republic, new paradigms of meritocracy and social mobility—embodied most notably by the Ferry educational reforms—enabled high school graduates from families of modest means to pursue careers in medicine and law for the first time. Enrollment in medical schools rose from 1,800 students in 1865 to 8,500 in 1913.[18]

The new medical schools were founded despite doctors' lobbying against their creation. Doctors argued that a rising flood of medical school graduates was hurting the profession.[19] They asserted that increased supply and competition did not have the same salubrious effects in medicine as in the marketplace.

Instead of creating a wider choice of services at lower prices, an oversupply of doctors, they claimed, forced them to resort to unseemly practices such as discounts, advertising, and falsified success rates. Doctors published articles in medical journals demanding that the state reduce the number of medical school graduates. The umbrella union organization, the Union des syndicats médicaux de France, exhorted parents to dissuade their high school–aged children from entering what they portrayed as an overcrowded and financially unrewarding profession.[20] The conflict between state authorities, who perceived a lack of health care practitioners, and medical unions, which insisted that there was a plethora of doctors, remained entrenched throughout the 1880s and 1890s.[21]

In reality, overcrowding was a dubious claim. Even though the number of medical doctors did increase steadily throughout the century,[22] a series of social developments in Third Republic France offset the growth, and any discussion of a plethora must take into account the disparate distribution of doctors across French territory. Cities well populated with doctors contrasted with a severe dearth of medical professionals in rural areas. Even within a single department, in the Haute-Loire in 1896, for example, the city of Le Puy counted one doctor for every 2,030 people, whereas in the rural cantons there was only one doctor for every 18,285 people.[23] Although health officers had been established specifically for rural populations, their numbers decreased steadily throughout the second half of the century, until the occupation was finally abolished in 1892. All historians agree that the decrease of health professionals created a major social crisis in the last two decades of the century: hospitals were dangerously understaffed, and during even the slightest epidemics, untrained medical students provided critical health care.[24] At the time, many doctors refused to acknowledge these factors, giving voice instead to an anticompetitive "Malthusian" discourse rather than envisioning an improved distribution across the country. The medical press consistently decried a labor oversupply even while mayors and prefects desperately advertised for medical graduates to settle in their areas,[25] a phenomenon that would repeat itself in the interwar period.

The main vehicles for propagating doctors' professional concerns about a perceived oversupply of doctors and unqualified health care practitioners were medical journals and professional associations, or unions. The second half of the nineteenth century saw an explosion of journals and associations focused on professional concerns. Some of the journals, such as *Union médicale* and *Le Concours médical* spread a discourse of defensive protectionism.[26] Doctors also began to found medical societies and associations as a way to unify practitioners locally, to share scientific ideas, and to defend professional interests. The primary goal of medical unions was to monopolize health care by restricting their own numbers and eliminating competition from other healers.[27] By 1884, seventy-four medical unions had been founded across France, which would become legally recognized in 1892.[28] The Union des syndicats médicaux de France, founded in 1884, would become one of the largest umbrella groups.[29] At the same time, the movement for professional defense, associated with working-class activism and protectionist self-interest in the minds of many doctors, contradicted their identity as a noble and charitable profession. The reticence of elite doctors accounted for less than explosive rates of medical unionization before 1900.[30]

By the second half of the nineteenth century, doctors as a profession had significantly increased their power and prestige in French society compared to their position at the beginning of the century. With the arrival of the Third Republic, doctors immediately became the second-most-prevalent occupational group in parliament, after lawyers. Their election gave them a powerful say in public matters. The law of 30 November 1892 was a watershed moment for the medical profession, satisfying a number of long-term demands. The profession of health officer was abolished, regulations on foreign doctors were tightened, illegal medical practice was made a misdemeanor, and medical unions were legalized. In addition, the Free Medical Assistance Act of 1893 made health care available to whole new swaths of the population previously uncared for, thereby enlarging the clientele of doctors, despite their resistance.[31] The programs instituted by such laws required the expertise of doctors, who became respected participants in national debates. The exposure served further to enhance their reputation in society. Finally, the young republican state conferred much attention and budgetary outlay in its first few decades on the medical profession: new medical schools were founded, professorial chairs were created, teachers' salaries were raised, hospitals were enlarged, laboratory equipment was updated, and educational standards were raised. As one historian has summed it up, "Never had any past regime done so much for medicine."[32]

Despite these gains, doctors harbored many anxieties in the early Third Republic. Criticism of socially progressive reforms took root among sectors of the medical profession with an undemocratic bent. Rather than a promotion of scientific medicine, medical assistance programs were perceived by these groups as depriving doctors of otherwise paying customers. Rather than a legitimization of the profession, democratization was perceived as diluting the quality of new doctors. Sociologists of French medicine have pointed out the expected reciprocity between the state and the medical profession in the 1890s: doctors were granted a monopoly over health care with the law of 1892, but this advantage carried duties in the form of the 1893 Free Medical Assistance legislation.[33] Some doctors feared an all-powerful state encroaching on their professional autonomy and the transformation of doctors into salaried state employees. Doctors' pessimism at this moment of real blossoming could be characterized, in Léonard's words, as "the Malthusian will to reserve the profits of a growing medicalization and of a more prestigious medicine to a deliberately reduced number of qualified persons."[34]

The Legal Field in the Nineteenth Century

Prior to the French Revolution, lawyers, like doctors, were largely governed by corporations, known as orders. To practice law before a court, a lawyer had to be a member of a law order or bar (*Ordre des avocats* or *barreau*). The right to the title *avocat à la cour,* which came with certain privileges and duties, was granted only to those registered with a bar.[35] The law bars, as masters of their membership registry (*maîtres de leur tableau*), made all admission decisions. The legal field itself was divided mainly among *avocats* (lawyers), *procureurs* (in 1791 reborn as *avoués* or solicitors),[36] and *notaires* (notaries). These three distinct professions were organized into separate orders which held well-defined monopolies over specific types of legal expertise: lawyers pleaded cases in court and consulted with their clients; *procureurs* were in charge of procedure, form, and assignment of cases; and notaries authenticated deeds and acts and handled inheritance and dowry affairs.[37]

Several reversals and new developments upset this arrangement during the Revolutionary and Empire periods,[38] pulling the carpet out from under lawyers' feet. Their formerly stable place in society and in the economy diminished. The law orders were dissolved in 1790 and later reestablished in 1810: there was to be one law order for every court of first instance, and each order was independent and drew up its own set of regulations. The Revolution opened up the traditional preserve of lawyers, the act of pleading cases in court (*la plaidoirie*), to other actors, in particular to *avoués*. Over the course of the century, lawyers reacquired their monopoly over pleading court cases, but it was a long battle that left the profession insecure. This development represented an unmistakable setback from lawyers' pre-Revolutionary monopoly of pleading cases in court.[39]

Moreover, after the Revolution, legal consultation with clients outside the courtroom remained unregulated and thus open to anyone, and business agents (*agents d'affaires*) rapidly entered this legal territory in direct competition with lawyers. Also known under different appellations such as legal counsel (*conseil juridique*) or accounting expert (*expert comptable*),[40] *agents d'affaires* generally held a law degree and offered legal advice and other services for a fee but were not registered with a law bar. Various types of legal practitioners therefore competed for legal consultation, but any legal consultation that entailed commercial business was off-limits for lawyers, forbidden by the law bar. The *agents d'affaires* therefore had much terrain to cover: advising clients on the legality of business practices; helping them to purchase and sell buildings and places of business; and performing the formalities of business transactions such as obtaining permits, collecting debts, and managing capital.

Lawyers also faced competition from courts of justices of the peace and new types of courts, such as commercial tribunals, which were created during the Revolutionary period, and where *agents d'affaires* and paralegal professionals known as *agréés* rapidly acquired dominance. The law bars forbade lawyers to plead cases in these jurisdictions, thus reducing the professional terrritory within which lawyers were allowed to practice. In addition, as of 1817, lawyers were excluded from the Cour de Cassation and the Conseil d'État, which were open only to members of special law orders. The nineteenth century also marked the beginning of an increased role for the state in the organization of the legal profession. As one historian has noted, "Though liberal, the legal profession in France has always been a regulated profession whose organization was dictated by state standards."[41]

Lawyers' Pursuit of Distinction

In contrast to the medical field, which lacked a corporatist structure to protect professional turf, the law bars sought to cultivate a distinctive and superior professional image for the legal profession. Lawyers lobbied to prevent the title of "lawyer" (*avocat*) from being used by those not registered with a law bar.[42] They cultivated an image designed explicitly to contrast with that of *agents d'affaires.* A critical element of the image was the notion of financial disinterestedness (*désintéressement*). The law bars publicized an anticommercial work ethic based on disdain for earnings. Lawyers portrayed themselves as advocates who worked selflessly for the sole benefit of "the people" and in the service of "the law." The publication of career manuals and guidebooks for the legal profession served this end, setting down on paper the rights, duties, and moral principles suitable for bar members. Such manuals were not so much a recording of established principles as "an invention of tradition."[43]

The principle of disinterestedness took on concrete forms: law bars forbade their members to handle clients' money, to publicize themselves, to hang plaques on their doorways identifying themselves as lawyers, to pass out business cards, and to send correspondence on letterhead stationery.[44] It was considered undignified for a lawyer to visit clients at their home because it gave the impression of soliciting business: all consultations had to take place in the office of the lawyer. Legal fees were considered to be "honoraria," voluntary offerings from clients to "honor" their lawyer. This notion was so critical to distinguishing lawyers that it proved to be the most difficult bar tradition to surrender in the move to modernization. In addition, law bars limited lawyers to providing legal counsel for individuals, leaving the entire market of legal services for businesses open to *agents d'affaires.*[45]

In keeping with the principle of disinterestedness, law bars also banned their members from arguing cases in new types of courts established after the Revolution. The activity in commercial tribunals, for instance, was considered debasing to lawyers since it brought them into physical contact with mercantile practices, and it required lawyers to contract with clients, an unacceptable surrender of a lawyer's independence.[46] In addition, the law bars forbade members to exercise certain other professions simultaneously. Internal bar regulations enumerated several "incompatibilities" with commercial activities. These served not so much to forbid lawyers from engaging in outside activities as to forbid *agents d'affaires* from becoming lawyers, even though they usually had no desire to join the bar and submit to its constraints. In the 1860s the list of incompatible activities increased significantly, demonstrating the long-term importance of this principle emphasizing disinterestedness and distinction.[47]

Lawyers also tried to raise the reputation of their profession by improving educational standards. In the Third Republic there was widespread agreement that French education needed overhauling after the defeat by the Prussians. Law studies in particular had a reputation for superficial teaching by unconcerned professors toward lackadaisical students. Not only would a more rigorous educational program help to raise the quality of the legal profession, but also, it was hoped, it would serve to limit the quantity of practitioners through a more rigorous selection process. During the Third Republic, law schools raised grading standards and implemented a more specialized curriculum.[48] At the same time, the introduction of the modern baccalaureate degree in the 1880s, with its increased emphasis on modern as opposed to classical languages and on math and science, represented to many traditionalists a lowering of educational standards in legal training. The defense of Latin and the classical baccalaureate was often a defense of traditional bourgeois values, and of theoretical over practical knowledge. To distinguish themselves and protect their professional turf, lawyers thus depended on both a policy of financial disinterestedness and elevated educational standards.

Unlike doctors, lawyers did not fear that republican efforts to democratize higher education in France would result in an oversupply of bar members, despite the fact that young men from the lower and middle social classes were studying law in French universities in record numbers. The number of law students grew from five thousand in 1875 to sixteen thousand in 1912. Not all of these students became lawyers, however; many law students dropped out before graduation or entered careers other than the bar.[49] Historians agree that there was never a plethora of lawyers: the number of lawyers did not keep pace with population growth, and as in medicine, the density of the legal labor market varied by region. The greatest concentration of lawyers was found in large cities where courts and universities were located: one-sixth of all lawyers practiced in Paris, which accounted for only 3 percent of the French population.[50] Mirroring urbanization trends, the numerical dominance of the Paris bar increased over time vis-à-vis other law bars in France. Whereas the total number of lawyers in France remained steady from the founding of the Third Republic to the outbreak of World War I, the number of lawyers in Paris more than doubled from 600 to over 1,500.[51] Furthermore, lawyers were well protected against overcrowding by bar admission standards. In contrast to medicine, which was open to anyone with a medical diploma, the obligatory membership in a law bar served as a formidable barrier to professional practice. The bars required of their candidates not only a law degree but also "good moral standing and honorability," granting a fair amount of subjective decision making to the corporatist bars. Traditionalist lawyers were concerned with the social makeup of newcomers to the profession in the early Third Republic, and lamented that new lawyers were of lower "quality." When they used the term, it was supposed to imply intellectual capacity, but most often it disguised a notion of social privilege that was threatened by the new classes entering higher education.[52] Lawyers were especially dismayed by an influx of two new social categories into law schools: foreigners and women.

The law bars' pursuit of strategies for professional protection—based on the principle of disinterestedness with the aim of preserving the prestige of the profession—did not garner total support from lawyers. More concerned about survival than prestige, some resisted the bar's ban on commercial practices and covertly collaborated with *agents d'affaires.* Just as doctors worked side by side with nuns and folk healers despite their publicized disdain for them, lawyers recognized the benefits of collaborating with other legal practitioners. It was only through referrals from *avoués* and *agents d'affaires* that many lawyers were able to survive their first years in practice and establish a clientele. Most clients in need of legal advice went first to an *agent d'affaires* because they were intimidated by lawyers, and the *agent* then sent them to a lawyer if they were to go to trial. Although law bars expressly forbade this, it was common practice.[53] As sanctions by the Paris bar council (an elected body that led the bar) increased in the late nineteenth century, so too did lawyers' appeals of the council's disciplinary actions, challenging from below the validity of the rules themselves.[54] The image of lawyers as the antithesis of *agents d'affaires* was at stake.

The reality of the legal field thus differed from the principles of the bar. Distinctions between lawyers and other legal practitioners were not as sharp as law bars wished; unregistered bar members called themselves *avocats,* and bar members did commercial legal work. Attempts to restrict *agents d'affaires* met with little success. Resistance to traditional bar ethics and rules eventually snowballed into a reformist movement which contested the principles behind the traditional identity of the law bars. As the century progressed, the official discourse resonated with fewer bar members. As the legal system diversified, the bar's purposeful withdrawal from particular courts worked against its strategy of restricting competition: by abstaining from certain legal activities and leaving significant professional terrain open to others, law bars in fact contributed to the creation of *agents d'affaires*.[55] The law bars' official identity was becoming less representative of lawyers as a whole.

Not quite a social movement, pockets of criticism nevertheless began appearing within the legal profession in the late nineteenth century. Encouraged by republican paradigms of social mobility, reformers in the legal profession sought to modernize, rationalize, and commercialize the field, countering the core identity of the law bars. Reformist lawyers, particularly the younger middle-class newcomers, began articulating arguments in pamphlets and journal articles against the bar's anticommercial regulations.[56] Reformist goals of financial self-sufficiency directly challenged the official professional strategy of distinction and disinterestedness. The Conférence des bâtonniers, founded in 1902, organized the presidents (*bâtonniers*) of the provincial bars to address concerns common to all of them, and to overcome the decentralized nature—each bar having its own regulations—of the legal profession. The Conférence was meant not as a federalist organizational challenge to the bar structure but as an authoritative response to reformist demands. In 1906 the Cercle d'études professionnelles was established by young Parisian lawyers as a discussion group. It proposed several daring changes: payment for legal assistance cases, a different mode of election for bar council members, a larger range of activity for lawyers, and permission to require clients to pay legal fees.[57] Tension between traditional and reformist groups was growing within the bars.

Some reformist demands found an echo in parliament. In 1906 Deputy Alphonse Chautemps proposed a law to reduce the authority of the bar over admission decisions and to limit the number of "incompatibilities."[58] A series of laws opened up new courts to lawyers: prefecture councils in 1889, courts of justices of the peace in 1905, labor dispute boards (*conseils de prud'hommes*) in 1907, commercial tribunals in 1911, rental and leasing jurisdictions and expropriation juries in 1918, and war damage jurisdictions in 1919.[59] These reforms remained highly contested by bar authorities.

There was therefore a whiff of reform in the Third Republic air. From 1886 to 1910, legislators proposed laws to abolish the law bars no fewer than seven times. Many of the deputies were lawyers themselves. Deputy Jules Coutant criticized the law bars as a vestige of the Old Regime and denounced them for prohibiting lawyers from being "active, intelligent, dynamic." His attack on the law bars, and in particular his singular concern about their social recruitment, was supported in 1906 by fifty socialist deputies, including the leaders of the Socialist Party, Jules Guesde and Jean Jaurès. None of these parliamentary efforts ever led to a vote, but they had the effect of launching a debate within the profession, and they ultimately gave rise to a 1920 decree that overhauled the legal profession, giving lawyers the right to appeal a bar rejection and obliging the bars to make their regulations transparent.[60]

The Republic of Doctors and Lawyers

By far the most incontrovertible evidence of the success and prestige of both the medical and the legal professions in the latter part of the nineteenth century was the number of doctors and lawyers elected to parliament in the Third Republic. "The Third Republic was the republic of lawyers and doctors: to say so seems banal," proclaimed one French historian.[61] In the 1881 Chamber of Deputies, 149 lawyers were elected among the 560 deputies: 27 percent of the house. The figure held steady into the twentieth century. Lawyers also dominated in the Senate. In the early 1900s, two-thirds of all ministers were legal professionals of some kind, especially in the Ministries of Finance, Interior, and Education, with the Ministry of Justice constituting a veritable lawyers' fiefdom.[62] In both the Chamber of Deputies and the Senate, doctors were outnumbered only by lawyers. Between 1877 and 1914, doctors averaged 10 percent of all members in the Chamber of Deputies (around sixty doctors).[63] One hundred and twenty-five doctors served as senators during the period, and thirteen doctors served as government ministers, including Georges Clemenceau and Émile Combes as prime ministers.

In local and departmental government, doctors also became politically active during the Third Republic: nearly every municipal council in France counted a doctor among its membership. Doctors served as mayors of hundreds of towns and villages as well as of large cities such as Bordeaux, Lyon, and Marseille, and they constituted about 13 percent of departmental legislatures (*conseils généraux*) by the 1890s. Doctors benefited from their local status and wide-ranging contact with the population, and a belief in the natural values shared by republicanism and the medical profession (education, hygiene) strengthened their place in the new regime. The leftist political leanings of many doctor- and lawyer-parliamentarians did not necessarily reflect those of the majority of their professional colleagues. Doctor-parliamentarians leaned generally to the left or center-left of the political spectrum.[64] Conservative right-leaning doctors were less dominant in politics, not because they did not exist but because rightist France preferred to elect notables other than doctors.[65] Similarly, lawyers elected to parliament were predominantly leftist and center-leftist, whereas practicing lawyers tended to be even more rightist than practicing doctors in the early Third Republic.[66] It was widely believed that French law schools were bastions of conservatism, as were the law bars. The anti-Dreyfusism and anti-republicanism to be found there contradicted the image of "la République des avocats."[67]

In part, at least, because of political differences, representatives of the professions in parliament often failed to act in direct accordance with the wishes of medical organizations or the law bars. Physician-legislators did bring medical issues into political debate and enacted into law some long-standing goals of the medical profession, such as the 1892 law that entirely reorganized the profession and satisfied many demands of doctors. The law abolished the profession of health officer, regulated foreign doctors, tightened penalties on illegal medical practice, and legalized medical unions. Doctors in parliament, however, did not always embrace the same views as the medical unions. When they legislated the creation of more medical schools in the 1870s, for example, they gave the medical unions denying that there was a shortage of practitioners "hardly a glance."[68] Medical activists were also excluded from the parliamentary debate over the 1893 Free Medical Assistance law.[69] The unions were unable to convince legislators that large numbers of doctors and socialized medicine were not in the national interest. Similarly, a parliament dominated by lawyers in the early Third Republic tended to favor reformist projects that challenged the authority of the law orders. It was only thanks to the French legislature that women were guaranteed equal access to the profession in 1900, a reform the law bars bitterly opposed. Fostering radical change such as democratization, the republic itself would become a threat to the traditional law bars.[70]

Women's Equal Access to Medicine and Law

Movements to exclude women and foreigners from the medical and legal fields in France at the end of the nineteenth century were inscribed in these conflicts between the state—often represented by members of the medical and legal professions—and groups of doctors and lawyers who were fighting to preserve the exclusivity of their occupational practice. To the extent that women and foreigners were allowed access to the medical and legal fields in France, progress was dictated by republican legislative reforms, despite strong opposition from various groups of doctors and lawyers seeking to exclude outsiders who might lower the prestige of their professions.

In the medical field, the primary key to professional access was a diploma from a French university. Women first sought higher education in medicine in France in the early 1870s with the advent of the Third Republic, far in advance of reforms in female secondary education, which would have facilitated their entry. Although women were not officially barred from French universities, formal education for women leading to the baccalaureate—the necessary requirement to enter university—was not enacted into law until 1924, and the transformation remained incomplete throughout the 1930s. Before then, those French women who did study at a university had to prepare for the baccalaureate on their own. In addition, a small number of women were admitted to French universities on a case-by-case basis, with the diploma offered in women's secondary schools in place of the baccalaureate.[71]

Because university regulations exempted foreign students from the baccalaureate requirement, and because access to higher education was limited in their home countries, the very first women to enter medical and law school in France were foreigners. They came mainly from Russia and eastern Europe, where educational channels were less open to them, especially for Jewish women.[72] In addition, the international reputation of French and also Swiss and German scientific medicine attracted women and men students alike from around the world.[73] In 1868 the first women entered the University of Paris medical school all at once: an American, Mary Putnam; an Englishwoman, Elisabeth Garrett; and a Russian, a Miss Gontcharoff. Garrett was the first woman to earn a medical degree, in 1870, followed by Putnam in 1871. The first Frenchwoman, Madeleine Brès, received her medical degree in 1875. By 1886, 3 percent of students at the Paris medical school were women, 108 women in all that year, of whom only seven were French, while eighty-three were Russian, eleven English, and three American.[74]

As women slowly entered university programs, male students and practitioners of law and medicine began campaigns against them. In medicine, it was the battle for women's access to the prestigious externship and internship (hospital training) programs in Paris that provoked the most hostility. After the first two women were admitted to the externship in 1882, Augusta Klumpke (American born) and Blanche Edwards (daughter of a French mother and an English father who was a doctor), various state organs such as the Board of Public Health's Surveillance Council, the Seine prefecture, the Paris Medical School, and the Ministry of Education were racked by infighting over whether women could advance to the internship. In 1884 the first act of the newly formed Association of Paris Interns was to mount a protest against the possibility of women interns.[75] Hospital chiefs publicly sympathized with the grievances of their male interns, and some senior doctors preemptively announced their refusal to work with women interns. Nevertheless, in 1885 negotiations between civil servants and doctors led to a guaranteed right for women to compete for internship programs. The final obstacle for women's full rights in French medicine was eliminated.[76]

The initial women pioneers paid dearly for their efforts. Augusta Klumpke scored the highest among all students on the 1885 written exam, only to be graded so low on the oral exam that she was nominated to be only a second-rung "provisional intern." The following year she became a full titular intern, the first woman to do so, but was subjected to resentment, stonewalling, and daily humiliations.[77] Blanche Edwards, who had been such an instigator of change that partisans of women's access to medicine were referred to as "blanchistes" and opponents as "anti-blanchistes," suffered worse treatment. Escorted by her mother, Edwards visited hundreds of municipal councilmen, deputies, senators, and ministers throughout the 1880s, lobbying for the admission of women to externships and internships. After overcoming numerous bureaucratic hurdles placed deliberately in her path and having her effigy burned on the boulevard Saint Michel before an exam, Edwards never became an intern.[78]

Unlike health care, the law field offered no comparable "natural" niches for women like gynecology and pediatrics. The question of women's access to law school was less contested than in medicine because of the additional barrier to practice posed by the law bars. To practice medicine in France, one needed a medical school diploma, but to practice law in court, one needed both a law school diploma and membership in a law bar. This corporatist barrier may have discouraged more than a few women from pursuing careers in law: no woman ever tried to join a law bar before 1897. As in medicine, the professional culture of law had long been masculinized; lawyers called themselves "master" (*maître*), one another "brother" (*confrère*), and the law bar a *confraternité*.[79] Women had never been officially excluded from the law bars by any written regulation. It was only when women began attending law school that the idea of their admission to the bar first surfaced.

As in the medical field, foreign women pioneered access to legal education in France, though later and in fewer numbers than in medicine. Compared to a medical degree, an education in French law was probably considered less portable by foreigners, women and men alike. The first woman registered in the Paris law school, in 1884, was a Romanian, Sarmisa Bilcesco, who earned her doctorate in 1890.[80] The number of female law students remained low until the turn of the century: in 1900, only five women, of whom three were foreigners, were studying in law schools in France.[81] In 1892, Jeanne Chauvin became the first Frenchwoman to graduate with a law degree. At her thesis defense, crowds of male students protested vociferously, but she passed with high marks. Chauvin initially wanted to teach law in a women's school but could not find work. She applied to the Paris bar in 1897. Debate over women's access to the legal profession immediately exploded, with Chauvin's case becoming an important cause for French feminists. The bar rejected her application, and the Court of Appeals affirmed the decision.[82]

Lawyers based their opposition to women's admission to the bar on several arguments: that women were by nature too emotional for the logic of the law; that women were unable to play the traditional lawyer role of protector of the weak; that they lacked the civil and political independence to act freely in the courtroom and in the profession; that women's presence would disturb the fraternal fellowship and virility of the profession; and that women lawyers would be inclined to seduce judges into unfair decisions.[83] Such rhetoric, according to the historian Sara Kimble, "signaled that more was at stake," since the legal field was closely associated in people's minds with politics: "Would female lawyers (*avocates*) catalyze the shift towards women's full equality in citizenship?" as many suspected.[84]

In reaction to the sexism of the law bars, influential figures in parliament took up the case for women's admission to the bar. Léon Bourgeois, Raymond Poincaré, and René Viviani—all three past or future premiers and practicing lawyers—together initiated legislation. With the Chamber of Deputies voting in favor 319 to 174 and the Senate 172 to 34, the law of 1 December 1900 guaranteed women's access to the law bars in France.[85] As in medicine, the republican state therefore played a crucial role in eliminating professional barriers for women. This trend illustrates not only the mechanisms by which politicians who were practicing lawyers or doctors used their political clout to address professional issues, but also the ideological diversity of these professional groups. Not all lawyer-ministers or doctor-deputies were as conservative and overtly protectionist of special interests as doctor-senator Raymond Armbruster (who would lead the campaign against foreigners in medicine). Some of the leading representatives were progressives.[86]

While the most significant changes favoring women's access to the medical and legal fields were state-driven, it is important to note that there were voices within the professions that spoke out in support of women's access. Klumpke, Chauvin, and other women pioneers had male professors who mentored them; some student petitions circulated in favor of women; and as we have seen, a number of government officials and legislators, many of whom were doctors and lawyers themselves, were committed to legalizing women's full access to the professions. In fact, France was one of the first European countries to open the field of medicine to women. The historian Thomas Neville Bonner has argued that centralized medical education was a crucial factor: "American women had to fight a thousand different battles on a variety of terrains to win the same advantages as a single political victory in Paris or Berlin."[87] France was also one of the first European countries to open the law bars to women, after only Sweden and Finland.[88] Credit is due, however, not to the French medical and legal corps, who were in the majority opposed, but to the state, in the form of a republican regime that guaranteed free public education for all and inevitably had to recognize women's rights to professional equality as well. Although women's entry into the professions in France and into the educational channels that provided such access was fraught with difficulty, it nonetheless occurred, at the very dawn of the twentieth century.

Having entered these professions, women met new challenges and advanced slowly. Both the high level of education required to practice medicine or law, and the limited income derived from their practice, ensured that these professions would remain the preserve of the independently wealthy, masculine elite until after the Second World War, despite shifts toward democratization and feminization. Codes of masculinity in the professions and in bourgeois society in general further served to alienate women who wished to enter these fields. For some, medicine was perceived as less of an old-boys' career than law, but for others, the common thinking was that medicine was too gory for women. The historian Robert Nye has demonstrated how dueling, smoking, drinking, and swearing constituted informal masculine honor codes and practices that excluded women from French medicine.[89] As Nye describes it, "When women began to enter the professions in significant numbers, a hierarchy of disincentives, ranging from brutal to subtle, was firmly rooted in the culture of masculine sociability."[90] For example, how women doctors would be titled ("Madame le Docteur" had a strange ring for some men) and how women lawyers would dress underneath their attorneys' robes stirred much concern among men. Although sexist sentiment was ingrained in the professional culture, doctors' and lawyers' opposition to admitting women was rooted primarily in fears about economic survival and major shifts in professional identity. While male doctors and lawyers generally tried to limit the number of women in their fields, the French state nonetheless allowed for moderate, steady progress toward equality.[91]

Foreigners

In the last few decades of the nineteenth century, French doctors and medical students mobilized to protect their field against foreigners. Their lobbying led to legislation in the 1890s that abolished recognition of foreign medical diplomas and added many obstacles for foreign medical students in France. Women of foreign origin were doubly designated for exclusion. It was not uncommon to hear xenophobic discourse melded with sexism, for instance, when medical men suggested that closing medical training to women would kill two birds with one stone.[92] The law bars were largely unaffected by these concerns. Although legal education was open to foreigners, French nationality had been required for access to the law bars since 1864, so foreigners did not pose a competitive threat to lawyers. In the 1920s, though, lawyers would join doctors in focusing their ire on "French of foreign origin."

Beginning in the 1880s, medical unions and medical journals led a campaign against the right of foreigners to practice in France.[93] Their frenzied lobbying, abetted by unrest in the medical schools, was the origin of restrictions on foreigners.[94] The 1892 law on medical practice provided for new regulations on foreign doctors in France.[95] No longer could doctors with foreign diplomas practice in France with the simple consent of the government. These foreigners now would have to obtain the French medical doctorate, the *diplôme d'état,* but they could obtain partial credit for their studies abroad. Although French universities required the French baccalaureate as an entry qualification for its own citizens, foreign-student candidates would be evaluated and granted equivalency for secondary studies done abroad. By instituting a formalized procedure for foreigners, as opposed to an arbitrary system of tolerance, the 1892 law effectively gave foreigners the right to practice medicine in France. The law also reaffirmed that the state was the ultimate authority on professional access to the medical profession.

The medical establishment was initially content with the new stipulations. But as foreigners continued to pursue French medical degrees and the Ministry of Education continued to grant transfer credit for secondary and medical studies done abroad, French medical students and doctors revived their demands for protection. With the other major desires of the profession finally satisfied by the 1892 law, doctors and medical students turned their attention to foreigners as the cause of a supposed labor surplus. Articles appeared in medical journals, and petitions landed on the desks of medical school deans. Students complained about overcrowding in classrooms and stiff competition from foreigners for externships and internships. Some were moderate in their objections—that credit for studies done abroad should be granted less liberally—while others rejected the principle of transfer credits altogether and demanded that the French baccalaureate be required of foreign medical students.

Critics drew distinctions between two types of foreign medical students. Foreigners who came to study French medicine and returned to their home countries once their studies were complete were considered inoffensive, even desirable. They acted as French cultural and scientific emissaries abroad. By contrast, foreigners who remained in France after graduation, intending to practice medicine in France, competed with French doctors for limited career opportunities. Many suggested that French education should remain open to foreigners but medical careers should not.

Practical training in hospitals was an integral aspect of medical education. The competitive forms of this training, hospital externship and internship programs, constituted an especially disputed nexus between study and practice. French medical students wanted foreigners banned from competing for internships, and in 1885, students sent a petition to the Paris Municipal Council demanding as much.[96] The rights of foreigners to participate in externships and internships were to be keenly debated for decades.

While medical school professors and deans were sympathetic to French students' demands, they did not lose sight of their post-1871 mission to educate and indoctrinate foreign students in the ideals and principles of French science. In response to the minister of education's 1896 survey of medical school deans, a faculty commission at the University of Lyon Medical School expressed its regret over the protectionist wave and asserted "that the practice of medicine by foreigners does not merit the excessive emotion that it currently arouses." The commission urged that transfer credit continue to be granted and that hospital externships and internships remain open. The commission advised nonetheless that medical civil service jobs be reserved for French nationals and that some kind of compensation be given to French male students for fulfilling their military service obligation.[97] Some broadminded medical academics proffered a solution calling for more schools, more professors, and more resources, so as to provide education to the broadest range of students, French and foreign alike. Other academics played an influential role in eliminating foreigners from French medicine, especially in the interwar years.

An 1896 Ministry of Education circular created a *diplôme d'université* in addition to the existing *diplôme d'état* in all academic disciplines.[98] The *diplôme d'université* (or *diplôme universitaire*) was offered only to foreigners as a way to educate them in France but without granting them the right to practice medicine. Only a *diplôme d'état* accorded that right. The coursework and exam requirements were the same for the two diplomas; the only difference lay in the entry requirements. Foreign students studying for the *diplôme d'université* could have their secondary studies deemed equivalent to the French baccalaureate, thereby permitting them to enroll directly in medical school. Partial credit was also granted for medical studies undertaken abroad. Foreign students were still officially allowed to sign up for the *diplôme d'état,* but they would have to fulfill the same stringent entrance requirements as French students: the French baccalaureate as well as a one-year program of premedical studies in physics, chemistry, and natural sciences (PCN). No transfer credit for study done abroad would be granted. Nevertheless, foreign students could obtain the *diplôme d'état* in four other ways without clearing the baccalaureate and PCN hurdles. First, all nationals of countries with which France had reciprocal international conventions were exempted from the new regulations, notably Romanian and Mauritian students. Their baccalaureates were considered equal to the French baccalaureate; thus they could register directly for the *diplôme d'état.*[99] Second, foreign doctors already fully trained abroad could receive partial credit for their studies and go on to obtain the *diplôme d'état* (this exemption would end with attrition). Third, the non-retroactivity of the 1896 circular allowed for all students already enrolled in a French medical school under the previous system to continue studying toward the *diplôme d'état* without fulfilling the new requirements. And fourth, foreign students who were eventually naturalized could transform their *diplôme d'université* into a *diplôme d'état.*[100] These four "loopholes" would continue to stir up controversies until World War II. Indeed, administrators of the Paris Medical School did not think the 1896 restrictions went far enough. Viewing overcrowding as a specifically Parisian problem and hoping to shift foreign students to provincial medical schools, the faculty voted in 1896 to unilaterally ban foreigners entirely.[101] This infuriated local officials at the Municipal Council and the Seine prefecture.[102] The council predicted that foreign students banned from studying in Paris would go not to Nancy but to Vienna, Berlin, or London.[103] The ban was dropped.

Abroad, reaction to the *diplôme d'université* was one of resentment. Professor John Matzke of Stanford University expressed disappointment and, regardless of French assurances, doubted that the diploma would carry as much prestige as the *diplôme d'état*.[104] Because the national laws in Switzerland, Belgium, and Luxembourg recognized foreign diplomas only if they granted the right to practice in the country of the degree-granting institution, the changes meant that their nationals returning home with a French *diplôme d'université* could not practice in their own countries.[105] This rendered the *diplôme d'université* useless for them, and hindered France's purpose of promoting its reputation abroad.[106]

For the next ten years, as fewer foreigners were able to pass through the expanding web of obstacles put in their way, French doctors and medical students continued to protest "leniencies" granted to foreigners in medicine. Minister of Education Aristide Briand responded to the pressure and further reduced foreigners' rights. A 1906 decree restricted the ability of naturalized citizens to transform their *diplôme d'université* into a *diplôme d'état,* thus closing up the fourth loophole. Such a transformation would be possible henceforth only if the naturalized French citizen passed the French baccalaureate and redid the final years and exams of medical school. These regulations for foreigners in medicine remained in place until after the First World War.[107]

From 1892 to 1906, therefore, legislation increasingly reduced the ability of foreigners to practice medicine in France. The restrictions were a government response to the relentless lobbying of French doctors and students. Doctors and medical students significantly muted their protests after 1906, a silence that was all the more puzzling given the continuing growth in the student population, including the foreign student population, in France. The exclusionary movement would spring to life again in the interwar years.

In the legal profession, secondary sources have alluded to xenophobia at the turn of the century, but little sign of it appears in primary sources.[108] In the law schools, the number of foreign students increased in proportion with the overall number of French law students.[109] This growth was minor compared to that in medicine.[110] Proportionately fewer foreign students came to study law in France, partly because an education in the intricacies of French law was not very useful outside France, and partly because law practice in France was off-limits to foreigners. Foreigners were not a competitive threat to lawyers because since 1864, French nationality had been required for access to the law bars.[111] When the *diplôme d'université* was created in 1896, little changed for the legal profession, since foreigners previously earning the *diplôme d'état* had not been admitted to the bar anyway. For this reason, xenophobic discourse in the legal profession at the turn of the century did not compare to the mobilization against foreigners in medicine.

★ ★ ★

In post-Revolutionary France, the law profession contrasted sharply with medicine in that the legal field was clearly delineated into areas of activity reserved for specific actors, and lawyers purposely removed themselves from much of the action in an attempt to define a particular professional image. The medical field, however, was characterized by competition among healers for recognition and monopoly. The corporatist structure of the legal profession constituted a particular advantage for lawyers over doctors. The law bar was both a sovereign authority over the independence of its members and a barrier against unwanted entrants. The institution of the Law Order, which defined the discipline and image of the profession and determined membership in its body, significantly influenced processes of professionalization, democratization, and exclusion in law. The medical profession, by contrast, was regulated by state legislation alone: access to the field was open to all who possessed a medical diploma issued by a state university. To counteract the vacuum of corporatist authority, the medical profession pursued unionization as a means of professional defense until a Medical Order was finally established by the Vichy regime in 1940. Despite these differences, the *agent d'affaires* was to lawyers what the *charlatan* was to doctors: an unregulated competitor who threatened to steal clientele.

Unlike doctors, who were relatively newly arrived, lawyers had long enjoyed a privileged place in French society. As a result of reforms begun under the French Revolution and the law bars' deliberate attempts to preserve the exclusivity of the legal profession, however, they had lost some ground in terms of professional monopoly and social prestige by the second half of the nineteenth century. Lawyers often perceived the changes instigated by the new republic as threats to their professional prestige: the democratization of education diminished the law career, which had been reserved for a wealthy few. Nonetheless, the bar's antimodern conservatism harmed some lawyers professionally. Divisions appeared within the profession between young and old, reformist and traditionalist, over issues such as free legal assistance, which challenged the very identity of the profession. And although the Third Republic was supposedly "the Republic of Lawyers," there was much public resentment of them. As political scandal and instability rose, lawyers' reputation fell with the fortunes of the republic.[112] The Dreyfus Affair engendered bitter animosity among lawyers, and because the bar's majority position was outspokenly anti-Dreyfusard, the entire profession was disgraced by the affair. The historian Christophe Charle has characterized the law orders at this time, and in particular the Paris bar, as "both the cradle of the Republic of Lawyers as well as the hotbed of end-of-century pessimism, fertile ground for exclusionary ideologies (anti-Semitism, xenophobia) to which some lawyers would subscribe."[113]

The professions used their influence with leaders of the French state as one strategy for obtaining their goals of delimiting boundaries between an established corps and undesirable outsiders, and of conserving their professional prestige. On the one hand, these two *professions libérales* par excellence—whose desire for autonomy had its roots in the corporations of the Old Regime—resented any interference of the state in their affairs. On the other hand, the medical and legal professions did not hesitate to request state legislation when it served their purposes. The French medical profession, according to the historian Matthew Ramsey, "had the best of both worlds. Although the state administration oversaw education and admission to practice, the medical practitioner, once established, was free from corporate or bureaucratic oversight. The profession did not have to give up anti-quack laws in return for its liberty...nor did it sacrifice its independence in return for monopoly."[114] In many ways, one might argue that successful professionalization and doctors' eventual monopolization of medical practices by the end of the nineteenth century were due less to their own efforts than to external factors, such as reforms in medical education, the bacteriological revolution and pasteurization, the Ferry educational laws, urbanization, and medical welfare programs.[115] Like doctors, lawyers solicited government intervention for protecting their title but resisted intervention in granting equal access for women. As one historian put it, "All the while defending their independence, law professionals never broke with the state, from which they almost always demanded protection of their monopolies or recognition of their rights."[116] This kind of relationship was beneficial to the state as well: Napoleon had reestablished the law bars in 1810 to help maintain the functioning of the judicial system, to free the state from petty concerns, and to keep the law orders in line.[117] But the gray area of authority remained a battlefield over control between the state and the professions into the twentieth century.

In the context of these larger developments shaping the professions, the exclusionary sentiment addressed toward women and foreigners in the late nineteenth century can be seen as a professional reflex in response to a perceived state of siege. In the interwar years, doctors and lawyers would target foreigners anew, as well as naturalized French citizens, as intolerable infiltrators in their narrowly conceived professions.

 CHAPTER 2

Defense of the Corps

The Medical Mobilization against Foreigners and Naturalized Citizens

The decade of the 1920s was one of enormous postwar recuperation, demographic growth, and modernization. Rebuilding and repopulating the country were top priorities, and France attracted thousands of immigrants with opportunities for work. In 1927 the French government passed a major nationality law that liberalized nationality and naturalization requirements. To create a fast track to citizenship, the law reduced the residency requirement for naturalization candidates from ten years to three. For those who had earned a diploma from a French institution of higher learning, the residency requirement was shortened to one year. The legislation was grounded in the belief that the cultural assimilation of foreigners could be completed after French citizenship was conferred. Passed by the leftist coalition known as the Cartel des gauches, the legislation was meant to encourage a continuous flow of immigrants to keep the economy moving and to boost demographic growth in the wake of World War I. But almost as soon as the law began to take effect, all sectors of the French economy were struck by unemployment. The worldwide depression that had been raging since 1929 hit France in late 1931; it was severe and lasted until 1939. Instead of providing an appropriate blueprint for France's reception of immigrants for the coming decades as it was meant to do, the 1927 law, its critics on the right argued, left French society vulnerable to a massive influx of undesirables during a major economic crisis. Whereas the 1927 law propagated the notion of "immigrants into Frenchmen," public reaction to the law rapidly grew negative and took the form of "France for the French." Indeed, in compensation for the nationality law—which the political scientist Patrick Weil has called "the most liberal legislation that the French Republic had ever known"[1]—and to placate restrictionist sentiment, legislators added important civil and professional *incapacités* for recently naturalized French citizens: ineligibility for elected political office and for labor representation for ten years after naturalization. The law also instituted the possibility of denaturalization for criminal acts. It was because of these restrictive clauses that legislators ultimately voted in favor of the 1927 law.[2] The rights of naturalized citizens were further reduced throughout the 1930s, and some of the restrictions imposed on them during this period remained in place until the 1980s. It was during the 1930s that naturalized citizens became a distinct social and political category in France.[3] In many ways, the restrictions imposed against them, which are described in this chapter, were a reaction to the liberalism of the 1927 law. This process of undoing culminated with the law of 22 July 1940 that legislated a systematic revision of all naturalizations accorded since 1927. From 1940 to 1944, more than fifteen thousand persons lost their French nationality and were rendered stateless.[4]

The contraction of the 1930s differed starkly from the boom of the 1920s in France. Several crises culminated at the same time: the worldwide economic depression, instability in French domestic politics, a deteriorating diplomatic climate in the wake of the First World War, and the arrival of waves of European refugees in France. Government policies for bringing the country out of depression—which hit France later than other nations but lasted longer—only exacerbated the crisis, which in turn led to tremendous political instability. Political parties were obliged to create coalitions that were not ideologically coherent and were thus incapable of shaking the country out of the economic depression before the outbreak of World War II. The Stavisky scandal of 1933–34, a noxious brew of political corruption, financial dealings, and anti-Semitism, enraged the political right and was partly responsible for the 6 February 1934 riots, which in turn frightened and rallied the left. When the Popular Front election of 1936 brought a coalition of communists, socialists, and radical socialists to power, led by Léon Blum, it would last only one year. In 1938 the radical Édouard Daladier's government undid many of the Popular Front's reforms, such as the forty-hour workweek, and cracked down on foreigners and refugees. The 12 November 1938 decree-law, in particular, reduced the rights of naturalized citizens in France regarding residency, marriage, and voting. The political strife caused many French to lose faith in the Third Republic and its parliamentary ideals.

The domestic turmoil hurt the nation's ability to develop decisive and coherent responses to international threats. The rise of fascism in Italy, Nazism in Germany, and totalitarianism in Spain threatened French national security and the status of France as a European leader throughout the 1920s and 1930s and engendered divisiveness among French citizens. With the large influx of refugees in the early 1930s, the European conflict was brought inside French borders well before "the debacle" of defeat and occupation in 1940. Jews fleeing discrimination in Germany, Romania, Austria, Czechoslovakia, Poland, and other eastern and central European countries, as well as Spanish refugees escaping Franco's authoritarianism, sought protection in the land of the rights of man. Under these circumstances, French persons quickly eyed the refugees with suspicion and resentment.[5]

The combination of an influx of foreigners and refugees and the economic downturn sparked a reflex of self-protection and nationalism. French industry, commerce, artisanry, and the liberal professions were considered saturated employment markets. Drawing inspiration from government measures protecting French manual laborers from employment competition with foreigners,[6] various middle-class groups began to demand that the state restrict the rights of foreigners to participate in certain sectors. The government responded to this mobilization with protective legislation: the Laval government passed laws in 1935 requiring foreign artisans to apply for prefectural permits and imposing quotas on them,[7] and similar regulations were imposed on foreign merchants.[8] The medical and legal professions, though they considered themselves an elite in French society, joined the lower- and middle-class protests against foreign competition and were also granted legislative protections.[9]

The crises of the interwar period in France were particularly difficult for the medical profession. French doctors returning from the front in 1918 encountered special challenges: the reestablishment of lost clientele, reclamation of hospital and salaried posts, the outpacing of medical fees by inflation, and the obligation of providing medical assistance to millions of war victims newly eligible for free care. At the same time, doctors worried about competition within the profession and loss of autonomy due to the welfare initiatives. Under the pressure of these professional challenges and the larger interwar circumstances, doctors quickly blamed foreigners. Foreign medical students and doctors were accused of crowding French universities, of stealing jobs that Frenchmen thought should be reserved for them, and more broadly of debasing the medical profession.

At first, the French medical corps called for the elimination of certain perceived advantages for foreign and naturalized doctors. Soon, though, the agitation intensified, and the identification of more and more types of competitors of foreign origin to be restricted from medical practice took on a certain predatory quality. Once foreign doctors were effectively barred from the medical field, French doctors turned their ire against naturalized doctors. By the late 1930s, before the Vichy period, the movement to exclude unwanted foreigners and naturalized citizens had spiraled into a discriminatory frenzy. Throughout, French doctors and medical students led the way, and the state followed.

The Myth of Professional Overcrowding

Not long after the end of World War I, the first complaints about overcrowding were uttered in French medical circles, and by the 1930s the perception of an educational system pushed beyond its limits was commonplace. During the 1930s parliament regularly debated regulations for admission to university studies and for access to various professions, while the mainstream press often wrote about overcrowding. In late 1934, Minister of Education Anatole de Monzie created the Bureau universitaire de statistique (BUS) for the purpose of alleviating "intellectual unemployment," deemed a problem of national importance. It was hoped that collecting statistics about students and professionals would ensure a better policy of population management in certain fields. The Confédération des travailleurs intellectuels (CTI) had been founded after the war by academics, scientists, artists, journalists, and professionals as a kind of trade union to represent the interests of the professional classes.[10]

There was indeed significant growth in the populations of both French and foreigners in medical schools and in the medical profession in France throughout the Third Republic. Foreigners, however, were not the main source of this growth, and the increase in the numbers of medical students and doctors was mitigated by other factors. Nonetheless, many of the most vocal actors in the profession asserted repeatedly that overcrowding was an acute problem and that foreigners were responsible for it. In reality, in French medical schools, all categories of students had increased since the beginning of the century, as table 2.1 illustrates.

The total medical student population nearly doubled from the year 1900 to just before World War II. The number of French males in medical school increased by about 50 percent, thus confirming that democratization was particularly significant in medicine: more French men from the

Table 2.1   Students registered in French medical schools

YEAR	FRENCH MEN	FRENCH WOMEN	FOREIGN MEN	FOREIGN WOMEN	TOTAL
1900	7,614	350	639	178	8,781
1910	8,013	565	634	509	9,721
1920	9,735	1,022	1,094	139	11,990
1925	7,924	1,761	1,336	229	11,250
1930	9,905	2,471	3,279	591	16,246
1935	11,206	3,372	3,486	695	18,759
1939	11,088	3,010	1,606	323	16,027

Source: Adapted from *Recueil des statistiques,* 60.

lower classes were attaining higher levels of education over time. The representation of other social categories in French medical schools also increased. Women—French and foreign together—increased from 6 percent of all medical students in France in 1900 to 22 percent in 1935. Foreigners—women and men together—increased from 9 percent of medical students in 1900 to 24 percent in 1930, but fell back to 12 percent of all medical students in France in 1939. The marked decline in the number of foreign students in medical schools after 1935 was the result of the medical profession's deliberate shutting down of educational and professional channels to foreigners in French medicine. For example, between 1932 and 1933, the number of Romanian medical students in Paris dropped from 711 (in all degree programs) to 532 as a result of restrictions placed specifically on their right to study in France.[11]

Table 2.1 may give a falsely elevated impression of the number of foreign medical students who could have become doctors in France. First, the enrollment statistics include students aiming for degrees in dentistry and midwifery as well as for both the *diplôme d'état* and the *diplôme d'université*. Few foreigners pursued degrees in dentistry and midwifery, and the *diplôme d'université* did not confer the right to practice medicine in France.[12] In the 1934–35 academic year, almost half (62) of the foreign women enrolled in the Paris Medical School were matriculated for the *diplôme d'université*. In the same year, 924 foreign men were matriculated for the *diplôme d'université* and 488 for the *diplôme d'état*. Furthermore, enrollment statistics include auditors; a large proportion of foreign students in French universities audited classes for a semester or a year with no intention of earning any diploma.[13]

Over the course of the interwar years, the greatest number of foreign medical students came consistently from Romania, Poland, and Russia. In the first half of the 1930s, there were between five hundred and seven hundred Romanians in the Paris Medical School, between three hundred and four hundred Poles, and a little more than one hundred Russians every year. Iranian and Greek medical students were the second-most numerous populations of foreigners.[14] Other nationalities that were dominant (between twenty and fifty students per year at the Paris Medical School) were Egyptians, Swiss, Hungarians, Turks, Americans, British, Bulgarians, Indochinese, and Colombians.[15] Special historical relationships between countries explain why some nationalities arrived in relatively large numbers (Romania), and geographic proximity explains others (Switzerland, Britain), while underdeveloped medical education abroad (Latin America) and anti-Semitic discrimination in some countries (Romania, Poland, Russia, and Hungary) account for still others.[16]

The medical *diplôme d'état* was required to practice medicine in France, and so statistics on it give some indication of the number of practicing doctors. In 1900, French medical schools awarded a total of 1,129 *diplômes d'état*. This rate remained steady until 1934, when about 1,400 *diplômes d'état* were awarded each year until the outbreak of war. The vast majority of these graduates were French men, amounting to between 82 and 89 percent of all *diplômes d'état* from 1937 until 1940. Only 138 foreigners earned the medical *diplôme d'état* in all of France in 1937 (10 percent of all graduates), and foreigners accounted for fewer than 5 percent of such graduates in the following three years.[17] The notion of an "invasion" of foreign doctors in the mid-1930s was therefore false. As this chapter will illustrate, after passage of the Armbruster and Cousin-Nast laws, foreigners holding the *diplôme d'état* were not permitted to practice medicine in France anyway because French nationality was also required.

The number of practicing doctors in France more than doubled from the beginning of the Third Republic (11,000 doctors) to the 1930s (25,000 doctors), a time when the entire population increased only from 38 million to 42 million, giving doctors grounds for complaint about an overcrowded profession. Indeed, in 1866 there was one doctor for every 3,395 inhabitants in France, whereas in 1931 there was one doctor for every 1,645 inhabitants. Yet was there really a plethora of medical doctors? A lower doctor-to-inhabitant ratio can simply attest to progress in public hygiene, especially since the disappearance of health officers left a significant void in the medical field. There were 5,500 health officers in the late 1860s and none by the late 1930s.[18] In comparison to its neighbors, France was far from overserved by doctors. In a 1930s survey of eighteen countries, France ranked twelfth highest in the proportion of doctors per capita. Hungary was first, followed by Italy, Switzerland, Japan, Latvia, Denmark, Norway, Belgium, Czechoslovakia, Germany, the Low Countries, and then France.[19]

Statistical evidence from the period points more to a problem of distribution of doctors and medical students than to one of widespread overcrowding. Practicing doctors were unevenly distributed across French territory. Whereas large cities and spa regions registered a high proportion of doctors per capita, rural areas in France rarely had enough doctors to care properly for their population. The Seine department counted one doctor for every 801 inhabitants in 1938, but the Morbihan department in Brittany registered only one doctor for every 2,899 inhabitants.[20] In 1934, almost one-fifth of all doctors in France (5,385 out of 25,470) practiced in the Seine department.[21] In the French colonies in 1931, one doctor was available for 50,637 inhabitants in Madagascar, one doctor for 68,392 in French West Africa, and one doctor for 86,245 inhabitants in Indochina.[22] Distribution appeared to be a problem with medical students as well. While medical schools in Paris, Lyon, Bordeaux, and Nancy were full, other medical schools such as those at Tours and Clermont-Ferrand had difficulty attracting enough students.[23] As the medical professor and future dean and rector Gustave Roussy summarized, "In terms of student overcrowding in universities, only one school is affected: Paris."[24]

Statistics on the number of foreign and naturalized doctors practicing in France in the interwar years are lacking. The historian Ralph Schor asserts that in the early 1930s, there were 750 practicing foreign doctors in all of France, approximately 3 percent of all doctors. In the Seine, by contrast, 530 of 4,993 doctors were foreign, representing 10 percent.[25] Naturalized doctors are even harder to account for since their origins disappear in the statistics.[26] A French law school dissertation from the 1930s reported that, of a total of 1,166 foreigners naturalized as French citizens in 1937, thirteen were doctors. Of a total of 1,352 newly naturalized citizens in 1938, eleven were doctors, and in 1939, of 2,178, two were doctors.[27] Medical unions—not a reliable source—claimed that forty-eight doctors were naturalized in all of France in 1936, and ninety-four in 1937.[28] Despite the discrepancies, these figures are remarkably low.

Nevertheless, most French doctors and medical students of all political, social, and economic persuasions believed that there was a plethora of medical practitioners. They further believed that foreigners were the main cause of this overcrowding, even though the number of foreigners earning the *diplôme d'état* was probably never more than one or two hundred per year for all of France and decreased to around fifty per year by the late 1930s. The dean of the Paris Medical School, Victor Balthazard, asserted in an official report, "We have shown from a study of precise statistics that *without the influx of foreigners registering for the diplôme d'état, the medical plethora in France would be nonexistent.*"[29] The medical community was able to convince representatives in parliament of such beliefs. Senator Georges Dentu, for example, proclaimed, "We are in the middle of abnormal growth, of a veritable hypertrophy of expansion."[30] Deputy Louis Bonnefous asserted, "One of the principal causes of this malaise resides in a 'veritable invasion of foreigners very often considered undesirables in their own country' and is continuing to increase in our universities."[31]

In general, French doctors perceived their professional potential in Malthusian terms: sick people constituted a fixed and limited quantity. So in the context of an increase in the number of practitioners and changes wrought by the development of socialized medicine, they saw themselves as having to devise new ways to divide up existing pieces of the pie and to protect themselves from an influx of foreigners. Doctors' understanding of their situation in interwar France, however divorced from reality it may have been, constitutes a prism through which to observe the importance of Frenchness to their professional identity.

The Scapegoating of Foreigners

The scapegoating of foreigners as the cause of overcrowding and the source of unfair competition in the medical profession was triggered anew in the aftermath of World War I. Fifteen thousand doctors had been mobilized over the course of the war, leaving few practitioners to care for the civilian population. To alleviate the dearth, the French government had temporarily allowed Belgians without a French *diplôme d'état* to practice in France.[32] The Paris regional medical union protested this, but the Ministry of the Interior refused to sacrifice the public interest to satisfy the medical unions.[33] After the war, French doctors returning from the front lost little time in trying to eliminate those who had ensured civilian health care in their absence.[34]

As peacetime returned to normal, French medical student associations, medical unions, and medical journals kept their focus on foreigners. French doctors and medical students insisted on the right of French nationals to a protected job market. They argued that it was in the national interest for France to maintain a small professional medical corps of native French, untainted by the nefarious effects of overcrowding. The public would benefit in turn from a morally upstanding corps of doctors freed from the taint of commodification. National and professional interests were thus merged into a single demand to reserve medical opportunities for French citizens.

Most French medical leaders recognized, however, that it was also in the national interest to attract foreign students to study in France, learn French methods from French *savants,* and later act as emissaries of French intellectual, scientific, and medical renown abroad. Therefore, most agreed that foreigners should be welcomed into French centers of higher education.[35] As Dean Henri Roger of the Paris Medical School proclaimed in 1928, "The constant growth of foreigners gives us great satisfaction; it proves that, despite the criticism, our medical education continues to have an excellent reputation."[36] The creation of the *diplôme d'université* in 1896 was precisely for the purpose of attracting foreigners to French universities, but without granting them the right to practice medicine in France.

Doctors and medical students distinguished between foreign students who went home after their studies—emissaries of French medicine abroad—and those who stayed, who were considered embryonic competitors. While agitating for restrictions against the latter, they regularly affirmed their acceptance of the former. It became a commonplace to refer to those foreign students who planned to leave France as *étrangers* and to those who planned to stay as *métèques.* This ancient Greek term, introduced in French by Charles Maurras in 1894 at the outset of the Dreyfus Affair, had become a popular slur in reference to foreigners as well as to Jews in interwar France: its usage was current even among the medical leadership. For example, Dr. Paul Guérin, a well-known union activist, stated, "How many colleagues, who became the honor of their medical corps in faraway lands, have remained our great and dear friends with whom we always reconnect with pleasure: these colleagues easily understand the motives behind our actions, for they are the first to wish to differentiate themselves from this legion of *métèques* who will never go back to the steppe where they were born."[37]

The core of the issue centered on regulations for obtaining the *diplôme d'état,* the document that granted its possessor the right to practice medicine in France. At the end of the First World War, various categories of foreigners could still practice in France under several conditions. First, nationals of certain countries (Romania and Mauritius), and students at the French medical school in Beirut,[38] were granted automatic equivalency for secondary studies in their native countries and had the right to earn the *diplôme d'état.* Second, foreign doctors already fully credentialed abroad could obtain the *diplôme d'état* after taking the French baccalaureate and fulfilling some exam requirements, being granted partial credit for their foreign diplomas. Third, foreigners who possessed a French *diplôme d'université* in medicine could transform their diploma into a *diplôme d'état* after becoming naturalized, if they retook the French baccalaureate and the final years and exams of medical school. Fourth, those who had started their studies for a *diplôme d'état* before 1896 were permitted to continue under the old system and practice in France. This category would exist only for the lifetime of those persons eligible as of 1896. By the 1920s, such doctors were in their forties. Fifth, foreigners who had studied in French *lycées* and earned the French baccalaureate could earn the *diplôme d'état.*[39] Finally, foreign doctors with foreign diplomas in frontier regions (Belgium, Luxembourg, Spain, Italy, and Switzerland) were allowed to practice in French municipalities along the border with reciprocity for French doctors in those frontier regions. French doctors and medical students viewed each of these categories as threats, and as causes of professional overcrowding. They complained that regulations regarding equivalencies, naturalization, and military service made it easier for foreigners than for French students to earn the *diplôme d'état.*

Resentment Coalesces, 1928–1933

Burgeoning agitation erupted in 1928, when the government granted increased freedom to foreigners wishing to practice medicine. Minister of Education Édouard Herriot's decree of 17 August 1928 made it easier to transform a *diplôme d'université* into a *diplôme d'état* for students and graduates who naturalized. Whereas before only partial credit was given for studies done toward a *diplôme d'université,* the new regulations granted full credit for studies and partial credit for exams. The 1928 decree was meant to standardize requirements for foreigners according to recent changes made for French students, and to legitimize French propaganda abroad claiming that the *diplôme d'université* program was exactly equal to the *diplôme d'état* program. It stirred the medical corps into a protest movement that was to endure until the Fourth Republic.

French doctors and medical students feared that the 1928 decree would allow a flood of foreigners to earn the *diplôme d'état* and the right to practice medicine in France. They argued that because of the liberal nationality law of 1927, it was easier than ever for foreigners to naturalize, and that fulfilling the baccalaureate requirement (necessary for naturalized citizens to transform a *diplôme d'université* into a *diplôme d'état*) was a cinch for foreign students already in possession of a *diplôme d'université*. The Confédération des syndicats médicaux français—which had replaced the Union des syndicats médicaux de France in 1929 as the umbrella medical union organization and counted 80 percent of doctors as members in 1930[40]—demanded the abolition of transfer credits, of transformations of the *diplôme d'université* into the *diplôme d'état,* and of all treaties that granted exemptions.[41] In other words, they wanted only French citizens who possessed a French *diplôme d'état* to practice medicine in France. A more restrictive naturalization policy was also demanded.

Some French doctors suspected the state of ulterior motives. The Nord Department Federation of Medical Unions and the Paris Medical Union suggested that the government had passed the 1928 decree to ensure that a sufficient number of doctors would participate in the new medical welfare program in case the medical unions refused.[42] In 1928 parliament had also passed a landmark law that provided health insurance to a third of the population, or 13 million people. The law took effect in 1930 and was "the most important piece of social legislation in the history of the nation to date," according to the historian Timothy Smith.[43] With the creation of a Ministry of Health in 1930, doctors feared losing control of major aspects of medical care. The doctor–patient relationship seemed to be ineluctably transforming itself into a triangle, with the state dictating the rules. Foreigners, therefore, became the scapegoat for a host of unwelcome changes. One doctor denounced a spate of "hasty and multiple naturalizations (forty-nine doctors in 1929), in the unconcealed goal of finding multipurpose doctors so as to break French doctors' potential resistance to medical insurance."[44] Another doctor, disapproving of both the 1928 decree and the social welfare law, depicted foreign doctors as strikebreakers and sneered, "Since the 'crazy' law is of foreign creation, it is not at all surprising that foreigners are ready to implement it."[45] In addition to raising doctors' ire against foreigners, then, "it was the 1928 decree that reignited the conflict between doctors and the state."[46]

The burgeoning movement against foreigners in French medicine quickly found a spokesperson in power. In late 1928, doctor and senator Raymond Armbruster, armed with reports and reactions from the medical unions, called for the Parliamentary Medical Coalition to discuss the issue.[47] Having rallied over eighty of his fellow senators into co-sponsorship, he proposed a comprehensive law to parliament on 8 April 1930 that would not only repeal the 1928 decree but also overhaul all regulations regarding foreigners' freedom to practice medicine in France. In his testimony before the Senate, Armbruster, politically unaffiliated with any party, cast doubt on the ethics and competence of foreign doctors "who did not succeed in their own countries for professional or other unknown reasons, and who were obliged to expatriate sometimes because of defects or misdemeanors."[48]

Specifically, Armbruster's proposed law called for the following changes. First, foreigners possessing the *diplôme d'état* had to naturalize before age thirty, in order to fulfill military service requirements. Second, foreigners from countries that demanded naturalization for French doctors practicing there had to naturalize as French to practice medicine in France. Third, foreign doctors who worked in any institution of social medicine had to naturalize. And fourth, medical positions in the civil service had to be reserved for French citizens who had been naturalized for at least five years.

The legislative proposal exuded a particular conception of naturalization, not as a confirmation of assimilation but as a professional barrier. In order to circumvent the 1927 nationality law's reduced pre-naturalization residency requirements, Armbruster proposed the novel idea of a waiting period *after* naturalization for specific socioeconomic categories of doctors to be allowed to work. This 1930 proposal to reduce full occupational rights for naturalized French citizens appeared in a legislative initiative a decade before the Vichy regime institutionalized the prioritization of "native French" in various fields of employment. The Armbruster proposal thus constitutes the beginning of a paradigm shift toward *jus sanguinis* conceptions of French nationality that culminated during Vichy.

Taking care to convince senators that French universities would continue to attract foreigners who would spread French scientific prestige abroad, Armbruster admitted that the medical unions' demands were "too protectionist" and risked diplomatic reprisals. "It is therefore indispensable," he asserted, "that we establish a rigorous selection process on foreign students and doctors, without being accused of xenophobia."[49] The strategy worked: Armbruster persuaded his Senate colleagues to put the exclusion of foreigners from French medicine onto the legislative docket.

The Movement "from Below"

Armbruster's proposition lent structure to the agitation against foreigners in student associations and medical unions. The mobilization of French doctors and medical students after 1930 became more organized, public, and militant. All the medical unions supported the Armbruster proposal. They published in their bulletins long articles in favor of restrictions on foreigners as well as regular updates on the vagaries of the law proposition. In the absence of a Medical Order, doctors were dependent on state regulations for determining access to the profession. Lobbying of government and parliament for legislative change, through local medical unions, was thus their primary means of action. The Confédération preferred to centralize lobbying within its own apparatus and discouraged individual actions that might render the campaigns ineffective.[50] Senator Armbruster himself had been a very active member of the Aube medical union.[51] But the medical corps were not always satisfied with their political representation. Whenever doctors felt neglected by parliament throughout the 1930s, the unions protested, blackballed individuals, and launched investigations into possible illegal medical practice by foreign doctors.[52] As one union leader dissatisfied with parliament warned, "The Seine-et-Oise Union intends whenever possible to do what is necessary to expurgate undesirable *métèques* from the profession."[53]

Student groups also leaped into action in support of the Armbruster proposal. The Association corporative des étudiants en médecine de Paris actively took up the cause.[54] At the annual congress of the Union nationale des étudiants de France in April 1931, student representatives from all French universities discussed the rise in the number of medical students and especially the influx of foreigners and the leniency of naturalization regulations. At the end of 1931, the Section corporative des étudiants en médecine de Montpellier hosted a conference on the supposed plethora of medical practitioners. One speaker claimed that foreign doctors were making a fortune off France's ill; that they competed with French doctors; that they were failing to assimilate French habits, mores, and language; that they had low standards of living and engaged French doctors in price wars over clients; and that most foreign doctors, especially those from central Europe, never intended to return to their native countries.[55] The discussion over the Armbruster law at this conference was "frenetically" applauded by the five hundred students present, and the congress as a whole declared itself in favor of the law.[56]

Even when foreigners endeavored to pass the French baccalaureate, French students denounced two aspects of this process as favoritism. First, they complained that foreigners' mother tongue fulfilled the requirements for a second language. Demanding a language requirement for foreigners more exigent than that required of French students, they insisted that foreign baccalaureate takers should have to know French and a second foreign language in addition to their mother tongue. Second, French students griped that foreign students could study for the baccalaureate while simultaneously fulfilling their medical school requirements, giving foreigners a two-year advantage over them.[57]

Naturalization policy was a crucial concern for both student groups and medical unions. They demanded naturalization as a requirement for the right to practice medicine in France, hoping that this would stop most candidates, or at least ensure their assimilation into French culture. Others asserted that naturalization should not be required but should rather be discouraged. They complained that the lower residency standards of the 1927 nationality law was allowing a flood of foreigners to come to France, naturalize within one year, and fulfill the academic requirements quickly. "We know the routine," one critic argued. "First naturalization, then transfer credits, then transformation of the *diplôme d'université* into a *diplôme d'état,* and finally setting up practice in our country, with all the same advantages as our nationals, but without having to fulfill the obligations that the state imposes on its own nationals, the baccalaureate and military service."[58]

The question of when foreigners should initiate their naturalization was the focus of much attention, because the timing of naturalization affected whether newly naturalized men would be obliged to perform military service. It was widely believed that foreigners pursuing medicine in France purposefully waited to initiate naturalization proceedings until after their thirtieth birthday so as to avoid military service. Armbruster asserted before the Senate, "Many foreigners wait until they are twenty-nine years old to apply for naturalization...[and] when they submit their request, they purposefully omit some necessary identification documents so that their dossier is delayed."[59] Depending on whether foreigners naturalized before, during, or after their medical studies, they would be subject to three distinct sets of regulations regarding the right to earn the *diplôme d'état.* Such details were the subject of an inordinate amount of discussion throughout the 1930s.

While student groups and medical unions led and sustained the anti-foreigner movement, other actors such as professors of medicine and members of elite medical associations lent their support, demonstrating that the issue crossed hierarchical lines. Dean Roger of the Paris Medical School, for example, argued that Armbruster's proposal was not xenophobic but merely fair in its quest to subject foreigners to the same requirements as French students.[60] The prestigious Académie de médecine also supported restrictions against foreigners in French medicine.[61] In 1931 the academy established a special commission to study the issue and included three of the most rabid anti-foreigner activists: Drs. Victor Balthazard, Émile Sergent, and Jean Quénu. Blaming professional overcrowding solely on foreign doctors, the academy pledged its support for the Armbruster proposal and added a suggestion to limit the Romanian privilege to fifteen students per year.[62] One highly placed doctor—a medical school professor, hospital doctor, and president of the Rhône medical union—exhorted his fellow doctors to rally to the cause of Armbruster's proposal: "Each one of us, using our networks and our means, must put pressure on legislators to bring this about."[63] To this end he published a sample lobbying letter for unions to send to their senators.

The Armbruster Law of 1933

Practically all the parliamentarians who were doctors supported the proposed Armbruster law.[64] As medical unions and student groups gradually increased their demands, the doctor-senators driving the anti-foreigner law proposition—Armbruster, Dentu, and Chauveau—recognized the need to propose more moderate legislation that would be acceptable to fellow senators. For example, while doctors and medical students wanted the transformation of a *diplôme d'université* into a *diplôme d'état* rendered "impossible,"[65] the doctor-senators proposed to render the transformation "more difficult."[66] While the Confédération's position was to grant the right to practice medicine only to French citizens, native or naturalized, who possessed a *diplôme d'état* and had fulfilled their military service obligations, doctor-senators thought it was excessive to require naturalization in all cases. They proposed naturalization only if doctors wanted to practice before age thirty (so as to fulfill their military service obligation) or if other nations required naturalization of French doctors practicing there.[67]

Armbruster tried to prove to his fellow senators that he was not defending a special interest but rather was acting in the national interest, for the good of all French citizens: "The proposed law submitted for your deliberation has the objective of instituting a rigorous selection process on foreigners who want to practice in France and of avoiding, in the interest of the sick, the grave problems of overcrowding in the medical profession. The proposed law will certainly have even greater consequences for the safeguarding of public health."[68] In addition, doctor-senator Chauveau argued that the state had always acted to protect French interests from foreign influences and that their proposed law simply followed in the same natural vein: "[The text of the law] is not as innovative as it seems at first glance.... [It] is simply the culmination of this evolution in our thinking."[69]

Although the doctor-senators mediated between the profession and the state in their stance, they were not above insinuating an occasional threat. Armbruster argued, "A vote on this proposition is even more opportune, at this time . . . when the implementation and success of the social security law depends especially on the complete and loyal collaboration of our medical corps, whose scientific merits are incontestable."[70] In this way, doctor-senators reminded elected officials of the necessity of doctors' cooperation if state initiatives in public health were to succeed. Ultimately, some eighty senators co-sponsored the bill.

The medical unions were restless during the slow parliamentary progress of the Armbruster law proposition. "Before the Senate and then the Chamber [of Deputies] have finished, we will have let all the beggars get their *diplôme d'état*," complained one physician.[71] A number of amendments had slowed its passage, such as a proposal to make the classical Latin-Greek baccalaureate a prerequisite for medical school, a solution that would diminish not only the number of foreign applicants but also the number of French applicants from lower social classes. Certain doctor-parliamentarians explicitly advocated this method for its efficiency in reducing the "plethora" of doctors.[72] Other doctors expressed frustration that some of the original restrictions had been watered down in later proposals.[73]

Finally, after three years of debate and modification, the Armbruster law was passed on 21 April 1933. The law required doctors, first, to possess the *diplôme d'état*. For foreigners to earn this degree, they had to pass the French baccalaureate, and they were not granted credit for partial medical studies done abroad. Partial credit was, however, awarded to foreign students already holding a French *diplôme d'université* and to foreign doctors already holding medical diplomas from abroad. Second, the law required doctors to be French citizens, subjects, or natives of a French protectorate.[74] Exceptions were made for foreign students already enrolled in French medical schools or foreign doctors already practicing in France, foreign students covered by a diplomatic convention between their country and France, and ten Romanian or Mauritian students per year. Furthermore, in order to practice in public medicine, the law required doctors to be French by birth or naturalized for at least five years, unless they had voluntarily served France in the First World War. This last measure was a significant step toward reducing full rights of citizenship for naturalized French.

As the Ministry of Foreign Affairs had feared, foreign reaction to the Armbruster law was negative. The Romanian government responded by declaring that the French *diplôme d'état* was no longer going to be valid for medical practice in Romania. French officials worried less about the effect this would have on French citizens practicing medicine in Romania than about its potential to encourage all the Romanian medical students currently in France, estimated at about three to four hundred, to remain in the country.[75]

The Romanian Exception and Anti-Semitism

In their quest to exclude foreigners from the medical field, French doctors and students had concentrated many of their efforts since the early 1930s on repealing the "Romanian privilege." As we saw in chapter 1, students from Romania had long been granted automatic baccalaureate equivalency for their secondary studies and thus were permitted to prepare for the *diplôme d'état*.[76] At the conclusion of World War I, Romania's aggrandized territory and increased population meant that more students were eligible to benefit from France's diplomatic agreements. As early as 1922, French student groups accused Romanian students of abusing their privilege by coming to France in large numbers.[77] Officials of the Paris Medical School recommended in 1923 that the Romanian privilege be revoked, noting in particular that the majority of Romanian students in France were "Jews."[78] In fact, although anti-Semitic quotas in Romanian medicine had not yet been established, student violence and faculty hostility toward Jewish medical students in Bucharest and other cities may have encouraged medical students to pursue their studies in France. Some came to France after attempting a year of university in Romania only to be shocked by the animosity they found there; others came directly from their baccalaureate studies. Some spoke excellent French, others not a word. Would they stay in France or return to Romania after medical school? As the historian Henri Nahum lucidly puts it, "Who knew?" They were eighteen years old and living in a volatile Europe.[79] Although most lived frugal and hardworking student lives in France, they were hardly welcomed with open arms. Citing the danger of a "veritable Romanian invasion," French doctors and students concentrated their efforts in the early 1930s on repealing the Romanian privilege at the same time that they were lobbying for the Armbruster proposal.

Senators Armbruster and Dentu brought the issue to the floor of parliament in the early 1930s.[80] In March 1931, Dentu pointed out to his fellow senators that whereas before the war the number of Romanians taking advantage of the privilege was limited to around fifty, since the war the numbers had exploded to 436 Romanians studying for a medical *diplôme d'état* in Paris. He further railed against the fact that Romanians were awarded French government scholarships.[81] In his arguments, Dentu cited a report by Victor Balthazard, professor and later dean of the Paris Medical School, and a major Parisian medical unionist. Balthazard wrote: "In five years, five hundred Romanian doctors will practice in our countryside and especially in our cities. How many will there be in ten years, if we do not decide quickly to dispel the danger?"[82] Balthazard was not above claiming in public, in print, and in high-level government circles that Jews constituted a large majority of the Romanian medical students in France, and furthermore that Romanian Jews were inferior students.[83] In preparing an official Ministry of Education report on medical education reform, Balthazard garnered information about the religious affiliation of the 436 Romanian students in the Paris Medical School. He reported that 377 of them were "israélites." The anti-Semitism of the future dean of the Paris Medical School went fully unconcealed later in the report: "Is it for this legion of Jews that the French government conceded this privilege to Romanians in 1857 and 1866? If we look at the history of the privilege,... it applied to Romanians of old stock from Moldavia-Valachia and not to Jews, who are only recent Romanian citizens, if they even really are."[84] Other doctors shared Balthazard's anti-Semitism. One wrote in a medical journal: "One must have the courage to say that the Romanian *numerus clausus* is particularly aimed at Jews. Romania reserves its universities for students of the Romanian race. All others go elsewhere: Jews forever, Romanians yesterday, they will be French tomorrow (and doctors in France), Bolshevists the day after. The eternal wandering Jew is just one step away."[85]

Historians have demonstrated that anti-Semitism was a driving force behind the exclusion of Romanians from French medicine,[86] yet it is important to note that the focus of French medical unions on the abrogation of the Romanian exception also had a certain strategic logic. Romanians were by far the largest group of foreigners to seek medical training in France. With Romanian students occupying so many seats in medical schools, the strategy promised a high return on investment. Of all the anti-foreigner proposals, this goal was the most defensible in parliament because the exception for Romanians was considered unfair to other foreigners. Add to these factors the common perception that most Romanian medical students were Jews, and Romanians were the perfect target.

As the Armbruster proposal shuffled around parliament, the Ministry of Foreign Affairs tried to talk Romanian officials into amicably accepting an inevitable abrogation of the privilege.[87] The parliamentary Commission of Foreign Affairs proposed a quota on the number of Romanians who could benefit from the exception. Despite the infinitesimal numbers of Mauritians, who had until then benefited from a similar diplomatic convention, the final legislative proposal also addressed their case. The 1933 Armbruster law revoked the privilege and replaced it with a quota: every year, just ten Romanians or Mauritians would be allowed to register for the *diplôme d'état* without the French baccalaureate, while all other Romanians and Mauritians would be treated like other foreigners and steered toward the *diplôme d'université*.[88] The change was nonretroactive, so those who had already begun could continue under the old system.[89]

The French medical profession's targeted campaign against Romanians shows the interconnectedness of various medical demands and how they escalated during the 1930s: arguments about overcrowding led to demands to preserve the limited number of jobs for French doctors and deteriorated into xenophobia and ultimately anti-Semitism. On 22 April 1933, one day after the passage of the Armbruster law, Adolf Hitler instituted the first of many discriminatory measures against Jewish doctors. Throughout the 1930s, as the German Reich gradually increased its territorial sovereignty over more and more Europeans, it tightened its grip on Jewish doctors, banning them first from state medical health care institutions, then from "Aryan" hospitals and private practices with "Aryan" clientele.[90] Facing the emigration of German Jewish refugees to France, a significant and multifarious camp of French leftists rallied to their aid, including political parties (communists and socialists, as well as liberal radicals), trade unions, nongovernmental groups (League for the Rights of Man and Citizen), national daily newspapers and journals, and spokesmen for the Catholic Church. Precisely because these groups discounted the notion of a medical plethora in France and recognized that a majority of the Jewish refugees tended to be professionals, they argued for concessions. Vicki Caron has demonstrated that this coalition sustained pro-refugee sentiment longer and more vigorously in France in the 1930s than historians have previously believed. She also reevaluates the record of the Popular Front in 1936 by highlighting several of its measures such as granting work permits to refugees and increasing rates of naturalization.[91]

French medical unions and student groups, by contrast, reinforced their campaign against admitting Jewish refugee doctors. The Syndicat médical de Paris, led by a Dr. Hartmann, immediately formulated the medical corps's reaction to the Jewish refugees: "Whatever sympathy they might feel for Jewish or socialist doctors deprived of their means of existence in Germany, [French doctors] still resolutely oppose any attempt that might be made to allow these doctors to practice in France. . . . In the case of a massive invasion of our universities by German students, even if in good standing, there is reason to foresee new measures of prevention." This vow was seconded by numerous medical unions and student groups.[92]

The Ministry of Foreign Affairs weighed the possibility of allowing the refugees to practice medicine in the French colonies.[93] The 1892 law required the *diplôme d'état* for doctors to practice medicine in the colonies, and regulations in Morocco, Tunisia, Syria, and Lebanon closed the door to refugees there.[94] Unofficially, however, foreign doctors with foreign diplomas, notably Europeans, commonly practiced in these countries, and French doctors had already been agitating to have protections applied to the colonies.[95] During negotiations over the proposed Armbruster law, French legislators debated the issue, but Minister of Education Mario Roustan protested strongly, arguing, "You know very well that in the colonies, we lack doctors."[96] Yet the Confédération protested continuously to various ministries against the idea of sending European refugees to the colonies.[97] After several years of medical union agitation, the restrictive 1935 Cousin-Nast law (discussed later in this chapter) was applied by decree to Algeria and the French colonies, protectorates, and mandates.[98] A resettlement program in the colonies for Jewish refugee doctors thus never came to fruition. The argument that there was an actual shortage of doctors not only in the colonies but in rural France as well was drowned out by the calls for protectionism.

At several junctures during this ongoing German refugee crisis, French political leaders sounded out medical opinion on possible aid for refugees in the medical field, for instance, allowing German and Austrian doctors to care for their fellow nationals in Paris and the opening of a German hospital in Paris, but the response was always negative. Though initially ready to consider certain relief measures, the French state chose to consult medical opinion and backed down in the face of its objections, ultimately doing nothing.

French medicine was hardly being "invaded" by refugees.[99] Only twenty-six Germans registered for medical studies in France between April 1933 and January 1935, and only one applied for the *diplôme d'état*.[100] The French consul in Lwów, Poland, however, signaled that many Polish Jewish students, in response to anti-Semitism at home, were applying for visas.[101] In 1930 he signed visas for 157 Polish Jews planning to study medicine in France and for 166 Polish students the following year, 93 percent of whom he claimed were Jewish.[102] Tighter restrictions on Jews in Romanian medicine in 1938 precipitated their emigration as well.[103] Nonetheless, the German, Polish, and Romanian student populations in France had decreased by the mid-1930s.[104] The restrictions on medical practice were too insurmountable, and the medical unions' sway over the government was too influential, to offer any hope for the Jews.

Restrictionism Intensifies, 1933–1935

Although the Armbruster law did much to limit the possibilities for foreigners to study medicine and practice in France and should have placated fears of overcrowding, the anti-foreigner movement in medicine did not subside with the passage of the law. In fact, the mobilization against foreigners and naturalized citizens intensified in medical circles. Many doctors, judging the law too limited, renewed their complaints. Critics decried three main weaknesses in the law. First, it was not retroactive and thereby allowed all foreign students who had already begun their medical studies to continue to do so under the old regulations.[105] This meant that foreign doctors who were already practicing and foreign students already registered for the *diplôme d'état* as of 21 April 1933 could practice medicine in France for the rest of their lives without ever naturalizing.

Second, the Armbruster law did not address the gray area of practical training between school and career. The most successful medical students competed in exams known as *concours* to become externs and interns, prestigious positions that provided practical experience before they became full doctors.[106] Clinical rounds, externships, internships, and replacements of absent doctors remained open to foreign medical students. The distinction that many French wished to make between foreign students who returned home ("*étrangers*") and foreign doctors who stayed in France ("*métèques*") was not so sharp in reality. French doctors and students complained that foreign medical students were participating in hospital rounds (which were getting more crowded as the student population grew) and were beating out French students in the extern and intern competitions. They wanted these intermediary training opportunities reserved for French citizens. Replacing absent doctors was another area of practical training that French students wanted reserved for themselves. Advanced medical students had the right to practice medicine in France in cases of epidemic disease and to stand in for vacationing or ill doctors for short periods of time. A circular of 15 November 1913 had already reserved the replacement service for students of the *diplôme d'état* program, effectively reducing the number of foreign students. But medical unions and student associations considered enforcement lax: doctors did not always verify the eligibility of replacements and did not register them with the department prefect. The lobbying had led to the passage of a 6 May 1922 law requiring the presentation of certificates of scolarity.

The profession's third major critique of the Armbruster law concerned naturalization and military service requirements. Given that the law had effectively restricted foreigners from practicing medicine in France, after its passage the focus shifted to naturalized citizens as the principal source of overcrowding in the profession. Medical groups began to call for both a reduction in the number of naturalizations and a long probationary period before naturalized citizens could actually practice medicine in France. The movement's change of focus in the mid-1930s manifested itself in a small but significant linguistic turn: medical discourse had begun to use the term "non-naturalized" (*les non naturalisés*) to denote foreigners.

Issues of fairness and cultural assimilation came to the fore in discussions about specific naturalization requirements for doctors. Student groups and medical unions debated the question of when medical students should be required to attain French citizenship through naturalization. Proclaiming that naturalized citizens owed their new country "the blood tax,"[107] they lobbied for earlier naturalization obligations and later military service age cut-offs so that naturalized citizens would be required to fulfill military service obligations.[108] They pointed out that military exemptions for those naturalized after the age of thirty gave naturalized medical graduates a head start on medical practice and thus an unfair career advantage over native French. Although the vast majority of doctors wanted naturalized doctors to perform military service, others hesitated to billet "our French soldiers with foreigners, with their different mentality."[109] At the same time, student groups used the assimilation argument to demand longer naturalization delays. "It is necessary that a French doctor—friend and counselor to French families—have a French name, a French sensibility, a French soul," declared one medical student association.[110]

The issue of mandatory waiting periods for naturalized citizens to practice medicine intensified after 19 July 1934, when the French parliament enacted a law that banned naturalized citizens from practicing law and working in the public sector until ten years after the date of their naturalization. The law was passed quickly and with no public debate. The medical unions, hearing of it after the fact, were dismayed that this protection did not apply the ten-year waiting period to doctors, except for positions in the burgeoning public health sector. The Armbruster law of 1933 had already instituted a five-year delay after naturalization for the functions of court medical expert and all medical positions awarded via *concours* or *sur titre*. This practice had been interpreted to include medical school professors and teaching assistants but not interns, hospital doctors, or clinic heads.[111] The 1934 law prolonged the waiting period from five years to ten and restricted more public service positions, though there was much debate afterwards over which positions were covered. Using the opportunity to complain about the state's growing social assistance program, medical unions argued that every medical treatment reimbursed by the welfare program was a public service that should be reserved for doctors who had been French citizens for at least ten years. In its interpretation of the 1934 law, the Council of State claimed, however, that the terms "civil service remunerated by the state" did not include any public function remunerated by departments, municipalities, or colonies, nor by public establishments having a juridical personality distinct from the state, even if such organizations were partly funded by the state. This excluded hospitals, leaving them open to naturalized doctors and even foreign doctors. The council also determined that the 1934 law was not retroactive: French citizens of less than ten years' duration already employed in the public service could retain their position.[112]

French doctors were dissatisfied with these provisions and especially felt slighted by their second-class treatment vis-à-vis lawyers. Immediately the medical unions adopted the ten-year waiting period as their rallying cry and began to lobby for such legislation.[113] "Because of our services rendered to humanity," they claimed, "we have the right, even more than messieurs the lawyers, to demand what they obtained."[114] Doctors also noted that the law passed so easily because lawyers benefited from a corporatist order to protect access to their profession. Without such an order, medical doctors were especially reliant on state regulation.[115] As the activist Dr. Querrioux saw it: "It is necessary to defend French doctors. The law of ten years of naturalization concerning lawyers was voted in eleven days by the Chamber and the Senate because there is a Law Order. And hence the benefit of an Order... to defend ourselves against the Staviskys of medicine."[116]

Thus the exclusionary movement shifted significantly in the mid-1930s. The focus of the medical corps fixed on another, more specific category to be excluded from its profession. It was no longer the "non-naturalized" or even "naturalized" but now the "recently naturalized" (*naturalisés de fraîche date*) who became the target for discrimination.

The medical unions debated the most efficient way to have a ten-year delay legislated: a decree applying the 1934 law to the medical profession, or the inclusion of medical practice into a revised version of the 1934 law. Parisian deputy René Dommange, an independent, proposed such a revision.[117] But with so many other complaints about the incomplete aspects of the 1933 Armbruster law, combined with a student strike that broke out in early 1935, and competing legislative proposals emanating from various deputies and senators in 1934 and 1935, union leaders began to push for a new law specific to medicine, which would be more far-reaching than the Armbruster law. To this end they lobbied their ally, the minister of public health, to introduce a new bill. In response, the minister warned medical leaders that the Chamber of Deputies would be less receptive to the medical profession's demands than it had been to the law bar's. Whereas law school graduates had other career opportunities outside the law bar, medical school graduates would be truly destitute if barred from practicing their trade for ten years, and apparently this gave the lawmakers pause. Not to be deterred, doctors led a battle on both fronts, executive and legislative, lobbying doctor-deputies for a *proposition de loi* as well. The Medical Union of the Western and Northern Suburbs of Paris notably chose this dual approach. Unusually, however, it tried to keep its lobbying campaign out of the press this time.[118]

While organizing this second round of the anti-foreigner movement, doctors debated when the ten-year delay should begin: after naturalization or after completion of the medical degree. Many preferred whichever event came later, to prevent naturalized citizens from practicing their profession for as long as possible. Since existing legislation required naturalization in order to obtain the *diplôme d'état,* the most restrictive way was to begin the ten-year waiting period after the dissertation defense, not after naturalization. For the Syndicat médical de Paris, the best—that is to say, most time-consuming—trajectory was naturalization, baccalaureate, medical school, ten-year waiting period, and military service, with no temporal overlap for fulfilling each requirement.[119]

Medical Students Strike

In early 1935, the exclusionary agitation shifted into the student camp. The activism snowballed into a nationwide student movement against foreigners in all disciplines that was to last throughout the spring semester. On 31 January, students at the Montpellier Medical School took to the streets to protest against foreigners in French medicine. The movement spread to other university cities—Marseille, Toulouse, Grenoble, Tours, Bordeaux, Lille, and Nancy—and picked up in Paris the following day. Parisian medical students distributed tracts demanding stricter equivalency requirements and limits on naturalization. Agitators occupied the rue de l'École de médecine and blocked access to classes. Fights broke out. One teacher was attacked, and students were injured. A group of about 250 demonstrators, mostly from the medical school, descended upon the Paris Law School, interrupting classes and shouting slogans. Less belligerent students sent petitions to the rector of the Académie de Paris, head of all levels of education in the Paris region. University authorities took rapid measures to try to extinguish the tumult. The next day, classes were canceled, and in the following days, student identity cards were checked at the entrance to classrooms.[120]

The Paris strike was led by various student associations: the Union nationale des associations générales d'étudiants de France (UNEF), the Association corporative des étudiants en médecine de Paris (ACEMP), the Association amicale des étudiants en médecine de Paris, the Association amicale des internes en exercice, and the Association professionnelle des externes en exercice. On 2 February the strike committee, together with the student delegates to the Conseil de l'Université, announced their demands to the Ministry of Education and in press releases. It was a summary of all the unsatisfied demands of the past few years complemented by a few innovations: that the Armbruster law and naturalization laws be strictly enforced; that transfer credits and the transformation of *diplômes d'université* into *diplômes d'état* be forbidden; that the 19 July 1934 law be extended to the medical profession; that foreigners be restricted to separate, unpaid internship programs; that the role of medical replacement be reserved for French students; that military service be obligatory for naturalized foreigners until the age of forty-eight; and that higher guarantees of morality be required of those entering the medical profession.[121] Medical students from Nancy and other cities across France seconded the demands.

Some student groups wanted even more. The Association amicale des étudiants en médecine de Paris urged that foreigners be barred from externship programs.[122] The ACEMP wanted foreigners to naturalize and obtain the baccalaureate *before* they began their studies for the *diplôme d'état*. They further demanded that a ten-year waiting period for the right to practice medicine begin not at the moment of naturalization but at the time of the dissertation defense. The association even demanded revisions to French nationality law: that the naturalization process take more stringent account of the morality of candidates, that quotas on naturalizations be instituted, and that the required period of residence before naturalization be lengthened.[123]

The medical students were joined by students from the law school and other university disciplines.[124] The historian Pierre Péan has documented the participation of François Mitterrand, then a first-year student at the Paris Law School and at the Institut d'études politiques, in these student demonstrations against *métèques* in early 1935, notably as a member of the Volontaires nationaux of the Croix-de-Feu group of Colonel François de La Roque.[125] It is well known that political groups and leagues seized upon the anti-foreigner student mobilization of 1935 to achieve their own ends.[126] The Étudiants d'Action française du groupe de médecine were largely responsible for encouraging violence during the demonstrations and for keeping the anti-foreigner flame alive in the Latin Quarter throughout the spring semester.[127] As the Paris rector recognized from

the beginning, "the goal of the agitators is without a doubt to sustain fermenta-
tion in the neighborhood so that the disorder will last until the sixth of February,
the day that extreme-right students intend to force the universities to close as a
symbol of mourning."[128]

Although student agitation continued regularly throughout the spring
semester, the street demonstrations terminated for the most part on the evening
of 2 February, with the publicizing of student demands.[129] University and government officials appeared to take seriously student claims about excess numbers of foreigners and unfair competition. In the immediate wake of the protests, the deans of all the medical schools and combined medical and pharmacy
schools seconded the French students and reproached those foreign students
"who, through the path of naturalization or via the administrative dispositions
which are currently insufficient or too liberally interpreted, will compete with
French persons in the practice of the medical profession. New regulations,
under review at this time, will put an end to these abuses."[130] Just days after the
protest, officials at the Ministry of Justice received representatives from unions
and student associations; the general director of Public Assistance met with
Maurice Mordagne, student leader of the ACEMP, and pledged his commitment
to remove foreigners from hospital externships and internships; and Minister of
Education André Mallarmé received a delegation of the ACEMP,[131] expressed
his sympathy with the medical students' cause, and promised to convey their
demands to other ministers and parliamentarians.[132] Weeks later, Mallarmé proclaimed before the Chamber: "Problems related [to foreign students] have come
to light from this very human, very understandable movement of French medical students, who fear that jobs for doctors are being taken by foreign students
in abusive proportions. I received these young people, and I was compelled, as a
university professor and as a minister, to show them my support. We must not
discourage our youth, even when their demonstrations are excessive."[133]

In response to the student strike, parliamentarians also intensified their work
on legislative proposals to further restrict foreigners in French medicine. Doctor-
deputy Georges Cousin from Paris had already proposed a very restrictive law
completely banning the transformation of *diplômes d'université* into *diplômes d'état,*
imposing a ten-year delay after completion of the degree before naturalized citizens
could practice medicine, and barring foreigners from medical posts remunerated
by the state or by communes (in order to address the issue of hospital positions).[134]
After the student strike, Cousin's proposition was reviewed in committee. Deputy
Dommange renewed talk of his proposal applying the 1934 law's ten-year post-
naturalization waiting period to medicine.[135] Deputy Charles Pomaret sought
an audience with Minister of Education Mallarmé to stress the importance of
protecting French youth from competition with foreigners in higher education
and in the liberal professions.[136] And on 14 February, Armbruster proposed a new

law to revise and complement his own 1933 law. Parliament, like the government, legitimated student demands with their official attention in those February days: students such as Maurice Mordagne and Georges Laffitte were received by Deputies Cousin and Dommange and by the Chamber's Commission of Hygiene.[137]

Most concretely, Minister of Public Health Henri Queuille gave quick satisfaction to the student strikers regarding the eligibility of foreign medical students for replacements and internships with his 4 February 1935 circular. Granting ultimate decision-making control to the prefects and emphasizing that anyone could be refused authorization to act as a replacement for almost any reason on the grounds of "general interest," the minister explicitly asked prefects not to grant authorization to foreign students. More implicitly, he encouraged prefects to exclude even those foreign students in the *diplôme d'état* program, who by law had the right to serve as replacements.[138] In addition, Queuille advised prefects to ask hospitals in their departments to bar foreigners from regular internships and to organize separate intern programs for them, unranked and unremunerated. While not having the force of law, this government initiative sent an administrative signal in favor of a nationalist conception of hospital internships and replacements. The ministerial circular reproduced almost word for word the ACEMP's demands of 2 February, revealing the willingness of state officials to cater to student groups.[139] Medical organizations were impressed with the rapid government response to the student demonstrations.[140]

In yet another example of the discrepancy between rhetoric and reality, however, Queuille's circular raised an oft-unspoken problem: that there were not enough French students to fill replacement positions.[141] Doctors conjectured about the causes of this shortfall: some French students chose a theoretical orientation to their career, and some were too busy with other medical work, while still others had personal wealth that made replacement work financially unnecessary; and some doctors favored foreigners because they accepted lower pay than French students. In order to provide a sufficient contingent of French replacements and to encourage doctors to choose French candidates, the Aube medical union proposed two solutions: the establishment of a corps of full-time permanent replacement doctors who would make a career of substituting around the nation, and the creation of a centralized registry of eligible replacements, compiled by the Confédération, with a system for rating their professionalism and morality.[142]

Not all government and university officials were sympathetic to the medical students, however. Sébastien Charléty, rector of the Académie de Paris, was particularly suspicious of the anti-foreigner mobilization. Scribbled notes in the margins of documents describing the mobilization which passed over his desk testify to his position: "This letter is an infamy"[143] and "Payback for his 'anti-*métèque*' campaign??"[144] and "Yeah, right! Except when chanting '*métèques* in the toilet'!"[145] Officially, the university condemned xenophobia among French students, but in fact did little to oppose it. Apart from Charléty, and his successor Gustave Roussy, who were both disappointed by the anti-foreigner mobilization in the 1930s but unable to exert much of a moderating effect, University of Paris administrators were more concerned with maintaining calm in the Latin Quarter than with punishing student outbursts against foreigners.

There was some evidence of pro-foreigner sentiment among some French medical students in 1935. Leftist student groups denounced the strike, especially the Union fédérale des étudiants (UFE), affiliated with the Communist Party. Representatives of the UFE were received by the Commission of Hygiene at the Chamber of Deputies, where they expressed their opinion that the 1933 Armbruster law sufficiently protected French doctors and asked legislators to help medical students in nonexclusionary ways, for instance, by eliminating the patent tax for doctors' first two years of practice and by fighting more diligently against charlatanism.[146] This meager protest from the left was drowned out by calls for nationalistic protectionism.

Anti-foreigner agitation continued sporadically throughout the spring semester but erupted violently again in late March and early April, when Parisian medical students, fearing that legislative deliberations had come to a halt, revived their protest. The associations that had led the strike committee in February now coalesced into a group called the Comité d'entente des étudiants en médecine and called for a general student strike in the Latin Quarter in order to renew legislative projects left languishing. The strike was widespread, and a few episodes of violent xenophobia received negative press coverage. In response to this second round of student agitation, state officials again appeared to take the students' demands seriously. Minister of Education Mallarmé, along with the dean of the Paris Medical School, Roussy, received a student delegation, and in turn pressed parliamentarians to renew their legislative projects.[147]

Although student groups insisted that they were not xenophobic, several anti-Semitic incidents were documented in this strike, including a physical attack on a pharmacology professor, Jeanne Lévy, who was a member of an antifascist group. The Association of Paris Hospital Externs and Interns ultimately apologized for its role in xenophobic and anti-Semitic acts of violence. The Comité d'entente denied any role in the incidents, which they attributed to non-student political groups. In fact, it is likely that extremist groups such as Action française played a significant role in the student strikes. The group was particularly active in medical and student milieux: it published a student newspaper, *L'étudiant français,* its association was the Groupement médical corporatif, and it published the professional journal *Le médecin*.[148] Demonstrators regularly affirmed that their movement was not aimed at foreign students who came to master French medical techniques and return home after completing their studies.[149] Nevertheless, when a hundred foreign students in Nancy met to discuss how to respond to the agitation, their meeting was brutally invaded by members of the Action française and the Jeunesses patriotes.[150] Xenophobic language intensified in May and June. One group proposed not only to force foreign doctors to naturalize but also to have those who were rejected for naturalization "taken *manu militari* to the border," where the French medical corps would organize "a *cordon sanitaire,* so that they would not be able to recross the border into France."[151]

Nearly all of the medical unions declared their solidarity with the student movement.[152] Some doctors urged unions not to let the ball drop. "It is important," wrote one doctor, "that . . . the students feel supported by their elders. It is not enough for us to give them our moral agreement. . . . Students are not rich; it is our role to give them the money. . . . Student interests are our interests. . . . The senators, deputies, ministers, those who fabricate public opinion, must know that doctors and students are one bloc, one unwavering bloc."[153] Immediately after the January–February strike, the unions met with student groups, helped frame their disparate demands, arrived at broad agreement on principles, and together initiated a lobbying campaign.[154] As one doctor noted, "Students have a major advantage over us, they are able to go into the streets; doctors will never go into the streets."[155] Dr. Hilaire, a leader in the Confédération, proposed to lobby parliament for an even tighter restriction than the one granted to lawyers in 1934, that is, a ten-year waiting period beginning after completion of the medical degree, not after naturalization. He concluded, "The student mobilization has been very useful for us."[156] The excitement over the student strike inspired practicing doctors to offer more openly xenophobic proposals. In May 1935 the two major Parisian medical unions demanded the expulsion from French territory of foreign doctors illegally practicing medicine and of those practicing legally but "in morally suspect conditions."[157]

Parliament Responds Again: The Cousin-Nast Law of 1935

By the spring of 1935, several important developments had fueled the growth of the anti-foreigner movement into a widespread and often xenophobic mobilization: the influx of refugees from the educated and professional classes of eastern and central Europe, the 1934 law excluding recently naturalized lawyers from the legal profession, and the medical student strike. The French parliament became convinced that stricter anti-foreigner legislation was necessary to placate the French medical corps.

The anti-foreigner movement found active supporters in parliament, most notably Victor Le Gorgeu, Raymond Armbruster, and General Jean Stuhl in the

Senate; Albert Nast, Georges Cousin, and René Dommange in the Chamber of Deputies. As in 1933, practically all the parliamentarians who were doctors supported more restrictions. Corporatist, protectionist, and even xenophobic rhetoric spread inexorably from union meetings and medical journals to parliamentary commission discussions and floor debates. Senators and deputies appropriated many of the most restrictive measures promoted in medical circles directly into their legislative initiatives. Some of them cited at length Balthazard's report about the large numbers of Jews in the Paris Medical School.[158]

But not all parliamentarians believed the "plethora" rhetoric. Deputy Joseph Archer argued that "in the countryside, it is reckoned that there are not enough doctors, so the law we are discussing is going to aggravate the situation."[159] Negotiation among lawmakers was substantial, and the resistance of various legislators succeeded in reducing the restrictiveness of the final provisions. Senator Maurice Viollette, a Paris lawyer, rendered the legislation more moderate.[160] In general, it was the leftist leaders who tried hardest to tone down the anti-foreigner legislation.[161] Nevertheless, on 26 July 1935, parliament passed a new law against foreigners in medicine.

The 1935 Cousin-Nast law reaffirmed the provisions of the 1933 Armbruster law and added more restrictions.[162] Most notably the new law addressed the issue of naturalized citizens who had not fulfilled their military service. According to the new law, naturalized doctors who had performed active military service in France or fought for France in World War I could begin to practice medicine immediately. Naturalized citizens who had not done so would have to wait a specified amount of time after receiving their medical degree before they could practice medicine. The point was to eliminate the supposed career head start of foreign-born doctors over native French. The length of the delay depended on the reason for the exemption. Naturalized citizens exempt from military service because of gender (all women) or health reasons would have to wait two years (the duration of normal military service) before they could practice medicine. Naturalized citizens exempt because of age (over thirty years old) would have to wait four years (double the duration of normal military service) before practicing medicine. The severity of these restrictions was intended to penalize immigrants who purportedly waited until after their thirtieth birthday to naturalize. The waiting period began from the date when naturalized citizens received their diploma, not from the date of naturalization.[163]

Second, the law barred naturalized doctors from all "functions or employment in public medicine" until five years after they gained the right to practice medicine. The "function of public medicine" was interpreted after the passage of the law to mean all permanent medical employment remunerated by a *collectivité publique* at the state, department, or municipal level.[164] Overall this expanded the scope of medical civil service positions barred to recently naturalized citizens but still did not put hospital externships and internships out of the reach of foreigners. Two exceptions to this provision were permitted: if naturalized doctors had voluntarily fought for France after 1914, or if the Ministry of Public Health declared a health emergency.[165] In an attempt to tighten control over medical doctors, the law stipulated that all practicing doctors had to register with their prefects. The Ministry of Public Health would maintain a nationwide list that would contain the names, nationalities or dates of naturalization, and types and dates of diplomas of all doctors authorized to practice in France. Medical unions were granted a role in collaborating with the prefects in the verification of diplomas.

The contrasting provisions of the Cousin-Nast law toward Romanians and Saarois embodied the increasingly common distinction drawn between good immigrants (pro-French, not Jewish) and suspect ones. On the one hand, the law dropped the ten-person quota for Romanians and Mauritians altogether.[166] On the other hand, doctors from the Saar territory, which had been returned from its League of Nations mandate to Germany in 1935, were permitted to practice in France with their German medical diplomas.[167] This concession to pro-French Saarois doctors (their number was estimated at four persons) was included in the law only after intense lobbying of parliament by the Ministry of Foreign Affairs, backed by support from some deputies.[168] The stipulations were inspired by those used in 1914 to reincorporate doctors from Alsace and Lorraine with German diplomas back into French medicine.[169]

The most discriminatory aspect of the Cousin-Nast law, which took effect immediately, was its retroactivity. Although no naturalized citizens already practicing medicine in France lost their right to practice, medical students who had begun their studies under the old system were required to abide by the new rules. This issue had been a source of conflict among senators. Le Gorgeu and Armbruster were not eager to continue the grandfathering of current students into medical practice under the pre-1933 system, as they had done with the Armbruster law. They claimed that this "mistake" had left French medicine open to so many foreign students that the 1933 law had yet to take effect and would do so only after 1940. Yet Senator Viollette warned that the withdrawal of rights explicitly granted two years earlier—which in some circumstances would affect the same students who had been permitted to stay in 1933—would reflect negatively on France abroad. Ultimately, parliamentarians appeared convinced by Le Gorgeu's Manichaean argument that they must choose either Frenchmen or foreigners, and the retroactive interpretation prevailed. Current students, no matter how far along in their studies, had to abide by the new regulations.[170] This decision would serve as a precedent for officials of the Vichy regime to follow five years later, when many acquired rights would be rescinded and the principle of nonretroactivity would be stricken from French legal tradition.

From the debates over the Cousin-Nast legislation, a conception of naturalized citizens as foremost and permanent "foreigners" permeated even the upper reaches of the legislature. This shift was evident in slips of the tongue whereby naturalized citizens were referred to consistently not just as "naturalized foreigners" but sometimes simply as "foreigners." Le Gorgeu made this error several times. Furthermore, he searched desperately for official statistics about naturalized doctors in the French medical corps. To his chagrin, naturalized French doctors were not counted separately from "French doctors."[171] Behind the use of these labels among political leaders of the Third Republic lay an unspoken notion of *jus sanguinis* as the basis of citizenship.

Exclusionism Rages, 1935–1940

While the Cousin-Nast law offered the most far-reaching defense of the medical profession against competition from foreign students and new immigrants, several doctor-parliamentarians still believed that the restrictions did not go far enough.[172] Medical unions and student groups expressed disappointment with the new law, and their dissatisfaction grew until the outbreak of war. The greatest source of disgruntlement was that, despite their frenzied lobbying campaign, the French medical corps had not been granted the same ten-year waiting period protection as the legal profession. Only much shorter delays were instituted, based on nonperformance of military duty. Furthermore, in fact, for the few medical posts in the public service sector that had been covered by the 1934 law, it was possible that the 1935 law actually reduced the waiting period, for although the Cousin-Nast law broadened the restrictions to include departments and communes, it cut in half the waiting period for jobs subject to the provisions of the 1934 law.[173]

Meanwhile, medical unions strategized to broaden the definition of medical posts in the civil service to include all medical treatment of the publicly insured. The Cousin-Nast law's definition of medical civil service was clarified by an administrative ruling, but it remained murky in practice. The Syndicat médical de Loir-et-Cher, for example, protested to its prefecture that a French doctor who was a military veteran and a recipient of the Legion of Honor for his actions during the war had been fired as a public-service doctor for war orphans and replaced by a foreigner.[174] In the Seine-et-Oise in 1938, unions loudly denounced the prefecture for appointing a naturalized doctor as a medical inspector of newborns. The unions threatened a strike by all doctors in public service positions. They referred to the appointed doctor as a foreigner, not as a naturalized citizen.[175]

Doctors were also angry about other issues that had gone unaddressed despite heavy lobbying. The law still did not regulate medical practice in the French colonies. *Sujets* and *originaires* from protectorates were still allowed to practice medicine in metropolitan France. Naturalized citizens could still pursue the French baccalaureate and the one-year premedical certificate program in physics, chemistry, and natural sciences simultaneously with their medical studies. The *diplôme d'université* was not abolished, transformations to the *diplôme d'état* were still possible, naturalized citizens could receive transfer credit, and all foreign and naturalized doctors who were already practicing medicine in France retained their right to practice.[176]

Externships and internships still were not officially closed to foreigners nationwide, and doctors were especially offended that positions in the *clinicat,* the highest level of the training program that followed the internship, remained open to naturalized citizens.[177] In one shocking incident, distinguished leaders of the Parisian medical corps engaged in threatening and abusive actions to dissuade a naturalized intern from competing for the *clinicat*. Andrée Abadie, a superior medical graduate (*doctorat mention très honorable,* scoring eighth out of the eight hundred who took the Paris internship exam that year), naturalized French (an English subject born in Cairo), was to take the *clinicat* admission exam on 22 October 1937. The night before, however, she was summoned by the president and former president of the Association of Paris Interns, Drs. Georges Labey and Regaud, who told her that they opposed her candidacy and threatened violent "street fighting" if she showed up for the test the following day. In the face of this nocturnal warning, Abadie renounced taking the exam for which she had been preparing, but not without notifying the president of the exam jury of the incident.[178] Labey himself reported on this activism in his presidential farewell speech before the interns' association: "Taking matters into our own hands, we have found ways either to warn professors who had the intention of hiring as clinical chiefs naturalized foreigners who had promised to leave France, or to warn such persons directly that they were exposing themselves to certain forms of reprisal which could lead to regrettable incidents. In this way, we persuaded some candidates to withdraw from the clinical competitions for which they are morally ineligible."[179]

Despite complaints by the French medical corps that the law did not go far enough, the situation for foreigners and naturalized citizens in French medicine had tangibly worsened. The Cousin-Nast law had placed substantial obstacles in their path toward making a living through the practice of medicine. Many found themselves well along the path, just about to earn an income after long years of study, and suddenly faced with years of forced inactivity. In reaction, a group of about seventy Romanian *diplôme d'état* graduates sent a plea to the French prime minister. They claimed that they had long ago demanded naturalization and were ready to perform military service, but that their naturalizations had been delayed and often denied unreasonably, especially under the influence of the medical unions. The Romanians asked to be permitted at least to serve as replacements, warning that in the coming recruitment cycle there would not be enough candidates, and the public would suffer grave consequences.[180]

Native French First

Because the Cousin-Nast law essentially required naturalization for the practice of medicine, student groups and medical unions focused increasingly on the inadequacy of naturalization as a protective barrier for entry into the medical corps. Doctors' complaints fell into two categories: the excessive number of naturalizations, and the inadequate degree of assimilation of naturalized doctors. French doctors were particularly resentful of the shortened residency requirement mandated in the 1927 nationality law (from ten years to one year) for those who held French diplomas. In July 1936, in December 1937, and again in 1938, the Confédération, impelled by its smaller member unions, called on the government to halt all naturalizations of doctors and medical students.[181] Doctors argued that because of overcrowding, naturalization should be a rare favor granted to only the most worthy; native French deserved the right to earn a decent living, and the government owed them that protection.[182]

French doctors also complained that naturalized doctors were not assimilated enough. They argued that to help the ill in France, doctors needed to speak French and understand French customs. As Querrioux proclaimed, "It is logical to ask a doctor to be French and to have French parents before caring for a disabled veteran, someone who has given his blood for his country."[183] Senator Armbruster spoke of naturalized doctors before parliament: "We would hope that they would perhaps feel, after a long time, united with their patients by links of national solidarity which might awaken in them particular feelings of altruism, feelings that might have previously left them indifferent."[184] Some expressed doubt that satisfactory assimilation could ever be possible: "After all,... do we really want them to come and penetrate into the intimacy of French families?"[185]

Comments such as this, which demonstrate fears of foreign invasion or even "rape" of a private and pure national space, and the evolution of terminology used by French doctors and medical students, reveal shifts in French thinking about nationality and origins. We have already seen a rhetorical shift in the mid-1930s from "foreigner" to "non-naturalized" as the focus on naturalization took shape. But in the later 1930s, the terms "non-naturalized foreigner" and "naturalized foreigner" appeared in medical discourse, emphasizing the biological origin of these doctors rather than their actual nationality, and signifying that, in the mind of such speakers, naturalized doctors were in fact forever foreigners.

Xenophobic rhetoric in the medical corps during the interwar period was often marked by contradictory suspicions: either foreigners were unable to assimilate, or they assimilated too smoothly, with ulterior motives.[186] Some French doctors worried that a certain foreign cachet could seduce potential patients, especially naïve French women. One doctor railed: "Once set up, these colleagues with their sternutatory names quickly figure out how to gain favor with people since the crowd, and the feminine element in particular, generally adores Exoticism in all its forms. And so those with last names like Durand, Dubois, or Dupont who are withering away would find quick success if they changed their names to Durandoff, Duboisoff, Dupontiff."[187]

In late 1935 the medical unions scored a significant victory for which they had heavily lobbied. Minister of Justice Léon Bérard, who had been active in promoting the 1934 legislation against naturalized citizens in the legal profession, granted a consultative role to medical unions in the naturalization process of doctors and medical students. Unions were permitted to examine the files of applicants for naturalization and convey their opinion to the ministry, which would take such an evaluation into consideration in its final decision.[188] Medical unions rushed to form commissions to weigh in on candidates. Their recommendations were most often negative.[189] Some available statistics concerning the most populous department, the Seine, allow for a case study, although they were published by the Seine Medical Union itself, so they should be regarded with considerable reserve. Only 40 of 166 doctors or medical students who were candidates for naturalization in 1936, and 78 of 227 candidates in 1937, were eventually granted naturalization by the French state.[190] The government did not always follow unions' recommendations regarding candidates for naturalization, but it did not ultimately approve many more candidates than the unions approved.

The unions nevertheless complained loudly about the discrepancy between their opinions and the state's final decisions, as well as about the large number of candidacies not even submitted to the medical unions by the state.[191] One doctor argued: "The *union* is alone competent to do a complete investigation.... A *judgment of peers* is alone able to furnish the state not only with the requested information but also with conclusions for a *judicious and equitable opinion*....This opinion should be the preponderant element in according or refusing naturalization.... What is the point of requiring unions to do long, fastidious, and always onerous investigations if the state can, with the flick of a pen, annihilate a careful reflective opinion?"[192] A report of the Seine Medical Union read, "It seems that consultation with the unions was granted more to flatter our pride than to take our information and professional conclusions seriously, which nevertheless are inspired by tolerance and impartiality."[193] The Union-Association of Doctors of Meurthe-et-Moselle, for its part, gloated that its departmental authorities always seconded its opinions about naturalization candidates.[194]

The Seine Medical Union proposed other strategies: developing contacts with civil servants dealing with naturalizations, monitoring the activities of pro-naturalization groups in France, and establishing a doctrine for all medical unions to follow in issuing naturalization opinions.[195] In an attempt to standardize union action, the Paris Medical Union recommended to other unions that they give negative opinions for all *diplôme d'université* graduates and for those whose age would preclude them from military service (this after the 1935 law instituted waiting periods for such cases).[196] In fact, one naturalization candidate was officially refused because he had a *diplôme d'université,* a justification that found no basis in any French law.[197] Other medical candidates were refused naturalization for not possessing the French baccalaureate, for being married to a non-French wife, for having no children, and for being too old to perform military service.[198] Regardless of how much weight the government gave to the unions' opinions, the implications are important. The French state allowed professional interest groups to participate in one of the state's basic functions: determining nationality regulations.[199] In fact, this state policy extended to other occupations: artisans and merchants groups were also invited to weigh in on naturalization candidates in their fields.[200]

It is important to situate the medical corps's increasing protectionism in the late 1930s within the context of radicalizing nationalism in French society as a whole. Naturalization policy became more restrictive overall with the decree-laws of 1938 and 1939. A delay of five years was imposed before naturalized French citizens had the right to vote, and the legal procedure for revising naturalizations was simplified in the last years of the Third Republic. Parliament raised the pre-naturalization residency requirement to five years,[201] instituted French language exams, and made medical exams for candidates for French citizenship more rigorous.[202] In fact, French doctors participated in these processes by performing medical exams on immigrants before their entry into France and on naturalization candidates.[203] Doctors had long used their role as the caretakers of public health to portray foreigners as carriers of contagion. The Paris Medical Union declared in its journal in 1935: "All the scum from other countries, all the undesirables in their own countries, head for France. Our ancient French race is beginning to be submerged by this influx of polluted blood, by the growing mass of millions of individuals, very often with physical and moral defects."[204] Doctors thus used their expertise to implant xenophobic sentiment in French society.

In this protectionist context, medical doctors drew inspiration from government measures protecting French manual laborers from competition with foreigners, equating their own struggle with that of less elite occupations.[205] Parliament heeded the point. Senator-doctor Dentu argued before his colleagues, "Without wanting to compare two things that are not very comparable, why not envelop into one protection both manual labor and intellectual labor?"[206] In 1938, inspired by the *carte de travail* required for shopkeepers and manual laborers, some doctors called for similar measures against foreign doctors.[207] The historian Vicki Caron has documented in rich detail the larger middle-class protest during the 1930s.[208]

At least two dissertations were defended in French law schools in 1939 that focused on the question of access to the medical profession for foreigners and naturalized citizens, suggesting that legal scholarship was paying attention to the new precedents being set by the restrictive legislation.[209] In two blatantly anti-Semitic dissertations defended at the Paris Medical School in 1939, Albin Faivre called for the blanket revision of all naturalizations conferred since 1918,[210] and Jacques Boudard linked malpractice cases with foreign doctors. Of dubious research, Boudard's thesis was chaired by Victor Balthazard.[211] That such dissertations received advice from faculty and were approved by deans and rectors demonstrates that anti-Semitic discourse was becoming acceptable in the year before the collapse of the Third Republic.[212]

Despite the mounting restrictions of the 1930s, the French government maintained diplomatic conventions with several nations that allowed exceptions for their citizens to practice medicine. Diplomatic conventions took two forms: an agreement to regulate the practice of medicine by the nationals of two countries in regions that shared national borders, or an agreement to institute reciprocal parity of doctors in each country. Agreements of the first type existed between France and Belgium, Luxembourg, Switzerland, Italy, and Spain. In the 1930s, French medical unions in regions bordering these countries fought doggedly against these exceptions, which affected their members directly. In the Moselle along the Luxembourg border, five French doctors scattered throughout the countryside complained of unfair competition from fifty-six Luxembourgeois doctors from large urban centers across the border.[213] Along the border with Switzerland, the Syndicat médical de Mulhouse lobbied the government to renounce its 1889 convention.[214] Despite prefecture surveys revealing that French public opinion and even a majority of French doctors were satisfied with the convention, the Ministry of Foreign Affairs revised the 1889 convention in April 1933 and forbade Swiss doctors from practicing in certain key areas along the French side of Lake Geneva.[215] French doctors complained that Belgian doctors were violating the 1910 convention by practicing in French communes where French doctors resided, and they lobbied to reduce the list of French communes open to Belgian doctors.[216] As chapter 7 shows, however, the shared experience of war and occupation may have quelled the competition between French and Belgian doctors: in more than one instance in 1940 and 1941, French doctors in the Nord department proactively defended doctors of Belgian origin in the face of Vichy exclusionary legislation.

Although the Armbruster and Cousin-Nast laws both allowed for diplomatic conventions of parity, no such convention existed until the Principality of Monaco initiated one in 1934. Eighteen French doctors practiced in the principality, whereas no Monegasque doctor practiced in France. The Syndicat médical de la Savoie resisted reciprocity and was defended by the French Ministry of Public Health. The Ministry of Foreign Affairs, however, pushed for a convention, which was signed in 1938 only after Monaco threatened to ban French doctors from its territory.[217] Although French state officials generally abided by diplomatic commitments—as well as acted to protect French patients' access to health care regardless of the provider's nationality—they did make extraordinary efforts to appease a minority of complaining French doctors. These examples challenge the growing notion in interwar France of selective immigration, whereby citizens from culturally proximate and neighboring nations were more favorably welcomed in France than others. When direct occupational competition with French citizens was at stake, the state was remarkably receptive to the demands of a minority.

The Irony of War: A Dearth of Doctors Reverses Restrictionism

As another European war became likely in the late 1930s, French nationalism in the medical field manifested itself in the fear that if French doctors were to be mobilized in great numbers, foreign doctors not only would avoid the battlefield but also would steal the clientele of French doctors fulfilling their patriotic duty.[218] One doctor reported to the minister of the interior that foreign doctors were "war profiteering" by practicing medicine in his town of Oisement in the Somme.[219] This concern had already arisen in 1935 during negotiations over the Cousin-Nast law.[220] In 1940 Senator Armbruster urged the prime minister to take action.[221] The Confédération proposed a compromise to the government: to mobilize foreign doctors as civilians,[222] and to station them "at least 25 kilometers from their residence" so as to prevent them from caring simultaneously for their paying clientele.[223]

As early as September 1938 this professional fear took a punitive turn when Dr. Hilaire, a leader of the Confédération, proposed that in case of war, foreign doctors who held citizenship in enemy states be placed in concentration camps.[224] The Paris Medical Union seconded Hilaire's proposal.[225] The medical unions of the Seine-et-Oise and the Aube likewise called for foreign and naturalized doctors to be forced into concentration camps.[226] Several of these groups also proposed that naturalized doctors originally from non-enemy states should be subjected to obligatory mobilization in a combat unit.

The outbreak of war and the general mobilization greatly disrupted the delicate balance of turf-sharing among doctors in various localities. Mobilized doctors worried not only about foreign doctors taking their places but also about competition from non-mobilized French doctors. Some doctors were mobilized in their own localities and thus could maintain their civilian clientele. Many accusations of intra-French poaching of clientele flew around the medical corps, and the Confédération soon lobbied for an end to *mobilisation sur place* for French doctors.[227]

And yet, even as French doctors were calling for the internment of foreign and naturalized doctors and accusing their French colleagues of poaching their patients, the military mobilization created an enormous shortage of medical care for civilians. Northern France faced an especially dangerous dearth of doctors during the "phony war." The death rate in the Nord department, where one commune of 32,000 inhabitants counted a single doctor aged seventy-two, tripled in the winter months of 1939–40 compared with the year before.[228] What the medical unions in the Nord department called for was not, however, temporary assistance from any qualified practitioner in the interest of public health and national defense, but the demobilization of the department's native French doctors.[229] In January 1940, in desperation, some doctors supported granting permission to "one or two Belgian doctors" to care for indigent recipients of medical welfare, but others disagreed with even this concession.[230]

As an emergency response to the shortage of medical professionals in certain regions, the decree of 15 May 1940, passed as German troops invaded French territory, gave authorization to practice medicine in France to all *diplôme d'université* graduates, to foreigners holding *diplômes d'état* who were not already allowed to practice, and in special cases to foreign doctors holding foreign diplomas (those who held special titles or had rendered special services to France). This decree thus represented a total reversal of the restrictionist legislation of the 1930s and essentially reauthorized all the categories of nationality and medical degree that had been so carefully excluded one by one from medical practice in France. But the 15 May decree was not a blanket liberalization: doctors were to be authorized individually after an investigation; the measure was temporary and revocable; and the reauthorized doctors were permitted to practice only in certain localities. The Confédération was offered one representative on the eleven-member interministerial commission to decide each authorization.

The Ministry of Foreign Affairs, noting the urgent need for doctors, intended to interpret the 15 May decree liberally, and it established an order of priority for authorizations: first, French nationals holding *diplômes d'université* (their number was insignificant); then foreign doctors holding either kind of French medical diploma who were natives of the Allied nations of Belgium, Luxembourg, Holland, Poland, and Czechoslovakia; and finally foreign doctors holding either kind of French diploma who were natives of neutral nations. This last category had to produce a one-year residency permit and was subject to a "very severe" investigation before authorization.[231] Obviously the ministry's hierarchy of authorizations was designed with foreign policy interests in mind.

These state measures regarding military and civilian medical care demonstrate rational policymaking in a time of national emergency. By reauthorizing foreigners to practice medicine in France after years of increasing restrictions against naturalized French, the state restrained protectionist tendencies in the interest of national security and public health. At the same time, without negating the new authorizations elaborated in the 15 May decree, six days later the government passed a decree-law forbidding the opening of new medical offices during hostilities "so as to preserve the rights and interests of mobilized doctors."[232] Under the strain of war, the French state was still responding to the demands of medical unions.

★ ★ ★

Through an analysis of the motivations and strategies of medical professionals, this chapter has examined a social movement from its genesis to its crystallization. French doctors had long strategized to protect their turf and exaggerated the plethora of professionals in order to defend their interests; but the interwar years brought many new challenges, such as the establishment of a new medical welfare system, the democratization of higher education, the depression, the arrival of refugees, student unrest, and an ideology of xenophobia that was being propagated on the political right. In this cauldron, the medical corps targeted foreigners and naturalized citizens as scapegoats. The movement was initiated and led from below, and it prospered in the near-absence of government correctives.

The state's role is not insignificant. The French parliament was ultimately responsible for the laws against foreigners and naturalized citizens in medicine, and the Ministry of Public Health and the Ministry of Education, as well as university administrators, all participated in various ways in implementing restrictionary policies. Some state actors, most notably the Ministry of Foreign Affairs, dissented in the interest of international relations, an important reminder that the state was not a monolithic entity pursuing a single coherent policy. But as medical unions and student groups pushed for more restrictions throughout the 1930s, the state continuously responded by legislating increased protections for medicine, though never to the complete satisfaction of the medical corps. One notable measure in this evolving process was the state's granting in 1935 of a consultative role to medical unions in weighing naturalization candidacies, which can be seen as a precursor to the republican abdication of 1940.

One of the most important developments during the 1930s was the slow but manifest paradigm shift that saw the republican principle of *jus soli* revoked. Naturalized citizens came to be viewed as second-class citizens at best, but most commonly as permanent foreigners. As a member of the Paris Medical Union put it plainly when planning protectionist strategies, "We will divide foreign doctors into two categories: naturalized doctors and non-naturalized doctors."[233] Throughout the 1930s, the idea of blood-based citizenship gradually but palpably gained ground in the medical community. This made it easier for Vichy to go further in its exclusionary policies after the defeat, though only after the remarkable interlude of the phony war and the Battle of France, when out of sheer necessity the government eased restrictions to deal with the emergency shortage of doctors.

Xenophobic sentiment can be partly attributed to a characteristic Malthusian conception of medical practice held by many doctors, a notion of a limited market of sick people that doctors had to fight over in order to maintain a share. Conspicuously absent from ordinary practitioners' thinking were innovative possibilities for finding new needs for medical care. As one doctor admitted: "There is a notable decrease in the number of sick people. That is good for the general population but unfortunate for us."[234] Vicki Caron argues that the depression, which created fears of unemployment and of downward social mobility, was a critical factor behind the middle-class uprising against foreigners and Jewish refugees.[235]

The quest for professional prestige was an additional factor that pushed doctors into protectionist reactionism. Even parliamentarians appealed to the importance of the healing profession to justify protection for French doctors. Deputy Dommange called medicine "a career that is, most often, a veritable apostolic mission,"[236] and Senator Dentu declared, "Medicine is a priesthood."[237] Even in a secular republican regime, these proclamations that preserving the honor of the medical profession was for the good of the public essentially endowed medical interests with national interests. Eliminating foreigners, naturalized citizens, and other undesirables was seen as a primary means of protecting the prestige of the profession. As one medical union congratulated itself, "The medical corps of Meurthe-et-Moselle constitutes an elite that has not yet grown gangrenous from the Slavic or Danubian invasion; we have so far been able to contain the infection."[238]

CHAPTER 3

The Art of Medicine

Access and Status

Although the movement to exclude foreigners during the interwar years was the most important manifestation of medical protectionism, doctors pursued other strategies for professional survival that call into question the notion that the anti-foreigner movement arose simply from xenophobia. Merging protectionism with professionalization, doctors strove to reduce the number of medical graduates by raising qualification standards. Three main proposals were advanced: a return to the classical baccalaureate, quotas on medical students, and more rigorous exams. This strategy was aimed at reducing the number of French citizens, not foreigners, entering the profession. Because educational trajectories were strongly determined by social origins, controversy emerged over the discriminatory effect of this strategy on the lower and middle classes.

The medical profession also sought to protect itself through distinction. By clearly defining and staking out their professional terrain, doctors hoped to elevate their status by distancing themselves from other health care providers. Manifestations of this strategy included the repression of charlatanism and illegal medical practice by non-doctors, protection of the title of "doctor," and campaigns against dentists, pharmacists, nurses, and midwives to preserve doctors' professional domain. Turf protection also led to battles among doctors themselves. Evidence of competition between private practitioners and state-salaried doctors, and between generalists and specialists, especially when the field of medicine was being altered by the institutionalization of medical welfare, demonstrates that the family of doctors was not immune to internecine feuds. Finally, two specific categories of French citizens were blamed for dragging down the profession and were targeted for exclusion: women and elderly doctors. Like foreigners, Frenchwomen were especially singled out as scapegoats whose legitimate presence in French medicine could be challenged when professional survival seemed to be at stake.

These proposals to restrict the access of French people to the medical profession attest to the existence of larger protectionist mechanisms beyond the scope of mere xenophobia. By providing a more complete picture of exclusionary practices in the medical profession in interwar France, they add nuance to the arguments presented in chapter 2 without diminishing the primacy of the anti-foreigner movement. Before analyzing these various strategies, I first examine the opinion of a small minority of doctors who rejected the myth of overcrowding altogether.

There Is No Plethora

A handful of medical professionals responded to the widespread panic over the supposed glut of doctors with detachment, believing that there was no plethora of doctors at all, given the infinite possibilities of scientific discoveries for improving health care and the democratic value of providing an excellent education to the maximum number of citizens. Several medical professionals acknowledged that more doctors were needed in rural areas of the country. These points of view effectively undermined all the premises behind the anti-foreigner mobilization, although they had little actual impact on it. A few French doctors and students even took an actively pro-foreigner stance and publicly criticized the exclusionary movement. Such resistance to the predominant thinking in the medical profession thus took three forms: rejection of the plethora myth, recognition of a professional distribution problem, and a welcoming acceptance of foreigners.

Determining the appropriate number of health care providers for a society was, of course, a subjective undertaking.[1] In response to the Malthusian stance embraced by most medical unions, which maintained that excessive competition led to the commercialization of medicine, with nefarious effects on patients, progressives argued that there could never be too many doctors. In favor of both social mobility and patient rights, such thinkers promoted accommodation of the maximum number of doctors. One doctor ironically lamented doctors' "financial situation, already compromised by the decrease in sick people. The medical profession is the only one, to our knowledge, that works against its direct interests and we are proud of it."[2] For the successful implementation of Jules Ferry's educational principles, *laïque, gratuite, et obligatoire,* such thinkers advocated for increased government funding to expand the infrastructure of the university system in order to serve the largest possible student body.[3]

The preceding chapter revealed that France did not have too many medical practitioners but, in fact, needed more of them in rural areas. Drastic differences in the doctor-per-inhabitant ratios between urban and rural regions attested to a sufficient number of doctors in Paris and other large cities but to a real and occasionally dangerous dearth in many other regions. In 1941 there were over three thousand inhabitants per doctor in the departments of the Ardennes, Nord, and Pas-de-Calais, whereas in the departments of the Alpes-Maritimes, Haute-Garonne, and Seine there were fewer than nine hundred inhabitants per doctor.[4]

The problem of geographical inequity in medicine began at the level of education. Provincial medical students often began their studies near home but transferred to Paris or another large city for the final years of medical school. The Paris Medical School awarded 52 percent of all medical *diplômes d'état* granted in France in 1937.[5] Students who finished medical school in the big cities generally preferred to remain there. Many presumed that an urban practice, even with supposedly stiffer competition, would be easier to manage successfully than a rural practice characterized by few clients, low fees, long travel distances, and loneliness. This typical educational trajectory contributed to the lack of medical practitioners in small towns and rural areas. As one observer pointed out, "If students stayed close to their families, regularly passing by the clock tower, they would be more likely to set up practice in their native towns."[6] The Ministry of Education had already tried to counteract the problem in the nineteenth century by creating more provincial medical schools, but it persisted into the twentieth century.

The state recognized that the medical profession was characterized by an unequal and inefficient distribution of doctors. The Ministry of Education organ, the Bureau universitaire de statistique (BUS), led the way in publicizing the problem and pushed for medical unions to cover costs for doctors willing to settle in less populated areas.[7] The BUS also collected job offers for doctors in rural areas of France and posted them on student bulletin boards.[8] Some municipal authorities in towns lacking in doctors also took initiatives to attract doctors with financial aid for lodging and travel. Deputy Charles Pomaret of the Popular Front coalition also attempted to address the unequal distribution of doctors. Article 22 of his 1936 proposed law called for state subsidies to match communal subsidies aimed at luring young doctors to small towns and rural areas.[9] The BUS also urged the government to create more civil service jobs for doctors in the colonies, which were in dire need of health care providers,[10] and propaganda from the Colonial Exposition of 1931 encouraged doctors to establish private medical practices in the colonies.[11]

A handful of medical professionals spoke out honestly about the dearth of doctors. One medical dissertation in 1939 declared, "Not only is professional overcrowding implausible, but we should worry that the number of doctors is falling beneath a minimum figure necessary for the maintenance of public health, especially in the countryside."[12] The communist student group Union fédérale des étudiants (UFE) argued candidly that medicine was characterized by a distribution problem.[13]

Although these examples show that exclusionary sentiment was not unanimous in French medicine, they had little impact in a sea of protectionist activism. Medical unions paid no heed to the unequal distribution of doctors across France and continued to insist that the profession was overcrowded. In the mid-1930s, the Confédération des syndicats médicaux français, which counted 80 percent of all doctors as members, proclaimed, "The medical plethora is a universal fact clearly established and proven by the statistics."[14] A few medical student groups and doctors' unions—for example, the Union nationale des étudiants de France—paid occasional lip service to the distribution problem, all the while battling fiercely to exclude foreigners and naturalized citizens.[15] In one medical journal, a writer advocated that overcrowding could partly be solved by "a plan . . . for decentralization or for better distribution, but especially by an all-out war against foreign elements."[16] The initiative to redress the uneven distribution of doctors was a top-down effort, originating with the state, but government efforts were meager and sporadic, and none met with much success.

Not every French medical student and doctor demanded the exclusion of foreigners. Some recognized that since there was no plethora of doctors in France, foreign doctors should be welcomed and even encouraged. Others criticized the xenophobic tide overtaking the medical corps on moral grounds, ignoring practical questions of supply and demand. The UFE was a champion of the foreigners' cause. In an internationalist spirit, the organization called for equal rights for foreigners to study and work. A UFE tract from 1931 proclaimed, "Down with the Armbruster exclusionary measure copied from the fascist universities in the Balkans."[17] Other student groups were founded in the 1930s for the purpose of promoting Franco-foreign cooperation, and they often spoke out against the exclusionary legislation of the 1930s.[18] Such countervailing ideas, however, attracted few medical students.[19]

A couple of practicing doctors also spoke out against the anti-foreigner movement in French medicine. In a 1922 meeting of the Paris Medical Union, a Dr. Levassort asserted that the panic over foreigners was unwarranted. The number of diplômes d'université transformed into diplômes d'état by naturalized French was minimal, he noted, and rumors of special exceptions granted to foreign students by the ministers of education and foreign affairs were completely false.[20] While Levassort succeeded in bringing a rational, calming influence to at least one medical union meeting, this lone measured perspective from the early

1920s did nothing to stop the acceleration of the anti-foreigner mobilization in medicine.

For other French medical professionals, their openness to foreigners was more strategic, justified by a concern for France's scientific reputation abroad as well as a fear of reprisals. It was considered a matter of national interest that French education remain open to foreigners, who would then act as ambassadors of French values in their native countries. Even some of the more virulent advocates of restrictions against foreigners recognized the value of this policy. The Association of Paris Interns was another active leader of the anti-foreigner mobilization, yet in one instance it made a pretense of international goodwill and Franco-Romanian solidarity by inviting a Professor Daniel, who had been educated in France, from the University of Bucharest to speak at its 1936 annual banquet.[21]

Many French expressed concern that German universities would profit from French exclusionism. Since the French *diplôme d'université* was no longer recognized as valid for practice in Belgium, more and more Belgian students in the first decades of the twentieth century sought a German medical diploma, which was accepted in Belgium.[22] Competition with Germany thus served to temper extremism in the interests of France's scientific reputation abroad. After all, the memory of the Franco-Prussian defeat, which was largely attributed to the decay of French scholarship, was only some sixty years old. A Dr. Hartmann noted, "If the recent demonstrations occur again, they will convince people that there is a xenophobic mobilization going on, which our neighbors—desiring to attract our foreign clientele—will not fail to exploit."[23] Others worried that the hostility toward foreigners in French medicine would incite foreign governments to enact reprisal legislation, hurting French doctors practicing abroad.[24]

Examples of pro-foreigner solidarity are extremely rare compared to the tide of anti-foreigner activism in the interwar period, but a study of any social movement must account for this quiet form of resistance. If French students and doctors saw no threat from foreigners in their classrooms or professions and even disdained the xenophobia exhibited by their more vocal colleagues, they remained largely invisible in the historical record. The few examples cited here were informed partly by generosity of spirit, partly by an accurate grasp of the professional market, and partly by calculated "public relations" concerns.

Quality Control

On one issue all doctors in interwar France agreed: that raising the level of educational and practical training would improve the quality of doctors and the reputation of the profession. Doctors also universally understood that raising standards (*relever le niveau*) would automatically decrease the number of doctors, and few were against that. The link between improved quality and diminished quantity of medical school graduates was so obvious to everyone that the discourse often inverted the ends and the means. The desire to alleviate supposed overcrowding often became primary, and raising educational standards was simply a means to reduce numbers, not an end in itself. As Jacques Léonard observed in 1981, "To deflate this supposed plethora—a sturdy trope lasting until today—doctors always invoked the necessity of a strict qualitative selection."[25] In this sense doctors engaged in another strategy of self-protection: professionalization.[26] Even officials at the BUS, which as a state organ of the Third Republic was officially in favor of the democratization of education and social mobility, worried in the 1930s that rapid social change in combination with a depressed economy meant that a university diploma no longer promised economic security. They feared the creation of an "intellectual proletariat."[27]

Doctors disagreed, however, over how to raise the level. The endless stream of legislative projects to reform medical studies in the interwar period attests to the importance of this issue. Determining access to the profession affected the core identity of medicine, which was in the midst of an evolution during the interwar years from its pre-Revolutionary values based on honor and prestige to its post–Le Chapelier principles based on education and professionalization. Because the profession was caught in the middle of a major transformation in which its elitist, traditional conservative identity was being replaced, with difficulty, by a more republican and democratic identity, the attempts to raise standards touched a sensitive sociopolitical nerve: class conflict.

Shortly after World War I, medical unions proposed three solutions to reduce the number of French medical students: requiring the traditional Latin-Greek baccalaureate, instituting a *concours* system of competitive exams, and raising educational requirements within the existing curricular structure.[28] Only the third solution elicited agreement. The first two were considered discriminatory by some, who argued that secondary and superior education should be open to all who were interested, and furthermore that more scholarships should be offered to needy students to guarantee free access for all social classes.[29] The Latin-Greek baccalaureate had long been a traditional prerequisite for medical studies, but educational reforms establishing the *école unique* unified the several types of baccalaureate degrees that conferred the right to enter a university. Traditional conservative doctors considered the other baccalaureate degrees to be inferior and held this change responsible for the invasion of medicine by many new students considered ill-prepared for university. Because of the historical association of the various baccalaureates with particular social classes, competing visions of social mobility and democratization were at stake in this debate.

The debate began when Senator Charles Debierre, from the department of the Nord, successfully inserted an amendment into the proposed Armbruster law in 1930 to reinstate the Latin-Greek baccalaureate requirement for entry into medical school.[30] Debierre argued that during his forty-plus-year tenure as professor at the Lyon Medical School, and later at the Lille Medical School, he had witnessed firsthand the decline in the intellectual abilities of students.[31] Senator Raymond Armbruster shared Debierre's esteem for the classics: "The practitioner must not only find the problem in the flesh of the patient, but must also read in his soul to know of his secrets. . . . It is a very delicate and complex role which requires a refined critical eye softened by the study of psychology, which forms, with the study of Greek and Latin, the core of our humanities. . . . It is said that medicine is a science, but its practice is an art."[32] Claiming that all doctors and medical school faculty councils shared his point of view, Debierre acknowledged that this measure would have the added advantage of reducing overcrowding.[33] Indeed the proposal would have dramatically reduced the number of medical students: records show that out of 762 first-year Paris medical students in 1931–32, only 177 had a Latin-Greek baccalaureate. Some senators worried that the amendment would create a sudden drop in the number of medical students and proposed a transition period to allow students to switch secondary education tracks.[34]

Medical unions and student groups such as the Confédération and the Association corporative des étudiants en médecine favored reintroducing the humanities into the training of medical professionals.[35] But medical opinion was divided, and in turn, political will was too weak to pass Debierre's amendment. A survey of 318 medical professors concluded that only 130 favored requiring the Latin-Greek baccalaureate exclusively, while 119 favored a limited choice between the Latin-Greek and Latin-sciences baccalaureates.[36] Some doctors and medical academics argued that a complete overhaul of medical studies was needed, not this single measure which would only continue the decades-long incoherent, piecemeal improvements. Parents' associations also rallied against requiring the Latin-Greek baccalaureate.[37]

After much debate, the Chamber of Deputies eliminated Debierre's amendment from the proposed Armbruster law in February 1933. Senator Alexandre Bachelet had resisted the senatorial tide with a plea not to discriminate: "I believe, on the contrary, that in a democracy we must try to lower the barriers that separate our primary from our higher education so that all those who are worthy can reach the highest roles in the social hierarchy."[38] Armbruster himself asked the Senate to withdraw the controversial amendment in order to focus on the essential goal of his law: the restriction of foreigners.[39] More doctors were in favor of barring foreigners than were in favor of barring French students of diverse socio-educational backgrounds.

For another solution to reduce the number of medical students, Senator Georges Portmann from the Gironde proposed a law in late 1934 to institute a numerus clausus, or quota, on medical students. A professor of otolaryngology at the Bordeaux Medical School, Portmann suggested that there be two competitive exams: one after the preparatory PCB year (physical sciences, chemistry, and biology) and another after the first year of medical school. The number of students allowed to continue their schooling after each exam would be predetermined by the Ministry of Education.[40] The Confédération, the Section corporative des étudiants en médecine de Montpellier,[41] as well as student representatives of the medical schools of Lille, Toulouse, Nantes, Limoges, and Clermont-Ferrand at the annual congress of the Union nationale des étudiants de France in 1932 all supported an admissions quota decided by exam (*concours*).[42] It would reduce the number of foreign medical students, they noted, implying that their intellectual level was inferior to that of French students. The Strasbourg medical students' association proposed that "naturalized foreigners [*sic*] should be chosen for their professional value, and as a way to evaluate them, a medical *concours* for all candidates should be instituted in order to limit entrance in the medical corps only to an elite."[43]

A significant portion of the medical corps, including members of the Confédération, however, rejected the idea of quotas for various reasons. Many doctors took issue with the problem of determining an appropriate number of future doctors in theory and in practice. Some stated that it was impossible to judge good from bad future doctors so early in their medical studies. Some believed that since the PCB and first year of study did not cover material pertinent to becoming a practicing doctor, competitive exams should not be based on those subjects.[44] Some worried about the fairness of grading within and across medical schools.[45] Some wondered how future medical vacancies could be predicted when retirement was random and war was unpredictable.[46] Others were concerned that determining a specific number of medical professionals for society's future needs would imply a quasi-promise of career opportunities. They feared that the state would be dragged into designating medical jobs and that medicine would become a bureaucracy.[47] Some resented the generational rift inherent in Portmann's proposal since it was aimed at the young for the benefit of older, voting doctors.[48] Several student groups were against the Portmann proposal.[49] Some professors thought a reduction in the number of students would hurt medical schools.[50] Because the Ministry of Education would control the determination of the number of doctors under Portmann's proposal, a numerus clausus represented to some doctors a more threatening possibility: the *étatisation* of French medicine.[51]

No quota or *concours* was instituted in French medical education in the interwar years. While all doctors favored raising the quality of medical graduates, and most doctors favored reducing the quantity, a quota was nevertheless distasteful to a medical corps whose supreme professional value was to be "liberal." Even

Victor Balthazard admitted that a *concours* "is repellent to our ideas about free access to higher education."[52] That a majority of the medical corps disapproved demonstrates that professional Malthusianism had its limits.

A third solution for raising the quality of doctors was easily agreed upon: rendering medical studies more difficult. In 1932 the Confédération called for more rigorous medical school exams; specifically, anonymous written exams were to replace orals, following the example of law schools, which had recently switched to this system. Anonymity was considered the only purely merito-cratic means of evaluating students in a field known for its socio-professional "reproduction."[53] The state did not disagree. Parliamentarians, the Ministry of Education, and the BUS all advocated raising standards by imposing tougher exams.[54] With such broad consensus, medical exams were made more difficult in the 1930s.[55]

While the strategy of "quality control" could be efficiently aimed at the most numerically significant source of growth in the population of medical students, namely young French students from classes not previously represented in universities and the professions, the strategy met resistance from those mind-ful of the Third Republic values of democracy and social mobility. A significant proportion of medical professionals rejected some of the tactics for raising edu-cational standards because they perceived the strategy as a mere screen for class discrimination. Although university schooling was theoretically free, the cost of administrative fees and books, not to mention the loss of income during long years of study, significantly deterred students from less fortunate families from attending medical school. One student group fought for greater educational democratization. In an early 1930s tract the UFE proclaimed: "'Daddy's boys' hold a quasi-monopoly over medical studies, which are long and costly. Let us open access to the sons of laborers by offering them generous scholarships." In particular, the UFE urged that state subsidies for student associations, notably for the Association générale and the Association corporative des étudiants en méde-cine, whose members the UFE labeled "semi-fascists," should be discontinued and used instead to fund more scholarships for needy students.[56]

Strategies of Distinction

Chapter 1 traced the evolution of the professionalization of French medicine throughout the nineteenth century and described, in particular, how doctors tried to assert their identity as unique, highly trained, scientific professionals, superior to all other health care providers. Their strategies included suppressing folk healers, eliminating the role of health officers, and distinguishing between themselves and paramedical healers such as midwives and nurses. These issues had not disappeared by the mid-twentieth century, although it is clear that foreigners had become the primary object of doctors' hostility in the twentieth century. In the interwar period the profession's desiderata still included the repression of illegal medical practice and charlatanism, as well as protections against the use of the title "doctor" by non-doctors and the distinction of medical doctors as superior to other legitimate health care professionals.

Since the nineteenth century, doctors had sought to criminalize the practice of medicine by those not possessing a *diplôme d'état*. What constituted illegal medical practice? The definition included midwives, nurses, health officers, or pharmacists performing medical treatments outside the range of their prescribed duties; folk healers performing any act that claimed to heal a physical ailment; medical students practicing medicine who had not yet graduated; and doctors with medical diplomas from non-French schools practicing medicine. The strategy of protecting doctors' occupational turf against these encroachments had the support of the entire medical corps, even the UFE.[57]

Over the years, medical unions lobbied the state to expand the list of illegal medical practices, to render judicial pursuit easier, and to increase penalties (prison terms and fines) for the guilty. To make it easier to pursue illegal practitioners, one proposal involved identity control. Doctors had long been required to register their medical diploma with the departmental prefecture, but new proposals emerged in the 1930s to include additional notification of the mayor and judiciary officials, strict notification procedures for moving from one town to another, and penalties for failing to follow these procedures.[58] Parliament often heeded the call and tried to oblige with legislation.[59]

Medical unions also took matters into their own hands and pursued individual illegal practitioners themselves. Many unions had special sections devoted to this activity. Doctors in the Medical Federation of Finistère pursued two cases of illegal practice in 1936.[60] The Seine Medical Union opened sixty-three investigations of illegal medical practice in 1927, forwarded twenty-seven complaints to the prefecture, sent seventeen cases to court, and congratulated itself for twenty convictions.[61]

While doctors sought to bar non-doctors from performing medical acts, they also sought to bar non-doctors from using the title "doctor." The so-called *usurpation du titre* issue was a battle for terrain that touched on professional identity: the fear that quacks operating under the guise of doctors would harm the prestige of legitimate physicians.[62] Although the 1892 law condemned illegal medical practice by non-doctors, it did nothing to criminalize the misuse of the title. It was legal for non-doctors to distribute business cards, correspond on letterhead stationery, and hang wall plaques identifying themselves as doctors.[63] In 1924 parliament passed a law penalizing the usurpation of titles belonging to doctors, lawyers, and other professions. This satisfied the medical corps up to a point. Usurpation of the title *docteur en médecine* was now prohibited, but using the title *médecin* or the colloquial term *docteur* (whether by itself or preceding a surname) was not banned by the law. Case law in the later interwar years, however, did provide a few victories.[64]

Two of the stickiest problems surrounding the title issue involved foreigners and auxiliary medical personnel, who were targeted in this campaign. French doctors worried that foreigners who might have been legitimate doctors in their native countries were continuing to use their title in France even when they were not permitted to practice medicine. Some French doctors proposed that the name of the medical school follow that of the doctor, for example, "Mr. X, doctor of medicine of the University of Paris." This usage, however, created problems of distinguishing themselves from medical school graduates with French *diplômes d'université,* almost all of them foreigners. If the same formula of mentioning the medical school in the title were applied domestically, the title for holders of university (not state) diplomas would be *docteur en médecine de l'Université de Paris*—not obviously inferior enough to the real *docteur en médecine.*[65]

Auxiliary medical personnel such as pharmacists, veterinarians, and dentists, by their very closeness to the medical profession, often raised the ire of doctors eager to distinguish their supposed superiority. This was particularly true because the officially appropriate forms of address, "Madame Dupont, docteur veterinaire," "Monsieur La Fontaine, docteur en pharmacie," and "Madame Roche, docteur en chirurgie dentaire," slid inexorably into the more handy "Docteur Dupont," "Docteur La Fontaine," and "Docteur Roche." A long, bitter battle over the issue led the Fédération corporative des syndicats médicaux de la Seine to quit the Confédération des travailleurs intellectuels (CTI), which represented many kinds of professions, in 1933.[66] The medical profession had little judicial recourse against these infractions even after the 1924 law went into effect.[67] The case of entirely nonmedical professionals whose doctoral degrees earned them the titles of *docteur en droit* or *docteur ès lettres,* even though such persons were never referred to as "docteur" in common parlance, also gave pause to parliamentarians deciding whether to restrict the title exclusively to medical doctors.

The amount of attention that doctors paid to the title issue was connected to their larger dissatisfaction with the lack of corporatist structure in French medicine. In the absence of a Medical Order, the title of "doctor" was the only boundary, albeit a linguistic one, delimiting membership in the medical corps. To lobby the state for protection of the title, medical unions used the classic argument that defending professional interests was in the public interest. Doctors tried to convince legislators that of all the professions, "the healing art" was most deserving of title protection since clear identification of doctors was essential for the public, which might otherwise be susceptible to chicanery. The importance of medicine, they argued, should be reflected in the penalty for appropriating the title. The medical corps were successful at persuading state authorities to merge professional and public interests in this way, as more and more court cases applied Article 259 of the penal code to the medical profession.[68]

In addition to battles over illegal medical practice and title usurpation, doctors fought other types of medical practitioners for professional turf left unclaimed despite processes of professionalization and increased government regulation. Dentists, pharmacists, nurses, midwives, and even veterinarians represented threats for doctors.[69]

Dental care was an unregulated area of expertise disputed by narrowly trained and uncertified *chirurgiens-dentistes* on the one hand and, on the other hand, doctors looking for new professional outlets. With the growing trend of medical specialization in the early twentieth century, doctors calling themselves *médecins stomatologistes* sought to elevate their dental expertise into an area of specialization that involved all oral and facial health, including surgery, and not just the care of the teeth. Such doctors wanted their specialty to be officially recognized by an additional diploma and title, *doctorat en médecine mention stomatologie*. This solution was not favored by all doctors, many of whom were fighting against the trend toward specialization.[70] Arguing that problems of the mouth were not medically integral to the body, still others proposed that dentistry be reserved exclusively for dentists on the condition that they stop using the title *docteur*.[71] The stomatologists were concerned that dentists who falsely called themselves *docteur en chirurgie dentaire* would appear to patients as better educated and more prestigious than doctors.[72] The issue was further complicated by the American influence on dentistry in France. Since training in dentistry was still being developed in France, many French traveled to the United States to earn the American doctorate of dental surgery, or D.D.S.[73]

As the historian George Weisz has shown, medical specialization became an important question in the organization of French medicine only in the late 1920s, and went completely unregulated until 1947. Although by the 1930s almost half of all French doctors claimed a specialty for themselves, specialization was not formally recognized and did not yet confer elite status, which remained in the hands of those holding hospital and medical school posts. A French *diplôme d'état* gave doctors the right to perform all medical treatments. Specialization, therefore, was perceived as voluntary self-limitation, though this view was on the verge of changing.[74] Still, the trend toward specialization provoked a sense of competition among doctors, especially with the concomitant growth in the medical welfare system, which was beginning to pay higher fees to specialists than to generalists for the same treatments.[75] Medical unions and state actors were starting to address the issue during the 1930s, but from a turf standpoint this competition was just beginning.[76]

Territorial battles between doctors and pharmacists dated back to the sixteenth century in France.[77] In the 1920s and 1930s, doctors regularly accused pharmacists of dispensing medical advice and refilling prescriptions without a doctor's authorization, that is to say, without the patient's making a second, paid visit to the doctor.[78] Bypassing a doctor's visit occurred especially when a pharmacist was widely recognized for inventing a special formula. Pharmacists, for their part, accused doctors of trespassing on their terrain.[79] In fact, *médecins pro-pharmaciens* had long been permitted to prescribe and dispense medication in remote rural areas.[80] At the same time, doctors and pharmacists had an interest in working together, just as lawyers and *agents d'affaires* referred clients to each other. Such favoritism was known to extend to the practice of *compérage:* contractual agreements whereby a doctor would provide a free medical consultation as long as a prescription was filled at a certain pharmacy, and the pharmacist would share the profit with the doctor. Medical union discourse disdained this practice, although it remained quite common in the interwar years.

During that time, medical unions regularly brought cases against nurses for illegal medical practice.[81] With the growth of the medical welfare system, the need had grown for nurses and *assistantes sociales* to serve the poor in hospitals and dispensaries. Private practitioners felt threatened not only by fellow doctors working for salaries in such institutions but also by the auxiliary medical personnel who seemed to be taking over more and more of doctors' traditional tasks. Midwives also were regularly accused of encroaching on doctors' terrain.[82] A certain amount of turf protection against nurses and midwives had misogynist overtones.[83] As primarily female auxiliary personnel assisting doctors, nurses and midwives provided a contrast to the legal profession. No equivalent female assistant figure existed for lawyers.

Doctors were, in fact, quite active in urging and developing regulations for nursing, midwifery, dentistry, and veterinary medicine during the interwar years as a means of distinguishing their profession from these others.[84] Sociologists have studied the tendency of individuals and groups to use distinction as a strategy of social definition and assertion of prestige.[85] For the French medical corps in the 1920s and 1930s, distinction as a professional strategy served to maintain the reputation of medicine and to mitigate the supposedly deleterious effects of democratization.

Endogenous Turf Wars

In addition to their conflicts with other health care providers over staking out medical terrain, doctors also battled among themselves for internal professional turf. Doctors' strategies for economic survival included discouraging potential medical students, instituting limitations on multiple medical positions, and emphasizing the division between private practitioners and medical civil servants. These strategies were all meant to improve doctors' economic opportunities.

Established doctors frequently dissuaded students from pursuing medical careers. In April 1930 Victor Balthazard, dean of the Paris Medical School and president of the Confédération, and Paul Cibrie, its secretary-general, published an open letter to high school students and their parents and teachers discouraging future baccalaureate graduates from taking up medical studies. They cautioned youngsters about the difficulties of going into medicine: professional overcrowding, rigorous exams, the high cost of medical school, and the threat posed by social insurance programs to the prestige of medicine. The letter was published in the national journal *Le médecin de France* and reprinted in many medical journals.[86] The BUS also engaged actively in efforts to redirect students. In cooperation with university rectors and deans and with organizations such as the Confédération, the Confédération des travailleurs intellectuels, the Fédération des associations de parents d'élèves des lycées et collèges, and the Union nationale des associations générales d'étudiants de France, the BUS hosted conferences for high school students and their parents at which it deliberately discouraged young people from pursuing medical studies. Statistical analysis of medical school enrollments demonstrates that this campaign had little effect.[87]

The medical welfare program initiated in 1930 provoked accusations that social welfare had stolen clients from private practitioners.[88] Posing as defenders of egalitarian values, doctors argued that even indigent patients under the care of free state health programs deserved the same rights as the paying upper classes to choose their own doctor and not to be limited to a salaried doctor chosen by the health program's administration. Doctors succeeded in persuading the state to operate medical welfare under such a stipulation. This issue provides an example of how defense of professional interests was most successful when argued coherently in terms of a greater public good.

Ordinary private practitioners considered three types of civil service doctors to be competitors: medical professors, hospital physicians, and military and civilian medical bureaucrats, all of whom pursued private clienteles outside their salaried occupations. Many independent doctors believed that, especially during the economic crisis of the 1930s, salaried doctors should be satisfied with their job security and should leave private clients to private practitioners. Private-practice doctors saw the loss of patients to collective health care centers as outright robbery, especially when well-to-do clients turned to these collective institutions for free care. The BUS also favored limits on holding multiple positions (*cumul*) in the liberal professions.[89] Student groups were particularly active in denouncing the practice in the hope of expanding opportunities for graduates.[90]

The wish to create a sharp division of labor between private practitioners and salaried doctors, however, did not gain majority support within the medical unions because many private practitioners benefited from temporary or part-time appointments in schools, hospitals, and other civil services. When parliament threatened to include the medical profession in a law limiting *cumul* as a means to alleviate unemployment in many economic sectors, the Confédération, in coordination with the hospital and professorial corps, lobbied swiftly and successfully to remove medicine from the law's provisions.[91] In this sense, the *cumul* issue created a generational rift between established doctors who rejected restrictions on holding multiple positions and students who had everything to gain from such restrictions. The *cumul* debate demonstrates that foreigners were not the only target of resentment in French medicine

The struggle for economic survival engendered not only intra-French competition but also intra-medical conflict. In the most literal sense of a turf war, many doctors brought lawsuits against other doctors who started a practice within a certain radius of the established doctor's staked territory. Medical unions often had to step in to resolve conflicts among their members.[92] These struggles within the family of doctors highlight the economic difficulties encountered by physicians during the 1930s and point to an explanation for exclusionism that goes beyond xenophobia alone.

French Scapegoats: Women and the Elderly

Despite a significant increase in the number of female medical students, women doctors accounted for a minority of practicing professionals. As we saw in chapter 1, women had been able to practice medicine since 1870 (when the first *diplôme d'état* was awarded to a woman) and law since 1900,[93] but women's thirty-year head start in medicine did not translate into significantly higher numbers of practitioners. From fewer than 100 women doctors in 1903, only about 320 women were practicing medicine in France by 1922. By 1928, the 556 women doctors[94] still represented only 2 percent of all doctors.[95]

Fewer foreign women in medicine came to France over time in the early twentieth century, for various reasons: France began to restrict foreigners in medicine as early as 1892; Germany's scientific reputation increasingly attracted foreigners; and American medical schools began to admit women.[96] Nevertheless, foreign women still came to France because the reputation of French medicine remained esteemed and because discrimination still existed in Russia and eventually became a problem in Nazi Germany. As the historian Nancy Green has noted regarding the significant numbers of Jewish women from eastern Europe, especially from Russia and Romania, studying medicine and law in Paris, "Emancipation through education and emigration were fundamental means of liberation for many women."[97] French women experienced emancipation through education only after World War I.

Women doctors tended to enter specific specialties. One of the few sources available, a 1931 survey of the 275 members of the French Association of Women Doctors, reveals that the largest concentration of women doctors worked in the field of gynecology and obstetrics (forty-five of them), followed by thirty-seven women doctors who worked in various functions in the civil service (schools, hospitals, laboratories), thirty-one women doctors in pediatrics, twenty-eight as general practitioners, nineteen in dispensaries for the poor, and seventeen at mineral spas (a medicalized field in France). Fifteen women reported that they did not practice but worked at charitable institutions.[98]

Discrimination hindered women doctors from achieving high-ranking medical positions in significant numbers, but a few managed to obtain elite positions by the 1920s and 1930s. Marie Long-Landry was the first woman nominated to the prestigious post-internship *clinicat* in 1911. The first woman (Dr. Tixier) was appointed hospital doctor in 1913, the first woman (Dr. Condat) became an *agrégée* in medicine in 1923, the first woman (Marie Curie) was elected to the Academy of Medicine in 1922, and the first woman (Dr. Jeanne Lévy) became a professor at the Paris Medical School in 1934.[99] The number of women interns in Paris hospitals began to grow significantly in the 1920s.[100] In 1937 the Association of Paris Interns celebrated the fiftieth anniversary of women's admission to the Paris hospital internship program by honoring Dr. Blanche Edwards, who had never been accepted into its ranks. In his laudatory remarks tracing the history of women's battle for access to internships, Dr. Georges Labey, president of the association, acknowledged "the poorness and childishness of the excuses used to bar women in the past, which hid rather mean intentions of, let us admit it, egoism and masculine pride."[101] In the Paris hospital system in August 1939, 10 percent of interns and 25 percent of externs were women. This constituted measurable progress, but still only one of 330 *chefs de service* in Paris hospitals was a woman, and there was not a single woman surgeon.[102]

Women doctors founded professional solidarity associations. The French Association of Women Doctors, comprising nearly three hundred members in 1933, published a journal, organized lectures, funded scholarships for women, provided an employment service for its members, and pressed the government to create medical services headed by women doctors for women and children in the French colonies.[103] As a member of the Association internationale des femmes-médecins (composed of some five thousand individuals representing nearly thirty countries in 1931),[104] the French association participated in a relief effort for women doctors who were victims of anti-Semitism in Germany by helping with job placement and fellowships.[105] Women doctors such as Madeleine Pelletier and Madeleine Thuillier-Landry were also activists in feminist movements.[106]

At the same time, discrimination continued to affect women in medicine. In the interwar years, several civil service medical positions were reserved for men only, while others admitted women under a quota system.[107] Until 1938, married women who wished to work were required by law to procure their husband's authorization.[108] In addition to this overt discrimination, the harsh economic climate of the 1930s provided a context that reignited hostility toward working women. Campaigns against the decrease in the birthrate intensified during the interwar period, wherein doctors, most notably, used their medical expertise to support sociopolitical platforms urging women to stay at home and produce large families.[109]

After the significant advances made by women in medicine, the depression set off a backlash against working women. For male doctors who perceived the medical market as overcrowded, the context allowed them to feel comfortable targeting women, whose recent access to the field was still fresh in the collective memory. When basic economic survival was at stake and waning honor-based occupational identities needed reinvigorating, male students and doctors easily relapsed into traditional concepts of gender roles.

Professional discourse about overcrowding from women and other new categories of practitioners was carefully framed not in terms of economic protectionism but around the need to preserve professional quality and integrity. Most often the discourse against feminization was masked by a general lament over a supposed decline in standards of competence, to be remedied by stronger educational requirements. Some student groups complained about the occasional exceptions made for women to enter a university without a baccalaureate and demanded that women's diplomas no longer be accepted as a prerequisite for university study.[110] That women's secondary education in France was unequal to men's, at least until World War II, was often cited as justification for the continued exclusion of women from French universities. Such circular reasoning clearly attests to anti-woman sentiment and exclusionary intent, but it must also be understood in the context of French educational policy. In Third Republic France, Latin- and Greek-based education was being replaced by modern subjects such as math, science, and modern languages, as we saw earlier. This trend, along with the democratization of education, threatened those who wished to safeguard the traditional educational priorities and social order,[111] but it also reinforced the discursive association of women's achievements with declining standards.

Professional men argued that some kinds of discrimination against women were actually forms of favoritism. For example, some student and medical groups complained that women's ban from military service constituted an advantage, since it permitted women to begin their careers earlier than male graduates.[112] The Association of Marseille Interns protested: "The stronger sex demands equal rights, which seem in this case to be breached in favor of the weaker sex. Nothing would be easier than to make the baccalaureate and military service obligatory for women; it would be more difficult to make maternity obligatory for men."[113] In addition, some male doctors complained that since women were paid less for the same work, health care institutions preferred to hire female doctors for salaried positions.[114]

Nor was discourse proclaiming women's intellectual inferiority absent from the French professional press during the interwar years. In one instance, the Medical Union of the Eighteenth Arrondissement of Paris published in its monthly journal a supposedly humorous compendium of aphorisms by famous thinkers denigrating women; for example, Joseph de Maistre commented, "Women's greatest achievement in science is understanding what men do."[115] After an apologetic nod to the sole female member of the union in a subsequent issue of the journal, the same medical union published an article a few years later arguing against women's right to vote.[116] Such commentary was quite common in the student, professional, and mainstream press, and was also to be found within academia. Dean Balthazard of the Paris Medical School acknowledged that women medical students were generally as competent as their male counterparts, but he expressed consternation as to why they were rarely able to achieve elite positions.[117]

Male doctors especially feared that the presence of women colleagues would undermine their professional values of masculine honor and traditionalism. In a 1931 conference in Paris, for example, Professor Émile Sergent remarked with false humor on the difficulty of addressing women doctors: "Madame le Docteur, why not Madame la Doctoresse? Shall we write 'Dear brother-colleague, Madame' or 'Dear fellow-sister-colleague'?" (*"Mon cher confrère, Madame," ou "ma chère...consoeur"*).[118] Such declarations from professional leaders helped legitimize a rethinking of women's professional access in the 1930s.[119]

Although no effort to restrict women from entering the liberal professions ever came to fruition in the interwar years, antifeminist discourse had become commonplace again within the medical corps, which surely had the effect of discouraging women from becoming doctors before World War II. What is important, however, is that antifeminist sentiment in the professions remained on the discursive level and did not go further. True, many blustering editorials can be found in the archives, but women's professional rights in medicine were never rescinded once they were established.

In June 1936 a new strategy to relieve the supposedly saturated medical field surfaced: a mandatory retirement age for doctors. This idea originated not from within the medical corps but "from above," with legislators—leftists this time—and addressed not just doctors but also lawyers, ministerial officers, veterinarians, dentists, pharmacists, midwives, architects, geometers, engineers, accountants, bankers, salaried bosses, company administrators, and university professors. Deputy Charles Pomaret, a republican-socialist, proposed the idea of an age ceiling of sixty-five years, arguing that the retirement of elderly professionals would alleviate the unemployment of French youth.[120] "The needs of a thirty-year-old man, who is starting a family," he declared, "seem to me much more compelling and urgent than those of an old man of seventy years."[121] Pomaret argued, "If we want to regulate and harmonize the labor market in the professions... we must accept the elimination of seniors."[122] He also believed that it was in the public interest to remove older doctors from practice because of their diminished intellectual faculties.[123]

The medical corps's response to Pomaret was overwhelmingly negative. Even medical students, who would have benefited directly from the early retirement proposal, were almost universally against the idea. Only the UFE welcomed the measure,[124] but most others, including the Association des étudiants en médecine de Paris, protested indignantly against it.[125] Medical groups argued that the *diplôme d'état* was not meant to be a degree with an expiration date and that doctors had the right to evaluate their own abilities. Doctors remarked further that medical geniuses like Louis Pasteur and Édouard Branly who were over sixty-five years old and were still at the height of their careers would be summarily put out of work. Medical unions also argued that doctors only began their careers in their thirties, having costly years of education behind them, and that having started their families late, doctors in their sixties were still financially responsible for their children.[126] In their battle against Pomaret's proposal, doctors also proffered a demographic argument: the number of doctors in their sixties in the mid-1930s was very small. They had started medical school around 1890, a time when student numbers were quite low compared to those of successive generations. In the interim, many of them had never graduated, had left medicine, or had died, especially given the losses of World War I. Hence, Pomaret's proposal would not alleviate the plethora, they argued.[127] One union, noting that this particular generation included those who had fought for France during the First World War, remarked sarcastically, "What recognition!"[128]

The Confédération, in quick and decisive response to Pomaret's idea, declared publicly, "It would be truly unacceptable if French doctors were forced into retirement in order to make room for foreign doctors" and called instead for the cessation of naturalizations.[129] This demand had immediate resonance with medical unions across France, which hastened to second the motion that foreigners, not elderly Frenchmen, be the first targets for elimination.[130] Xenophobic remarks surfaced over this issue. At a large meeting of the CTI, an important group representing most professions and intellectuals, Dr. Pochon, the medical

Confédération's representative, railed that a "multitude of foreign parasites, very often undesirable types," would be permitted to practice while loyal Frenchmen would be forced out of work.[131]

Throughout the second half of the 1930s, the Pomaret initiative remained a source of public debate within medicine and other professions. Despite the hostility of medical unions, Pomaret, who became minister of labor, as well as the BUS continued to support the idea up until the outbreak of war.[132] The retirement age proposal is another example—albeit one initiated by the state—of how socioeconomic fears resulting from the depression and not just xenophobia were at the root of various exclusionary measures in the professions. The Pomaret episode clearly manifests the conflict between the state and the medical profession. Although medical unions and student groups demanded protection from the state against foreigners, they were decidedly opposed to state intervention in setting a retirement age. In strategic response they discursively pitted elderly French against foreign youth.

Sexism and ageism were two forms of exclusion that, in addition to xenophobia, contributed to a comprehensive mobilization among doctors to reduce the size of the medical population. Whereas some doctors were ready to eliminate women from the profession, the state refused to undo republican advances. Whereas the state was ready to impose obligatory retirement on the liberal professions, doctors successfully rebuffed the initiative. As we saw in chapter 2, the state and the profession together approved the strategy of barring foreigners and naturalized citizens from medicine. Exclusion of particular social categories was successful only when there was a confluence of both corporatist and state goals.

★ ★ ★

The medical corps pursued a number of solutions to alleviate the supposed overcrowding in the university and the profession. Strategies of quality control and distinction, internal turf battles among French doctors, and the scapegoating of women and the elderly constituted a much broader exclusionary movement than one based merely on xenophobia; measures that were aimed at various portions of the French population itself—secondary students, women, the elderly—illustrate more fully how the medical profession engaged in a many-sided strategy of professional defense in the years between the wars.

While these factors are important taken together, a certain hierarchy of exclusion emerged during the period. Foreigners were the top-priority scapegoats, followed by naturalized citizens. Foreigners were an easy target because they had little social or political clout with which to fight back. Xenophobic discourse had become more socially acceptable, too, rendering foreigners vulnerable. The other professional strategies described in this chapter were fueled by concerns for economic self-defense and for professional image and identity. The shift from a conservative, traditional identity to a modern, democratic one touched many raw nerves when new social categories began to seek access to the profession. The targeting of reputedly ill-prepared secondary students in the strategy to raise the intellectual standards of the profession stemmed from conservatives' fear that democratization was diminishing the prestige of medicine. Likewise, proposals that questioned women's right to access stemmed from fears that the classic medical professional identity based on masculine pride and honor was being undermined by women's inroads.

Differences arose over each issue: educational traditionalists versus modernists, pro- versus anti-woman activists, youth versus seniors. In many medical circles it was still acceptable to discriminate against women, but there was some dissent, and women doctors also became more active in protecting themselves. The proposal to raise the level of training and qualification was a response from the traditionalist faction to what they perceived as professional decline, but ultimately their efforts to reinstate the Latin-Greek baccalaureate and to institute an entry *concours* for medical school met resistance from a new generation in the field.

Strategically, it made sense to prioritize the exclusion of foreigners because the medical profession was most united behind that goal. Non-xenophobic strategies that targeted professional outsiders such as dentists, nurses, and folk healers similarly found easy agreement among the majority of doctors and were successful. The hierarchy of exclusion was based more on professional consensus and prevailing social custom than on numerical efficacy. Statistically, the growth in the number of medical students and practitioners by the interwar years resulted far more from the influx of French males from the lower classes who had not previously entered higher education than from the entry of women or foreigners. But in the context of the 1930s, it was more acceptable to target foreigners and, secondarily, women, two groups that lacked social worth in the eyes of the middle-aged men who dominated the profession. Sensitivity over class conflict kept in check efforts to restrict access for the new social classes.

The material presented in this chapter regarding the indifference to or tolerance of foreigners and naturalized citizens in French medicine shows that an openness to foreigners was possible in the 1930s, albeit among a minority. This makes it clear that xenophobia was a consciously embraced choice, an outlook that was not automatic but was one point of view among others.

 CHAPTER 4

The Barrier of the Law Bar

During the interwar years, the decree of 20 June 1920 defined the rules of access to the legal profession. Lawyers themselves had lobbied for such legislation to back up their internal rules with the force of law, but the bars still deemed themselves "masters of their registry" (*maîtres de leurs tableaux*), in charge of granting access to the profession. The 1920 decree enumerated the requirements for entry into all law bars: a French *licence en droit*, French nationality, and three years of practical training (*stage*) in the office of either a lawyer, an *avoué*, or a notary, or with a tribunal. There were approximately 375 law bars in the late 1920s. They were attached to the twenty-seven courts of appeal. Every bar had the same structure (a president and leadership council elected yearly by universal suffrage), but each had its own set of internal regulations, was largely responsible only to itself, and had the power to determine subjective criteria for admission such as the moral standing of candidates.[1] The tug-of-war between the state and the corporatist bars over control of the legal profession was ongoing. Criteria for access were far from settled in the interwar years. Old and new exclusions of unwanted categories continued to be debated throughout the course of the 1920s and 1930s.

Because of its corporatist structure organized around bar membership, the legal profession, unlike the medical profession, wielded a major weapon against unwanted practitioners in the field. While foreigners were free to earn a *licence en droit* from a French law school, they were blocked from membership in a French law bar and, therefore, from the practice of the *profession d'avocat*.

Foreigners had essentially never been permitted to practice law in France, and this practice was concretized by the decree of 20 June 1920.[2] In 1934 French lawyers also succeeded in excluding recently naturalized citizens from their profession. But the nationalistic vision of bar membership was only one element in a larger context of professional protectionism during the interwar years. Like doctors, lawyers pursued many other strategies to reduce their numbers, to raise their prestige, to marginalize professional competitors outside the bar, and to exclude various categories from their membership. Their strategies included improving legal education and training, directing law school graduates toward careers away from the bar, denigrating competitors such as *agents d'affaires,* and challenging the rights of women and the elderly to bar membership. This broader context is necessary to a better understanding of the mobilization against foreigners and naturalized citizens that will be examined in the next chapter.

Barriers to Professional Overcrowding

During the interwar years the number of law students grew significantly in France. But because of the barrier created by the law bar, lawyers were much less concerned than doctors about overcrowding. As Table 4.1 indicates, the number of law students in all categories—men, women, French, foreign—increased during the first forty years of the twentieth century. The number of French male law students doubled between 1900 and the mid-1930s, and the increase in the number of French women was exponential. The doubling of the number of French male law students was at a much higher rate than that of overall population growth, confirming that democratization processes were particularly important in French law schools. The rise in the number of French women is due partly to the fact that the democratization trend affected women too, but other sociopolitical factors were also at work. The granting to women of equal rights to compete for the baccalaureate beginning in 1924 was a watershed moment for their push into higher education in all fields. Women (French and foreign) constituted just 8 percent of all law students in 1925, a figure that jumped to 19 percent by 1939.

The number of foreign men studying law peaked in the early 1930s, reaching almost three thousand in 1930, but then dropped markedly in 1935 and declined steadily thereafter. At the beginning of the century, foreign women were more numerous in French law schools than French women. The number of foreign women increased steadily until a peak was reached in 1932 with nearly four hundred students, and decreased sharply after 1933. If men and women are added together, the greatest number of foreigners studied in French law schools between 1930 and 1932.

Except for French women, the number of students in all other categories, including the total population of French law students, dropped in the late 1930s. The same

Table 4.1   Students registered in French law schools

YEAR	FRENCH MEN	FRENCH WOMEN	FOREIGN MEN	FOREIGN WOMEN	TOTAL
1900	9,285	2	419	3	9,709
1910	15,706	51	1,057	101	16,915
1920	12,025	518	1,365	40	13,948
1925	13,414	1,248	1,768	87	16,517
1930	14,339	1,967	2,970	309	19,585
1935	18,865	3,458	1,766	237	24,326
1939	17,031	4,049	1,236	154	22,470

Source: Adapted from *Recueil des statistiques,* 12.

reasons that explain a similar drop for medical students are valid for law students and, more generally, for all university students. The decline in the birthrate during World War I meant that there were fewer seventeen- to twenty-year-olds in the mid- to late 1930s (*les classes creuses*), and the economic depression necessitated life-choice sacrifices for many would-be students. Foreign students were probably discouraged from undertaking law studies in France for other reasons as well. Although the law restricting naturalized citizens from entering the law bars was not passed until 1934, the decline in the number of foreigners had begun in 1932, possibly because the atmosphere in the Latin Quarter was already palpably hostile to foreigners. Furthermore, the worldwide economic depression prevented many foreigners from studying abroad. At their peak in 1930, foreigners constituted 17 percent of all law students. By 1939 their numbers had declined to just 6 percent of law students.

For comparison's sake, foreign students in French law schools were proportionately fewer than those in French medical schools (24 percent of the medical student population in 1930). The universality of medical education compared to the more nation-based approach of legal education provides one explanation. There were also proportionally fewer women law students than women medical students. Medicine was perceived as less of an "old-boys" network than was law, and it also offered "natural," socially acceptable niches for women in fields such as gynecology and pediatrics, whereas no such equivalent existed in law.

Over the course of the interwar years, the greatest number of law students in Paris came consistently from Romania, Germany, Poland, Russia, Yugoslavia, Greece, Egypt, and China. By far the largest number of foreign students came from Romania: at their peak in the 1929–30 academic year, 433 Romanian students were registered in the University of Paris Law School. Other nationalities that were well represented (between twenty and fifty students per year) were Bulgarians, Turks, Swiss, and Persians. Among colonial populations, Indochinese and Tunisians were best represented.[3]

Many of the same reasons that explain why particular foreigners came to France to study medicine are also valid for law, such as a special historical relationship between countries (Romania, Egypt), geographic proximity (Germany, Switzerland), and anti-Semitic discrimination abroad (Poland, Russia, and Hungary, as well as Germany in the 1930s). Nevertheless, some differences become apparent. For instance, because German medicine was highly regarded in the interwar years, very few Germans studied medicine in Paris, whereas Germans were among the most numerous foreign groups in the Paris Law School. Also, many more Yugoslavs studied law than studied medicine in Paris. And while Chinese studied law in Paris in significant numbers, there were barely ten students per year in medicine. By contrast, many more Romanians, Poles, Hungarians, Russians, Tunisians, and Americans studied medicine in Paris than studied law.

Student populations varied greatly according to the law school. The 1936–37 school year can serve as a basis for comparison. Paris had by far the largest law school, with 10,048 students. The next-largest law school was at Lyon, with 1,408 students, followed by Aix, Algiers, Bordeaux, and Toulouse with nearly 1,000 students each. Foreign students were also most numerous at the Paris Law School: a total of 804, followed by 130 foreign students in the Lyon Law School. Most other law schools registered foreign students in small numbers relative to their overall student population, except for Grenoble and Nancy, which attracted a fairly high number of foreigners. Whereas the Paris Law School accounted for 50 percent of all law students, 62 percent of all foreign law students studied in Paris in 1936–37.[4]

The law schools offered several diplomas: the *capacité,* a two-year program; the *licence,* the standard degree, taking about three years; and the doctorate (all of which are counted in Table 4.1, as well as auditors). The *licence* was the required degree for entry into the law bars. About 1,500 *licences* were awarded by French law schools in the year 1900. Increasing steadily from the beginning of the century, the number of *licence* law degrees peaked at nearly 3,000 in 1936, and declined thereafter to fewer than 2,300 in 1939.[5]

In terms of nationality and gender of law school graduates, the statistics are revealing. In 1937, French law schools awarded *licences* to 2,093 French men, 378 French women, 117 foreign men, and 15 foreign women, a breakdown that remained consistent through the outbreak of war.[6] In the late 1930s, therefore, foreigners accounted for just 5 percent of all law *licence* graduates, and their numbers declined thereafter. Although naturalized citizens were counted as French graduates, the vast majority of law graduates were French men: they averaged 80 percent of all *licence* graduates from 1937 until 1939. French women occupied a distant second place. Even though membership in a law bar required not only a *licence* but also French nationality, foreign law students could obtain French citizenship after graduation and join a bar. The 1934 law imposing a ten-year delay on naturalized citizens before joining a law bar—the focus of the next chapter—was passed precisely in order to reduce this possibility.

Unlike medical school graduates, who were apt to practice medicine exclusively, law graduates were qualified to work in a number of careers outside the law bar. The magistrature was a career open to law graduates, but only one to two hundred new positions across France opened each year in the early 1930s. Law students often began careers in *offices ministériels* as notaries, bailiffs (*huissiers*), judicial auctioneers (*commissaires priseurs*), solicitors (*avoués*), and court recorders (*greffiers*), even though such fields did not require a law degree. Their number was fixed by the state as a vestige of Old Regime corporations, and appointments were usually passed from father to son or from master to apprentice. Law graduates also pursued careers in the civil service: they were preponderant among candidates for numerous public administration entry exams. It was also common for law graduates to work in business and industry. Finally, law graduates could practice many forms of law besides pleading cases in court as members of a law bar. As legal advisers (*conseils juridiques*), tax advisers (*conseils fiscaux*), accountants (*experts comptables*), and business agents (*agents d'affaires*), they could offer legal consultations and represent clients in commercial tribunals, before justices of the peace, and in other types of jurisdictions without joining the bar.[7] In the 1930s, in a strategy beneficial to the law bar, the Bureau universitaire de statistique, the government organ in charge of helping French youth make the transition through university into a career, pushed the government to create more civil service positions for university graduates, in particular by banning the practice of allowing civil servants to hold more than one job (*cumul*).[8]

Unlike the steady career climb in medicine, entering the bar in interwar France was the beginning of a very long period of poverty with few guarantees. Some made it in law and others did not. Social reproduction was the norm in bar membership: because establishing a law bar career was financially difficult for recent graduates, new lawyers tended to come from bourgeois backgrounds. Bar membership figures in France between the wars held steady. In 1922 there were about 4,500 lawyers in all of France, translating to a rate of 8,900 inhabitants per lawyer. In 1931 the number of bar members remained the same, but because of population growth, the ratio rose to 9,200 inhabitants per lawyer. By 1941 the number of lawyers had increased to over 4,700 in France, with a ratio of 8,500 inhabitants per lawyer.[9] At these rates, there was no evidence of a plethora of lawyers.

A greater percentage of lawyers, however, actively practiced law after World War I compared to before. In 1912 it was estimated that one-third of registered lawyers (1,642 out of 4,928) actually worked as lawyers, while all other registered lawyers had the title but did not seek remunerative activity as lawyers.

Thus, in 1912 the field was less competitive than it appears from statistics. By 1931 the situation had reversed; it was estimated that two-thirds (3,040 out of 4,561) of registered lawyers pleaded court cases regularly.[10] A net decline in the number of lawyers to inhabitants therefore should not be overemphasized since competition for clients was increasing. Being a member of a law bar had not ceased to be an honorable pastime for *notables,* but it had become for many practitioners their principal source of income.

Geographical variation in legal coverage across France was significant. The number of lawyers in the Paris bar far exceeded that of any other.[11] Over the course of the 1920s, small cities in France experienced shrinking law bar membership, whereas Paris and the large provincial cities of Nice, Marseille, and Toulon registered moderate increases in bar registration. The Paris bar counted approximately 1,500 lawyers in 1922, 1,800 in 1931, and 1,900 in 1941. In light of the national average of one lawyer for over 8,000 inhabitants, Paris was a singularly competitive city. Lawyers in the Paris bar would have argued that even though the lawyer-per-inhabitant ratio did not seem excessive, bar regulations limited members to certain activities and jurisdictions, and *agents d'affaires* occupied much legal terrain outside the courtroom.

When a certain jurisdiction lacked a law bar, or when the law bar lacked sufficient members to cover the casework of a tribunal or court, *avoués* were permitted to represent clients in those courts, which were normally reserved for lawyers. In these situations, lawyers lost their monopoly on pleading cases. This was quite common in provincial areas in the 1930s. Even in areas less than one hundred kilometers from Paris, such as Corbeil with 280,000 inhabitants or Rambouillet with 110,000 inhabitants, no bar existed in several *arrondissements.* The department of the Seine-et-Marne lacked a bar altogether, despite a large and well-off population there and two second-instance tribunals in Meaux and Melun. Most cases that came before the department's criminal court were pleaded by *avoués.* In the Eure-et-Loir, the few lawyers in Chartres were not sufficient to retain a monopoly. The dominance of Paris did not necessarily cause this dearth, for in nearby Versailles a large law bar thrived.[12]

Compared to doctors, lawyers were much more likely to acknowledge the unequal geographical distribution of lawyers across France. As one activist lawyer noted, "Next to the plethoric bars where young lawyers are crushing one another, where legitimate ambitions are frustrated, do you know that there are rich lands, populated neighborhoods, *entire departments,* that are completely lacking in lawyers?"[13] He tried to rally lawyers to stake out virgin territory. His and others' willingness to consider a more equal distribution of lawyers across France as a solution to perceived overcrowding in certain areas was driven largely by the threat of the loss of *monopole de la plaidoirie* to non-lawyers. Because doctors could not be replaced by non-doctors when no doctor was present (especially after the profession of health officers was eliminated), there was no need to protect professional prerogatives and therefore less incentive than lawyers had to redistribute themselves geographically.

In summary, there was indeed significant growth in both French and foreign student populations in French law schools. Most of this growth occurred between 1900 and 1930. Because law graduates had several career options, and because the law bar constituted a sort of barrier to the profession, the number of lawyers did not grow in proportion to that of students. In fact, the number of lawyers remained stagnant throughout the first few decades of the twentieth century and even declined relative to population growth. At the same time, practicing law had become more competitive for three reasons: the fact that more bar members now pursued law as a professional practice for vital income, whereas in the past, lawyers frequently did not practice; competition with legal practitioners who were not members of the bar; and perhaps most important the contracting of the economy in the 1930s as a result of the depression. Lawyers sought to protect their professional interests during the interwar years in two ways: a reformist associative movement developed to defend lawyers' causes, and lawyers used their socio-professional networks with politicians to achieve protectionist measures through legislative action.

Networks of Lawyers in the Profession and Politics

Chapter 1 described the reformist movement in the law bars at the turn of the century, which resulted in the creation of groups such as the Conférence des bâtonniers and the Paris bar's Cercle d'études professionnelles. After World War I, the associative movement grew significantly in order to address more effectively the professional issues common to all lawyers. Several nationwide professional organizations were founded, notably the National Association of Lawyers (Association nationale des avocats inscrits aux barreaux de France, des colonies et des pays de protectorat et de mandat, or ANA), founded in Lyon in 1921, and the Union of Young Lawyers (Union des jeunes avocats, or UJA), founded in Paris in 1922. Another shorter-lived, less influential, and more radical group, the Jeune barreau français, was founded in 1934. Although no group could claim to represent the entire legal profession, some figures attest to the influence of these associations: the ANA counted over two thousand members in 1934, almost half of all lawyers.[14] And while other branches of the UJA were springing up in Versailles, Orléans, Lyon, and Montpellier, the UJA of Paris was steadily increasing its membership to nine hundred lawyers, or about a third of the Paris bar by 1937.[15] The Conférence des bâtonniers was still thriving in the interwar years. By 1934, 111 law bars had joined, totaling 2,461 lawyers, about half of all lawyers, plus 1,766 lawyer-apprentices.[16]

As bastions of tradition and privilege, the law bars were initially threatened by the ANA and other groups that called for modernization and reform. But the reform organizations were all careful to affirm their peaceful coexistence with the bars for the good of the profession.[17] Many influential bar members were, in fact, at the forefront of the reformist movement: Jean Appleton, a prominent lawyer and professor of law in Lyon, was the founder and first president of the ANA, and his cofounder and successor, Albert Rodanet, was a member of the Paris bar council. ANA vice president Paul Marchandeau had been finance minister, interior minister, budget minister, mayor of Reims, elected depart- ment council member, deputy, and president of the Reims bar at various points throughout the 1920s and 1930s.[18] By the 1930s, leaders of the law bars began to acknowledge the role of the ANA and UJA in professional affairs. In the later 1930s, important bar members and presidents began to attend their meetings regularly. This in turn gave more legitimacy to the associations, which lost no opportunity to mention in the legal press the names of the bar presidents and bar council members who joined them.[19] While reformist organizations challenged many of the law bars' traditional principles such as anticommercialism, both the bars and these legal associations agreed on the need to exclude naturalized citizens from the profession.

Lawyers continued to be elected to the French legislature and nominated to government positions in significant numbers during the interwar years. In the 1924 victory of the left-wing alliance between the socialists and radical socialists (Cartel des gauches), 167 or 28 percent of the 584 deputies elected were jurists. "Jurists" included all those who had a *licence* degree in law and who practiced some kind of legal profession: mostly lawyers, but also legal consultants, law professors, *avoués,* and magistrates. Although the "République des avocats" may have been fading after World War I—from 41 percent in the 1881 Chamber of Deputies, jurists declined to 21 percent after the Popular Front victory of 1936—lawyers were still the socio-professional group best represented in the Chamber.[20]

The historian Yves-Henri Gaudemet has argued that the decrease in the number of jurists in parliament exemplified the success of the Third Repub- lic: deputies from less privileged classes were being elected to the Chamber. With economic concerns being considered for the first time as political issues, the rising middle classes sought deputies who could represent their interests. Economists were increasingly elected as deputies after World War I, and jurists were coming to be considered by some as "too attached to outdated methods, incapable of renewal, and far removed from social realities."[21] Not only was the law bars' traditional conservative outlook hurting lawyers financially—as this chapter shows—but also it may have led to a loss of political influence during the interwar years.

Despite their decreasing presence in government ministries since the First World War, jurists nonetheless remained the dominant socio-professional group there as well. In fact, they wielded even greater influence in the executive branch: whereas one-fourth of deputies in the interwar year were jurists, no fewer than half the ministers and undersecretaries of state were jurists. Of the twenty-two prime ministers between 1913 and 1940, fifteen were jurists. Twenty-seven of thirty-four ministers of justice during the period were jurists. And in the Ministry of Education, the lawyers Anatole de Monzie and Jean Zay served for most of the 1930s.[22]

Lawyer-legislators came from the elite of the profession.[23] Various professional networks helped lawyers enter politics. For example, the Conférence du stage was a prestigious oratory competition among newcomers to the Paris bar: its twelve winners per year formed an elite circle, and many of them became important politicians. Raymond Poincaré, René Viviani, Louis Barthou, Léon Bourgeois, Jules Méline, Joseph Reinach, Jules Jeanneney, Anatole de Monzie, César Campinchi, and Léon Bérard had all been Conférence winners, known as secretaries. Between 1919 and 1940, fifty-three Conférence secretaries sat in the Chamber of Deputies, five served as prime minister, and twenty-four as ministers or undersecretaries of state. Five Conférence secretaries served in the Popular Front in 1936. So commonly did the secretaries go on to political careers that the Conférence could be considered "a sort of antechamber to the houses of parliament."[24] It was common practice for secretaries already in politics to choose recent secretaries as their assistants. As an open competition, the Conférence was a perfect means for meritocratic personal advancement—and it billed itself as such. It tended, however, to be an organ of social reproduction through which established elites most easily rose to the top. Like the Conférence du stage, the Conférence Molé-Tocqueville was a body for debate and colloquia dominated by young lawyers, many of whom played important political roles later in their careers. These groups and others like them were key Third Republic training grounds for the law bar elite, who moved seamlessly between the profession and politics.[25]

The law bars and legal associations were proud of their politically successful members, and they touted their elections and government nominations in the professional press.[26] As the Third Republic became tarnished by political scandal in the 1930s, however, practicing lawyers and their organizations began to distance themselves from the regime. A few months after the Stavisky affair and the 6 February 1934 riot, a debate arose over whether or not to prevent lawyers from holding multiple parliamentary offices simultaneously.[27] Some hoped that if lawyers who were elected parliamentarians temporarily renounced their bar affiliation, that would prevent political scandals from tainting the bar's reputation. The Rouen bar favored this position, although most bars ultimately did not.[28] No such change ever happened. Instead the law bars prohibited certain activities of lawyer-parliamentarians, such as pleading cases having to do with state affairs while holding a political office.[29]

Protectionist Strategies: Quality Control and "Distinction"

As noted earlier, the most important factor behind the growing ranks of law students was the democratization of education, evidenced by the doubling of the number of French men studying law from 1900 to the 1930s, far outpacing population growth. Social reproduction, however, was still the norm among the interwar generation of lawyers. The profession attracted bourgeois youth more than lower-class students because remuneration was minimal during the early career years and often longer. The BUS warned potential lawyers, "Make no mistake; to choose this profession without sufficient personal resources means to languish for a long time before making a living."[30] Of the 6,399 *licence* students in the Paris Law School in 1938–39, 1,904 had parents who were employed as civil servants, 1,896 had parents who worked in the liberal professions, 1,052 had parents who were heads of business enterprises, 690 were children of land-owners, 408 had parents who were employees, 25 were children of artisans, and 3 were children of manual laborers. The families of law students were thus highly concentrated in the liberal professions and the civil service (30 percent each), followed by "heads of business" at 16 percent.[31]

The professional ethics (*déontologie*) of the law bars also contributed to the social reproduction of lawyers. Bar tradition forbade members from engaging in all activity related to commercialism: advertising and soliciting clients, financial legal consultation of any sort, legal consultation for businesses, disputes over honoraria, and the *pacte de quota litis*—the practice of basing honoraria on the outcome of the case in court. Lawyers were not permitted to plead in commercial tribunals until 1911, and only then as a result of reformist pressure against bar regulations. Brand-new law graduates with no family money thus could hardly hope to survive in a profession that forbade most profit-oriented initiatives.

Many conservative members of the law bars nevertheless argued that such barriers were not adequate, on the grounds that democratization produced not only greater quantities of law school graduates but also lower quality in lawyers.[32] Standards were considered insufficient to maintain the prestige of the law: law studies had a reputation in the interwar years for being lax and irrelevant, despite the bar's self-laudatory rhetoric. Some lawyers proposed measures both to reduce the quantity and raise the quality of new entrants, such as adding a supplementary year of studies called the "pre-internship" (*pré-stage*), requiring a doctorate in law as opposed to a mere *licence,* or instituting a competitive *concours* and quota system in the law schools. By imposing more rigorous standards on potential entrants to the bar, conservative lawyers hoped to improve the reputation of the profession; and there were those among them who did not mind the side effect of reduced competition.

Other members of the profession saw class discrimination behind these projects to raise the entrance qualifications for the law bars. Because educational trajectories were strongly determined by social origins, the *concours* proposal would have adversely affected students from the lower and middle classes, who were generally shunted into dead-end secondary studies. The extra years of university study would put off further the moment when lawyers could start earning an income and would thus discourage such students from pursuing law. None of these proposals were ever put into place in the interwar years, largely because they met with resistance from members of the profession, although the pre-internship was instituted in 1941 by the Vichy regime. The strategies for quality control—promoted in terms of intellectual competence and rigorous training—demonstrate how processes of professionalization were inseparable from the aim of exclusion.

In another protectionist strategy, lawyers distinguished themselves from the despised *agents d'affaires.* As we saw in chapter 1, the law bars did not have a monopoly over all legal practice. Notaries and other legal experts all competed to provide legal consultation and representation in certain types of courts.[33] In the interwar period, lawyers' archenemy remained the *agent d'affaires,* who had generally earned a *licence* diploma, who offered legal advice and other services for a fee, but who did not join a law bar and adhere to its strict anticommercial professional ethics. *Agents d'affaires* were formidable competitors. Oftentimes they were established professionals, just as competent as lawyers but less expensive and considered more approachable by potential clients. Also known under different titles—*conseil juridique, expert comptable*—they were abhorred by lawyers for encroaching on their professional territory.[34] Lawyers were incensed by these unregulated professionals who stole their clients and sometimes posed as lawyers.

Bar regulations forbade members from engaging in the activities of an *agent d'affaires. Agents* could practice in commercial tribunals and other jurisdictions from which lawyers had purposefully withdrawn in the name of honor and anticommercialism, and were thus sought after by clients in need of such services. Furthermore, even though *agents* were forbidden from pleading cases in normal tribunals and courts reserved for lawyers, clients often hired *agents* instead of lawyers in situations where they hoped to *avoid* a trial. One lawyer complained: "Lots of young people join the bar, thinking they are protected by their university degrees for the practice of their profession. They agree to submit to severe discipline, and they are completely disillusioned when they learn that they must compete fiercely with persons who work on the edges of judicial organizations, and who are not bound by any obligation or onerous duties to the organized professions."[35] Since some of the activities of *agents d'affaires* were expressly forbidden to bar members (handling clients' money), and since others were in direct competition with those of lawyers (legal consultations), the *agent d'affaires* was both a hated nemesis and an indistinguishable competitor.

For some lawyers, the *agent d'affaires* represented the main threat to the bar, trumping naturalized citizens practicing from within. Marcel Bloch, on his resignation as president of the UJA in 1931, noted:

> It is commonly said that the number of lawyers in 1930 is higher than before the war, which is cited as the cause for professional overcrowding and the decrease in cases for each lawyer. This assertion is unfounded. There are fewer lawyers than before the war, the number of their cases has decreased, and the number of litigations has greatly increased. Why? The brutal truth is revealed by our colleague Robert-Martin in a recently published study. In 1866 the addresses of *agents d'affaires* took up six columns in the Paris phone book, whereas in 1929, tax counsels, *agents d'affaires* themselves, *conseils juridiques,* judicial consultants, litigators, foreign lawyers, and business counsels take up seventy-six columns.[36]

Whether or not Bloch's assertion was accurate (because they were unregulated, there are no statistics on these legal practitioners), the belief that such competitors were extremely numerous was entering the professional psyche of lawyers.

Agents d'affaires were considered not only a financial threat to lawyers but also a threat to the moral well-being of the profession. Lawyers claimed that *agents d'affaires,* capable only of shoddy work but passing themselves off as lawyers, brought down the reputation of the law profession. As the founder of the ANA, Jean Appleton, put it: "There are some perfectly honorable *agents d'affaires;* but it is quite certain that this profession, precisely because it resembles ours in some ways, must be carefully distinguished from us....Furthermore, their recruitment is not always perfectly satisfactory: the honest *agent d'affaires* is mixed together with the worst gold digger. It is understandable, therefore, that the bar councils wanted to create a sort of airtight barrier between the lawyer and the *agent d'affaires.*"[37] Another lawyer expressed the fear of indistinguishability: "There is an association that was founded, an extremely important and powerful association, which is called—pay attention—which is called the 'Association of Lawyers, Lawyer Counsels, and Judicial Counsels.' This association has a 'tableau' with its registered lawyers, its interns, its internal regulations....In other words, the average Frenchman would not be able to make any distinction between the registry of this 'Association'—completely unsanctioned—and the registry of our law bar."[38]

Agents d'affaires were a moral threat to lawyers because the traditional vision of the law profession eschewed commercialization.[39] *Agents* performed all kinds of commercial transactions that were forbidden to lawyers, for example, buying and selling property and basing trial fees on the success or failure of a case. In a professional manual for lawyers, Louis Crémieu insisted:

> A good *culture générale,* strong juridical framework, love of work, perseverance, an ease with words, a faithful memory, a sense of authority in the appearance and in the voice, a clear mind, a good education, robust health, probity... these are the qualities that have always marked and will always mark the irreducible difference, the impassable gulf, that the legislator has dug between the profession of lawyer and the trade of *agent d'affaires.* The worst danger that could threaten this noble profession is its commercialization, which would bring lawyers down to the level of *agents d'affaires* and would cause them to lose the esteem of the public.[40]

Lawyers engaged a double strategy to reduce the threat: they excluded *agents d'affaires* from the bar, and they sought state cooperation to marginalize and restrain their activities. Internal bar regulations enumerated and enforced several *incompatibilités* with lawyers' profession. In general, no other profession could be practiced simultaneously with the profession of lawyer. One of the bar's main principles was that a lawyer must truly and freely practice the profession. In other words, lawyers had to work full-time as lawyers, and had to be totally independent and not subject to the regulations governing other professions. Forbidden secondary professions included "any hired job for wages" and "any type of trade" such as *agent d'affaires,* shopkeeper, business head, newspaper manager, accountant, prefect, and civil servant, as well as magistrate (except as a temporary substitute), solicitor, court clerk, notary, or priest.[41] Lawyers were, however, permitted to serve as deputies, senators, ministers, even president of the republic. The law bars justified this exception by the fact that such offices were temporary.

In addition, those candidates for the bar *formerly* occupied as *agents d'affaires* were considered not compatible with the traditions of the legal profession. "It happens too often," charged Appleton, "that from their type of work they have acquired unfortunate customs that are irreconcilable with the customs that centuries of experience have wisely imposed on the law bars." Yet banning former *agents* violated the 1822 ordinance regulating the law bars and was generally condemned by case law. Appleton admitted, "Doctrine and case law today allow for the former *agent d'affaires* to be admitted to the bar," adding, "But, *bien entendu,* the candidate must show strong proof of morality and dignity; he must avoid all possible confusion between his former profession and the new one. For this reason, he cannot establish his law office in the same locale as his former agency."[42] In fact, throughout the interwar period, several bars continued to exclude former *agents d'affaires* on some pretext or another, and their decisions were sometimes confirmed by courts of appeal; at other times the courts of appeal rejected the law bar exclusions but the bars did not comply.[43] Furthermore, candidates for the bar whose spouse was an *agent d'affaires* or even a shopkeeper were often rejected for admission.[44]

To eliminate the influence of *agents d'affaires,* lawyers were compelled to do more than just exclude them from the bar, for most *agents* themselves did not want to join a bar and submit to its constraining regulations. Lawyers thus tried to exclude *agents* from the legal domain by differentiating the two professions more clearly in the public mind. Through a strategy of distinction, by asserting their own superiority and also by imposing the exclusive rights of lawyers over an ever broader area of legal territory, lawyers hoped to attract more clients for themselves. To accomplish this end, the legal profession had to turn to the state. French lawyers lobbied for legislative protection of the title *avocat à la cour* and for a protected monopoly in more types of courts.

After decades of lobbying, a 1920 decree made the use of the title *avocat* illegal for anyone not registered with a law bar; this was followed by a 1924 law that instituted a penalty for the illegal usage of the title. The 1920 decree was not retroactive, however, so all those who had regularly called themselves *avocat* without being a bar member were allowed to keep the title for the rest of their life. Throughout the 1920s and 1930s, lawyers in the bar demanded a retroactive interpretation of the law.[45]

Lawyers' second overall tactic was to seek legislation to reserve their monopoly over certain types of jurisdictions.[46] In 1935, lawyers at the ANA unanimously implored the minister of justice to ban all non-lawyers—solicitors and court clerks as well as *agents d'affaires*—from all French courts.[47] The BUS supported lawyers in their quest to diminish the rights of *agents* to represent clients in jurisdictions such as those of justices of the peace.[48] Minister of Justice Vincent Auriol put forward legislation in 1937 to grant lawyers a monopoly over representing clients before justices of the peace and commercial tribunals.[49] But these efforts were not successful.

Widening lawyers' legal terrain was a third strategy for competing with *agents d'affaires*. First, around the turn of the century, reformist lawyers had persuaded bars to allow members to plead in new jurisdictions, and such persuasion continued during the interwar years. Second, lawyers pushed to reduce bar restrictions on lawyers' activities, demanding revisions to bar regulations that would allow them to act as in-house counsels for businesses, to handle clients' funds, to advertise, to form law firms, to specialize in certain fields, and to demand honoraria for work performed. Such a relaxation of internal regulations would allow lawyers to compete on the same terms as *agents d'affaires* rather than differentiating and excluding them. This was not an exclusionary solution but, on the contrary, one that favored an opening up of the profession. Over time the law bars tended toward a relaxation of restrictions on lawyers, to the dismay of traditionalists proffering Malthusian solutions.

Designating Outsiders: Sexism and Ageism

Finally, the right of access to the law bar for two categories of French persons was called into question during the interwar years. French lawyers considered excluding French women, who had been enrolling in higher education in increasing numbers throughout the early decades of the twentieth century, and elderly French lawyers who had yet to retire. These other types of protectionist strategies illustrate an exclusionary movement much more complex than one based merely on xenophobia.

In 1900 there had been two French women and over nine thousand French men in law schools. By 1935, French women represented 15 percent of the French law student population.[50] Despite enormous growth in the number of female university students and guaranteed equal access to law bar membership as a result of the 1900 law, women accounted for only a small minority of lawyers. The provincial bars were starting to feminize by the interwar years, but women still constituted less than 8 percent of lawyers by the Second World War.

By the interwar period, many male lawyers had come to accept women's presence in the profession.[51] Summing up the first twenty years of women's access, Jean Appleton wrote: "The application of the law [granting women access to the bar] has shown that the main objections raised against it were unfounded. The bar did not become overcrowded with women lawyers. Their presence at the bar did not cause any scandal; their glamour did not divert justice from the course of its duty. The family was not sacrificed; couples were not separated by women's admission to the legal profession."[52] Two other leading lawyers publicly agreed: "The presence of women at the bar has not caused a scandal, and it is difficult for us to understand the long-lived exclusion of which they were victims."[53]

Once professional access was officially opened to women, prejudices and discriminatory practices nevertheless continued to exclude them from certain subfields and elite positions. In law as well as in medicine, women pioneers focused their professional practice on the needs of women and children. This was less a "natural inclination" than a strategy for keeping a low profile while entering the professions, and women professionals often relied on arguments about gender difference to make inroads where possible. It took time for women lawyers to break out of the one area widely deemed appropriate for them: juvenile court.

After the First World War, women were beginning to plead cases in civil and commercial tribunals, courts of first instance, and even courts-martial. Not only did women lawyers have to struggle against the prejudices of their colleagues, but also they had to overcome an additional challenge unique to the liberal professions: the hesitancy of clients to hire them. The gender stereotypes held by potential clients limited the competitive threat that women professionals posed to male colleagues.[54] Although the lawyer Suzanne Grinberg claimed in 1925 that more men than women were choosing women lawyers in divorce cases, lawyers Lucile Tinayre and Suzanne Blum countered that it was still quite difficult for women lawyers to obtain criminal cases.[55] In a compilation of sixty-one court cases argued by ten female lawyers in Paris between 1907 and 1939, two-thirds of the defendants were women.[56]

Although powerful female professionals remained the anomaly, some reached the elite professional echelons by the 1930s. A few women had begun to win the prestigious Conférence du stage.[57] In 1933, the first woman was elected president of a bar: Paule Pignet in Roche-sur-Yon (a small town in the western department of Vendée).[58] Women lawyers had also begun to be named to government posts, for example, Marcelle Kraemer-Bach as *chargée de mission* in Premier Édouard Herriot's cabinet in 1932.[59] The legal press saluted all of these advances[60] and regularly published laudatory articles about women lawyers.[61] On the one hand, the women's achievements highlighted here were negligible in the grand scheme and attest to a persistent bias keeping a critical mass of women from reaching parity up through World War II. On the other hand, these signs substantiate an increasingly favorable climate for women in law; given the low number of women in the professions, their success was impressive.

Women lawyers founded professional associations such as the Federation of Women Magistrates and Lawyers, the Group of Women Lawyers of France,[62] the Society of Women Intending to Work in the Liberal Professions,[63] and the Association of Women Jurists.[64] The associational phenomenon was a sign of both progress (women gathering forces and expressing a feminist message publicly) and blockage (women responding to continued discrimination and misogyny). In interwar France, women lawyers such as Marcelle Kraemer-Bach, Agathe Dyvrande-Thévenin, Suzanne Grinberg, Yvonne Netter, and Maria Vérone were also activists in the feminist movement.[65] With their oratorical skills and knowledge of rights and legislation, women lawyers in particular were apt leaders of larger feminist causes.[66] The career trajectory of Grinberg, a feminist activist and reputable lawyer, demonstrates that "both the professional and feminist women's association movement served to integrate and not ghettoize women."[67]

At the same time, other forms of discrimination impinged on women trained in medicine and law. Female law graduates were denied access to the corporatist legal fields of notaries, solicitors, and court clerks.[68] And because women were banned from the magistrature until 1946, female lawyers could not fulfill one particular role, otherwise obligatory, of the legal profession in France: to substitute for judges whenever needed.[69] Until 1938, married women who wished to work were required by law to procure their husband's authorization.[70] In addition to these concrete discriminatory measures, the harsh economic climate of the 1930s provided a context that reignited hostility toward working women.

Women's professional progress in the French Third Republic had reached a sort of midpoint—marked by their significant advances in law and yet by entrenched limits to their success—when a backlash against working women was triggered by the depression. For male lawyers who perceived the legal market as stagnant and overcrowded, the context allowed them to feel comfortable targeting women, whose recent access to the field was still fresh in the collective memory. When basic economic survival was at stake and waning honor-based occupational identities needed reinvigorating, male students and lawyers easily relapsed into traditional concepts of gender roles.

The renewed antifeminism was formulated through various arguments, most of which had been iterated originally to deny women access to the bar in the late nineteenth century. Although the aim of protecting male employment was often used to disguise a general resentment of working women, lawyers in particular were reluctant to couch antifeminist views in protectionist terms for fear of tarnishing their honor-laden image of financial disinterestedness. Not incidentally, such anticommercial values served to alienate younger lower-class professionals, male and female, and deny them the opportunity to earn a living wage for their work, as described earlier.[71] Professional discourse about overcrowding caused by women and other new categories was carefully framed not in terms of economic protectionism but instead in terms of the need to preserve professional quality and integrity. Most often the discourse against feminization was masked by a general lament over a supposed decline in standards of competence. Discourse proclaiming women's intellectual inferiority was not absent from the French student, professional, and mainstream press in the interwar years,[72] and it was also to be found within academia. The dean of the Paris Law School, Henry Berthélemy, in a 1932 student daily paper, admitted that female law students usually performed better on tests than male students, but proclaimed, "As civil servants, women are not as good as men; and they are too emotional to succeed at the bar."[73]

Male lawyers feared that the presence of women colleagues would undermine their masculine values of honor and tradition. One leading Parisian lawyer warned in a newspaper article: "Many young ladies (currently more than two hundred in Paris) are seeking in our profession a financial situation which they seem unable to achieve through marriage. Without a doubt, such a transformation in our recruitment will profoundly alter the traditions of the bar, for which we will pay dearly."[74] These declarations from professional leaders helped legitimize a rethinking of women's access to the professions in the 1930s. The exclusion of women, however, never became a concrete initiative as had the exclusion of naturalized citizens. Anti-female discourse was less socially acceptable than discourse against naturalized citizens in the French legal profession in the 1930s. Yet entrenched discrimination against women accounts for one factor in a broader movement of exclusionism.

Even older lawyers, however distinguished and thriving, were not immune from exclusionary sentiment in the professions. In 1936 a plan was floated to impose a retirement age for the liberal professions in order to allay the unemployment of recent graduates. Young lawyers-to-be in the 1920s and 1930s faced financially dire career prospects, as we have seen. They tended to come from less well-off backgrounds than their predecessors, were burdened by the law bars with unpaid pro bono cases, and went unremunerated as they apprenticed with established lawyers. Most women professionals fell into this struggling subset. The Union des jeunes avocats and the Association corporative des étudiants en droit lobbied for solutions. Eventually their demands found a receptive echo. Lawyer-deputy Charles Pomaret and several other lawyer-deputies in 1936 proposed a law to institute a mandatory retirement age of sixty-five for lawyers, doctors, engineers, and other professionals. Thus, as a result of an ad hoc alliance of youth groups and parliamentarians, elderly professionals became a target of exclusion.

Mobilization against the proposed mandatory retirement age was swift and strong. The law bars did not intend to be told what to do by the state. Groups such as the ANA, medical unions, and student associations rallied.[75] Ultimately, the organizations that had originally supported the proposal backed down.[76] Yet the idea of obliging older lawyers to make way for the young became the subject of lively debate, won over more adherents than were probably willing to admit it, and remained on the table through the late 1930s.

★ ★ ★

These examples of antifeminism and ageism contextualize the larger reality of professional exclusionism aimed at naturalized citizens, to be examined in the next chapter. Employment concerns and fears of a changing professional identity best explain male lawyers' opposition to outsiders. Factors including economic depression, university demographics, educational reform, and professional modernization fomented an internal crisis in the legal corps, which manifested itself in various exclusionary tendencies. Determining access to the professions affected lawyers' core identity, an identity in the midst of a difficult transition from corporatist orders based on honor and tradition to republican *professions libérales* characterized by meritocracy and professionalization. Traditional professional identity, with its fundamental values of masculine pride, French nationality, and bourgeois belonging, was undermined by the arrival of members of the lower classes, women, and naturalized citizens.

 CHAPTER 5

Citizens into Lawyers

Extra Assimilation Required

Unlike doctors in the years between the wars, lawyers already possessed an airtight barrier against foreigners in their field through the formidable tool of the law bar. French nationality was required for bar membership. But beginning in the 1920s, recently naturalized French citizens became the new target of lawyers' exclusionary sentiment. French lawyers demanded that new citizens be banned from practicing law for a fixed period following their naturalization. They argued that "freshly naturalized" foreigners suffered from a lack of assimilation into French culture and should not have immediate access to the sensitive function of lawyering. Much of the exclusionary discourse exaggerated the number of naturalized citizens entering the bar. The term "invasion" was used regularly. The proclaimed need to maintain the lofty reputation of the French legal profession often masked a practical fear of competition for clients. Despite the real increase in the number of law students, the ranks of practicing lawyers in fact declined relative to population growth in the first half of the twentieth century. Lawyers' economic survival was at stake not because of professional overcrowding caused by naturalized citizens, but because the profession had painted itself into a corner through anticommercial policies such as bans on advertising, on forming law firms, and on working in commercial courts. These professional strictures impinged on the ability of a critical mass of newly arrived young lawyers from the lower and middle classes to earn a living, and ultimately served to reduce the bar's purview over the legal field as a whole. To a large extent, as the previous chapter elucidated, lawyers ignored the real socioeconomic developments that affected their profession; instead they focused their attention on naturalized lawyers.

A New Threat in the Interwar Period: Naturalized Lawyers

Foreigners had long been banned de facto from French law bars and thus unable to practice law as *avocats à la cour*. Whether the ban on foreigners dated from 1620, from the post-Revolutionary reestablishment of the Law Order in 1810, or from an 1864 Court of Cassation ruling,[1] the requirement of French nationality for the right to practice law in France was formalized into official legislation by the decree of 20 June 1920 that reorganized the legal profession.[2] Article 22 of the decree stated, "All those seeking admission to a law bar must furnish to the bar council: a bachelor of law diploma, proof of French nationality and civil status, and a police record."[3] Of course, foreigners with legal training could practice law outside the law bar structure as *conseils juridiques* or *agents d'affaires*. These areas of legal consultation were unregulated and left open to foreigners. As described in the previous chapter, the freedom of foreigners to work in these roles served to bolster French lawyers' enforcement of their distinction within the legal field.

In the same way that doctors regarded medical students, French lawyers distinguished between foreign students who wished to study law in France and return to their native countries upon graduation and foreign students who intended to remain and practice law in France. University officials historically promoted a policy of welcoming foreign students in all disciplines—law, medicine, science, letters—motivated by the reputation of French intellectual prestige abroad. In 1920, the dean of the Paris Law School, Ferdinand Larnaude, proclaimed about foreign students: "To attract and retain them, we must multiply the means of fellowships. Let us not forget that these students constitute the best agents of French influence."[4] Thirteen years later it was still a priority. His successor as Paris Law School dean, Edgar Allix, recognized that attracting foreign students would increase France's "worldwide influence," and, like Larnaude, asked the government to augment the budget for the law school's personnel and physical plant for this very purpose.[5] Many services were available to foreign students in French law schools: residency in the *cité universitaire,* courses in the French language at the Alliance française and the Sorbonne, as well as a mentoring program unique to the Paris Law School, whereby each law professor was in charge of advising foreign students from certain countries.[6]

At the same time, French law students had begun to complain about overcrowding in their schools and accused foreign students of monopolizing their professors, libraries, and classroom seats. The Association corporative des étudiants en droit called for a law regulating transfer credit equivalencies for foreigners, for the creation of a separate diploma for foreigners, and for the abolition of "advantages" accorded to foreign students.[7] Two associations founded within the Paris law bar to cater to the needs of young lawyers, the Union des jeunes avocats (UJA) and the Jeune barreau français (JBF), nurtured close ties with students and focused their attention in particular on the issue of overcrowding in law schools. The two associations, in fact, competed with each other to recruit members while designating foreigners as outsiders, all the better to create a boundary around their initiates. The UJA lamented that "through the trick of credit equivalencies" for law studies completed abroad, foreigners could get a French law degree, naturalize, and join a bar in only one year's time.[8] The JBF also called for a limitation on equivalencies.[9] The campaign against foreigners and naturalized citizens was practically the raison d'être of the short-lived JBF, which was founded in 1934 and disintegrated by the end of the war (but not without inducing a postwar criminal investigation into the group's collaborationist activities).

Lawyers had first manifested protectionist sentiment during the parliamentary debate over the 1927 nationality law. The reduction of the residency requirement from ten years to three worried lawyers, especially the reduction to only a one-year residency for naturalization candidates if they earned a diploma from a French university.[10] Thus all foreign students at a French law school could naturalize and enter the bar shortly after graduation. Lawyers denounced the process by which foreign students who were granted transfer credit for law studies in their country of origin (the ease of which was another source of discontent) could complete the final year of the law degree (*licence*) at a French law school, fast-track their naturalization, and enter the bar in as little as one year after their arrival in France.[11] French lawyers feared that such a short period of residency would not give naturalized citizens time to acquire a French mentality, which could be particularly harmful to the law bars. In fact, even though it was true that foreigners who had already had significant legal training abroad were required to fulfill only the requirements of the last year of the *licence* degree, and that this one year of residency crowned by a French diploma gave foreigners the right to apply for naturalization, it was an exaggeration to suggest that the entire process of graduation, naturalization, and bar admission could be concluded within twelve months from the date of arrival in France.

In May 1927 the Parisian Cercle d'études professionnelles (CEP) submitted a formal request to the *colonnes* (subgroups of lawyers within each bar) to lobby government and parliament to counteract the 1927 nationality law by imposing a five-year waiting period on naturalized citizens before they could register with a law bar. Once the CEP garnered enough support from the rank and file of the profession, the association pressured the Ministry of Justice.[12]

The idea of a naturalized citizen without full citizenship rights was not entirely new. The principle already existed for candidates for political office but not for labor or economic purposes. The 1889 nationality law was the first to institute the notion of withholding certain citizenship rights after naturalization: a ten-year waiting period for election to parliamentary assemblies. With this late-nineteenth-century provision, the historian Gérard Noiriel has stated, "the 'internal boundary' between the French national and the foreigner was distinctly drawn."[13] In the 1927 nationality law, legislators expanded the ten-year withholding of rights from new citizens to apply to *any* elected position. This was done to compensate for the new leniency of naturalization requirements embodied in the 1927 law. Because of compromises such as this and the possibility of being stripped of French nationality in the first ten years, the parliamentary majority finally agreed to vote for the liberal 1927 nationality law.[14] During these negotiations, legal professionals tried to persuade legislators to expand the category of delayed rights beyond elected positions to include membership in law bars.[15] This attempt represents the first time lawyers publicly called for a dual-class concept of citizenry for lawyers. Their efforts were brushed aside by the legislators, but only until 1934.

The Power of the Word: Xenophobic Discourse toward Lawyers of Foreign Origin

Throughout the late 1920s and 1930s, exclusionist lawyers criticized the 1927 law for its "dangerous" leniency regarding the naturalization of un-"Frenchified" foreigners into the French nation and the French law bars. French lawyers justified banning "freshly naturalized foreigners" from the practice of law for a supposed lack of assimilation into French culture, mores, and traditions. Louis Sarran, a Parisian lawyer and founding member of the ANA, exclaimed, "Foreigners... have taken advantage of the exceptional easing made possible by the 10 August 1927 naturalization law to solicit... their registration [with the law bar], sometimes while butchering the basics of our language."[16] Albert Rodanet, member of the Parisian bar since 1893, founding vice president and second president of the ANA, and former member of the Paris law bar council, wrote a series of articles in the journal *La vie judiciaire* in 1933 and 1934 about the "grave peril" posed by naturalized citizens in the bar. He asserted: "Freshly naturalized citizens, for whom French culture and the genius of our race are unknown, are noisily invading us. Not only do they speak our language poorly, but what is much more grave is that they do not have any consciousness of our historical role. Because of their insufficient adaptation, they cannot understand the essential characteristics of our profession, which is the handmaiden of Justice and the guardian of our oldest national traditions."[17]

Professional protectionism was thus masked behind calls to protect the national interest: naturalized lawyers constituted a danger for the French client and thus for the collective good. Such rhetoric was widespread. Sarran, in his presidential speech at the annual ANA congress in May 1934, argued, "Without suggesting the slightest sentiment of xenophobia and without renouncing our traditional right of asylum, it is legitimate, in the interest of justice, to require that all those who participate in the realm of justice possess not only the guarantees of knowledge that diplomas confer, but further that they are immersed in our traditions and our national mentality."[18] Jean Appleton, Lyon lawyer, professor at the Lyon Law School, and founder of the ANA, declared about naturalized lawyers, "Defendants and claimants, and the public in general, in the numerous situations in which they require legal advice for conducting business and defending their interests, have the right to be protected against the ignorance, greed, and lack of integrity of intermediaries."[19] UJA leader Gustave-M. Rémond stated, "The national interest, which incited the legislature to forbid naturalized citizens from immediate access to certain elected functions, also holds for the legal profession."[20] Dozens of similar claims can be found in legal journals and publications from the period.

Much of the exclusionary discourse grossly exaggerated the proportion of naturalized citizens entering the bar. Rodanet warned, for example, "In the near future, the Palais de Justice could be submerged by these new arrivals who possess a conception of neither our profession nor our way of living."[21] In another instance, he bordered on extremism: "Naturalized people, thanks to the improvident law of 10 August 1927, are invading the bars; before long they can constitute a grave danger for the very existence of our constitutions.... We must not let foreigners [*sic*], sometimes of dubious origin, come and modify our customs and our traditions, all the while appropriating clientele that had legitimately belonged to fellow colleagues."[22] Behind the proclaimed need to maintain the elevated reputation of the French legal profession is thus revealed a more practical fear about the loss of professional turf. Rodanet merged the two concerns into one: "Lawyers would lose doubly. From a personal point of view, they would be unjustly plundered, and still more seriously from a general point of view, the Bar, with a declining level of corporatism, would cease to be an appreciable element in the state."[23]

French lawyers also justified the temporary exclusion of naturalized citizens by linking the legal profession with service in the public sector. All lawyers were obliged to substitute for magistrates whenever necessary in courts and tribunals. Therefore lawyers could be considered "occasional" magistrates, it was argued, and thus members of the civil service. As Appleton wrote in 1923: "Justice is a civil service. Although not a civil servant, a lawyer contributes to the administering of this service in a very important way. The Law thus requires of a lawyer knowledge and guarantees, of the sort needed to ensure the steady course of the service in which he is called to collaborate.... These reasons explain that the access to and the practice of the legal profession must be regulated."[24] Twenty pages later he concluded: "In a word, the Law Order is one of the essential organs of a great civil service. The principles of French public law reserve the right to collaborate in the management of public services for French nationals only; foreigners thus do not have access to the legal profession."[25] Another lawyer argued that a ten-year waiting period for naturalized citizens to practice law was as important as the existing delay for an elected position: "Before ten years, [a naturalized citizen] cannot be a municipal representative of the smallest town in France, but he can be a court lawyer. He is considered incapable of deciding the paving of a small side road or the purchase of hoses for a firehouse, but we allow him to argue before the Prefecture Council in favor of the nullification of the election results of all the municipal representatives."[26]

Lawyers further likened the legal profession to the civil service through the professional obligation of all lawyers to defend the poor, and recently naturalized citizens were considered unworthy of the task of providing pro bono legal assistance. "It is an honor for our profession, and it singularly aligns the profession with a public mandate," professed Rodanet.[27] This was a particularly weak argument, since it was well known that the professional obligation of legal aid was pushed off almost entirely onto the most junior members of the bar. The bar presidents (*bâtonniers*) were responsible for assigning the cases of the needy. The unremunerated work, shunned by all, invariably went to struggling neophyte lawyers and even to *stagiaires,* lawyers in training. But the argument was used nonetheless to justify the exclusion of recently naturalized French citizens. Sarran warned of the danger of investing recently naturalized lawyers with this important task: "The Bar, a participant in the administration of justice, should be a career reserved, like other important state services, for Frenchmen of a certain date. This goal would be reached by imposing on naturalized citizens a trial period of several years."[28]

On the strength of all of these arguments, French lawyers called for the exclusion from the bar of new French citizens for a period of ten years after their naturalization. This delay would constitute, it was argued, "a certain training period for the freshly naturalized citizen that would allow him to have direct contact with French life, of which the Bar is one of the highest and most vital expressions."[29] Lawyers recognized that such a demand, contrary to basic principles of citizenship, could not prevail in the form of a mere internal professional regulation, so they worked toward the passage of legislation.

Strategies and Mechanisms of Exclusion

French lawyers' strategy for promoting legislation to exclude recently natural-ized citizens from their profession entailed a basic rallying and lobbying mecha-nism. The movement developed as such: several committed individuals, usually of leadership stature such as Louis Sarran, Albert Rodanet, and Jean Appleton, roused their fellow lawyers by publicizing their views in legal journals. While the seeds of discontent were being sown in the press, law associations were rally-ing their members to their official points of view. The ANA and the UJA both held multiple meetings on the subject and regularly had members vote on types of actions to be taken by the group. The UJA authored a proposal that eventu-ally became the exact text of the 1934 law.[30] Meanwhile, within the individual bars and on their own initiative, the bar councils were meeting on the issue. The Paris bar council had been trying to remove recently naturalized lawyers from the profession since 1927, as we have seen.[31] At the same time, the subgroup-ings of lawyers in each bar known as the *colonnes* were drafting formal requests to submit to their bar councils. This is a telling point concerning the breadth of the movement, since every lawyer was necessarily a member of a *colonne,* and presence at meetings and votes was mandatory. Pushed by the CEP in late 1933,[32] several *colonnes* in the Paris bar voted to ban naturalized citizens from the bar for ten years.[33]

Widespread support among the rank and file of the profession gave senior members of the bar the legitimacy to voice their demands in parliament in the name of the entire profession. Lobbying of government and parliament was logical and simple, since lawyers were the socio-professional category holding the most parliamentary and government positions in interwar France. Their actual presence in the Chamber of Deputies and the Senate evidently eased the passage of a law in favor of the legal profession. If not holders of political office themselves, many lawyers, especially in Paris, had political clout through friendships and professional connections. Thus the mechanism used by the legal profession to promote exclusionary legislation took the most efficient form of quiet "lobbying" among colleagues of similar socio-professional backgrounds.

Léon Bérard, a senior member of the Paris bar, solicited the minister of justice and the Senate in May 1933 to push for the ten-year delay. Himself twice min-ister of justice under Prime Minister Pierre Laval, in 1931 and 1935, Bérard was careful to assure senators that his proposal was not based on any kind of interest-group protectionism but rather that instituting a "trial period" for naturalized lawyers was necessary for the protection of the public interest. To emphasize the civil service nature of the legal profession, Paris bar president and senator Man-uel Fourcade made sure to mention the magistrature in the same breath as the bar and to link the two functions. Minister of the Interior Camille Chautemps, a lawyer himself, was more frank. He admitted that naturalized French citizens had already fulfilled a waiting period in France before their naturalization, and that if a foreign accent remained by the time of naturalization, it would probably remain forever. Chautemps also acknowledged that if a citizen had completed legal studies, he had a right to practice law, and restricting that right would condemn many to penury. He further noted that it was in the interest of France to have its naturalized citizens *working*. In spite of his own arguments, Chautemps supported the proposed reform because of the "particular character of the profession, the very legitimate traditions."[34]

The minister of justice and members of parliament then left the issue on the back burner until early 1934, and constant changes of government leadership slowed the momentum that was being stoked by lawyers. But legal professionals pressed on in their campaign. The members of the UJA Paris office adopted the following resolution in 1934: "The General Assembly of the Paris UJA allies itself completely with the formal request made by Monsieur the Bar President to the Minister of Justice regarding the admission of naturalized citizens to a trial period. We express our gratitude to Monsieur the Bar President for having interceded with the Authorities so that a bill may be presented and voted without delay by the two Chambers."[35] The ANA called on its president, Sarran, to intervene with the justice minister in order to get the waiting period passed into law.[36] The Paris law bar president, Émile de Saint-Auban, successor to Manuel Fourcade, also pressed the minister with the unanimous backing of his membership.[37]

Exclusionary activists were careful to apply political pressure appropriately. One of the more extremist lawyers, Rodanet, wanted all non-French-born citizens to be permanently excluded from practicing law (a demand that was eventually satisfied by Vichy legislation in 1940), since "nothing replaces familial upbringing." But he recognized that "such a law will not be passed in the current climate."[38] Other lawyers wanted a ten-year delay with no exceptions allowed, but strategically renounced this wish in order to speed up the legislative process.[39]

The Arrival of Jewish Refugees

Hitler's rise to power and persecution of Jews in German society led to an influx of some 25,000 asylum seekers in France.[40] Whereas the French medical profession responded to this humanitarian crisis by defending itself against the possibility of Jewish refugees being permitted to practice medicine in France, the legal profession was already protected by the barrier of the bar, which excluded all foreigners. For this reason, French lawyers were less prone than French doctors to manifest anti-refugee and anti-Semitic sentiment publicly in the 1930s.

Nevertheless, Jewish refugees in France with legal training from abroad represented a threat to the French law bars in two ways. First, refugee lawyers could conceivably offer legal advice as *conseils juridiques* or *agents d'affaires,* professions completely open and untouched by 1930s protectionist legislation requiring work permits for artisans and shopkeepers, for example. Second, Jewish refugees could apply to become naturalized French citizens, and thus threaten to swell the ranks of the bar. In fact, the 1934 law banning recently naturalized citizens from the profession was voted on at a crucial moment when Jewish refugees were arriving in France in large numbers, and it is possible that this perceived threat spurred lawyers to pass their exclusionary legislation.[41] Dr. Fernand Querrioux claimed as much in a jealous rage over the fact that the 1934 law did not apply to medicine, asserting that the law resulted from fear of a supposed group of three hundred Jewish German lawyers coming to France.[42] Indeed, a rumor had spread, initially publicized by legal associations that had procured university statistics, that three hundred German students (not identified as Jewish except by Querrioux) were registered in the law schools of Paris, Strasbourg, and Nancy. Lawyers used this information to raise fear that a mass of foreigners would naturalize and join the bar within a year.[43] Exclusionary initiatives had already begun well before 1933, but the Jewish refugee wave served to further heighten lawyers' alarm about professional invasion by foreigners. Fears about an influx of Jewish refugees also extended to other European countries where anti-Semitism threatened law professionals in the mid-1930s. In Romania in 1937, for example, forty-six of sixty-six law bars voted at a legal congress to exclude lawyers of "non-Romanian blood" from the profession.[44]

While some lawyers in interwar France certainly were prejudiced against Jews, barely a single instance of blatant anti-Semitism emerges from the journals and archives of the legal profession. Various lawyers of the period have noted in their memoirs, however, that a quiet anti-Semitism permeated bar culture. Jacques Isorni, who would later defend Philippe Pétain and Robert Brasillach after the war, claimed that in the 1930s there was an unspoken quota on Jews in the Paris bar's Conférence du stage, the oratory competition for new lawyers. Of the twelve winners (*secrétaires*) chosen each year, never were more than two of them Jewish. A Parisian lawyer, Raymond Hesse, also noted such a practice in his postwar memoirs, claiming that the custom was to nominate one woman, one colonial subject, and one Jew per year.[45] Isorni wrote that it was his task as the Conférence's top winner, or first secretary, in 1935–36 to select the twelve winners for the following year, who would then be confirmed by the Paris bar council. Isorni reported that his list included four and possibly five Jews, one of them a woman, Lucienne Scheid, who deserved first place in his view. He wrote that he understood the risk he was taking with his nominations: only once before had a Jew been chosen as first secretary, Pierre Masse in 1906, and no woman had ever been first secretary. Isorni claimed: "I fought for her, Lucienne Scheid, because she deserved it. . . . It was a sense of justice, perhaps a sense of dignity, that caused me to battle against the unwritten racism of the law courts.... Who would have had the courage of opinion to say publicly, 'There are too many Jews,' which is what many thought privately?"[46] Isorni, who had been a member of the extreme right and xenophobic Lycéens d'Action française, was likely promoting himself as anti-anti-Semitic in his postwar memoirs. Nevertheless, Lucienne Scheid was elected first secretary of the Conférence in 1936–37.[47]

On 6 June 1936, upon Léon Blum's accession to the post of prime minister, Xavier Vallat, member of the Paris bar and deputy from Ardèche, notoriously declared before the French Chamber of Deputies, "For the first time, this old Gallo-Roman country will be governed by a Jew." This was not the first time that Deputy Vallat had insulted Blum, a fellow Paris bar member, nor the first time Vallat made anti-Semitic statements in parliament, but it was a critical moment in Third Republic politics. Booed by the left and applauded by the right in the Chamber, Vallat's statement was notable for its premeditated and implacable character. The subsequent speaker at the podium, Deputy René Dommange, who was a leader of the anti-foreigner legislation in medicine, stated his appreciation for the preceding "courageous and eloquent speeches."[48]

What is not well known about the spectacle of Vallat's speech in the Chamber is that two weeks later the members of the Paris bar elected Vallat to their bar council. His candidacy likely resulted directly from his recent notoriety for his anti-Semitic remarks in parliament. Contrary to bar traditions, Vallat's candidacy was wanting in several respects: his youth, his undistinguished record as a bar member and practicing lawyer, and his current political mandate (never before had an acting deputy been elected to the Paris bar council). Robert Badinter, former justice minister, has remarked that Vallat's professional merits were well below bar council standards.[49] Furthermore, Vallat's opponent for the bar council seat was Étienne Caen, a Jewish lawyer. Vallat was elected to the twenty-four-member council, but with difficulty: only on the ninth round, by 471 out of 940 votes. He was reelected in 1937, 1938, and 1939, but reelection was part of bar tradition, and Vallat's reelections were not won with ease. Does Vallat's election to the bar council in 1936 signify that anti-Semitism was widely shared in the Paris law bar? Vallat himself saw it that way. Others have argued that his election signifies the law bar's political rejection of the Popular Front.[50] Whereas Vallat's anti-Semitism was known for being "flagrant," and even "maniacal," according to Badinter, who gained privileged access to bar archives in order to write about his profession's attitudes toward Jews, there reigned in the Paris law bar during the interwar period "a measured anti-Semitism," but toward foreign and naturalized Jews there was a "fierce and xenophobic anti-Semitism."[51] In this sense Badinter reifies the distinctions made by French lawyers in the 1930s and early 1940s between French Jews and foreign Jews. Still, it has been suggested by a contemporary member of the UJA that the rival group, the Jeune barreau français, was founded because they claimed there were too many Jews (that is, French Jews) in the UJA.[52]

Some French Jews had attained important positions in the legal field, proving that if a glass ceiling existed, it was not impenetrable. Pierre Masse, first secretary of the Conférence, a deputy and senator, had regularly published articles in the legal press,[53] and was resoundingly elected to the Paris bar council in 1932.[54] Kadmi Cohen of the Paris law bar was a cofounder of the UJA and received favorable reviews of his books, *L'abomination américaine: l'essai sur l'âme juive* and *L'état d'Israël,* in the journal *La vie judiciaire.*[55] Marcel Bloch, who was blind, was elected president of the UJA in 1930 and was lauded publicly by bar president and member of the Académie française Henri-Robert.[56] René Idzkowski, a Paris lawyer and deputy justice of the peace in Nogent-sur-Marne, was publicly commended by his colleague Vincent de Moro-Giafferri, member of the bar council and former undersecretary of state in the Ministry of Education.[57] André Lévy-Oulmann was honored publicly by César Campinchi, former member of the bar council and deputy from Corsica.[58] Louis Crémieu, Aix bar president, professor at the Aix-Marseille Law School, author of an important and lauded treatise on the legal profession, was a respected leader of the profession.[59] Although these examples of Jewish lawyers who gained respect and success within the French law bars concern French Jews, the distinction between French and foreign Jews would not matter in just a few years' time. Eight years after his election to the prestigious Paris bar council, Pierre Masse would be sent along with other Jewish lawyers from the Paris bar to the Drancy transit camp for deportation and then killed. Idzkowski would be dead in less than ten years, sacrificed by his law bar. Although Crémieu's powerful colleagues in the profession saved him upon his arrest during the German occupation, he was victimized professionally by the anti-Semitic laws of Vichy.

In the mid-1930s some bar members, however, spoke out in favor of even refugee Jewish lawyers. In January 1934, Vincent de Moro-Giafferri wrote to Prime Minister Camille Chautemps requesting that German refugees who had refused to join the Nazi Party and had fled to France without proper passports and visas be welcomed.[60] Moro-Giafferri's appeal conspicuously avoided the term "Jewish" and alluded rather to political refugees. The Strasbourg law bar made an official plea to all French lawyers in favor of Jewish lawyers in Germany who unfortunately "were not, in their distress, finding from their fellow colleagues nor from their corporatist organizations the assistance that, in all countries and in all times, lawyers have always been honored to bring to those in need of justice and pity." The Strasbourg bar council did not go so far as to call for allowing Jewish refugee lawyers to join French law bars, but it did call on French lawyers to support charitable organizations and to alert them of any positions in commerce, industry, litigation, or translation. The gesture found little resonance. Leaders of the ANA permitted the Strasbourg appeal to be read at the 1933 annual congress, and although applause followed, the gathering moved on to the next item on the agenda without further comment.[61]

Just as some humanitarian groups pushed the French government to find positions for German refugee doctors in the colonies, there was some debate within the Ministry of Foreign Affairs in 1933 as to whether German refugee lawyers could practice law in the mandate territories of Lebanon and Syria.[62] Not only did all lawyers in these territories have to fulfill age and diploma qualifications, be fluent in French and Arabic, and gain admission to the local law bars, but also the bars there had in place a quota on foreign lawyers: one-eighth of the total bar membership. Because of these restrictions, and because the legal profession there was considered "more overcrowded than ever," the ministry ultimately decided to dissuade German refugee lawyers strongly from going to these territories in an attempt to establish a career.[63]

Parliamentary Response to Professional Mobilization

By 1934 lawyers convinced legislators that naturalized citizens ought to be excluded from the legal profession. In response to the profession's multipronged lobbying approach to both parliament and government, a *proposition de loi* (a bill initiated by the legislature) was launched by Félix Aulois, a lawyer and unaffiliated deputy from the Nièvre, and supported by deputies Pierre Baudouin-Bugnet, Alcide Delmont, and Albert Sérol (all four of them lawyers), and a *projet de loi* (a bill initiated by the government) was submitted by Minister of Justice Henry Chéron.[64]

Immediately evident in the proposed legislation was the link that lawyers wished to highlight between their profession and public service. Political leaders seemed readily convinced that the exclusion of recently naturalized citizens was justified because the legal profession was integrally linked to the public order and the functioning of the civil service; thus only French citizens "of long duration" could master all the intricacies necessary to practice law. In the preamble to his March 1934 bill, Chéron favored the facilitated naturalization process inaugurated by the 1927 nationality law, but he argued that because in some cases the assimilation level was quite imperfect on the date of naturalization, it was natural to allow for a sort of intermediary period, whereby the naturalized citizen was temporarily barred from certain functions that required a complete assimilation to the ideas and habits of France. He argued that a temporary ban should be applied to civil service positions and to *offices ministériels* (quasi-public professions such as notaries, *greffiers, avoués, huissiers,* and *commis-greffiers assermentés*). While admitting that a lawyer was certainly not a civil servant, the minister claimed, nevertheless, that a lawyer was an "unceasing representative of the public service of the law" who could be called upon to serve on a judicial tribunal or even on an interdepartmental prefecture council. Furthermore, a lawyer could be asked to consult dossiers concerning national defense, which required a longer presence in the French nation. For these reasons, the minister proposed that the "incapacities" enumerated in the 1927 law for naturalized citizens be extended to include three additional categories: law bar membership, civil service positions, and *offices ministériels.*[65]

The justice minister's bill went unaddressed for several months. Then in June 1934, Deputy Aulois, feeling that the matter presented "a certain urgency notably from the perspective of national defense," proposed a similar measure to the Chamber. Like the justice minister, Aulois paid lip service to the benefits of the facilitated naturalization process instituted by the 1927 law; but, he argued, the law should "temporarily exclude" new citizens from performing certain functions that required a complete assimilation to Frenchness.[66] A few days later, independent deputy Louis Rolland from the Maine-et-Loire and *agrégé* professor of law, presented to the Chamber his committee's report on the two legislative proposals. Given the similarity of the proposals, Rolland focused on two outstanding issues: when the ten-year delay should begin and what exceptions to allow. These issues were complicated because the legislation was meant to amend and attach itself to the 1927 nationality law, which had addressed these issues for elected positions. Article 6 of the 1927 law established a ten-year waiting period from the date of naturalization but eliminated the delay for those persons who had performed military service in the French army, and eliminated, or in some cases lessened, the length of the delay for those persons who were granted a special exemption by the Justice Ministry.

In Minister Chéron's bill, the start of the ten-year waiting period would not change for elected positions (the date of the individual's naturalization), but for membership in a bar, the civil service, and the *offices ministériels,* the delay would begin on the date of the decree. What was at stake here was the principle of non-retroactivity. Deputy Aulois's bill instead sought to change the 1927 law to make the delay for elective functions begin on the date of this new amendment.

As for exceptions, Chéron's bill would leave unchanged the exceptions to the delay for elected functions, but for the three new categories would allow no exceptions whatsoever. Aulois's bill would also undo those exceptions allowed for elected functions by the 1927 law. The parliamentary proposition, therefore, was much more restrictive than the justice minister's bill: it sought to toughen provisions of the 1927 law that had nothing to do with lawyers.

Deputy Rolland threw his committee's support to the parliamentary bill calling for the most restrictive legislation with regard to the starting date of the ten-year delay. His committee sided with the government's bill by not allowing any exceptions for the three categories of lawyer, civil servant, and holder of an *office ministériel*. Rolland's committee considered whether or not the new provisions should retroactively affect those who were naturalized before the signing of the new law. Both possibilities had precedents: the 1889 nationality law's delays for political eligibility were not retroactive, whereas the 1927 law's delays for legislative eligibility were. Rolland's solution was to create a blanket exception to the principle of retroactivity for all those already naturalized for five years.[67] But three days later the minister of justice pushed for "immediate discussion" in the Chamber of a revision that would entirely eliminate the committee's proposal regarding retroactivity. The new wording instituted a ten-year delay for law bar membership, civil service, and *offices ministériels* dating from the naturalization of each individual, allowing for no exceptions.

During the discussion that followed, the president of the Chamber asked on four separate occasions for comment from deputies, and four times no deputy asked to speak before the bill was put to a vote and adopted.[68] The same day the bill was sent to the Senate for deliberation,[69] and two days later Senator Manuel Fourcade, president of the Paris law bar, delivered his committee's report to the Senate. Misleadingly interpreting the text for his colleagues, Fourcade claimed that exceptions were allowed for naturalized citizens who had performed military service and for special cases allowed by the minister of justice, when in truth no exceptions were mentioned. Fourcade's declaration of urgency for both the reading of the report and the adoption of the bill was seconded by nineteen of his fellow senators, including Raymond Armbruster and General Jean Stuhl, who had been notably active in restricting naturalized citizens from practicing medicine. When no senators asked to speak at several opportunities, the Senate voted and adopted the text.[70] Two weeks later, on 19 July 1934, the "law on naturalized citizens' access to certain functions" was promulgated. Naturalized citizens were henceforth barred from the practice of law in France until ten years after their naturalization.[71]

Several historians have noted the rapidity and discretion with which the legal profession achieved passage of this momentous law.[72] No debate whatsoever took place in either the Chamber or the Senate on the day the text of the law was adopted, but one could argue that the call for a post-naturalization delay for membership in a law bar was an old issue. It had been launched during negotiations over the 1927 nationality law, and lawyers had been lobbying for it in a concentrated fashion since early 1933. The interconnections between the Palais de Justice and the organs of political power surely helped smooth the passage of exclusionary legislation. All of the parliamentarian and governmental activists were lawyers by profession. Over time, then, a few committed individuals were capable of rallying the rank and file of the legal profession, and a growing movement in turn influenced the upper echelons of the profession to lobby the government and parliament for the passage of a law.

Some historians assert that the main objective of the exclusionary law against naturalized citizens was to benefit the legal profession specifically, and that the other two areas of exclusion (civil service and *offices ministériels*) were added solely to camouflage the special interest benefit to the law bars. Ralph Schor, for example, has stated, "Nobody was fooled: it was a law made by lawyers, for lawyers."[73] It is difficult to confirm or refute this claim, owing to the lack of parliamentary discussion. Of all three functions in the legislation, however, bar membership was least obviously tied to the national interest.

Perhaps, too, what the minister of health had said to doctors wishing for a similarly rapid vote for exclusion in medicine was true: that parliamentarians were amenable to passing legislation for lawyers because, unlike in medicine, the profession of lawyer was not the only career path open to law graduates. Because naturalized law school graduates had other career opportunities outside the law bar, parliamentarians could stomach such a restriction, the health minister suggested, but they were reluctant to ban naturalized medical school graduates from practicing their trade for ten years because this would leave them truly destitute.[74] Indeed, one deputy presiding over a committee, Louis Gardiol, a doctor by profession and member of the Socialist Party, demonstrated sympathy for naturalized citizens in this regard, although his remarks were quickly shot down by another deputy, Jean Lerolle: "Do we need them in France? Are there not already enough French doctors?"[75] Lerolle, a lawyer in the Paris bar and member of the center-rightist *démocrate populaire* party, had supported a number of measures to protect French commerce from foreign competition in the 1930s. What is certainly true is that lawyers conducted their campaign for protection in an extremely discreet manner compared to doctors. Archival resources on the subject are significantly less rich for the legal profession, which testifies to lawyers' success in influencing politicians through direct and private channels.

Lawyers Interpret the Legislation to Their Advantage

The exclusionary legislation satisfied many in the legal profession, although it did not stop the xenophobic mobilization, which continued throughout the 1930s. The Association corporative des étudiants en droit called for the strict application of the July 1934 law,[76] and repetitively promulgated its "firm attitude, but always marked by just moderation" vis-à-vis the ten-year waiting period for naturalized citizens to practice law.[77] Some French lawyers continued to complain that the law did not go far enough. At the monthly general assembly of the Jeune barreau français, Alphonse Joffre declared that "despite this law, the bar is still insufficiently protected against foreign infiltrations." Inciting fear that in cases of espionage, recently naturalized lawyers would have access to documents concerning French national defense, Joffre claimed that "professional interest is closely allied with national interest." Speaking before many bar leaders and members of the Paris bar council, he argued that "a profound distinction must be established between the Frenchman from birth and the foreigner who recently managed to attain our nationality." After Joffre's talk, the JBF voted unanimously to give civil tribunals the ultimate say on naturalization rights as well as on questions regarding stripping individuals of their nationality, and to make all new legislation on naturalization retroactive.[78]

In one behind-the-scenes instance, the Paris bar council refused to admit a qualified German Jewish lawyer to the bar in the mid-1930s. Mr. M. J. B.[79] fulfilled all the "wrong" requirements: as a German national, he had benefited from transfer credit in order to earn his French law degree; as a Jew removed from the Frankfurt law bar in 1933 by Nazi purges, he could claim French nationality (thanks to the 1919 Treaty of Versailles, which granted, without expiration, automatic reintegration to those who had lost French nationality in the Franco-German Treaty of 1871); and as a man over the age of thirty-five, he was not obliged to fulfill French military service. The Paris bar council bitterly resented B.'s nationality switch, which, though completely legal, they deemed "self-interested." The bar council rejected him for admission, claiming that the ten-year delay for naturalized citizens in the 1934 law was equally necessary for this Treaty of Versailles case, for as "B. proved that he does not have a sufficient use and pronunciation of the French language to permit him to be admitted to the bar, his admission is not acceptable."[80] B. appealed his rejection, and the Court of Appeals overrode the Paris bar council's decision. This set the council in furious motion. Bar president William Thorp took an exceptional measure, *tierce opposition,* an extraordinary legal procedure that allows a third party, in this case the bar president as an individual, to request that a case be reheard.[81] In a final striking and arbitrary legal twist, the Court of Appeals overruled its own initial decision and decreed that a three-year delay would be imposed on B. so that he could properly assimilate, even though he was found to speak French correctly. B. could reapply to the bar after three years, but there was no guarantee of admission. He was also found liable for all court costs. The thick dossier on B.'s case in the archives, including a 1936 secret police investigation of his "morals, habits, and lifestyle," which shows the involvement of the minister of national education and the minister of justice, is a testament to the lengths the Paris bar was willing to go to block one German Jew's application for bar membership.[82]

The Paris law bar's response to B.'s application for admission seems extreme, and yet it may have been the norm. Law bar archives are privately held, and only fragments of internal proceedings in the bar councils have been deposited in public archives to this day. In another example of the discretionary power the law bars wielded with regard to bar admissions, the Paris law bar rejected a naturalized Frenchman in December 1933 (that is, before the 1934 law) "who had neither the knowledge nor the understanding of the French language that the profession of lawyer requires."[83]

As described in chapter 2, the passage of the 1934 law had repercussions on the medical profession's mobilization against naturalized citizens, and some lawyers participated in medical protests out of professional solidarity. After 1934, the demand for a ten-year delay became the adopted cry of the medical corps.[84] Law students participated in the medical students' cause and played a role in the 1935 student strike against foreigners and naturalized citizens. The historian Pierre Péan has documented the participation of François Mitterrand, then a first-year student at the Paris Law School and at the Institut d'Études Politiques, in the student demonstrations against *métèques*. At the time, Mitterrand was a member of the Volontaires nationaux of the far right Croix-de-Feu association of Colonel François de La Roque.[85] Student agitation in the law school in the interwar years was often colored by politics. Even more so than for medical students, the Action française had recruited student members from the law school after the First World War, as had other right-wing groups such as the Camelots du roi and the Phalanges universitaires des Jeunesses patriotes.[86] In fact it was prolonged agitation against two law professors, Georges Scelle and Gaston Jèze, minority leftists in a conservative law faculty, that gave form and continuity to the political demonstrations in the Latin Quarter throughout the interwar years.[87]

The Association corporative des étudiants en droit was partly responsible for launching the second wave of agitation in the spring of 1935. Its members called a new strike for April 4 to demonstrate their discontent and to press the authorities for measures "to ensure the future of law school graduates." Four of the law students' five demands concerned foreigners or naturalized citizens: a stricter law on transfer credit granted to foreign students, regulations on foreigners' use of French diplomas, strict enforcement of the July 1934 law, and elimination of all advantages for foreigners in general. The fifth demand called for the obligatory retirement of professionals, that is, the Pomaret proposal. In response to the strike call, the law section of the communist UFE circulated a tract encouraging law students to resist the ploy of scapegoating foreigners, concluding, "Down with the xenophobic strike." Because of the UFE's swift denunciation of the strike call, the Association corporative abandoned the idea and instead called for a press campaign of posters, petitions, and lobbying.[88]

Despite parliamentary debate over the matter, the 1934 law ultimately left the questions of retroactivity and exceptions unresolved. What about citizens who were already naturalized in 1934 but for less than ten years? In response to the law's ambiguity, and also in response to debate within the medical profession over provisions regarding medical civil service positions, the Council of State issued an interpretation of the 1934 law clarifying that the law was not retroactive: those who had been French citizens for less than ten years and who were already employed in the functions covered by the law could retain their positions.[89]

The Council of State further decreed that natives of French protectorates and mandates were subject to the provisions of the 1934 law, but that Algerians were not. The interpretation regarding Algerians was not uniformly respected by all law bars either before or after the council's ruling. Louis Crémieu, law professor and president of the Aix law bar, in his *Traité de la profession d'avocat,* argued in 1939, "The bar...must be protected against the infiltration of indigenous elements, whose loyalty is uncertain and who are not sufficiently evolved."[90] Although bar leaders such as Appleton, Payen, Duveau, and Crémieu insisted in their treatises that natives of French protectorates and mandates were ineligible to practice law in France,[91] actual jurisprudence revealed a murkier reality.[92] The rights of Algerians to practice law in France remained a controversial and unsettled issue. The same argument made about Algerians' lack of full voting rights had been made against women's access to the legal profession prior to 1900, when women were granted entry to the bar. French lawyers, attempting to deny the rights of Algerians to practice law in the interwar years, engaged in verbal acrobatics to explain women's access while opposing that of Algerians.

Despite the consensus that the law was not retroactive, some French bars and courts interpreted it retroactively. In the autumn of 1934, the Paris law bar rejected two candidates for admission who had been naturalized for less than ten years and who had not performed military service, and the bar's decision on this matter was confirmed by the Court of Appeals.[93] A 24 January 1935 *arrêté* of the Paris bar council finally chose this principle as a guideline: citizens who had been naturalized less than ten years before enactment of the 1934 law and who were already members of a bar would not be stripped of their right to practice; citizens who had been naturalized less than ten years before enactment of the law and were not yet registered with a law bar would have to wait until ten years after their naturalization to be admitted to a bar.[94] Furthermore, exceptions that were allowed for elective positions under the 1927 nationality law did not apply to the newly covered categories of civil service, *offices ministériels,* and membership in a law bar. This was confirmed by Louis Rolland on the floor of the Chamber in February 1935.[95] In contrast, the 1933 Armbruster law instituting restrictions on naturalized citizens in medicine exempted all those who had served in the French military.

Easing of Restrictions under the Popular Front

Shortly after the 1934 law passed, some French lawyers expressed dissent. Maurice Lansac of the Paris law bar wrote in *La vie judiciaire* that the law was contrary to French patriotism and, furthermore, was unnecessary, given that in the Paris region alone there lived over a million foreigners and colonial peoples who needed their own kind to represent them in the courts.[96] Eventually parliament, controlled by the Popular Front in 1936, was willing to rethink the policy.

Even before this sharp shift in political climate, however, after the doctors had succeeded in getting their demands for a ten-year waiting period in medicine to reach the floor of the legislature in 1935, parliamentarians looked back at what they had done for lawyers the previous year. For some it was with regret. Deputy Fabien Albertin and several of his socialist colleagues presented a bill to amend the 1934 law to add exemptions for military service. And socialist deputy Marius Moutet, also a Paris bar member, proposed to stop the law's retroactive effect against any citizen who either had naturalized or was in the process of naturalizing before 19 July 1934 and who had obtained a secondary school diploma leading toward the professions addressed by the law.[97] A few months later, when Deputy René Dommange was fighting for an extremely restrictive law for doctors, Albertin spoke out frankly about the left's mistake in 1934: "The law of 19 July 1934, which we passed under circumstances about which none of us, I am certain, retain the slightest recollection, bans naturalized citizens from the legal profession and from the role of *officier ministériel* for ten years beginning with their decree of naturalization. It is unfortunately true. Indeed, we committed this injustice."[98] In the Senate, too, there was regret over the 1934 law. After Raymond Armbruster reminded Maurice Viollette, as a way of justifying a similar restriction for doctors in 1935, that the Senate had voted for exclusionary legislation in 1934 for lawyers, Viollette responded: "You are completely correct, but because the bill was presented in such a way, many of our colleagues realized it had been passed only once it was already submitted to the other Assembly. Otherwise, I would have protested." Viollette was a member of the Paris bar.[99]

Student groups reacted to parliamentary proposals to reconsider the law in predictable ways. The Association corporative des étudiants en droit responded negatively to an easing of restrictions, and the UFE favored exemptions for naturalized citizens who had performed military service for France.[100]

On 28 August 1936 a new law passed which established exemptions from the ten-year delay for all those who had been naturalized before the 1934 law and who had completed their military service obligations or who had fulfilled at least five years of military duty, regardless of whether or not they had already begun to practice law. Also, naturalized citizens who were practicing law already but who had not fulfilled their military obligations could retain their positions.[101] The change of political regime that brought the Popular Front to power was to a great degree responsible for this 1936 legislation. Nevertheless, the 1936 law could be interpreted as an overall confirmation of the 1934 restrictions.

What real effect did the 1936 law have on naturalized citizens wishing to practice law? Minister of Justice Vincent Auriol defended the new law's revision of the 1934 law: "This law has in truth lifted the ban only for those who were naturalized before 1934 and have done their military service, or for those who naturalized after 1934 and have performed five or more years of military duty. The number of young persons registering for the bar [under these conditions] is low and actually negligible."[102] Nevertheless, the JBF expressed hostility to the Popular Front's easing of restrictions, noting, "We do not want to see our positions loopholed by the enemy, previously camouflaged as an accommodating legislator, who under the guise of amnesty would intend to impose on us colleagues judged unworthy by their peers, or who, on the pretext of internationalism, would claim to envelop in our tricolor flag men who speak our language poorly and who in all cases do not think French."[103]

The archival documents suggest that by the late 1930s, lawyers were expressing less resentment toward foreigners and naturalized citizens, most likely because these categories had been excluded from the profession to the greatest degree possible. At the 1937 and 1939 annual congresses of the ANA, for example, not a word was uttered about naturalized or foreign lawyers, quite a change from the discussions at the same congresses in the mid-1930s.[104] At the same time, however, whatever anti-foreigner sentiments were expressed had become virulently xenophobic. The *Bulletin* of the ANA in late 1935, for example, published a laudatory review of a book by a Paris lawyer, Henry Decugis, titled *Le destin des races blanches,* whose theme was the supremacy of whites over blacks, Asians, and Jews.[105] And the lawyer Auguste Vigne published a number of articles in *La vie judiciaire* in 1939 in which he complained about the "cosmopolitan underworld" of "undesirable foreigners" who "invade France." He declared that any naturalized Frenchman who refused to perform military service should be expelled from French territory or sent to a "special concentration center."[106] Vigne also railed against the Senate's vote in 1936 to allow foreigners to "Frenchify" their family names because this "could lead to dangerous consequences, not only from a penal point of view nor from concerns about international relations, but also in civil matters and regarding family relationships."[107] That some lawyers expressed anti-foreigner sentiments beyond the realm of professional concerns attests to a more visceral xenophobia, at least for a minority. Hints of anti-Semitism, for example, the use of the term *cosmopolitanisme,* are also detectable in this late 1930s discourse.

Expressions of Tolerance within Exclusionary Patterns

Despite the overall trend of nationalistic exclusion and xenophobia in the legal profession during the interwar years, some instances of pro-foreigner sentiment also emerged. Apart from the collective momentum that eventually led to the easing by the Popular Front of the 1934 law, manifestations of tolerance and solidarity were scattered and short-lived, usually shot down quickly by outspoken xenophobes or most often left unanswered by a silent professional corps. But their existence deserves mention since, in juxtaposition to the overall trend, even the faintest cries of tolerance mattered. What follows is a compendium of pro-foreigner expression, though the motives behind each vary significantly.

Displays of international goodwill came easily to French lawyers when it was a question of Francophile foreign lawyers who had returned to their native countries to practice law. In late 1934 a dozen Romanian lawyers had come to spend the holidays in France, led by Constant Ionesco, holder of a doctorate in law from the University of Paris, member of the Bucharest law bar, and member of the council for the Union internationale des avocats. Louis Sarran of the ANA and Marcel Fournier of the UJA invited them to a festive lunch, and the Versailles law bar invited the Romanian lawyers to a New Year's party, where they were applauded for "their admirable knowledge of French and their elevation of mind."[108] A complaint commonly leveled at foreigners who stayed in France after completing their university studies, as we have seen, was that they had not assimilated enough—quite a contrast with this example in which foreigners who had left France were highly praised for their Frenchness. Yves Ozanam, archivist of the Paris law bar, has observed that contrary to lawyers' arguments for exclusion based on a lack of assimilation, naturalized citizens were in fact serious competitors in the law bars; in general they spoke excellent French and were well educated and cultivated.[109]

The Union fédérale des étudiants, the communist-influenced student group that defended foreign students in medicine, did the same in the law schools in the 1930s. The UFE leveled a sharp accusation: "Everywhere, at the law school as at the medical school, smiling spineless deans are accomplices to the unrest against foreign students." Instead, the UFE urged fellow French law students and university leaders to show more solidarity and benevolence toward foreign students.[110]

One lawyer-deputy took seriously his professional role as a defender of the weak and vulnerable. Marius Moutet of the Paris bar and deputy from the Drôme had tried for several years to have legislation passed that would guarantee equal rights for foreigners in France, including legal representation for all foreigners subject to expulsion from French territory. Moutet succeeded in getting the ANA to adopt a public resolution to this effect at its annual congress in 1935,[111] but the legislation never mustered broad political support, even under the Popular Front.[112]

Before the 1934 ban on recently naturalized citizens, Henry Lémery, senator, minister, and member of the Paris bar, intervened with the naturalization service of the Ministry of Justice on behalf of a Romanian graduate of a French law school who wished to practice law. Boris Stark had tried to naturalize but had been rejected because he had been unable to perform military service because of flat feet. Lémery argued, "It would be truly excessive if this young man, who did not hide from his military duties and who offered himself there, were to have his career ruined and his future compromised because his feet do not correspond to military standards."[113] A director of the ministry told Lémery that Stark's candidacy had been adjourned because his whole family resided abroad and it was too soon to reconsider his case.

In October 1936 one law bar asked the ANA its opinion as to whether law bars themselves could make exceptions to the ten-year delay rule for admitting naturalized citizens, regardless of the legislation in force. In response, the leadership committee of the ANA "unanimously and very firmly declared itself hostile to any exceptions."[114]

In a final example, in 1939 the law bar of Perpignan sought to rally support within the legal profession for Spanish refugee lawyers in France. The leadership committee of the ANA debated possible action. While one lawyer insisted on some kind of modest gesture, bar president Desplats wanted to make sure that refugees could prove their status as real lawyers before helping them. Jean Appleton proposed passing the burden on to the International Union of Lawyers. In the end, the ANA leaders decided that they would do nothing, but that the Perpignan bar president would coordinate the transfer of any individual donations from lawyers to the needy Spanish refugees.[115]

In 1939–40 many lawyers were mobilized to fight for France. The Lyon bar noted that 140 of its 263 lawyers had been called to the armed forces, leaving the daily business of justice at a significant standstill,[116] just as the health care needs of the civilian French population were dramatically affected by the mobilization of doctors. But whereas French doctors in these circumstances expressed a reflexive paranoia that doctors of foreign origin would reinfiltrate the field in their absence and steal their patients, the law profession was already well protected by legislation that was significantly more restrictive than that covering doctors.

Perhaps fortified by their impenetrability, several law bars such as those of Toulouse and Lyon welcomed French lawyers from the northern law bars who had evacuated during the great exodus of the summer of 1940. Out of professional solidarity they allowed them to join their bars temporarily so as to continue to earn their livelihood. Not all law bars were so generous: the Marseille and Aix-en-Provence bars claimed that they needed to protect the clientele of their own mobilized and imprisoned lawyers. Finally a 31 October 1941 law obliged law bars in the free zone to accept the temporary registration of evacuee lawyers. But as the next chapter demonstrates, this assistance was not extended to Jewish lawyers.[117]

★ ★ ★

Consequential differences between the ways the medical and legal professions received professionals of foreign origin into their midst have by now become evident. To practice law in a French court, a French law degree and membership in a law bar were required. Foreigners and naturalized citizens could obtain the proper law diploma in France, even without taking the French baccalaureate,[118] but foreigners could not join a French bar, and after 1934 neither could recently naturalized citizens. Lawyers thus had the means to bypass all of the complicated entanglements that doctors encountered in their quest to restrict foreigners' access to medicine. That means was the law bar. Because a simple state diploma granted access to medicine, the legislation to protect the medical profession had to address both the schooling for and the practice of medicine. In contrast, the legislation regarding access to the law profession did not concern itself with any educational issues such as diplomas or transfer credits. Recognizing their weakness all too well, doctors lobbied during the first half of the twentieth century for a corporatist structure similar to the law bar.

Partly because the exclusionary movement in the legal profession focused on access to the law bars and not on diplomas, French law students played a lesser role than medical students. The leaders of the law bars achieved exclusion in an efficient and discreet manner in high-level professional and political circles; they did not need to rely on protests in the streets of the Latin Quarter. Although French law students did participate in some protests against foreigners and naturalized citizens, the agitation was much less widespread and less impassioned than it was among medical students.

The legal and medical professions fed off each other to achieve increased protection from legislation. Just as doctors argued that their profession deserved the protections afforded to lawyers by the 1934 law, lawyers had used the 1933 Armbruster law to justify their own protections against naturalized citizens. These discussions revealed each profession's view of the other. Practitioners of both medicine and law considered their profession more prestigious, and therefore more deserving of state protection against undesirable elements.[119]

Like the medical profession, the legal profession had to turn to the state to obtain what it wanted, despite the formidable barrier constituted by the bar. Lawyers recognized that to exclude recently naturalized citizens from a professional career was contrary to the basic principles of citizenship and therefore could not pass in the form of a mere internal professional regulation. Parliament obliged lawyers generously in 1934. The various governments throughout the 1930s also protected the legal profession, for example, by resisting the Principality of Monaco, which sought to establish permission for its citizens who possessed a French law degree to be admitted to French law bars.[120] Lawyers' influence on the political scene gave them significant advantages over doctors.

The legislation excluding recently naturalized citizens from the legal profession differed from the laws regulating the medical profession in that the 1934 law was attached to a major French law on nationality. It modified the 1927 nationality law, whereas the medical laws were concerned only with regulating the study and practice of medicine. The legal ramifications of this difference were great, as parliamentarians recognized. Deputy Rolland stated: "The nationality law is of a permanent nature. The measures concerning the practice of medicine by naturalized persons are motivated by risks judged particularly salient in recent times. The measures must be able to be modified if new circumstances arise and without the need to affect the law on nationality."[121] While legislators were hesitant to attach restrictions for medicine to the 1927 nationality law, they had no such scruples with regard to the practice of law.

The movement within the legal profession established a sort of hierarchy of exclusion that treated various persons in the category of naturalized citizens differently. Some lawyers considered certain naturalized citizens more acceptable than others. Those who had done their military service in France, or better yet had fought for France during World War I, were considered legitimate fellow members of the profession: "All those for whom France has been, since their birth, a second fatherland, and who spontaneously came to fight for her in the hour of danger. These ones, by the blood that they have spilt, became our brothers."[122] The revised law of 1936 was intended to compensate such veterans. Also, some exclusionary discourse hierarchized naturalized citizens by their country of origin. Americans who became naturalized French, for example, were less likely to be targeted for exclusion than were Romanians who became naturalized French, because of both national stereotypes and the numbers of emigrants from each country. In addition, certain types of people were considered especially excludable if they had more than one undesirable trait, for example, naturalized female lawyers or Jewish female lawyers.[123] Behind some of the discourse against naturalized lawyers in the 1930s was a prejudice against Jewish refugees from eastern and central Europe. While anti-Semitism alone did not drive the exclusionary movement, resentment toward Jewish refugees and immigrants provided additional impetus for lawyers' mobilization against naturalized citizens.

My findings demonstrate that the demand for the temporary exclusion of naturalized citizens issued from both higher and lower ranks in the legal profession. The movement succeeded because the senior leaders had the clout to get the law passed quickly through parliament, with the support of the rank and file of the profession behind them. These elements taken together constitute a vertical professional movement of exclusion. Although the primary sources from the legal profession's campaign against lawyers of foreign origin are meager in comparison to those for the medical profession, it is incorrect to conclude that lawyers were less xenophobic than doctors. Xenophobic discourse was minimal because public justifications for exclusion were unnecessary. Lawyers achieved their objectives without fomenting agitation as doctors did. Exclusionary legislation ended up being much more severe for naturalized lawyers than for naturalized doctors: a ten-year delay for lawyers compared to a maximum four-year delay for private doctors and a five-year delay for medical civil service posts. Exceptions for those who had performed military service were allowed in medicine, but not for lawyers until after the Popular Front imposed its will. Finally, the exclusions in medicine were nonretroactive, but not always for law. Lawyers' willingness to apply exclusionary legislation retroactively stands out as particularly significant, coming as it did from legal professionals in a republican regime.

 CHAPTER 6

Lawyers during the Vichy Regime

Exclusion in the Law

After the Nazi invasion of Poland, France declared war on the Third Reich in September 1939, but months of what became known as the "phony war" followed. In May 1940 Nazi Germany invaded Belgium, Luxembourg, the Netherlands, and France. Over 4 million women, men, and children fled their homes in France and pushed southward in a great exodus. Paris and half the territory of France were occupied in less than a month, leaving French society and the political leadership in panic and disarray. The government collapsed, a new government was formed and relocated to the town of Vichy, and full powers were voted to Marshal Philippe Pétain, who signed an armistice with Germany. French territory was divided in two main zones, one occupied by the Germans in the north and a southern zone controlled by the French, though in two years the Nazis would occupy most of France. In a complicated arrangement, French law would govern both zones but German law would take precedence. The Third Republic was effectively abolished. The national government was now called the French State. Its motto changed from "Liberty, Equality, Fraternity" to "Work, Family, Fatherland," symbolizing the reactionary orientation of the new regime.

As war continued to be fought on other European fronts, French society accommodated itself to a new reality. Independently of Nazi influence, the Vichy regime imposed its ideological program of National Revolution, which placed blame for the defeat on communists, foreigners, Freemasons, and Jews, and rejected them from the national community. If the Third Republic can be described as a duel between two Frances—a republican, Dreyfusard, universalist France on the one hand and a conservative, nationalist, and exclusionary France on the other—it was the latter that, in the vacuum of war, defeat, and occupation, prevailed and was incarnated in the Vichy regime. "Exclusion was consubstantial with the regime," the historian Denis Peschanski has maintained.[1] This exclusionary France denounced the supposed ills of republican France: denatalism, secularism, cosmopolitanism, feminism, urbanism, industrialism, communism, individualism, and democratization. The new values of the National Revolution would encompass a return to ruralism, corporatism, and Catholicism.

The new Vichy regime quickly imposed its view of French nationality as a status that could be granted and taken away—a throwback to the arbitrariness of the Old Regime, when withdrawing and conferring nationality was a system of punishment and reward.[2] As a means of repressing resistance movements, the laws of 23 July and 10 September 1940 stripped French persons of their nationality for having left the country without permission.[3] Some of the most notoriously xenophobic manifestations of Vichy's National Revolution began in 1940: the 16 July law easing procedures to strip people of French nationality; the 17 July law barring French persons born of a foreign father from the civil service; and the 22 July law undoing naturalizations effectuated since 1927. More than 15,000 persons lost their French nationality as a result of this last law, out of 900,000 who had acquired it between 1927 and 1940.[4] Forty percent of these denaturalized persons were Jewish (more than 6,000), whereas it has been estimated that Jews represented only 5 percent of those who were naturalized between 1927 and 1940.[5] As Catherine Kessedjian has pointed out, the legal term for loss of nationality, *déchéance de la nationalité,* exudes a "deep sense of degradation, of disgrace, thus of sanction."[6] Denaturalization was, for many Jews, a prelude to deportation.

Lawyers' and doctors' interwar mobilization against foreigners and naturalized citizens continued apace throughout the debacle and into the new regime. With discourse and strategy at the ready, their plans for eliminating outsiders fell on sympathetic ears within the Vichy regime, which had quickly implemented its own exclusionary agenda.[7] The Vichy regime sought to safeguard various occupational fields from the influence of suspect populations. The civil service was the first economic sector to be purged of persons of foreign origin, Jews, Freemasons, and women.[8] French persons "born of a foreign father" became a new target as Vichy legislation narrowed its exclusionary focus on ever smaller sets of outsiders. They were eliminated from the medical profession and from the law bars by the laws of 16 August and 10 September 1940, respectively. In total, about 1,400 doctors and between 200 and 300 lawyers were ousted from their professions for being born of a foreign father. Unlike earlier laws passed in the 1930s restricting the right of naturalized doctors and lawyers to practice for a certain number of years after naturalization, the Vichy exclusion from professional access was meant to be permanent. It therefore concretized into law a notion that cultural integration, or *francisation,* was never possible in the first and second generations of immigrant families.

The Vichy regime passed the Statute on the Jews (*Statut des Juifs*) on 3 October 1940 and the second Statute on the Jews on 2 June 1941, which excluded Jews from French civil society and led to their eventual internment, deportation, and mass murder.[9] Following the dictates of the second statute, the regime imposed a quota of 2 percent on Jews allowed to practice law and medicine. In all, approximately eight hundred Jewish doctors and two to three hundred Jewish lawyers were expelled from their professions.[10]

Vichy's homing in on persons born of foreign fathers and then on Jews can be viewed as the late Third Republic's exclusionary logic pushed to ever greater extremes once circumstances—defeat, occupation, an authoritarian regime—permitted. Indeed, the Vichy regime mounted a "veritable legislative arsenal" against French persons of foreign origin.[11] The dramatic anti-Semitic turn that exclusionism took beginning in 1940 was unprecedented, and yet at the same time substantially grounded in the xenophobic language and practices put in place under the Third Republic. Although anti-Semitic exclusion was aimed in part at native-born French Jews, the rise of anti-Semitism in the French professions cannot be fully understood outside the context of xenophobic exclusion of foreigners. Of course, these categories also overlapped: Jewish foreigners were doubly targeted by Vichy, and women Jewish foreigners triply so.

In telling the story of French lawyers' participation in the increasingly restrictive and racist policies under Vichy, this chapter explores the relationship between the state and professional interest groups. The Vichy regime passed a number of laws in 1941 significantly reorganizing the law bars and created a corporatist Medical Order in 1940, in both cases satisfying longtime professional demands to impose tighter restrictions on newcomers.[12] For both law and medicine, Vichy offered an opportunity to push through professional wish lists for membership control that had been awaiting action for years during the Third Republic. Hardly any lawyers or doctors publicly protested the anti-foreigner and anti-Jewish restrictions; many, in fact, did not hesitate to play an active role in their implementation.

Lawyers Born of Foreign Fathers

The professional ban on those with a father of foreign origin was imposed first on doctors, dentists, and pharmacists in August 1940. Some individual lawyers, a group of military veteran lawyers from Nice, and ultraconservative law associations such as the Jeune barreau français were calling for a similar ban on persons of foreign origin in the legal profession. In August 1940, Paris bar president Jacques Charpentier proposed legislation to the Ministry of Justice to limit access to the law bars to citizens with *two* French parents and not just a French father.[13] Ultimately the regime imposed a less radical ban on lawyers born of a foreign father, which was instituted the following month and modeled after the law passed for the medical profession.[14]

The 10 September 1940 law required French nationality "by native right, as being born of a French father" for admission to French law bars. The ban targeted naturalized citizens as well as persons born in France of a foreign father who had acquired French nationality at the age of majority (*par option*). Lawyers unable to prove that at the time of their birth their father was French were dismissed from the bar. Former minister of justice Robert Badinter has described this law as "an unheard-of text [*un texte inouï*]" and called it a form of "ethnic cleansing."[15]

The traditionalist ideology of the National Revolution gave structure to Vichy exclusionism. For example, lawyers born of a foreign mother and a French father were considered French persons of French origin, and thus not excluded from the profession, because the father's nationality determined the child's—an ironic form of discrimination since anti-immigration natalists often emphasized the critical role of the mother in shaping future French citizens. Persons born in Alsace-Lorraine and reintegrated into French nationality after 1918 (*réintégrés de plein droit*) were considered French.[16] Exemptions were allowed for children born without a recognized father, for those holding a military veteran's card (for having served in a combat unit in World War I or in 1939), and for those persons' descendants. As Badinter has pointed out, "The 'baptism by blood' cleansed the foreign-origin Frenchman of his impure lineage."[17] An additional exception was allowed for some foreign-fathered lawyers who did not fall into any of the previous categories of exemption; because of their stature or connections they could be nominated for special exemption by their law bar council and approved by the Ministry of Justice. The law bars were responsible for determining the exceptions.

I use the awkward term "foreign-fathered lawyers" to refer to the persons targeted by this legislation; the accuracy of the expression is important, because nearly all documentation from the period uses the incorrect term "foreigner." Well beyond the confines of the liberal professions, such misusages were common in interwar French society, and have been so ingrained, in fact, that some historians have unconsciously reified them. The legal scholar Richard Weisberg, for example, persistently refers to "foreign lawyers"—rather than foreign-fathered French lawyers—in his book on Vichy law and the Holocaust.[18] Because French nationality was a requirement for joining a law bar, as we saw in chapter 5, a "foreign lawyer" was a contradiction in terms.

In banning already established lawyers from the profession, the legislation violated the fundamental legal principle that laws should not be retroactive. Despite this illegality, however, the Paris bar council "swallowed the Vichy legislation and implicitly accepted the principle of retroactivity and discrimination, which constituted a violation of law without precedent in the history of the bar," according to the Paris law bar archivist Yves Ozanam.[19] In his postwar memoirs Jacques Charpentier, president of the Paris bar at the time, noted his surprise at the retroactive nature of the legislation, which he considered an "excess." And yet his comments show that what he regretted was not the principle of exclusion itself but rather the fact that the postwar regime annulled the law entirely. Charpentier implied that if the exclusionary Vichy measures had not been retroactive, then later regimes might have been more inclined to keep them in place:

> In 1940, a law excluded the sons [sic][20] of foreigners [sic] from the legal profession. For several years, this measure had been keenly desired by the Paris bar. If a country suffering from a birthrate crisis is obliged to favor immigration, certain professions, including ours, require a minimum of assimilation. Before the war, we had been invaded by recently naturalized people, almost all of eastern origin, whose language, highlighted by the popular press, made us the target of ridicule, and who brought their bazaar-like procedures and methods into their lawyerly conduct. In this respect, Vichy policy matched our professional interests. But I had envisioned the application of this measure only in the future; in my opinion, we had to respect vested rights. The government did not have the same scruples. The exclusions it enacted were retroactive; they struck some of our colleagues who had been honorably practicing their profession for many years. We were able to save only military veterans and a few others. Such excess led the government of the Liberation to radically abrogate the prohibition enacted by the preceding regime. Thus the problem is posed anew, which, with a little moderation, could have been definitively settled.[21]

Even in the years immediately after the war, therefore, Charpentier continued to defend the exclusionary Vichy legislation with a two-class conception of citizenship, while offering only the mildest criticism of its retroactive character. Furthermore, as the historian Catherine Fillon has pointed out, Charpentier had included the retroactive measure in his own draft of the law.[22]

Implementation of the Ban

The 10 September 1940 law stipulated that the law bar councils were to send a letter to all members asking them to prove their French roots. The required proofs were sometimes difficult to obtain: for example, Noël Verney, *doyen* (most senior member) and former president of the Lyon bar, attested that beyond producing his birth certificate, he could not provide further proof that his father and grandfather were born in St. Étienne in the Loire, such as voter registration cards or military service records, since during his father's era there was no military service and universal suffrage did not yet exist.[23]

As the law began to be implemented, lawyers were surprised to discover that the foreign-father ban affected colleagues whom they considered very "French." There was a significant disconnect between the law's approach to Frenchness—primarily defined by military service—and lawyers' alternative emphasis on their colleagues' professional seniority and cultural assimilation into bourgeois mores. Implementation of the ban was by no means consistent, since the legislation also bumped up against the long-standing customs of law bars close to France's borders, where Belgian or Swiss lawyers were traditionally welcomed in exchange for French lawyers' rights across the border.[24] Moreover, some law bars were beginning to take note of their members' Jewishness as they implemented the ban, even before the first Statute on the Jews was promulgated.

In the Paris bar, 239 lawyers were kicked out as a result of the ban on foreign-fathered lawyers.[25] Others were allowed to remain in practice because of their military service. Emmanuel Blanc, Jewish and born in Romania, might have been a near-perfect target for disbarment if it were not for his military record. Naturalized in 1931, he finished his French law degree in 1932 and was a lawyer-apprentice (the last stage before becoming a full member of the bar) in the Paris bar from 1935 to 1939. Blanc served in the French military in Lebanon in 1939–40 and joined the Paris bar in 1940. In September 1940 he was kicked out, but was reinstated on appeal because of his military service. Although his file contained such evidence, Blanc never declared himself as Jewish and was never expelled from the Paris bar as a Jew.[26]

Although he was Jewish and born of a foreign father, Raymond Rosenmark was also able to keep his legal career intact. He survived the foreign-father legislation and avoided being cut from the Paris bar thanks to his World War I mobilization. It was a close call: the bar council hesitated as to the adequacy of Rosenmark's military service, but in a rare instance of leniency the public prosecutor (*procureur général*) accepted his record as sufficient. When the anti-Jewish quota was established a few months later, Rosenmark was again in jeopardy because the quota required not just proof of military service but a veteran's card. To the surprise of the Paris bar council, Rosenmark produced an attestation of eligibility for a veteran's card.[27] He too remained in the Paris bar.

In Lyon, the bar obediently surveyed all of its members about their national origins after the new law went into effect. Catherine Fillon has claimed that geographical proximity, socioeconomic class, and religious affiliation gave foreign-fathered lawyers a greater chance of inclusion in Lyon.[28] The decree threatened only three lawyers there. The Lyon law bar council eventually authorized them all to remain, although only one of them fulfilled the criteria for an automatic exemption. They voted unanimously to maintain Marthe Keller, daughter of a Swiss father, and voted eight to three to keep Antonio Charles Navarro, son of a Spanish father. In presenting Keller's case to the minister of justice, Lyon bar president Claude Valansio relied on diplomatic arguments, noting that his bar council, "profoundly moved by the Swiss nation's very touching gestures of sympathy and tireless devotion to France, would like to see Mademoiselle Keller's exemption favorably approved." For Navarro, Valansio argued that he was born in Algeria, fought for France during World War I (which made him automatically eligible for exemption anyway), and was the grandson of a "*colon,* who lived with all his family in the French empire for nearly one hundred years." The Ministry of Justice allowed both Keller and Navarro to continue to practice in Lyon.[29] Their cases exemplify the growing currency in French society of the notion of selective immigration, which favored the acceptance of immigrants from neighboring and "culturally proximate" countries. The physician René Martial and the geographer Georges Mauco, respected immigration experts in the 1930s, argued that such foreigners were more "assimilable" and desirable than immigrants from eastern European countries.[30]

A third candidate, Béatrice Benaroya, born Jewish of a Bulgarian father, was not as "assimilable" as Keller and Navarro, and her exemption encountered more resistance. Since Benaroya's professional and personal record was so slim given her youth, the Lyon bar relied on the fact that she had siblings who had fought for France, married French spouses, and produced French children. Although Benaroya was born Jewish, as Valansio noted unnecessarily in his letter to the minister of justice a week after the Statute on the Jews was promulgated, she had converted to Catholicism, volunteered for the Red Cross in 1939, and was responsible for her aged mother. Valansio also did not neglect to note, in a probable attempt at sabotage, that Benaroya's father had been imprisoned for five years beginning in 1929 for "abuse of confidence."[31] The Lyon bar council voted seven to five to keep her, with one abstention.[32] Although the council was divided on Benaroya's case, the exemption it ultimately granted for her and for Keller, two young, women lawyers of foreign origin, was unusual.

A few months later in December 1941, however, Benaroya was removed from the Lyon bar in accordance with the anti-Semitic quota. The 2 percent quota allowed only six Jewish lawyers to remain in practice in Lyon. The Lyon bar council had ranked the Jewish lawyers by the sole criterion of seniority, according to their deliberations, and Benaroya was the seventh, and the youngest.[33] But when a new class of lawyers entering the Lyon bar the following year raised the quota to seven Jews, the tenacious Benaroya pressed her case anew and was readmitted. Bar president Valansio had lobbied against her, however, and continued to harass her with administrative problems after her admission.[34]

The Lille bar counted many members with one Belgian parent. The father of the bar president was not French, but the Lille bar council decided that this pillar of the bar for the last forty years had the right to stay. The unusual circumstances in the "forbidden zone," the northeastern departments of French territory that fell under special Nazi administration, and the upheavals of mobilization, imprisonment, and exodus endured by so many Lille lawyers contributed to the bar's willingness to admit two young women with Belgian fathers as lawyer-apprentices in December 1941, and these exceptions were accepted by the Ministry of Justice. More admissions of this sort followed in Lille.[35] As the next chapter shows, doctors in northern France were also unusually tolerant of their Belgian-fathered colleagues.

Another foreign-fathered lawyer who was granted exceptional authorization to remain in practice was Jacques Isorni in Paris. Born in France in 1911 of a French mother and a Swiss father who was naturalized in 1924, Isorni had been mobilized in 1939, but not in a combat unit. He was therefore not automatically exempt from the exclusionary law. Isorni reacted to the laws with shock: "We suddenly had the impression that, for no intelligible reason, without any reason for blame, we were excluded from the French nation by a strict form of nationalism and that we were no longer like everyone else.... In sum, I felt Jewish." He continued, "I felt as if I was naked before the [lawyer assigned to me], scrutinizing my young professional life and dissecting my family back to its oldest ancestors."[36] The Paris bar council nominated him for a special exemption, and the minister of justice approved the request in May 1941. Ironically, Isorni went on to become Pétain's defense lawyer in 1945. Until his death in 1995, Isorni continued to defend Pétain's honor, claiming that the Statute on the Jews was the first action taken by Pétain "in his willingness to protect the Jews and to shield them from the terror that had swooped down upon France," thereby contributing to the French postwar myth of Vichy as a lesser evil.[37]

In a striking demonstration of political support for Vichy policies, the Paris bar took unprecedented steps to expel two prominent lawyers, former Popular Front deputy and air minister Pierre Cot and former deputy Henry Torrès. The two had left France for the United States during the summer of 1940 and were subsequently stripped of their nationality under the terms of Pétain's special legislation targeting French persons who had left French territory in resistance to the armistice with Germany.[38] In an unusual, precipitate, and highly politicized move, the Paris bar council passed a resolution in February 1941 expelling the two lawyers on the grounds that French nationality was a requirement for bar membership.[39] Félix Gouin, one of the minority of parliamentarians who had refused to grant full powers to Pétain in 1940, was similarly expelled from the Marseille bar.[40] Although these expulsions were not a result of the ban on foreign-fathered lawyers, the measures taken by the bar councils manifest an obsessive legalism, a willingness to abide by Vichy's discriminatory policies and repression, and an alignment with Vichy ideology. It is possible, of course, that the bar councils were pressured by Vichy authorities to eliminate these prominent republican leaders. Torrès was an emblematic figure of the left: he had represented a number of anarchists and other defendants in politicized court cases throughout the 1920s and 1930s and was a well-known defender of Jewish rights and human rights. In any case, the disbarments probably mattered little to the politicians themselves; Cot, for example, was busy leading resistance efforts from abroad.

Lawyers had the right to appeal their expulsions to the appeals courts, and they were permitted to practice law pending the verdict. Most of the cases in Paris were adjudicated in the first half of 1941; in this period, forty-seven out of fifty-one appeals were rejected. Also in Paris, about ten banned lawyers were readmitted after they provided proof of military combat service for themselves or an immediate relative. In addition, the Paris bar council proposed thirty-two lawyers for special exemption on the grounds of family situation, patriotism, or professional merit, and the Ministry of Justice approved these exemptions. Eight of them had declared themselves as Jews, but the Paris bar council made no mention of this fact.[41] The anti-Semitic quota against Jewish lawyers was still to come.[42]

In the fall of 1941, a new law banning foreign-fathered lawyers from the profession abrogated and replaced the 10 September 1940 law. The 15 October 1941 law tweaked the exemptions. It narrowed the criteria for military service from "those who served in a combat unit" to those who had obtained "official recognition of combat status," in other words, a veteran's card. It added three new grounds for exemptions for those not born of a French father if they themselves had French nationality: if they were naturalized for exceptional services rendered to France, the conditions of which were to be fixed by a future law; if they were natives of a French protectorate and were naturalized French; or if they were parents, wives, widows, or descendants of recognized combatants. Lawyers expelled by the earlier law could request to be reinstated under the provisions of the revised law.[43] Several lawyers were able to be reintegrated into the Paris bar as a result of the supplementary exceptions, in particular spouses and parents, not just children, of former combatants.[44]

Although the revisions were more technical than meaningful, and little archival documentation attests to the rationale behind the revised law, three hypotheses can be put forward to explain this liberalization in the midst of 1941 Vichy repression. First, many legal professionals had been shocked, as Jacques Isorni claimed to have been, to find that the law had expelled very "French" colleagues whom few considered outsiders. The revised law could redress some of these situations. Second, law bar leaders may have discovered over the course of the year that the immediate departure of foreign-fathered lawyers had disrupted court cases, legal services, and the general administration of justice at a time of an explosion of new legislation and jurisprudence. Third, after the original law banning foreign-fathered lawyers, the decree imposing a quota against Jewish lawyers was passed in July 1941, with a different set of exemption criteria. The revision of the law against foreign-fathered lawyers aligned the two sets of legislation more coherently, though not precisely. Some law bar council members were surprised to find themselves in the position of expelling Jews while reauthorizing foreign-fathered lawyers.

Anti-Semitic Measures in the Professions

Even if the anti-Semitic quotas in the professions were legislated by Vichy officials with little direct input from the law bars, the lobbying of the 1930s had normalized xenophobic discourse and exclusionary attitudes. The Jeune barreau français, known in the 1930s for its rabid hostility toward foreigners, forwarded the results of its general assembly resolution to the Paris bar council on 28 August 1940—well before the first Statute on the Jews—calling for "the necessity, more urgent every day, of chasing away the Jewish and Freemason undesirables in order to render to lawyers the prestige of honor and honesty that was theirs for centuries."[45] The group sent the following missive to the Paris bar council in February 1941: "The Jeune barreau français takes orders from Marshal Pétain and is permanently opposed to the Union des jeunes avocats, whose members are naturalized citizens, Jews, and Freemasons, all adversaries of the Marshal."[46] This kind of language had become widespread in French society by 1941. In the Paris exhibition "The Jew and France" mounted at the Palais Berlitz, a large panel denounced the role of Jews in the French law bars, claiming, "The Jews have transformed our noble legal profession into a vile market in which clients are solicited in the prisons."[47] The exhibition drew some 200,000 paying visitors during its four-month run.[48] Often the discourse during the Vichy period distinguished not only between desirable (culturally proximate, non-Jewish) and undesirable foreigners, but also between good (French) Jews and undesirable ones. Of course, such distinctions were not clear-cut. In his book, *Un antisémitisme ordinaire,* Robert Badinter estimated that among the two hundred or so foreign-fathered lawyers ejected from the Paris bar, at least sixty were Jewish.[49]

The first Statute on the Jews, dated 3 October 1940, defined Jews as persons with either three Jewish grandparents or two Jewish grandparents and a Jewish spouse. It expelled Jews from the civil service, including jurists and doctors who were employees of the state. Law professors, for example, very often had private practices and were members of a law bar. The statute banned Jews from many private sector fields, and it announced that future legislation would address the rights of Jews to work in the liberal professions. Article 6 barred Jews from holding leadership positions in professions including law and medicine. (The Paris bar council included no Jews.)[50]

The second statute replaced the first. It widened the definition of Jewish persons, increased the number of forbidden professions, clarified exceptions to anti-Semitic restrictions, and addressed the question of pensions for Jews expelled from their employment. Article 4 specified that a decree would soon set the terms of a Jewish quota in the liberal professions. The second statute did allow for new exemptions based on "exceptional services rendered to the French state" or for those whose families had been in France for at least five generations, and instituted procedures for the arrest and detention of any lawbreakers, "even for those of French nationality." Two weeks after the second statute, Vichy legislated a 3 percent quota on Jewish students in French universities. Since the pipeline to the professions began in the law and medical schools, the quota was set at 1 percent above most of the forthcoming professional quotas, taking into account attrition rates.[51]

The second Statute on the Jews created an important gender discrimination regarding the exemptions for military veterans: whereas Jewish men could be exempted from the anti-Semitic legislation if they had military veteran status or war citations, women, who were forbidden to join the military, had to meet higher criteria by proxy; that is, a Jewish woman had to be the wife, daughter, or mother of someone killed in action, not merely of a veteran, in order to remain in the professions. This gender discrimination would have an effect on the Paris bar. Women accounted for about 29 percent of the ousted Jewish lawyers (approximately 60 out of 210),[52] but only 4 percent (approximately 2 out of 52) of those exempted. With a subsequent list established in October 1942, 21 percent of exempted Jewish lawyers (4 of 19) were women. More Jewish women lawyers may have been able to provide documentation of male relatives killed in action, but this authorization may have come too late for many.[53]

In addition to the occupational fields such as finance and communications where a total ban on Jews was ordered, the Vichy regime instituted anti-Semitic quotas in professional fields. The new regime viewed "justice" as a critical domain of the nation, which required leadership and patriotic devotion, a vision that excluded Jews.[54] Law was the first of the liberal professions to be purged of a supposed Jewish influence (in July 1941), followed by medicine (August 1941), then architecture (September 1941), then midwifery and pharmacy (December 1941), and finally dentistry (June 1942).[55] A very restrictive first draft of the decree instituting a quota on Jewish lawyers originated in the Ministry of Justice in the first month of 1941; when the Commissariat-General for Jewish Affairs (Commissariat général aux questions juives, or CGQJ) was created in March 1941, it took over the drafting.[56] After minor resistance from the Council of State, the decree of 16 July 1941 limited Jews to 2 percent of the total of non-Jewish lawyers in every Court of Appeals district.[57] Basing the quota on the total number of *non-Jewish* lawyers would yield a lesser figure.[58]

The total number of Jewish lawyers in any bar, furthermore, could not exceed the number of Jews registered there on 25 June 1940, the date of the armistice between France and Germany. By limiting the maximum number of Jewish lawyers per bar to the number of Jews practicing there as of a certain date, Vichy legislators stifled the potential movement of Jewish lawyers from urban centers to provincial law bars whose quotas had not been filled. The anti-Semitic quota affected mainly the bars of Paris and North Africa,[59] and only secondarily the large urban bars of Bordeaux, Lyon, Marseille, and Toulouse, which, like the smaller provincial bars, contained few Jewish lawyers.[60] Thus in areas where few or no Jews had been practicing in 1940, the bars were not allowed to fill their 2 percent quota. Since many bars counted fewer than fifty members, it was decided that computation would be centralized at the level of the courts of appeals, which had jurisdiction over a number of law bars. This meant that the law bars lost some autonomy over the elimination process and over their membership more generally. We must not make too much of this symbolic loss, however, since the bars were the ones that did the initial vetting of their Jewish members.[61]

Implementing the anti-Semitic quota violated a long-standing tradition of the law bars. The state-imposed criteria for exceptions placed a higher value on military service than on the professional value of *ancienneté,* or seniority. Priority for inclusion in the 2 percent numerus clausus was accorded to holders of a veteran's card, those with a Croix de guerre citation for combat in 1939–40, those decorated with the Legion of Honor or a military medal for war conduct, *pupilles de la nation* (children of certain categories of living or deceased veterans), and the parents, spouse, or children of a soldier who had died for France. The admission of such Jewish persons was allowed beyond the 2 percent limit. Although exceptions for Jewish lawyers of "eminent professional merit" and for "exceptional services rendered to the French state" were also allowed above the 2 percent limit, this left only a slim possibility for the law bars to nominate their distinguished and senior Jewish colleagues. During the draft phase of the decree, Minister of Justice Joseph Barthélemy protested to the CGQJ that the legislation would allow young, inexperienced lawyers with some military service behind them to remain in practice, to the detriment of senior and eminent Jewish lawyers without veteran status. This hierarchy would have concrete effects, especially in Paris, where it was widely estimated that Jewish lawyers with veteran status would more than fill the 2 percent quota and leave not a single space for non-veteran Jewish lawyers. Barthélemy warned that the elimination of experienced lawyers would harm the administration of justice.[62] Ministry of Justice secretary-general Georges Dayras also called the exemption criteria "unjust."[63] But Xavier Vallat, head of the CGQJ, was immune to such pleas to respect bar traditions, even though he was himself a member of the Paris bar council. His allegiance to the National Revolution apparently outweighed his lawyerly sensibilities.[64] Only on a case-by-case basis could non-veteran Jewish lawyers of "eminent professional merit" be considered above the 2 percent quota.[65] The conflict between the legal profession's value of *ancienneté* and Vichy's value of military duty was not resolved upon the signing of the legislation but continued throughout its implementation. In the spring of 1942, for example, the Aix Court of Appeals and the CGQJ clashed over ranking Jewish lawyers under the 2 percent quotas by these different values.[66] As Robert Badinter has pointed out, the very existence of the exceptions "even more cruelly emphasized that Jews were, by their essence, considered unfit to practice law."[67]

The anti-Semitic quota provoked hardly any protest in legal circles. In fact, French lawyers played an active role in its implementation: it was the job of the law bars to evaluate the personal, professional, and military credentials of Jewish colleagues and to decide whom to exclude from practice. The law bars—traditionally protective of their independence in matters of professional organization—demonstrated an extraordinary degree of compliance with the Vichy legislation instituting restrictions on bar membership. In anticipation of the quota and its implication of state control over bar membership, for example, five of the Lyon bar's seven *colonnes* (subgroupings of lawyers within the bar) debated the measure in October 1940 but ultimately declined to issue an opinion, saying they believed that the decision resided with the government.[68] The *colonnes'* inaction was not only an unusual acquiescence to the imposition of state authority but also a missed opportunity to take a stand against anti-Semitism. It was a sign that these members of the bar were not displeased with the expulsion of Jews from their profession.[69] The minutes of the Lyon *colonnes'* meetings provide an additional window into the larger protectionist zeitgeist of France in 1940: several voted not only to eliminate married women lawyers from the bar but also to forbid retired lawyers to rejoin the bar.

Implementation of the Quota

The law bars played three important roles in the implementation of the decree eliminating Jews from the profession. First, the law bar councils were required to determine which lawyers were Jewish. Articles 3 and 4 of the decree stipulated that all Jewish lawyers had to declare themselves to the law bar councils, and that the councils had to verify the declarations, deliberate on potential omissions, and disbar Jewish lawyers who failed to declare themselves. Suspected Jews who did not file a declaration were subject to police investigation.

Second, the bars evaluated and ranked their Jewish colleagues for potential exemption. The bar councils were to transmit the list of Jewish lawyers to the *procureur général* in their Court of Appeals, who would decide if any of them were eligible for the exceptions granted by the second statute. For each Jewish lawyer not benefiting from an exception, the bar council was to write up a reasoned opinion and submit it to the court. With this information from the *procureur général* and the bar councils, the Court of Appeals would establish a list of Jewish lawyers banned from practice for each law bar in its jurisdiction.

Third, according to Article 1 of the decree, the law bar councils could nominate Jewish lawyers of "eminent professional merit" to continue to practice law beyond the 2 percent quota. Regarding this prerogative, Badinter has emphasized that "it was no longer juridical, objective, and specific criteria to be applied as in the case of Jewish veterans or their relatives. Now the bar council was to choose who among its colleagues could remain lawyers on the basis of a vague notion of 'eminent' merit.... What remained of the traditional principle so proudly proclaimed by all law bars according to which all lawyers had equal rights?"[70]

Understanding French anti-Semitism in the legal profession during Vichy is not just a matter of examining the legislation. After all, similar anti-Semitic laws passed in Belgium and Italy were largely ignored, disobeyed, or tempered by legal professionals. Richard Weisberg has argued, "The inanimate ink of statutory law does not explain legal outcomes: people and institutions bring about these outcomes."[71] How did the French law bars make decisions about which of their Jewish colleagues to expel? What priorities did they use to rank fellow lawyers? How restrictively did they interpret the rules? Under what circumstances did they make efforts to nominate colleagues for eminent merit or exceptional service exemptions? Were the bars generally consistent, or did regional circumstances influence these decisions? Marseille's record is less glorious than Grenoble's, for example, but most bars chafed a little bit under the legislation because of their reflexive professional preference for seniority over military service as a credential for choosing which Jews to retain.

In October 1941 the CGQJ agreed to a more lenient way to calculate the 2 percent quota, which was codified in a Ministry of Justice circular on 12 November 1941. If non-Jews in any given law bar numbered twenty-five or more, the total would be rounded up to fifty, and if they numbered seventy-five or more, the total would be rounded up to one hundred. In one example, taken from the Lyon Court of Appeals, if non-Jews numbered fewer than 325 in the jurisdiction, then six Jews would be kept on; if non-Jews numbered 325 or more, a seventh Jewish lawyer could be kept under the quota without the membership's reaching the previously required total of 350.[72] In Toulouse, five Jewish lawyers among 227 non-Jewish lawyers were held to be within the 2 percent quota.[73] Rounding up fractions allowed a handful of additional Jews across France to remain in law practice. Archives explaining this liberalized procedure are sparse.

Implementation in the Court of Appeals of Aix-en-Provence, which centralized the anti-Semitic quotas for its nine law bars, proceeded in a more or less typical fashion. The court counted 775 non-Jewish lawyers in its jurisdiction, which meant that sixteen Jews would be allowed to remain in practice.[74] Selection began in the individual bars, the three largest being Aix, Marseille, and Nice. The Court of Appeals retained fifteen Jewish lawyers on account of their veteran status, leaving space for one more lawyer under the quota, who was chosen from the Aix bar. Of the sixteen Jewish lawyers kept, two were from Aix, six from Marseille, two from Toulon, and six from Nice.[75] Although this was a major Court of Appeals district, the number of Jewish lawyers was low to begin with.[76] The Marseille bar counted about eight Jewish members out of 211 lawyers; the Nice bar counted eight Jewish members out of 195 lawyers.[77] Yet according to historians, the Marseille bar council hounded its Jewish lawyers with "constant zealousness."[78]

The former president of the Aix law bar, Louis Crémieu, who was Jewish, had to resign from the bar council after the first statute banned Jews from holding leadership positions. Crémieu had been a stellar force in Aix: in addition to his bar stature, he was a professor at the Aix Law School and author of an important book on the legal profession. Ironically, he was also an outspoken leader of the movement to restrict naturalized citizens from the law bars. It must have come as a shock to him and his peers when he fell victim to policies of exclusion. The Aix bar council accepted his resignation from the council without comment. In January 1941, when new legislation allowed exceptions for military veterans, the council unanimously approved Crémieu's request for readmission to the council.[79] Because of his military credentials, Crémieu was also spared being expelled entirely from the profession under the anti-Semitic quota. According to informal accounts, he was arrested twice in 1943 and 1944, and bar council members made efforts to have him freed both times.[80] This evidence of professional solidarity was dismissed as mere politeness by one historian.[81] Badinter would cite Crémieu as an example of a small act in favor of an individual "good Jew."

Because there were no Jews among the ninety-four members of the Grenoble bar in 1940, not a single Jew could be included under the quota, according to the absolute maximum set by the decree. Nevertheless, when Gilberte Lévy-Darras requested admission to the Grenoble bar as a lawyer-apprentice, the *procureur général* made no objection. She consulted Professor Guyot, dean of the Grenoble Law School, who argued that the first paragraph of the decree allowing a 2 percent quota was the main legislative requirement and that the second paragraph limiting Jews to the total in 1940 was exceptional and could not undo the intent of the first paragraph. On the basis of this opinion, the Grenoble bar council admitted Lévy-Darras to the bar, justifying her admission as a case of "eminent professional merit," which at any rate allowed bar councils to exceed the quota, though the decision had to be approved by the CGQJ.[82]

In Lyon, the Court of Appeals counted 317 non-Jewish lawyers and eight Jewish lawyers in its bars. For one of the largest French cities, this low figure disproves claims that the law profession was dominated by Jews.[83] The quota allowed for six Jews, and as none of the eight practicing Jewish lawyers qualified for an automatic exemption, the bar council was to evaluate and rank all of them. In doing so, it followed a hierarchy based solely on seniority. Complications arose in that two were prisoners of war and so did not have to be counted initially, and an additional woman lawyer from the St. Étienne bar who was included in the quota was subsequently arrested. In the end, all the Jewish lawyers in Lyon were authorized to stay.

An additional case in Lyon concerned a lawyer-apprentice, Béatrice Benaroya, who, as we have seen, had managed to be exempted from the foreign-father ban. As the most junior Jew in the bar, she was originally not retained under the six-person quota, but she fought her case on the grounds that a new crop of lawyer-apprentices would be admitted to the bar before the end of 1941, bringing the total of non-Jews to 327 and allowing for a seventh Jew to be kept on. The Court of Appeals granted her an exception in January 1942. Since no Jewish prisoner of war returned to the Lyon bar, which would have jeopardized Benaroya's authorization, she was able to practice law through the end of the Occupation.[84] Because no Jews were ejected from the Lyon bar, the CGQJ suspected bar president Claude Valansio of protecting Jewish lawyers.[85] Later historical analysis has shown that this was not the case: it was simply by chance that the Jewish candidates did not exceed the number of spots available according to the quota. Given the Lyon bar's total lack of principled protest to the discriminatory legislation, former Lyon bar president Ugo Iannucci in 2001 called his bar's wartime record "legalistic and timorous."[86]

Implementation of the anti-Semitic quota in Paris got off to a rough start over the stipulation that lawyers must declare themselves as Jews to their bar council. It was estimated in 1941 that there were 300 to 400 Jewish lawyers in the Paris bar, out of a total of approximately 2,500 (including lawyer-apprentices),[87] but only 214 Paris bar members declared themselves as Jewish to the bar council.[88] Unsatisfied, the Paris *procureur général* Raoul Cavarroc established a list of 75 "suspicious" lawyers and 41 "suspicious" lawyer-apprentices and initiated a police investigation to determine if they were Jewish.[89] Suspect lawyers were described in these terms: "He seems to be of Jewish origin," "One supposes that she is Jewish," "People think he is Jewish but not established with certainty," "She might be Jewish," "probably Jewish," or "It seems that he should be considered to be presumed Jewish."[90] The results of the police investigation bespeak an absurd attempt to determine religious affiliation in a society officially imbued with secularism. Robert Badinter claims that ultimately 250 Paris lawyers declared themselves as Jewish.[91] The discrepancy between the number of presumed and declared Jews resulted from a combination of factors: the presumed figures were exaggerated; some Jewish lawyers were still mobilized or prisoners of war; and a number of Jewish lawyers born of a foreign father had already been eliminated from the bar.

The Paris *procureur général* completed the various lists by December 1941, and the Court of Appeals assembled in order to designate which Jewish lawyers were to be retained.[92] On 2 January 1942 the court rendered its decision: forty-eight Jewish lawyers would be kept on in the Paris bar as war veterans, according to Article 3 of the second Statute on the Jews. In addition, one female lawyer, Marcelle Kraemer-Bach, was temporarily retained until her son's reported death on the battlefield could be confirmed. As expected, the number of automatically exempted Jewish lawyers exceeded the 2 percent quota—forty-five Jewish lawyers—but not by much. In addition, twenty more Jewish lawyers were certified as prisoners of war, for whom a definitive decision would be made upon their liberation. Many prominent names in the Paris bar were retained, including K. C.,[93] former senator P. M., and former minister J. M.[94] The court's list of exempted Jews was continuously amended throughout 1942 and 1943. For example, shortly after the first list of exceptions was drawn up, it was determined that five more Jewish lawyers possessed veteran's cards.[95]

According to the decree, all Jewish lawyers not included on the list of exempted veterans and war wounded were to be notified, but before their definitive removal from their profession, their situations were to be evaluated by the bar council for a possible exemption for "eminent professional merit."[96] Such a recommendation would have to be endorsed by the Court of Appeals, proposed by the CGQJ, and accepted by the minister of justice before it could come to fruition. It was the Paris bar council's initial selection that would decide the fates of the 220 or so Jewish lawyers who did not have a military record. Even though many Jewish lawyers were still compiling their personal dossiers, the council wasted no time; it met on 6 January 1942, a mere four days after the list was drawn up.[97] The head of the CGQJ, Xavier Vallat, was a Paris bar council member, but he was not present at this meeting.[98] Of the 220 ejected Jewish lawyers, the Paris bar council eventually recommended fourteen for exemption on the basis of eminent merit, one of whom was a woman. These fourteen, as well as a fifteenth candidate from the Reims bar, all had common characteristics: they came from old French families; many had origins in Alsace or Lorraine; several had distinguished family relations in the army, magistrature, government, and liberal professions; and most of them had received awards and honors for their intellectual brilliance.[99] There was no doubt that they were all eminent.[100] The legal profession's principle of *ancienneté* also seemed to take priority: six of the Jewish lawyers were over sixty years old. In this way, the bar council tried to reestablish its traditional value of seniority after submitting to CGQJ criteria. Out of the rest of France's law bars, only a sixteenth Jewish lawyer, in Avignon, was nominated for a professional merit exception.[101]

The Paris Court of Appeals supported the fifteen recommendations. There was uncertainty as to whether the lawyers would have to stop practicing while waiting for the final approval from the CGQJ and the Ministry of Justice: the Court of Appeals counted them as already excluded, whereas the Ministry of Justice counted them as temporarily reinstated until their cases were definitively decided.[102] In any case, many of these lawyers were facing a far graver situation than being denied the right to practice. At least two of them were already arrested and imprisoned as the debate over their professional status ran its course.[103] Another, Lucien Vidal-Naquet, who detested the idea of exemptions but was recommended by former French president Alexandre Millerand, had taken refuge with his family first in Brittany, then in Marseille after the exodus. He was ultimately arrested with his wife, Margot, in May 1944 and sent to Drancy, then Auschwitz, where they were both killed upon arrival in June 1944. Their children escaped arrest.[104]

As the historian Joseph Billig noted in his vast 1955 study of the CGQJ, in regard to professional quotas, the issue of exemptions was the only source of debate among state authorities, and such exemptions provoked "incessant discussions" among the Germans, the French authorities, and the CGQJ.[105] After the Court of Appeals, it was the CGQJ's turn to evaluate the fifteen candidates. In April 1942, Vallat chose five of the fifteen to be retained.[106] Prominent family connections probably counted most in Vallat's selection.[107] In July 1942, Minister of Justice Barthélemy in turn recommended ten Jews to be retained. Involuntarily acknowledging how dire the circumstances were becoming for Jews in France at this time, Barthélemy wondered whether exempted Jewish lawyers would be more visible to the CGQJ and more vulnerable to arrest.[108] The fifteen candidates were in fact subjected to extra scrutiny: the CGQJ had them all investigated for membership in secret societies.[109] The Ministry of Justice's list of ten candidates for exemption was sent back to the CGQJ, now led by Louis Darquier de Pellepoix, who in August 1942 rejected every single one. Pierre Laval, himself a Paris bar member since 1909, concurred.[110] This marked the end of the eminent merit exception for Jewish lawyers in Vichy France.

The interaction of the various authorities over the merit exception resembled inglorious horse trading: the bar councils nominated fifteen Jewish lawyers, the CGQJ initially accepted five, the minister of justice proposed ten, and Darquier and Laval ultimately ruled against them all. In an October 1942 meeting, the Paris bar council expressed "its regret that the exemption for its fourteen members was rejected in a systematic way that does not seem to conform to the will of the law."[111] This was a notable expression of dissatisfaction. It was, however, a private statement within the bar council's closed meetings, and its portent was limited: it regretted only the disbarment of fourteen Paris lawyers. Badinter compared the Paris bar's unsuccessful selection of fourteen Jews (out of approximately 220) with the bar's thirty successful exemptions for foreign-fathered lawyers (out of 200) earlier in 1941 to argue that the law bars judged Jewish lawyers more harshly than foreign-fathered ones.[112] Yet this comparison does not take into account the accretion of fatigue and fear among French citizens by the time the anti-Semitic quotas were implemented, the increasing Nazi pressure, or, most important, the monitoring role of the CGQJ, which became even more hard-line under Darquier de Pellepoix. No equivalent state organ existed to enforce the foreign-father ban. The CGQJ was vigilant and effective in limiting the autonomy of law bars and the effects of legalisms in order to carry out its agenda.

A third and final possible exemption from the anti-Semitic quota stemmed from Article 8 of the second Statute on the Jews, for those who had "rendered exceptional services to the French state" or "whose family has been established in France for at least five generations and rendered exceptional services to the French state."[113] Compared with the exemption for eminent professional merit, Badinter notes, "in this case, the exception rewarded not the 'good lawyer' who was Jewish but the 'good Jew' who happened to be a lawyer."[114] Although no explicit procedure had been dictated by the law, the Paris bar council evaluated its Jewish members for this exception simultaneously with the eminent merit exemption in January 1942. The council established its own hierarchy of opinions: "very favorable," "favorable," "honorable professional practice," "without objection," and "unfavorable." Badinter calls the council members' act of judging their colleagues' and their colleagues' families' contributions to the French state "singular" and well beyond their authority.[115] Badinter and Weisberg were granted exceptional access to Paris bar archives regarding this question, but neither of them explains the history clearly.[116] Yves Ozanam has reported that forty or so Jewish lawyers nominated themselves for the "exceptional services to the state" exemption, and that the Paris bar council evaluated them beginning in January 1942 but approved none of them. Ozanam also notes that in a May 1942 meeting, the council declined to give an opinion requested by the Paris Court of Appeals on Jewish lawyers for whom an exemption was being considered.[117] Records of the bar council deliberations, if made available, would reveal whether the criteria used to judge lawyers' "service to the French state" differed from those used for the "eminent merit" exemption. For both types of exemptions, the law bars had dutifully assumed their prerogative—set out in legislation—to rank Jewish lawyers. They made a feeble attempt to protect fifteen of the most "eminent" among them and declined to name a single one for "exceptional service." More important, such archival records of closed-door meetings would elucidate how leaders of the Paris bar conceived of their participation in anti-Semitic measures.

In sum, not a single lawyer was exempted from the anti-Semitic quota on the grounds of professional merit or exceptional service rendered to France. About fifty Paris lawyers were retained as military veterans as of June 1942,[118] as noted earlier, a figure that went up at certain moments of the process, only to shrink again as repression continued.[119] An October 1942 document listed only nineteen Jewish lawyers in Paris permitted to practice under the quota.[120] Authorized lawyers had other problems that prevented them from practicing: about a dozen of them were imprisoned or deported, thus reducing the real impact of the veteran's exemption[121] and demonstrating that the Nazis, and in some instances the French police, disregarded exemptions entirely. In all, over two hundred Jewish lawyers were kicked out of the Paris bar.[122]

Several daily newspapers responded vociferously to the quotas on Jewish lawyers. The collaborationist *Le matin* titled an article "Fifty Jewish Lawyers Still in the Paris Bar: Is This How We Can Hope to Be Rid of Such Parasites?" and lamented that so many Jews "could continue to take care of the legal affairs of their Aryan clients."[123] *Le petit parisien* was more neutral in its report on the decisions, and *Les nouveaux temps* used measured language, even though it was obviously in favor of the anti-Semitic quotas.[124] An article in the collaborationist paper of Jacques Doriot's Parti populaire français, *Le cri du peuple,* accused the Paris bar of being "deficient" and "complicit" in protecting "Jewish lawyers of foreign origin." The article's wording, which repetitively emphasized that the problem with Jewish lawyers was their foreignness and which falsely asserted that the law targeted foreign Jews only, reveals that in early summer 1941, blatant anti-Semitism toward French Jews remained taboo in some quarters.[125]

Further complicating the implementation of the anti-Semitic quota in the law bars was legislation passed on 29 July and 31 October 1941 that allowed lawyers evacuated from the annexed and occupied zones of France to register temporarily with a law bar in the unoccupied zone.[126] Although several law bars declared their fraternal solidarity with "evacuee" lawyers from the bars of Belfort, Besançon, Lille, Metz, Nancy, and Paris, few set out the welcome mat for evacuees who were Jewish.[127] Their quandary, they claimed, was that they were required to accept Jewish lawyers from other regions as they were in the midst of expelling their "own" Jews. A debate ensued about whether exempted Jews could benefit from the law's provisions for transferring from a bar in the occupied zone to one in the free zone, just like non-Jewish lawyers. The CGQJ tried hard to impose a negative interpretation. One lawyer, J. S., who had been retained under the Mulhouse bar's 2 percent quota because of his veteran status, was temporarily admitted to the Limoges bar, with the approval of both the Limoges bar and the Limoges Court of Appeals.[128] The CGQJ and the *procureur général* intervened to reverse S.'s temporary admission, the CGQJ arguing that since there were no Jews in the Limoges bar on 25 June 1940, the stipulations of the 16 July 1941 decree must prevail, that is, 2 percent of zero lawyers equals zero.[129] The lengths to which the CGQJ went to eliminate individual Jews from the bar were often extraordinary.[130]

With the explosion of new and exceptional legislation during the Vichy era, the wording of laws was commonly ambiguous or contradictory. S.'s case exemplifies many situations in which individual fates were determined not by the letter of the law but by power relations among government organs. Whether the Limoges bar and Court of Appeals were protecting a Jewish lawyer or conforming to their technical approach to the legal text, they were willing to take a good deal of flak from the *procureur général* and the CGQJ in this case. The minister of justice finally declared authoritatively that the law allowed "all lawyers" registered in a bar in the annexed zones to join a bar in the free zone temporarily. This included Mr. S. To consider the total number of Jews on 25 June 1940 in the host law bar was, the minister of justice claimed, to apply the quota twice to the same lawyer, a legally unsound practice.[131] Because of the tenaciousness and concerted effort of the Limoges bar, the Court of Appeals, and the justice minister, S. was retained in the Limoges bar throughout the Occupation.[132]

The mixed reception that approved Jewish lawyers received from their southern colleagues in the free zone shows that sometimes a little pushback from lawyers and magistrates could thwart daunting Vichy authorities. In Marseille, for example, the bar council had refused the request for temporary admission of five Jewish lawyers who had been retained under the Paris bar quota for their veteran status, but who had nonetheless fled the occupied zone. In July 1942 the Aix Court of Appeals overruled the bar council and took the initiative to admit the five temporarily to the Marseille bar. Despite dogged protests by the Marseille bar council and the CGQJ, the decision of the court held.[133] The historian Liora Israël has asserted that the Marseille bar council's "relentlessness" toward approved Jewish lawyers looking for a temporary home was "without equivalent" in other southern law bars.[134] As the largest city in the unoccupied zone, Marseille was a destination for many Jews in flight.[135] Unlike Marseille, the Grenoble bar welcomed four Jewish evacuee lawyers from other French bars, above the quotas allowed by the legislation.[136] These examples demonstrate that bar councils and courts of appeals had more power than they thought or claimed when up against the CGQJ. In all, however, Badinter condemned the provincial bars as much as he condemned the Paris bar for their lack of protest against anti-Semitic exclusions: "Not a single declaration of principle was uttered, not a single gesture of collective solidarity was shown toward eliminated colleagues."[137]

The CGQJ continued throughout the fall of 1942 and the spring of 1943 to pressure Paris bar president Jacques Charpentier to confirm the names of Jewish lawyers who were actively practicing in the Palais de Justice, most likely with the intention of catching a few unauthorized Jews. Charpentier sometimes complied but sometimes resisted these efforts, and at one point was accused by the *procureur général* and the CGQJ of "bad will."[138] The CGQJ funneled German requests for the names and addresses of Jewish lawyers not wearing the yellow star down to the law bars and back again.[139] Like the rest of French society, the Paris bar took umbrage at the imposition of the yellow star on lawyers' black robes in the spring of 1942. In a rare instance of resistance, the Paris bar council refused to post the order to wear the yellow star in the cloakroom of the Palais de Justice, and Charpentier declined to denounce noncompliant lawyers to the authorities. There is evidence that some Jewish lawyers did wear it.[140]

Legal Expertise at the Service of Exclusion

Alexis de Tocqueville once said that "while lawyers may prize liberty, they generally place a far higher value on legality. They are less afraid of tyranny than of arbitrariness, and so long as the legislator himself sees to it that men are deprived of their independence, the lawyer is more or less content."[141] The participation of lawyers in Vichy anti-Semitism was not limited to their active role in excluding Jews from their profession. Leaders in the field also used their intellectual expertise and social influence to legitimize anti-Semitic measures affecting all of French society during the Vichy regime. Via legal doctrine, French lawyers contributed to the normalization of anti-Semitic law as a formal discipline with its own set of legal experts.[142] Doctrine consists of opinions written by law professors, legal experts, and lawyers that are published in law school text books and the legal press for experts. In the French legal system, judges use doctrine to interpret laws, and doctrine has more weight than case law. In addition to drafting discriminatory laws, lawyers participated in the banalization of anti-Semitic legislation by commenting on and interpreting them.[143] In law school lectures and in articles in law journals, bar members gave opinions on such issues as determining whether someone was Jewish, weighing the burden of proof of non-Jewishness, defining a Jew in a mixed marriage, and deciding cases of Aryanization of property and estate law for Jews.[144] The most infamous such article was written by Maurice Duverger in the *Revue de droit public,* but there were many others.[145] Legal and jurisprudence journals created new rubrics such as "Jewish Questions." The political scientist Dominique Gros has noted that "in flipping through the law reviews of the 1940s, all law students could perceive—albeit confusedly—the importance of the question." He asserts, "In sum, a new field of law was born, with its own specialists."[146]

In a seminal article, the legal scholar Danièle Lochak asserts that Vichy lawyers interpreted anti-Semitic law under the guise of neutralism, or positivism. Their resolute commitment to a supposed objectivity blinded them to the ethical and human consequences of discriminatory legislation. Lochak blames the positivist legal tradition itself for legitimating iniquitous law.[147] In response to this argument, the law scholar Michel Troper argues that, on the contrary, it was because the French judiciary had lost touch with its positivist heritage during Vichy that it supported legal exclusion. When authors of doctrine left the bounds of objective commentary and slipped into interpretation or justification of legislation, they violated the principles of positivism. Positivism itself, he argues, is not to blame.[148] Lochak counters that even objective commentary, by its very enunciation, reinforced the notion that the content of a law was acceptable.[149]

Under Vichy, the tools and methods of the French legal system—originally established on values of democracy and republicanism—were used toward unconstitutional and persecutory ends. Just as some doctors placed their credentials behind the promotion of racialist ideologies to put a "scientific" seal on Vichy policies of exclusion, lawyers lent their legal skills to the implementation of xenophobic and collaborationist laws. The Vichy regime used the French judicial apparatus to assert its authority and repress its enemies through the creation of a large number of courts of "exceptional jurisdiction": "special tribunals," "the State Tribunal," and the "special sections."[150] As Groucho Marx once said, "Military justice is to justice as military music is to music." By pleading cases in these judicial bodies—akin to military tribunals with little respect for legal guarantees—French lawyers were confronted with difficult choices. Even in regular courts, non-Jewish lawyers took on many cases dealing with anti-Semitic legislation, such as helping Jewish clients obtain certificates of non-Jewishness or working to liberate them from French concentration camps. All of these acts contributed to this new "field" of law.

The Effects of Exclusion and Evaluating Lawyers' Record

It is impossible to generalize Jewish lawyers' reactions to the anti-Semitic quota. Some rejected the idea of an exception made for them (Lucien Vidal-Naquet); some asked the Paris bar president not to protest in their favor (Pierre Masse);

others committed suicide (Jacques Frank). Many of them turned to the Resistance. As Israël makes clear, both the symbolic designation of "enemy of the regime" and the loss of one's livelihood made clandestinity seem the logical next step to many Jewish lawyers.[151] Examples include Joë Nordmann, Lucien Vidal-Naquet, and Marcel Willard. Nordmann's Jewish identity was known to the Paris bar, from which he was expelled, but he refused to declare himself in the Jewish census. In response to the bar president's form letter asking for any justifications to be kept on as an exception, Nordmann replied simply, "As a lawyer and son of a lawyer, I have practiced my profession honorably and I ask to be retained in the bar."[152] To no avail.

Some disbarred lawyers switched careers entirely. The well-known author Nathalie Sarraute, for example, entered the Paris Law School in 1922 and began her career in the Paris bar in 1926. Born in Russia of Jewish parents, she was subjected to the full array of Vichy exclusionary legislation.[153] She was expelled from the Paris bar by both the 1940 law banning foreign-fathered lawyers and the 1941 decree banning Jews.[154] She fled into hiding in the French countryside and, under an assumed name, survived the war with her husband and three daughters. She never returned to the legal profession.[155]

Lawyers eliminated from their profession had little resort to other remunerated work. The CGQJ explicitly forbade disbarred Jewish lawyers from becoming employees in their own law firms.[156] They could not join any paralegal profession such as quasi-government solicitors (*avoués*), notaries, judicial auctioneers (*commissaires-priseurs*), or legal consultants (*conseils juridiques*), since the number of Jews in those professions was also fixed. They could not work as government lawyers, since no Jews were permitted to hold jobs in the civil service sector. Furthermore, Vichy laws forbade Jews to start almost any kind of business.[157]

In the chaotic days of 1940 and 1941, with new anti-Semitic restrictions raining down, Jewish lawyers, whether or not they remained in the bars, suffered much from being in professional limbo. It is likely that practicing Jewish lawyers lost clients, who may have hesitated to employ their services if they risked disruption of their cases due to their lawyer's abrupt disbarment. For the two hundred or more Jewish lawyers and the two hundred or more foreign-fathered lawyers who were summarily eliminated from legal practice, their clients needed to find replacement lawyers. In a significant—though localized and abortive—show of pity, the *colonnes* of the Paris bar voted in favor of a measure to preserve the clientele of both groups of excluded lawyers, just as the law bars had taken steps to help mobilized lawyers maintain their cases and clients during their military service. In November 1941, however, the Paris bar council declined the proposal.[158]

In 1942 the question of retirement benefits for disbarred Jews arose among the law bars, the Ministry of Justice, and the CGQJ. Discussion ensued over whether Jewish lawyers, cut off from their source of livelihood, would have access to funds to which they had contributed throughout their career.[159] Even though the Justice Ministry and even the CGQJ determined that disbarred Jewish lawyers could receive compensation from their pension funds, the Paris bar council issued its own decision on the matter: Jewish lawyers who had served thirty-five years or more in the bar could receive their pensions. All others would receive nothing.[160]

The few lawyers authorized to remain in practice, after having endured a repugnant selection process by their colleagues, still faced the perils of daily life for Jews in occupied France, such as avoiding arrest and "Aryanization" of their property, as well as coping with the yellow star and the restrictions on movement. As one historian has pointed out, "For most Jewish lawyers, judges, functionaries, and legal assistants, the fight for life and death that failed in 1943 and 1944 began as a struggle for *professional* survival in 1940 and 1941."[161] In the Paris roundups in August 1941, in which over four thousand Jews were arrested, more than forty Jewish lawyers were arrested and interned at the Drancy camp.[162] Initiated by the Nazis in reprisal against communist agitation in the wake of the invasion of the Soviet Union, the roundup was implemented by the French police, who for the first time arrested French Jews, one year before the infamous events at Paris's Vélodrome d'Hiver.[163] The Nazis expressly targeted certain Jewish lawyers for arrest because of their influential leadership, such as former senator and former Paris bar council member Pierre Masse, Yves Jouffa (member of the Paris bar council, future president of the League of the Rights of Man), Gaston Crémieux, Théodore Valensi, and Edmond Bloch.[164] A triangular struggle ensued among Nazi occupiers, Vichy authorities (who were surprised by the prominence and "Frenchness" of the arrested personalities, and who subsequently protested to the Nazis), and activist anti-Semitic French lawyers (who had designated certain Jewish lawyers to the Nazis for capture and others for release). Nazi leaders opted to please the last group, what they called a "small circle of honest collaborators," and refused to free the lawyers.[165] The Paris bar president, Charpentier, went to the Drancy camp to inform the imprisoned Jewish lawyers that, in the meantime, they had been disbarred. He expressed not a word of regret or dissent. After his departure, several of the lawyers broke down in tears.[166] Sometime in early 1942, Pétain wrote to the German authorities requesting the liberation of Pierre Masse; the request was refused.[167] Masse was eventually deported on 30 September 1942 and died at Auschwitz. Twenty other Jewish lawyers arrested with him were also deported and never returned.[168] For these lawyers, "ordinary" French anti-Semitism contributed directly to the Nazis' "final solution."[169] The law professor Eric Loquin, in analyzing "the horrifying expansion of disenfranchisements and the perversity of their finality," concluded that the degradation of one's juridical personality

constituted a degradation of the personality of the human being, and the beginning of a process that could lead to genocide.[170]

What to conclude about lawyers' participation in the anti-foreign and anti-
Semitic policies that overrode the very rules and ethics of the legal profession?
Joseph Billig has shown that whereas the CGQJ played a direct role in the
Aryanization of property, when it came to implementing anti-Semitic quotas
in the professions, the CGQJ only "monitored rather than acted." It was the
professional organs that played the real role.[171] In the archives of the Paris, Lyon,
and Marseille bars, historians have searched fruitlessly for evidence of opposition
to the anti-Semitic quota.[172] Protest and noncompliance were not impossible:
after all, on numerous occasions bar leaders publicly objected to Vichy actions
and state interference in bar business, and they were not punished for expressing
their critical views. For instance, Charpentier and the Paris bar council passed
resolutions rejecting the oath to Pétain in 1941, demanding that the minister
of justice guarantee defendants' right to consult with their lawyers in 1942, and
refusing to readmit Pierre Laval's associate Jean-Charles Legrand to the bar in
1943.[173] These Paris bar protests were not confined to the elite but were widely
supported by French lawyers.[174] Yet French lawyers failed to protest in any significant way the state's expulsion of Jewish and foreign-fathered lawyers.[175]
Belgian lawyers, by contrast, simply refused to enforce the legislation against
their Jewish colleagues.[176]

Most historians have therefore concluded that members of the legal profession were content with the anti-Semitic quota. Joë Nordmann remembered,
"The malaise that certain colleagues felt about these measures of exclusion
expressed itself only very timidly. Many were satisfied with them."[177] Commenting on the minutes of bar council meetings between 1940 and 1945, Yves
Ozanam made this assessment:

> One can only be struck by the choices made by the bar president and
> council: they did not protest against the exclusion—without precedent in
> the history of the bar—of more than three hundred of their colleagues,
> victims of xenophobic and anti-Semitic legislation. This retroactive exclu-
> sion also flouts the most elementary principles of law, of which lawyers
> are by vocation the very defenders. On the contrary, they made decisions
> ensuring the application of the exclusionary laws and, by making selec-
> tions among excluded colleagues, engaged in discrimination that made the
> law bar an accomplice in the Vichy regime's work.[178]

Although this book is concerned with the social history of doctors and lawyers as a professional group, a few individual men of law during the Vichy period
played crucial roles, especially given the overlap between Paris bar council members and Vichy government officials. Government head Pierre Laval, CGQJ

leader Xavier Vallat, Minister of Finance Pierre Cathala, and Manuel Fourcade, who was a member of Vichy's pseudo-parliamentarian advisory National Council, were all members of the Paris law bar. Jean-Louis Tixier-Vignancour, an extreme-right deputy during the Third Republic and head of radio for Vichy, was also a lawyer. Minister of Justice Raphaël Alibert, a friend of Pétain's who began working on a Statute on the Jews as early as July 1940, was a former member of the Council of State and a professor of constitutional law at the Institute of Political Science.[179] Vichy's second minister of justice, Joseph Barthélemy, developed and signed the second Statute on the Jews as well as hundreds of laws discriminating against Jews. During his tenure, an average of one anti-Semitic law and one decree were passed each week. Barthélemy also established the "special section" courts, which violated many basic legal principles. Although in a few particular instances he tried to reduce the scope of anti-Semitic persecution, as head of the French justice system Barthélemy contributed enormously to the legitimization of anti-Semitism.[180] At the same time, the CGQJ was considered by all segments of the government to be the legitimate authority over anti-Semitic matters. Although the traditional ministries such as Justice and Health considered the CGQJ to be radically anti-Semitic and beholden to the German occupiers—a perception that flattered their own self-image of moderation—their officials nonetheless actively participated in the state machinery of anti-Semitism.[181]

In retrospect, it seems an obvious conclusion that leaders within the legal profession could have done more to counter anti-Semitism. Paris bar president Jacques Charpentier chose his battles, but defending the Jews in his bar was not one of them. Active in the Resistance, Charpentier opposed many Vichy policies without qualm, including the lack of due process during the Riom trial. He rejected a Vichy directive to denounce Jewish lawyers for not wearing the yellow star.[182] And yet, despite other acts of protest, Charpentier allowed and even actively participated in the persecution of foreign-fathered and Jewish lawyers.[183] As the leader of the Paris bar, Charpentier lacked the will to direct lawyers toward a more liberal and humanitarian mission during the Vichy period.

Of course, Vichy was an exceptional moment in French history. For years, people living in France had to cope with a new and authoritarian regime, an occupying force, civil war, food shortages, and arbitrary threats to life and livelihood. The French population was probably more preoccupied and self-centered than under usual circumstances. This may explain in part why lawyers did not protest or resist the anti-Semitic and xenophobic measures that affected their colleagues. And yet, as one historian has pointed out, the anti-Semitic laws were "pervasive. . . . They were implemented by agencies and courts, interpreted by hundreds of magistrates, utilized by practicing lawyers on behalf of clients, discussed for potential reform on the highest levels of government, as well as by scores of academicians."[184] It was simply not possible for lawyers to ignore them, or pretend to be unaffected by them. As Vicki Caron persuasively argues regarding middle-class professional groups,

> There was considerable popular support for Vichy's legislative measures against the Jews, including the two *Statuts des Juifs,* as well as a slew of anti-foreign measures that targeted Jews to a disproportionate degree. This support went well beyond extreme right-wing circles, and under no circumstances can it be called indifference, or even accommodation.... Rather, among certain sectors of the population, particularly various middle-class professional groups, there was strong support for Vichy's drive to restrict Jewish influence in French political, cultural and economic life.[185]

Even lawyers active in the Resistance—a minority of lawyers—did not rise up against the exclusionary measures.[186] The xenophobic and anti-Semitic purges figured hardly at all in the ideological battles of Resistance groups in the judicial and legal fields. Vichy anti-Semitism was hardly mentioned in the publications of *Le Palais libre,* one of the main Resistance journals maintained by legal professionals during the war. This is especially surprising, given that several leaders of the journal were themselves Jews who had experienced professional banishment. Liora Israël has argued that the absence of the subject from its columns constituted a "strategic orientation of *Le Palais libre* toward topics that were likely to rally jurists, in particular around professional norms and values. Such a will to unify necessitated the concealment of certain sensitive topics considered likely to upset this cohesion."[187]

★ ★ ★

Previous chapters have amply demonstrated that during the interwar period, it was *because of* demand from lawyers and doctors that exclusionary measures were put into place against foreigners and naturalized citizens. When the new political leadership of the Vichy regime quickly initiated xenophobic and anti-Semitic legislation in the fall of 1940, there was little time for the liberal professions to flex much exclusionary muscle. Of course, after years of their lobbying against outsiders during the interwar period, Vichy authorities knew they could count on cooperation from lawyers—and doctors—to participate in banning their foreign-fathered colleagues from the profession and probably suspected the same cooperation for their anti-Semitic measures. The presence of many lawyers in the Vichy state apparatus also signified a degree of pressure from below. Many of the same activists in professional interest groups in the 1930s, moreover, became administrators and lawmakers during Vichy, serving as human conduits between the two regimes, and indicating an alignment between the legal profession and Vichy ideology.[188] Xavier Vallat, for example, a Parisian lawyer, deputy from Ardèche, and future head of the CGQJ, along with a number of other lawyer-legislators, including Alfred Jourdan, president of the Aix-en-Provence bar, and Paris law professor Donnedieu de Vabres, had co-signed a tough law calling for the expulsion of foreigners in 1938.[189] Prior to that, as we saw earlier, Vallat had gained infamy for his anti-Semitic comment from the podium of the Chamber of Deputies against Léon Blum upon the election in 1936 of the Popular Front government.[190]

If we compare the exemption criteria for foreign-fathered lawyers with those for Jewish lawyers, we see that the anti-Semitic quota required more extensive military service credentials in order for a lawyer to remain in practice. To be considered for a special exemption, the trajectory of approval was much more lengthy and hazardous for Jews than for foreign-fathered lawyers. Jewish lawyers had to be nominated by the bar council, accepted by the Court of Appeals, approved by the CGQJ, and receive the blessing of the Ministry of Justice. Foreign-fathered lawyers had to clear only two hurdles: the bar council and the Ministry of Justice. Acquiring an exemption from the CGQJ was nearly impossible, and Nazi authorities pressed only for the elimination of Jews from the profession and did not care at all about the ban on foreign-fathered lawyers. The more restrictive exclusion of Jews compared to foreign-fathered lawyers clashed with the views of a majority of legal professionals: in the minds of many, a French Jew remained more "proximate" to French identity than a recently naturalized citizen, although this was not true for the real zealots like Vallat and Alibert.

As previous chapters have shown, control over professional access—determining membership criteria and enforcing professional ethics on lawyers already admitted to the bar—had always been a critical factor in the law bars' assertion of power vis-à-vis the French state. This struggle continued throughout the Vichy period.[191] When the new Vichy regime was rumored to have signed a law giving some control over bar admission to state courts, the Paris bar council protested immediately and resolutely. In contrast, the law bars offered no resistance during the same period to legislation that trampled bar regulations by summarily disbarring certain French lawyers.[192] These different reactions to Vichy measures reveal contradictory impulses concerning professional autonomy and bar membership. When it came to the state-imposed measures against lawyers born Jewish or of foreign fathers—measures that were both discriminatory and retroactive and therefore contrary to the professed values of the legal profession—the law bars showed no inclination to defend their autonomy.

 **CHAPTER 7**

L'Ordre des Médecins

Corporatist Debut and Anti-Semitic Climax

The medical profession as a whole responded to Pétain's accession to power with enthusiasm, for many reasons. Pétain chose a doctor, Bernard Ménétrel, as his personal secretary and chief of propaganda.[1] With his privileged access to the head of state, Dr. Ménétrel received hundreds of letters from doctors who hoped his place at Vichy would enhance the medical profession's prestige and meet their personal needs.[2] The regime would soon legislate the creation of a corporatist Medical Order, and a plan to reform and raise standards in medical studies was initiated. In addition, as the sociologist Francine Muel-Dreyfus has illustrated, the National Revolution's program to cure the social ills it identified, such as denatalism and military weakness, ushered in "the consecration of a new medical figure, that of the expert in national hygiene, which accompanied the growth of new fields of medical competence and the political uses of medical legitimacy."[3] Finally, Vichy measures to exclude foreigners from the profession surpassed the demands of doctors themselves. The exclusionary movement in medicine had for years been priming parliamentarians and ministers. Such propaganda and lobbying efforts fell on highly sympathetic ears in 1940 and fit seamlessly with the values of Vichy's National Revolution. Although not all doctors subscribed to an exclusionary vision of their profession, the archives record no public protest in response to the ban on foreign-fathered doctors or the anti-Semitic quota, but they do reveal several examples of outspoken approval and a willingness of the majority of doctors to participate in the implementation of discriminatory and racist policies.

The National Revolution not only targeted outsiders such as foreigners and Jews but also stoked a nostalgic ideology that excluded women from public roles and urged a return to an elitist Latin-Greek high school curriculum. In a letter to Education Minister Georges Ripert in October 1940, Maurice Mordagne, who had been a student leader of the exclusionary movement in the 1930s, urged that the classical baccalaureate be imposed as a prerequisite for medical school and advocated a male-only profession: "Morals demand an urgent measure: the prohibition of girls from attending middle and high schools for boys."[4] In another letter to Ripert written before the passage of the first Statute on the Jews, Mordagne railed: "The whole problem stems from this: since 1900 the Jews have invaded Freemasonry and taken on a mission to destroy the Latinist spirit in France. They succeeded. . . . If you return us to classical education, Mr. Minister, you will save France."[5] If Mordagne represented a marginal though attention-grabbing segment of the interwar medical profession, he incarnated the triumphant values of Vichy. The National Revolution wove various strands—nostalgia for a more rigorous, classical curricular past, a forced return of women to their domestic roles, explicit blame on foreigners, Jews, and Freemasons for having led France astray—into an ideology that fit well with dominant perceptions in medicine.

Prior to 1940, as noted in previous chapters, the medical profession had no central authority to unify the various career trajectories of doctors into a coherent profession or to set standards for medical practice. In October 1940 the Vichy regime finally satisfied long-term demands for the creation of a Medical Order (Ordre des Médecins), whose centralized corporatist structure would control the right to practice medicine in France. This seminal change in the structural organization of French medicine symbolized a return to Old Regime conceptions of privileged corporations and a rejection of the republican heritage of democratic, open liberal professions. Doctors' control over their membership was the most important prerogative of the Medical Order. The new Order was to be led by a national council (Conseil supérieur) and individual department councils. Doctors were to register with the Order council in the department in which their practice was established, though once authorized they could practice anywhere in France. Each department council of the Order was to draw up a public registry (*tableau*) of authorized doctors. The councils could refuse permission to doctors "if the required conditions of morality were not met."[6]

Many doctors were initially thrilled with the institution of a corporatist structure and the promise of increased power over membership in the profession, but they were quickly dismayed by the statism inherent in Vichy's style of corporatism. They were disappointed by the top-down manner in which the reform was enacted: Vichy authorities had not consulted any doctors when legislating the Medical Order. The law simultaneously dissolved medical unions, changing the professional structure of medicine in ways doctors had not anticipated. Until a process of elections could be instituted, the members of the department and national councils of the Order were to be nominated by the minister of the interior. The initial membership of the national council was disproportionately favorable to the elite Parisian university and hospital medical corps, leading critics to stew over their lack of representation in the new corporatist organization. A glaring absence in the national council of the new Medical Order was that of Victor Balthazard, who had led the interwar effort at corporatism. Balthazard, the dean of the Paris Medical School, had presided over the powerful Confédération des syndicats médicaux, and had spearheaded campaigns in Paris against foreigners in medicine. Balthazard's absence was understood as another sign of the new regime's intention to subsume the Order under its own authority. But feuds over corporatism and statism were of minor concern to Jewish doctors and those of foreign origin, who could not hope for better treatment from René Leriche, the first national council president of the Medical Order, any more than they would have expected from Balthazard. Leriche's views were made clear early on. In a memorandum to Ménétrel in July 1940, he expressed his wish to rid medicine of "undesirables" and to "de-Semitize" the medical profession.[7]

The myth of a plethora of doctors and the scapegoating of doctors of foreign origin continued unabated by war and occupation. Statistics were regularly abused to sustain the myth. Even Vichy authorities such as State Secretary of Health Serge Huard (a doctor by profession) promulgated exaggerated figures that inflamed public opinion. One historian writes, "An official claim that [six thousand doctors or] 22 percent of the medical corps was 'foreign,' repeated throughout the medical and mainstream press, had a fearful effect on even moderate doctors." A more reliable source showed that 319, or 5.7 percent of the 5,636 doctors in the Seine department in 1935, were foreign, and another source put the national figures even lower: 750, or 2.8 percent of the 27,700 doctors in France, were foreign.[8] Regardless, the links made between xenophobic rhetoric and fears of overcrowding, downward mobility, and loss of prestige in the medical profession were clear.[9] On the contrary, with thousands of doctors and medical students mobilized into military units or taken prisoners of war in 1940 and 1941, there was more than ever before a shortage of doctors to care for the French population.

Because of the exclusionary laws of Vichy obliging doctors to declare their national origin and religion, a novel opportunity for gathering such information presented itself. Still, the archives leave us with an incomplete statistical picture. As for Jewish doctors, it has been estimated that approximately 1,500, or 5 percent of the 27,700 doctors in France in the 1930s, were Jews.[10] Higher proportions of Jewish doctors practiced in the Seine department: nine hundred, or 15 percent of the six thousand doctors in the department, declared themselves as Jewish. The anti-Semitic quota expelled over seven hundred of them. In the rest of France, the percentage of Jews among doctors was much lower, between zero and 6 percent. Some Jewish doctors, to be sure, were banned from medicine for having a foreign father.

The Ban on Foreign-Fathered Doctors

On 9 July 1940, the day before the French parliament voted full powers to Marshal Pétain, the six hundred–member Seine-et-Oise Medical Union wrote to the new French leader, thanking him for saving France and expressing its six-part agenda for medical reform. Topping the list was a request for "the elimination of the innumerable unassimilated foreigners who have invaded France and especially the department of Seine-et-Oise in the last few years and who are the primary cause of the decline of medical morality."[11] This demand outranked the creation of a medical order, reform of the national medical insurance program, and the restructuring of hospitals. In another report sent that week to Pétain, the Seine-et-Oise Medical Union's secretary-general Dr. Robert Hollier raged against "the invasion of medicine by stateless persons with lowly mercantile mentalities." In making "foreigners" the first item on his eight-page agenda, Hollier lumped doctors of foreign origin in not only with swindlers but also with communists and abortionists.[12] Hollier would soon be nominated to the founding national council of the Medical Order.[13]

Hollier's department, the Seine-et-Oise, was the same in which the author of *Journey to the End of the Night (Voyage au bout de la nuit),* Louis Ferdinand Destouches (better known by his pseudonym, Céline), practiced medicine during the interwar years, specifically in the Paris suburb of Clichy. His character Bardamu also worked as a medical doctor in a fictional Paris suburb.[14] As a doctor, Destouches appropriated a medical position vacated by a doctor of Haitian origin in the town of Bezons in the fall of 1940, when the law banning doctors with foreign fathers took effect. Some of his anti-Semitic outbursts are chronicled in the archives of the Seine-et-Oise Medical Order.[15] In his 1938 book *L'école des cadavres* Céline mocked medical unions for no longer listing their members' place of birth, claiming they were doing so out of embarrassment that so many doctors were foreign-born.[16]

The law of 16 August 1940 dictated that only those "possessing French nationality in a native capacity as being born of a French father" could practice medicine in France and its colonies.[17] Medical doctors were required to declare their national origin, and the newly created Medical Order was assigned the task of eliminating colleagues. Another version of the law banning foreign-fathered doctors was passed a year later, following the passage of a decree establishing quotas for Jews in medicine.[18] Under the 16 August 1940 law, it did not matter if a doctor had been born in France or abroad. It also did not matter if a doctor's mother was French or foreign. It did not matter if a doctor's father had obtained French nationality after the birth of the future doctor. The only thing that mattered was the nationality of a doctor's father at the moment of the doctor's birth. And the law was retroactive: even if a doctor with a foreign father was already practicing in France, she or he could no longer do so.

Two exceptions to the legislation were allowed: for those who had served in an armed unit of the French military in the wars of 1914 or 1939, and for those who had "scientifically honored their country of adoption" (such wording dismissing the fact that those born in France of a foreign father might never have had another country from which to adopt France).[19] The law also exempted those from Alsace and Lorraine who were reintegrated into French nationality in 1918 (having lost it as a result of the 1871 Franco-German treaty) as well as children born in France of an unknown father. Ministerial circulars issued in the fall of 1940 further expanded the possibilities for exemption to include doctors covered by diplomatic conventions and doctors who had "assimilated" into French society.[20]

This was an extraordinary piece of legislation, which far exceeded professional demands. Anyone whose father was not born French was permanently forbidden to practice medicine. The Vichy regime had passed the same law for civil servants a month earlier, and would apply it to dentists, pharmacists, lawyers, veterinarians, architects, and midwives over the course of the year. The law was thus one of many legal texts that embodied Vichy's exclusionary principles, even though it catered to doctors' special interests and responded to cries of a medical plethora. Action française leaders Charles Maurras and Léon Daudet loudly celebrated the law in its publications and gave the league's medical section credit for years of successful lobbying.[21] Indeed, the law's total ban made the *diplôme d'université*—a diploma reserved for foreigners and the center of much interwar debate—moot: foreigners and naturalized citizens no longer needed to be barred from earning the *diplôme d'état* since they and their children could never practice medicine in France anyway.[22]

A decree of 28 October 1940 spelled out the process of requesting exemptions from the 16 August law.[23] Every request was to be reviewed by the department council of the Medical Order and by the department prefect, each of whom would submit an opinion on the candidate and forward the dossier to the Ministry of Interior. Doctors had one month from the date of the decree to submit an exemption request; doctors who were prisoners of war were granted one month following their return to France. Since the Medical Order had barely been instituted at this point, the decree stipulated that demands for exemptions would not include the opinion of the department councils of the Medical Order until they could be constituted. Though temporary, this was a loss of sovereignty for doctors. A Superior Inspection Commission (Commission supérieure de contrôle) composed of three members—a doctor designated from the national council of the Medical Order, the director of health from the Ministry of Health, and a member of the Council of State—would evaluate each case, and the minister of the interior would make the final judgment. With a single national medical council member as one of three decision makers on the Superior Inspection Commission, practicing doctors did not have an all-powerful representative at the level of appeals and exemption requests. This did not matter much, however, since the fundamental task of exclusion lay with the department medical councils.

In evaluating candidates for exemption, prefects were instructed to take into account a wide array of factors including diplomatic conventions (which were explicitly legislated in the second version of the law in 1941) and familial qualities. In a series of circulars, the minister of the interior urged prefects to consider complex realities ignored by the legislative text, notably to distinguish carefully among foreigners, naturalized French citizens, those born in France of a French mother, women doctors who had become French by marriage, and foreigners of either sex whose naturalized children may have "honored" their country of adoption. One circular also stated perfunctorily that the 16 August law was "not applicable to Italians." As a result of protests by Italian authorities, it had been decided to exempt Italians, meaning not only French persons born of an Italian father but also Italian nationals. This exception was not granted automatically, however; candidates had to apply.[24] This turned out to be just the first of several diplomatic conventions woven back into the legislation over time and reducing its impact. Doctors with a validated exemption request were permitted to practice medicine provisionally until their case was judged by the Superior Inspection Commission.

Ministerial circulars provided additional clarifications to the law, whose cryptic and vague articles continued to arouse questions and whose very intent perplexed those with a basic understanding of French legal principles. The 27 November circular confirmed that the law was indeed retroactive: it banned doctors already rightfully practicing. And by "born of a French father," the law's wording meant that the father must have been French at the moment of the birth of the son or daughter, not that the father had to be French from birth himself. By "French," the circular continued, the law meant a French "citizen" or "subject" but not natives of a French protectorate; *protégés* would have to ask for exemptions, but their requests would automatically be considered by the

Superior Inspection Commission. Dossiers of all those who had "been deeply integrated into the French community" were to be sent up for consideration, for example, doctors who had a French mother, a French wife and children, a history of French military service, or a French husband or father with a history of military service. Women who had lost their French nationality by marrying a foreigner (which had been the case until 1927 for women but not for men), and who subsequently became widowed, would have their exemption request automatically considered (with no guarantee, however).[25] Still, some questions remained about how women doctors were to be treated, and the national council slowed down appeals by foreign-fathered women doctors with a request that clarifications for women be added to the law.[26] Official and unofficial documentation consistently referred to the targets of the legislation as "*sons* of foreign fathers." Since the 16 August law was meant to be permanent, the circular prescribed that current and future medical students who were born of a foreign father and fulfilled the criteria should apply for an exemption once they had a diploma in hand. Finally, the prefects were to pronounce a favorable or unfavorable opinion on all cases, taking into account both services rendered to the French population and candidates' "morality and attitude toward their country of adoption," leaving the door open to a great deal of subjectivity. Candidates whose dossiers were not approved by the prefects were also permitted to appeal directly to the Superior Inspection Commission.[27]

By the spring of 1941, department medical councils were operational, and they had reappropriated from prefects some of the power over decisions to exclude foreign-fathered doctors. This marked an important consolidation of professional sovereignty, and the department councils took their role in determining membership seriously. Department councils' opinions on whether to approve candidates' claims to exemption were usually unfavorable. For example, the Gironde department council gave a negative opinion on eighteen of twenty-two requests for exemptions.[28] And yet, serving on a Medical Order department or national council from 1940 to 1944 did not automatically mean that one shared the exclusionary attitudes of the Vichy regime. Dr. André Lemierre, president of the Seine department council, who as a medical professor before the war had advised on a thesis refuting racial theories, voiced concerns about the exclusion of foreign-fathered doctors and was regularly accused by the right-wing press of being soft.[29]

Conflict often arose between the department and national councils of the Medical Order over implementation of the ban.[30] Archival sources indicate that in many cases the national council was more open than its department council colleagues to approving exemption requests.[31] In response to a barrage of complaints from department councils over delays, the national council accused department councils of underestimating the breadth and difficulty of the Superior Inspection Commission's dossier reviews.[32] Department councils such as the Maine-et-Loire council also accused the commission of granting too many exceptions. In order to publicize the interdictions—the better to enforce them—the Seine-et-Oise council asked to publish the names of banned doctors in the mainstream press. The national council forbade department councils from doing so. When the national council debated whether or not to print the names of banned doctors in its own Medical Order bulletin, one council member argued, without irony, "It would really weigh down the bulletin," and another retorted, "It would satisfy doctors' wishes." Ultimately the national council decided to publish only the total number of banned doctors in its bulletins, without their names.[33] Overall, department councils were more exclusionary than the national council of the Medical Order, although some department councils were more exacting than others.

Some department councils rejected candidates who should have qualified automatically for exemption, thus lengthening the national council's appeal docket. One member of the national council denounced the restrictive bent of the department councils, saying, "Most of them accuse foreign-fathered candidates of 'deplorable morality' without giving any reasons."[34] Frustrated with the department councils, the Superior Inspection Commission asked government authorities in March 1942 to clarify the role of department councils in the implementation of the law. In response, the state secretary for family and health issued detailed instructions, reminding department councils that their duties were limited and that many exemptions were automatic. In non-automatic cases, department councils were supposed to send the applications to the Superior Inspection Commission for a final decision. This was the crux of the problem, since the department councils controlled a critical filtering mechanism and could decline to send cases up. Even though individuals could appeal directly to the Superior Inspection Commission if they were rejected at the department level, the process surely had a discouraging effect on appeals.

Some Medical Order leaders in the national council recognized the unfairness of allowing foreign-fathered French persons to study medicine in France while barring them from practice. They proposed, to no avail, that such persons be permitted to apply for exemption to the ban before they began medical studies so as not to waste years in futile training.[35] Members of the national council also took note of doctors of Romanian origin who had volunteered for combat units in the French army: some regiments did engage in combat operations, while others did not. The president of the national council exclaimed in a meeting: "They joined a combat unit, it is not their fault if their assigned regiment was not sent to Flanders! If the law says that only those who engaged in combat are allowed, it is unfair; it was not up to them if they got beat up or not!"[36] One member, Dr. Jean Roux Berger, voiced resistance in national council discussions to measures against Jewish doctors and those of foreign origin, and was at one point exasperated by the exclusionary measures in which he was called upon to participate: "I am more generous than [all of] you; that is why I am not speaking; my opinion has no value at this time, given the current laws."[37]

Vichy officials tweaked the criteria to include more possibilities for exemptions all throughout 1941, often with the support of the national council of the Medical Order. In respect of preexisting diplomatic conventions, citizens of Monaco holding a French medical diploma were authorized to practice medicine in France without having to apply for exemption. All future Monegasque doctors wishing to practice in France also received a blanket authorization.[38] Other nationals from frontier states—Swiss, Belgians, and Luxembourgeois—were provisionally permitted to practice medicine as long as they held a French medical diploma, although they had to request an exemption. Both the Nord department council and the national council wanted such requests from "sons" of Belgian fathers to be considered with benevolence.[39]

Throughout 1941, as these examples show, there was a growing malaise among medical leaders that the legislation was eliminating "Frenchified" persons, and the national council and some department councils occasionally lamented such unwanted expulsions. As national council president Leriche noted: "In this affair there is a kind of cruelty that the law imposes on us. There is a side to this that is very shocking from a French point of view."[40] Although the 1 November circular had urged prefects to take family background into consideration, it did not have the force of law. In March 1941 the national council asked to add an exemption to the law in favor of foreign-fathered doctors with a French wife and children.[41] State Secretary for Family and Health Huard declined to go that far, but he granted the possibility of a *sursis* (temporary deferment of the ban) for certain doctors:

> Some practitioners, who fulfill none of the exemption criteria according to the law in its current form, are nonetheless in various ways worthy of particular consideration. For example, naturalized foreigners [*sic*] who married native Frenchwomen and had children, are heads of French families.... While the eight-day delay instituted by the 5 June 1941 regulation is enough time for a single person to liquidate his affairs, the same brutal treatment of families who, in fact, *are French,* inflicts grave harm on them. It is a good idea, taking into account the current impossibility for heads of families to leave France and return to their country of origin, to allow, as interdictions are pronounced, for a temporary deferment proportionate to the interest that doctors' family situations present.[42]

While this was a rare occasion in which a government official took action to address the humanitarian consequences of Vichy's growing restrictive legislation, Huard remained blind to the fact that many of the banned doctors had been born in France and had no "country of origin" to return to. Furthermore, a few months' respite was not going to make much difference. Ultimately, Huard discontinued the temporary deferment program around March 1942 because it "was having the effect of considerably attenuating the reach of the law," a point that highlights the high degree of assimilation among many "foreign" doctors.[43]

Despite the national council's request in favor of "heads of French families," the same leaders of the Medical Order felt no compunction about enforcing the legislation as harshly as possible in other respects. In the summer of 1941, the national council urged the department councils to flag for administrative authorities any banned doctors still practicing, and cited the "encouraging example" of an illegally practicing doctor who had recently been imprisoned in a camp.[44] Continuously pressured by doctors' complaints about lack of enforcement, Huard instructed prefects to remove professional plaques from the premises of banned doctors and to bring violators to justice.[45]

What these examples demonstrate is that doctors distinguished "good" foreign-fathered doctors from "undesirable" ones. The criteria established by the legislation did not always conform to their vision of insiders and outsiders, although in contrast to lawyers, doctors gave less weight to professional seniority (ancienneté) and more closely mirrored the values of the National Revolution. "Good" doctors of foreign origin were male, married to Frenchwomen, fathers of large families, and war veterans. "Undesirables" included almost everyone else, and especially lawbreakers who continued to practice after being banned. The term "undesirables" was bandied about regularly by national council members in their monthly meetings without ever being defined.[46] Even the arguments used in favor of banned doctors often "remained bounded by the ambient ideology" of Vichy.[47] In the eyes of many French doctors, cultural and linguistic proximity distinguished good doctors of foreign origin from undesirable ones. For example, the Nord department council urged regularly that French doctors with Belgian fathers who had practiced in the border towns for many years be viewed favorably, "with a large spirit of understanding and solidarity."[48] Georges Mauco, who emerged in the mid-1930s as an expert in the new field of immigration studies in France, was the first to establish the concept of ranking foreigners by national and ethnic origins. He gave Italians, Swiss, and Belgians the highest scores on criteria such as good work habits and physical being. Mauco was also an innovator in his field in distinguishing between desired and imposed immigration, a concept that led him to categorize eastern European Jewish refugees, especially urban professional ones, as undesirables.[49]

Despite the recurrence of the plethora theme and continuous denunciation of the invasion of French health care by foreigners, by the fall of 1941 the national council of the Medical Order claimed in its monthly bulletin that "medical care was not assured in several regions as a result of the ban on foreign [*sic*] doctors."[50] This may explain in part why the 16 August 1940 law was replaced by a 22 November 1941 law increasing possibilities for exceptions.[51] Another explanation for the revision might be the realization that foreigner was not the same thing as foreign-fathered, and in fact many doctors who had been kicked out under the original law were very "French" indeed. Their elimination was shocking to their colleagues and patients alike. Reports of angry patients of ousted doctors reached the national council, which noted one case in which a replacement doctor who had taken over the practice of a foreign-fathered doctor was blackballed by the local population.[52]

The revised law expanded the categories for exemption to six: those who were naturalized for reasons of exceptional services rendered to France (the conditions of which would be settled by a future law); French *protégés* or *administrés* from countries under the purview of the Ministry of Colonies; those who had served in the French military and earned a recognized status of combatant; the parent, spouse, widow, or child of someone covered by the previous exemption; those from Alsace and Lorraine who had been reintegrated into French nationality in 1918 (having lost it as a result of the 1871 Franco-German treaty); and those born in France of an unknown father. Article 3 further allowed for an open exception left entirely to the discretion of the Superior Inspection Commission; it replaced the prior law's exception for those who had honored France in science. Article 4 permitted doctors who were banned by the prior law and who were eligible under the new exemptions to request their reintegration. Such candidates were not, however, allowed to practice medicine until a final decision. Finally, Article 5 opened opportunities for *foreigners* to practice medicine. It authorized foreigners covered by diplomatic conventions, with some restrictions, and it provided a general dispensation that was bound to anger many French doctors: any foreigner from any nation could apply for special permission to practice in France.[53]

This apparent easing of restrictions in the 1941 revised law banning foreign-fathered doctors did little to change the reality on the ground. With all the educational and nationality requirements now stacked up against doctors since the 1933 Armbruster law, there was little chance that anyone with fewer than three generations of French ancestors could practice medicine in Vichy France. Referring to the anti-Semitic quota of 11 August 1941, which had been legislated between the two versions of the decree banning foreign-fathered doctors, the state secretary for family and health further specified that the quota against Jews would be taken into account in determining new exceptions to the foreign-father ban. "As this decree deprives a certain number of French Jews of the right to practice medicine, it would be abnormal for such a right to be liberally accorded to foreign Jews," he stated.[54]

Dr. Raymond Grasset, who replaced Serge Huard as state secretary for family and health in April 1942, stated in a speech to a congress of Medical Order department councils that his interpretation was to apply the law restrictively, despite the diplomatic interventions that foreign embassies had made to "fiercely defend" their citizens.[55] He proclaimed that he personally believed that "foreigners [sic] who were harbored in France and who did not perform their duty as combatants in either war should not compete professionally with French practitioners, the majority of whom were combatants." Medical Order council members in attendance responded to this news with "intense and prolonged applause."[56]

Implementation of the Ban

Scholars have published varying statistics on the effects of the foreign-father ban, but none are nationwide or conclusive.[57] The names of banned doctors were published in the government legislative register, the *Journal officiel,* but at this writing no researcher has yet totaled definitive numbers. It is unclear whether these *Journal officiel* figures account for only the appealed decisions or for all doctors affected by the foreign-father ban, many of whom never requested exemptions. Monthly figures of banned doctors were included as appendixes to Medical Order national council circulars issued to department councils and were also published in the *Bulletin de l'Ordre des Médecins,* but such archives have been incompletely conserved.[58] Moreover, documents from official Vichy organs can be unreliable. For example, State Secretary of Health Grasset claimed in August 1942 that 1,853 foreign-fathered doctors had requested an exemption to the ban, and that of these, 1,388 were definitively banned, 400 were definitively authorized, and 65 requests were pending. Grasset was quick to emphasize in a speech to Medical Order department councils that "certain authorized foreign [sic] doctors will never practice because they are Jewish and subject to department quotas."[59] The health secretary's numbers are dubious because they may have included only appeal cases, because the national council commonly reinstated doctors who were wrongly banned by department councils, and because other sources reveal that many more than sixty-five cases were still pending in August 1942.[60] Given the sources, it is not possible to make a conclusive claim as to the number of foreign-fathered doctors who were expelled or retained during Vichy.

Many foreign-fathered doctors struggled for months and even years to be declared exempt from the exclusion. Their cases' winding trails through French bureaucracy reveal much about the zeitgeist of the time: general confusion over how to oust established doctors from their profession; scuffles over professional leadership after the prewar medical unions were dissolved; tensions between the nascent department and national medical councils; conflicts among Vichy organs and personalities; and surprise over the sudden dearth of health care personnel. These factors added to the traditional structural discord that had always existed in the French medical profession between Paris versus province, specialist versus generalist, and practitioner versus elite. A review of a few individual cases will exemplify these tensions and elucidate how the fate of individual doctors often depended on factors unrelated to their personal profiles.

Dr. D.'s profile was the very model of the potential for exemption. Born in Mauritius, he benefited from a nineteenth-century diplomatic convention according Mauritians the right to practice medicine in France. D. was a Catholic who had come to France in his twenties in 1925. Naturalized French in 1934, he earned the French medical *diplôme d'état* with honors in Montpellier in 1935, married a Frenchwoman whose father was a World War I veteran, fathered three French children, and was mobilized in 1939–40. D. had been practicing medicine in Caderousse in the Vaucluse since 1935, where he was the only doctor in town. He was appreciated by the population, and had received a favorable recommendation from the Vaucluse department medical council.[61] He was also the president of the Caderousse Association of Large Families. Nonetheless, his request for an exemption was rejected by the Ministry for Family and Health in August 1941.[62] As the head of a large French family, he was, however, granted an exceptional deferment of the ban for a few months. (Such deferments were the purview of the state secretary for family and health and sparked much protest from French doctors.) Dr. D. dutifully reapplied once the November 1941 revision of the legislation rendered him even more eligible for an exemption. Another recommendation from the Vaucluse department council of the Medical Order praised D. for being an upstanding citizen and doctor, as well as someone free of "any Judeo-Masonic connection."[63] The mayor of the town of Orange also intervened.[64] D.'s case was finally approved. With over two years of uncertainty, Dr. D.'s experience reveals that even a solid case like his was subject to vicissitudes and rejections. Many individuals would not have been able to withstand the two-year wait. Another Mauritian, Dr. Samboo, was of English nationality, but his father was French. Having completed his medical studies in France, he practiced in the Saint-Denis arrondissement of the Seine department, married a Frenchwoman, volunteered for military duty in 1938, and received a recommendation from the mayor of Pierrefitte. Samboo succeeded in having his case supported by a high-level official in Pierre Laval's office, who asked the Superior Inspection Commission to allow Samboo to practice medicine, "at least until the end of hostilities."[65]

Dr. N. F. was initially rejected for exemption despite his stellar profile according to Vichy standards. He was not Jewish. He was born in Paris and resided in the eastern suburb of Rosny-sous-Bois. His mother was French, his father Greek.[66] He was married to a French woman who was a war orphan from World War I. They had four French children. He had been a Paris hospital intern in 1935, and was mobilized in 1939–40 as a lieutenant-doctor. F. was French in every possible way except his father's origins. Yet when F. succeeded in having his dossier brought to the attention of Pétain's secretary, Ménétrel, what made his case so compelling to the secretary was not the risk that a French national would be cut off from his livelihood as a second-class citizen, but that if F. were to be banned, his *wife,* who was also a medical doctor and "100 percent French," would take over the family practice, thereby "reversing the social roles in this family."[67] Ménétrel took this threat to the patriarchal order seriously enough to request that the Superior Inspection Commission consider F.'s case favorably.

Dr. Boris de Lutomsky, an orthodox Russian naturalized French, a graduate of the Montpellier Medical School, and a practicing doctor in Pau, had somehow survived the vise of legislative exclusions tightening around him during the interwar years. Lutomsky saw himself as a well-meaning Russian student who had arrived in 1924 hoping to establish himself in France. Eligible, as a foreigner, to study only for the *diplôme d'université,* he hoped that upon his naturalization he could transform that degree, according to the legislation in place at the time, into a *diplôme d'état,* which granted the right to practice medicine in France. He had taken immediate steps to naturalize, but the lengthy bureaucratic process lasted until 1936, by which time the transformation of diplomas had been forbidden by legislation. Lutomsky felt that he had diligently followed the rules. French medical unions in the 1930s would have painted an entirely different picture of him. They would have seen him as a wily foreigner who had misrepresented himself from the start: he should never have planned to stay in France. As a student of the *diplôme d'université,* he was supposed to immerse himself temporarily in superior French medical culture and return to Russia as an emissary of French science. For the medical unions during the interwar years, the ever-tightening limitations on transformations of *diplômes d'université* into *diplômes d'état* were meant to protect French medicine precisely from people like Lutomsky. The medical unions would have interpreted Lutomsky's tardy naturalization as a highly suspect attempt to avoid military service. Despite the odds, Lutomsky had managed to eke out a medical career with his French citizenship and *diplôme d'université,* working in sanatoria and hospitals since 1936. In 1939 he was offered a job as surgery assistant at a hospital in Pau. When the 16 August 1940 law banned foreign-fathered doctors, it seemed that Lutomsky's medical career in France was finally over. He applied for exemption and beefed up his dossier with numerous attestations to his honor and service. Having served as a doctor in the French army in 1939–40, and being supported by a Captain Beigbeder, *chargé de mission* at the Ministry of the Interior, Lutomsky was able to have his exemption request seconded by the minister of the interior, who pressed the minister for family and health to rule in his favor.[68]

Personal contacts were extremely important for candidates seeking an exception to exclusionary legislation, but doctors also sought help from higher-ups to single out colleagues for exclusion or to advance their own careers at the expense of foreign-fathered doctors. Dr. F. of Lyon wrote Ménétrel in January 1941 to ask the secretary to intervene on his behalf. The prefect of the Drôme department had offered F. a job, thanks to the departure of a Romanian doctor who had been working there a number of years. Dr. F. was about to step into the serendipitous vacancy when the banned Romanian doctor began to resist, citing the 27 November 1940 circular that might allow him to remain in practice because of his marriage to a French schoolteacher. F. wrote to inform Ménétrel of the "audacity of such *métèques*," and requested his help. No sooner said than done. Two months later F. was thanking Ménétrel for his "immediate help."[69]

Ménétrel did not know Dr. F., but personal relations definitely mattered.[70] Ménétrel was willing to help Dr. W. S., who had been a friend of Ménétrel's father. Dr. S. was a Romanian naturalized French in 1908, a Catholic married to a French Protestant, a father of three, a former Paris hospital intern, a recipient of medical honors, and a published author. He had also participated in World Wars I and II, but not enough to earn the veteran's card. In response to S.'s request for help, Ménétrel assured him that his qualifications were sufficient for exemption and promised to speak with the Ministry of Health.[71] Jewish acquaintances of Ménétrel, however, did not always obtain satisfaction from their connections.

By the late summer of 1942, the majority of foreign-fathered doctors had been eliminated from the medical profession, and many of the requests for exemption had been dealt with. Absent a definitive record of the expulsions, statistical samples give an indication of the processes at work in determining doctors' fates. What is clear is that exceptional authorizations of foreign-fathered doctors were rare and that foreign-fathered doctors who were born in France had a greater chance of authorization. The *Journal officiel* figures mention only doctors' birthplace. Place of birth is not the same as father's nationality, which was the basis of the law, but it can be indicative. Those born in Romania were more often among the banned than the exempted. For example, in the months of June and July 1942, fifty doctors were banned, thirty-three of whom had been born in Romania and two in France. Those born in Belgium and Switzerland, though limited in number to begin with, were more likely to be exempted,[72] a factor which suggests that cultural and geographic proximity mattered in the subjective determinations made by department councils and the Superior Inspection Commission. At the same time, those born in the French empire (mostly from the mandates and protectorates of Syria, Lebanon, and

Tunisia) were disproportionately less likely to be authorized than Russians and Armenians. One statistical sample indicates that those affected by the ban were primarily eastern European. Of all doctors born of a foreign father, 70 percent were themselves born in a European country: 42 percent were born in Romania, 12 percent in France, 11 percent in Russia, 5 percent in Poland, and 3 percent in Armenia.[73]

From Xenophobia to Anti-Semitism

Even though in confidential meetings, medical leaders expressed interest in attenuating the impact of the law on "assimilated" doctors, the archives record no public protest against the ban on foreign-fathered doctors. Examples of outspoken approval, often tinged with anti-Semitism, were common. Pierre Mauriac, dean of the Bordeaux Medical School and president of the Gironde Medical Order department council, gave a speech in 1942 declaring: "During the Third Republic, our profession, more than any other, was invaded by more and more *métèques*. The numbers are alarming. We use the word *métèque* deliberately for its pejorative meaning. It establishes the distinction between the scum dumped by their various countries into ours and certain other foreigners whom France can and should welcome, if deriving advantages and honor in exchange for hospitality."[74] Mauriac was the head of a medical school and a department medical council; his audience consisted of forty delegates from department councils, thirty of whom signed his petition; and his speech was reprinted in toto in the *Journal de médecine de Bordeaux*.[75] Although it was possible not to sign the petition, three-quarters of the doctor-delegates did, testifying to the widespread acceptance of Mauriac's views within medical opinion.

Dr. Fernand Querrioux—already an interwar leader of the movement to eliminate naturalized citizens from French medicine—became an even more prominent spokesman once xenophobia and anti-Semitism became the cornerstones of the Vichy regime in 1940. In his book *La médecine et les juifs,* he lambasted his scapegoats for "commercializing" medicine, for "infiltrating" unsuspecting French families with charlatan promises, and for being communists.[76] He claimed, "All French doctors, the real ones, are waiting impatiently for the implementation of this law [banning foreign-fathered French doctors] which targets foreigners only and not Jews. It is true that most *métèque* doctors are Jews."[77]

After the passage of the revision of the foreign-father ban in November 1941, Querrioux objected furiously:

The author of this law is a standup comedian or a clown who wanted to entertain himself at the expense of French Aryan doctors.... A naturalized

Jew remains an unassimilable Jew. And why should French *protégés* and *administrés* have the right to practice in France? Let them go practice in the place of their protection or their administration, but not in France. A Tunisian, Syrian, Moroccan, or Algerian Jew is a Jew vomited up by the Arabs, and cannot consequently claim to practice in France. A military veteran remains a Jew, just as negroes will always be negroes. As a result, there should be no exception for them. As for parents, spouses, widows, and children of veterans? Why not the whole tribe?![78]

Against the fifth article of the law authorizing exceptional foreigners to practice medicine, Querrioux railed, "We know all too well, alas, what the word 'exceptional' means in our still Judaized country."[79] Querrioux's anti-Semitic attacks were all the more striking since the law he was referring to applied only to foreign-fathered doctors. The law had nothing to do with Jews. Yet officials in some of the highest offices of the Vichy regime—the head of state, the prime minister, the head of the CGQJ, and the French ambassador to the occupied territories—passed around this document and discussed Querrioux's views, demonstrating that such discourse was becoming normalized in political channels. Again, the state secretary for health and family gave assurances that the new permissions would not undo the anti-Semitic restrictions enacted in the meantime by an August 1941 decree.[80]

Querrioux was named to head the Institut d'étude des questions juives (IEQJ), the propaganda arm of the regime's CGQJ.[81] A cornerstone of the IEQJ's wartime activity was the mounting of the exhibition "The Jew and France" in Paris's Palais Berlitz in 1941, which included an exhibit on Jews in medicine. It accused Jews of having invaded French medicine and of being charlatans. The panels alleged that 50 percent of doctors in some Parisian neighborhoods were Jewish, and that many doctors found guilty of medical malpractice were Jewish. Querrioux gave a presentation on Jewish doctors and called for their total elimination.[82]

The Groupement corporatif sanitaire français wanted "abortionists," "charlatans," and *métèques* to be banned and indicted.[83] Their brochure called for "the immediate elimination of harmful elements, which the medical corps must rid itself of just as a father expels unworthy sons. Immediate application of the 16 August 1940 law in all its severity to *métèques;* no delay, no misplaced softening will be tolerated for much longer. Revision of the Statute on the Jews and extension of a *numerus clausus* of 3 percent to the liberal professions in favor of Jews with sufficient moral guarantees."[84]

Although the Groupement corporatif sanitaire was a relatively small group of five hundred doctors, dentists, pharmacists, and students, it nonetheless possessed influence via its monthly medical page in the journal *Je suis partout.* One of its leaders was Dr. Paul Guérin, a leader of the 1930s anti-foreigner mobilization, an active member of Action française, the Croix-de-Feu, and Jacques Doriot's Parti populaire français, and a friend of Ménétrel.[85] Dr. Robert Hollier, member of the national council of the Medical Order, was a member.

Another conglomerate of doctors, the Federation of Clubs and Associations of Doctors from the War Front, issued propaganda that consistently amalgamated foreigners, naturalized citizens, and Jews. The federation demanded the establishment of a numerus clausus on Jewish doctors, communicated its platform widely to the Medical Order and medical press, and obtained an audience with the secretary-general for health in January 1941.[86] In February the federation, along with the Union médicale française[87] and the Groupement corporatif sanitaire, was again received by the secretary-general for health and by the Medical Order national council. Together these groups urged the Superior Inspection Commission to minimize exemptions to the foreign-father ban: "The level of a candidate's 'integration into the French community' is a criterion that should be interpreted in a very restrictive sense (as Dr. Huard believes, moreover), and should be concerned only with cases of Belgian, Swiss, White Russian, Native Polish [polonais de race], Mauritian, etc. doctors—easily assimilable elements— and be maximally limited, on the other hand, when concerned with Jewish doctors (Romanians, Polish, or otherwise)."[88] Such a comment exemplifies the burgeoning of a public mélange of xenophobia and anti-Semitism, as well as an ethnicized hierarchization of foreigners.

Such strongly voiced opinions remained at the margins of French medicine: at one point in national council deliberations, one member asked, "What is this Groupement corporatif sanitaire?" to which another member responded dismissively, "They are political-agitator nobodies."[89] The historian Joseph Billig has asserted, however, that extremist professional groups, such as the Association amicale des anciens combattants médecins des corps combattants, were influential in making the anti-Semitic quota in medicine a reality.[90] Anti-Jewish sentiment, moreover, was reflected throughout the medical community among ordinary doctors, especially in instances in which doctors denounced other doctors on the basis of their Jewishness even before a quota against Jewish doctors was enacted. In an August 1940 letter, for example, a Dr. O. from the small village of Entraigues in the Vaucluse wrote to Ménétrel, whom he did not know personally, to complain about a certain Dr. B., a "Tunisian Jew," who had not volunteered for military service and who had allegedly "drained" all the clientele of the region while Dr. O. was mobilized in 1939–40. (Such fears of protecting the professional turf of mobilized doctors were flashpoints during the war and were commonly raised by department medical councils.) Dr. O. described to Ménétrel how Dr. B. was "cunningly practicing his little commerce (you know as well as I do that there is no other way to characterize the 'trade' of these people)."[91] Dr. O. had already complained about B. to the department health inspector and local medical leaders. O.'s focus on Dr. B.'s Jewishness, before even the first Statute on the Jews was promulgated, shows that anti-Semitism was coming out into the open at this critical juncture in the summer of 1940, in a phenomenon known as "anticipatory compliance."[92] What is more, O.'s requests for protection from professional and state authorities, all the way up to Pétain's office, signified an acute economic competitiveness within the medical profession, but also an expectation of state protection, as well as a subscription to Vichy's ideology of national and religious preference.[93]

Anthropological and biological anti-Semitism were also making their way into medical discourse in France. Just as lawyers applied their legal expertise to develop and legitimize exclusionary legislation, doctors during the Vichy era put their credentials behind the promotion of "scientific" racialist doctrines, a practice familiar to medicine since at least the late nineteenth century. The first published assertions in France that Jews were biologically different or inferior appeared in the mid-nineteenth century. As the Dreyfus Affair exploded, respected medical doctors such as Jean-Martin Charcot used "scientific evidence" to claim that Jews had higher incidences of various pathologies. French medical school dissertations were defended on blatantly anti-Semitic topics. Fifty years later during Vichy, such anti-Semitic propaganda served as a historical reference.[94]

Dr. George Montandon took on the mantle of race science. Having studied medicine in Switzerland, he published a book titled *How to Recognize a Jew,* contributed to the Berlitz exhibition "The Jew and France," and directed the journal *L'ethnie française* from 1941 to 1944. He earned a good deal of money doing anthropometric exams, inspecting circumcisions, and delivering "certificates of non-belonging to the Jewish race." Ironically, just days before Montandon was to begin teaching his first course, "Racial and Ethnic Elements of Prehistoric and Contemporary France," at the Paris Medical School in the fall of 1940, he was barred from doing so: born of a Swiss father, he was struck by the foreign-father ban and was not allowed to teach in a French university.[95] Having been nominated by Vichy authorities for this adjunct teaching position without consultation with the medical school faculty, Montandon would probably have faced a cool reception from medical professors and students, as had been the case for a similar nomination of a Professor Labroue to teach a course on the history of Judaism in the Paris School of Letters.[96] Instead, Montandon took over the IEQJ from Captain Paul Sézille in 1943. The following year he was shot by resistants in Clamart.[97]

Another specialist in racial science was Dr. René Martial. Widely recognized for his theories on immigration, sanitary concerns, and racial heredity and mixing, Martial succeeded in teaching an open course on the anthro-biology of race at the Paris Medical School in 1938. During Vichy, Martial was nominated to the CGQJ's Institute for Anthro-Sociology. In immigration debates during the period, his work, like that of Mauco, contributed to a growing consensus that favored a white European immigration over all others.[98]

Dr. Alexis Carrel also played a significant role in putting a medical seal of approval on Vichy policies of exclusion. Trained in Lyon hospitals with experience in the United States, Carrel was awarded a Nobel Prize in medicine in 1912. Pétain appointed him to the new French Foundation for the Study of Human Problems, which was "an attempt to turn wartime France into a huge laboratory of sociobiological experimentation and human engineering," according to the historian Andrés Reggiani.[99] While eugenics never evolved into practice in France as it did in Germany, and while Montandon, Martial, and Carrel were not typical of practicing doctors in France, their concepts of selective immigration and racial biology were taking root in political and scientific discourse and having an impact on medical beliefs.[100] The first French legislation informed by eugenics ideology was the 1942 law mandating a premarital medical examination for both women and men.[101] Gérard Noiriel has noted the significance of the rise of the medical "expert" in elite and powerful sociopolitical networks and the political use of scientific expertise to develop hygiene, immigration, and pro-natalist policy—in short, social Darwinism—during the 1930s and 1940s in France.[102]

Late 1940 and early 1941 were months of uncertainty for Jews in medicine after Article 4 of the first Statute on the Jews presaged a quota in the liberal professions. In fact, the exclusion of Jews from the medical field took place gradually and resulted from a succession of legislative and administrative acts beginning with the banning of Jews from the civil service, then a quota of 3 percent on the number of Jewish students, including medical students, in French universities, and then finally a 2 percent quota on the number of Jews allowed to practice medicine, modeled after the quota for Jewish lawyers.[103] The anti-Semitic quota was signed into law by the decree of 11 August 1941.

Prior to that, in October 1940, the first Statute on the Jews banned Jews from holding positions as civil servants. In the medical field, this raised the question of how to classify hospital doctors, who had multiple functions: tending to hospital patients, teaching medical interns, and maintaining private practices. The common thinking had always been that hospital doctors and surgeons were not civil servants but were merely entrusted with a civil service function. "They earned meager compensation for the patients they treated there, they generally did not have retirement rights, and nearly always had private clients outside the hospital. Therefore their hospital employment was rather an accessory to their profession," argued the state secretary for family and health during vigorous debates among Vichy officials over the issue.[104] The second Statute on the Jews in June 1941 settled the issue. Article 3 explicitly barred Jews from serving in any "public administration or any organization benefiting from state or public concessions or subsidies." Thus Jewish hospital doctors were banned like all Jewish civil servants.[105] Jews holding ministerial medical positions and faculty positions in French medical schools or working in social insurance capacities and as school doctors were also ousted.[106]

Still, discussion between hospitals and the CGQJ continued well into 1942 on how to interpret the rules for hospital personnel.[107] One particular problem centered on whether interns and externs were to be considered civil servants (full ban), doctors (2 percent quota), or students (3 percent quota). The state secretary for family and health argued in July 1941 that it would be "illogical" to ban Jews from these training opportunities since the medical profession was not entirely off limits to them.[108] But after a summer of muscular correspondence with the CGQJ, the secretary ultimately backed down.[109] The ban was implemented retroactively: employed interns were given two months to vacate their positions.[110] By 1942, there were only four Jewish interns (exempted because of their military service credentials) still working in Paris hospitals, including Alexander Minkowski.[111] Born in Paris of a foreign father, Minkowski survived as long as he did in the Paris hospital system partly because he had never declared himself born of a foreign father. By early 1944, all four interns had left the hospital.[112] Over time, Vichy and Nazi authorities transferred Jewish doctors still authorized to work in Paris public hospitals, along with Jewish hospital patients, to the Rothschild Hospital in the twelfth arrondissement, which became an antechamber for Jewish prisoners at the Drancy transit camp.[113]

Vichy next turned to limiting the number of Jewish students at French universities. State Secretary for National Education Jérôme Carcopino justified the anti-Semitic student quota to Pétain in these terms:

> The great principle of justice that gave all French persons equal access to state functions was very often violated by the Jews. For them, civil service and the liberal professions held a special attraction, especially because they were high-ranking and important careers. Against this continuous intrusion, recent laws have been enacted in reaction. The laws banned Jews from high state positions; they excluded them from most of the civil service; and finally they equitably reduced their numbers in the liberal professions. It was the duty of the state secretary for national education and youth to draw the necessary consequences from these measures. If the number of Jewish doctors or lawyers is reduced, if their admission to government positions is limited, there is no

point in allowing them to earn diplomas, which for them would just be empty titles. Since Jewish doctors are not tolerated as doctors, it is useless to let them study medicine.... Such are the considerations which have ordered the present law. Its purpose is to institute a numerus clausus on students since one exists in the professions to which such studies lead.[114]

The law of 21 June 1941 imposed a 3 percent quota on Jewish students in French universities.[115] Carcopino considered that the "Aryanization" of medical studies should be prioritized over other disciplines,[116] probably because it was believed that more Jewish students studied medicine than other fields.[117]

After the student quota, ambassadors from Egypt, Hungary, the United States, Uruguay, Brazil, Turkey, and Holland confronted the CGQJ and the French Ministry of National Education, protesting the treatment of their Jewish nationals in French universities.[118] Asked by diplomats to "favor" foreign Jewish students by exempting them from the quota, Vichy officials were drawn back into prewar debates about the role of foreign students in French universities.[119] Some considered ranking foreign Jewish students over French Jewish students. A report from an interministerial conference held at the CGQJ in November 1941 stated: "The application of the Jewish legislation risks reducing French influence.... There is good reason to make a distinction between foreign students chased from their own countries by laws against Jews and those who come from countries which have no such legislation. For the latter, who are attracted by the brilliance of our culture, we need a special law to grant them exceptional permission."[120]

As we saw in chapter 2, legislation in the 1930s had already isolated foreign students in French medical schools into the *diplôme d'université* program rather than the *diplôme d'état* program, which gave the right to practice in France. Even the state secretary for national education recognized that adding the anti-Semitic quota to the arsenal of existing barriers against foreign medical students would have been overkill, and suggested as much to the CGQJ. But the CGQJ insisted that an interministerial conference in August 1941 had already resolved that the anti-Semitic quota would apply to every degree program.[121] The CGQJ reasserted the quota's stipulations: "The proportion of 3 percent instituted by the law of 21 June applies to all Jewish students whether French or foreign. No measure of discrimination has been envisaged for the latter."[122]

The Anti-Semitic Quota in Medicine

Within confidential meetings, two or three members of the national council of the Medical Order voiced disapproval of the notion of an anti-Semitic quota as it was being drafted into legislation in the spring of 1941. Dr. Henri

Grenet stated, "I find it abominable, because there are surely French Jews who have conducted themselves properly; I believe that taking away the means to work from such people is abominable; they are French and they have the right." Another national council member, Dr. Paul Giraud, countered: "I am very opposed to the Jews and I believe they have caused much harm in the nation, and I did everything possible to prevent them from taking over leadership positions. Those who have been in France for several generations have caused much harm, but ultimately, they acquired rights and we cannot put them out on the street."[123] In the following monthly meeting, Dr. Roux Berger derided the anticipated quota's conditions: "It is hypocrisy! An *état-civil* that dates to 1790? How could one know? Five generations? This means going back to about 1750. It is monstrous!" He went on to note, "I claim that if we had waited to chase out all the foreigners that we had to chase out before making the Statute on the Jews, since surely three of every ten foreigners are Jews, there would not have been a need for a numerus clausus, and we would have avoided all scandal and all kinds of injustice in France."[124] These individual reactions found no echo beyond the private deliberations of the national council.

The council also debated ways to evade the impending measure. Council members hoped that an anti-Semitic quota would instead be imposed at the beginning of medical studies rather than retroactively upending the established careers of Jewish doctors. They wrote to Health Secretary-General Huard in May 1941: "It would be unfair to halt the studies of Jews already admitted to medical school and also to forbid a segment of French Jewish medical doctors to continue practicing their profession. Furthermore, it seems that the law against foreigners [*sic*] will reduce the number of Jewish doctors practicing in France by a significant proportion."[125] The council's proposal was circulated among various government organs in the spring of 1941 as the legislation was being drafted. In May 1941, Huard wrote to the CGQJ, seconding the opinion of the Medical Order's national council: "I allow myself to add that it does not seem to me that this legislation is welcomed very favorably by the French medical corps. All of the conversations I have had on the topic with different medical groups, in particular with the Medical Order, confirmed for me that the general wish was for a numerus clausus on admission to medical school, without modifying the situation of Jews currently practicing. As for foreign Jews or Jews born of a foreign father, I remind you that they are subject to the 16 August 1940 law and their eviction is being carried out accordingly."[126] The proposal, which was contained in interministerial communication and ultimately went unheeded, was the sole expression of misgivings about the anti-Semitic quota in medicine. Huard's qualms should not be overestimated since he immediately went on to comment, article by article, on the draft decree, thereby conceding its existence and legitimizing it with his input.

Yet the proposal is significant in that Huard included a reminder to the CGQJ that Jews of foreign origin were already being evicted by the 16 August law, and emphasized that *foreign* Jews were the most unwanted category in French medicine. Once foreign-fathered doctors were banned, the profession as a whole did not have a burning desire to exclude French Jews. The medical councils were in fact still in the midst of implementing the foreign-father ban when the regime started drafting the anti-Semitic quota. At the Seine department medical council meeting in August 1941, a member responded to the quota, "It is shocking to take such measures against French Jews while foreigners, Jewish or non Jewish, continue to practice illegally."[127]

Whereas some doctors on the national council genuinely believed that a quota on Jewish students would be more equitable than a quota on Jewish doctors, it is obvious from national council deliberations that getting another authority besides themselves to implement the anti-Semitic quota was the main motivation behind their proposal. Dr. Marc Nédélec of the national council said, "If this all comes to pass, it is necessary that one has the sense that it does not come from us."[128] In his communication to the CGQJ, Huard focused on Article 8, which spelled out who was responsible for designating the Jewish doctors to be authorized or expelled. He rejected the idea of having such responsibility given to doctors: "Article 8 will not be accepted by the national council of the Medical Order. The term 'will designate' will cause doctors to bristle." Instead, Huard proposed to reverse the language of the law so that the department councils "*will be authorized to designate*... Jews who *will be admitted* to practice medicine in the department."[129] The CGQJ had no patience for such niceties. The final text of the law stated, "The council will designate... Jewish doctors... who must cease practicing their profession." The Medical Order councils were going to implement the anti-Semitic quota, and the CGQJ was not going to euphemize their role.

After much expectancy, the decree regulating Jews in French medicine was signed on 11 August 1941.[130] It was lengthier than the Vichy law against French doctors with foreign fathers, largely because a 2 percent quota entailed much more detail compared to an outright ban. Provisions also needed to be spelled out for future Jewish doctors, since the anti-Semitic legislation was deemed permanent.[131]

The quota capped the number of Jewish doctors allowed to practice medicine at 2 percent of the non-Jewish doctors in a given department. Explicitly modeled on the legal quota passed one month earlier,[132] the quota stipulated that the number of Jewish doctors in each department could not exceed the number of practicing Jewish doctors as of 25 June 1940, the date of the armistice. This meant that Jewish doctors excluded from urban areas could not move in order to practice in departments where there were fewer Jews. Military veterans would be retained even if their numbers exceeded the 2 percent quota, but they could not exceed the total number of Jews practicing medicine as of 25 June 1940. As in the legal profession, the second Statute on the Jews created an important gender distinction regarding the veteran exemptions: whereas Jewish men could be exempt from anti-Semitic measures for veteran status or war citations, women—who were forbidden to join the military—had to fulfill stricter criteria by proxy: Jewish women doctors had to be the wife, daughter, or mother of someone killed in action, not merely a veteran. In addition, the decree authorized an exemption for doctors of eminent professional merit.

If there was any room left under the 2 percent quota after war veterans were included, the Medical Order department councils, like the law bars, decided which Jews to expel and which to retain. The leaders of the local corporatist organs were thus the ones to rank their Jewish colleagues, leaving "an open door for personal enmities, professional rivalries, and the temptation to eliminate a competitor."[133] Jewish doctors' appeals of department council decisions would be considered by the national council of the Medical Order. Cases of eminent merit would have to be proposed by the Order, approved by the CGQJ, and enacted by the Health Secretariat.[134]

In the December 1941 meeting of the Medical Order's national council, members expressed exasperation over the size and complexity of the task demanded of them. Because the appeal process was going to take a long time and was going to hobble Jewish doctors' careers, one council member drafted a proposal to the Ministry of Health requesting that Jewish doctors be authorized to practice until their appeals were ruled upon. This provisional permission was granted to foreign-fathered doctors but not to Jewish doctors.[135]

As we have seen, Huard had asserted during the drafting of legislation that doctors would scrupulously resist the responsibility of designating Jewish colleagues for elimination. On the contrary, Medical Order department and national council members implemented the quota thoroughly and to completion. Some members of the national council, however, did privately reiterate reservations—as they had done during the drafting of the decree—once they were faced with an actual caseload in early 1942. Although the national council of the Medical Order did not make the initial decisions on Jewish doctors (the department councils did), the national council was required to rule on each appeal and to propose exemptions. In a January 1942 national council meeting, Dr. Charles Gernez-Rieux objected, "I find this very disturbing, very unjust, and it is not our role." Dr. Armand Vincent asked, "Can't we simply declare ourselves incompetent to decide?" Dr. Gernez-Rieux stated, "I insist that I do not accept to judge." Council president Leriche responded to these qualms, "We must accept our responsibilities, and it is our taking of responsibility that will establish our authority." Secretary-General Charles Laurent offered council members a way out: "You will not be judging the thing in itself, but you will simply be saying, 'The department council has ruled properly or improperly.'" After more expressions of discomfort, Nédélec spoke: "Let's consider the worst. If we all agree not to do it, it means resignation." Leriche responded:

> This is not a medical question, it is a political question. We must apply the law by thinking that it is perhaps the best way to protect the interests of those whom we are here to defend. Each of us, as a member of the council, is only just obeying the law. If each of us consults the cases coming from our regions, this will give a certain sense of security. I will propose another solution:...If there are any dossiers that seem particularly interesting to us, we can write a letter to the minister of health...who will pass it to the CGQJ, which will likely respond in the negative; we will have done what we were able to.

Laurent finally proposed a way to shift the blame: if the national council consulted the Medical Order's legal advisers to ensure that the law was being followed properly, the council could conclude each case by saying, "This is the opinion of our legal experts." Leriche settled the discussion: "It is thus decided. Next item on the agenda."[136]

Despite this momentary uncertainty, Nédélec's suggestion of a mass resignation was rapidly dismissed, and the national council of the Medical Order duly assumed the task of implementing the anti-Semitic quota in medicine. The council never once publicly denounced the quota. No council member resigned in protest. By August 1942, an update on the quota published in its bulletin proclaimed: "The national council has recognized that according to the decree, the department councils, and itself in cases of appeal, are masters of the entire issue of the numerus clausus. Consequently, we are in charge of verifying the calculations and rankings done by the health inspector. . . . In addition, the national council has decided that its corporatist bodies are themselves directly in charge of evaluating the quality of Jewishness in regard to the laws in question."[137]

Implementation of the Quota against Jewish Doctors

Although the archives rarely disclose the ultimate fate of individual Jewish doctors, they do reveal the dominant hierarchies and values of the Vichy regime. From the ways in which the exemptions were prioritized, from the ways in which Jews presented their credentials, and from the inexhaustible debates among the Medical Order leaders and Vichy bureaucrats in the Health Ministry and CGQJ over the fates of individual doctors, one comes to understand how the possible and the impossible were defined for Jews in France in 1940–41.

Given the long-standing French ban on the official gathering of statistics regarding religion, no one knew how many Jews were practicing medicine in France in 1940. Propaganda from groups such as the Action française could be relied on for inflated numbers. The Vichy decree of 11 August 1941 establishing the anti-Semitic quota and requiring Jewish doctors to declare themselves to their Medical Order marked the beginning of a new era. As a result of this novel census, the national council of the Medical Order learned that out of 5,980 doctors in 1940 in the Seine department, 918, or about 15 percent, were Jewish.[138] In less urban areas, the percentage was much lower: 8 of 154 doctors (6 percent) in the Nièvre were Jewish, 19 of 638 (3 percent) in Alpes-Maritimes, and 3 of 198 (1.5 percent) in the Pyrénées-Orientales.[139] In the Seine, the quota's absolute maximum—the number of Jews in practice as of 25 June 1940—was moot since Jewish doctors in the department numbered over 2 percent on that date. Since the Seine department quota was entirely filled by veterans, however, no Jewish doctor without military credentials could be retained. This had a particularly nefarious effect on women doctors, who had to have had a male relative killed in action in order to qualify for exemption. Although women made up 12 percent of the declared Jewish doctors in the Seine, they were only 3.5 percent of the exempted doctors.[140]

Of the 918 Jewish doctors in the Seine department before the quota, the Seine council eliminated 712 and allowed 203 to remain in practice as of January 1943. Every one of the 203 authorized Jews had military credentials,[141] but 320 Jewish doctors in the Seine had veteran status, and so, according to the letter of the law and the ideological precepts of the National Revolution, all 320 should have been authorized.[142] The Seine department council strictly implemented the quota even beyond the dictates of the law. Of these Jewish doctors authorized to practice in the Seine, 189 were exempt because of veteran or other military status, 7 held the Légion d'honneur, and the rest filled the other automatic exemption criteria. About 50, or one-fourth, of the exempted Jewish doctors in the Seine were born outside France, with the largest numbers coming from Romania (19) and Russia (13).[143] According to Vergez, another 13 percent of the automatic exemptions in the Seine department were accorded to Jewish doctors born in Algeria, having been stripped of French nationality.[144] As the historian Bernard Laguerre has proven, the number of Jews denaturalized by the Vichy regime was vastly disproportionate: whereas 5 percent of all naturalized French citizens since 1927 were Jewish, 40 percent of those who were denaturalized were Jewish.[145]

Veterans or not, at least 250 of the 712 Jewish doctors who were expelled from the Seine department appealed to the national medical council.[146] Some tried to be nominated for the eminent merit exception.[147] The CGQJ warned the Seine department medical council not to propose too many names or else risk having them all rejected. Ultimately, the Seine council gave more weight to family background and length of family residence in France than to professional merit, on the understanding that this was in line with CGQJ prerogatives and would yield the greatest number of approvals. This hierarchization had two implications. First, it meant that any Jewish doctor of foreign origin who had managed to survive the foreign-father ban in the Seine department was unlikely to be proposed for exemption from the anti-Semitic quota. Second, by prioritizing heredity over meritocracy, the medical leadership agreed to define its "insiders" according to Vichy's ideological terms rather than the traditional principles of the medical profession. Wishing to be ready with a list when the CGQJ called, the Seine council multiplied its meetings in late 1941 and early 1942. During this process, as Nahum shows, "step by step, they entered into the system of exclusion and they accepted measures which they had initially considered iniquitous; they actively collaborated with their implementation."[148] By the end of 1942, the question of how to remove Jewish and foreign-fathered doctors, which had previously dominated Seine council meetings, no longer appeared in the minutes.

The Seine-et-Oise department counted 874 non-Jewish doctors, which meant that seventeen Jewish doctors could be retained under the quota. The number of Jewish doctors practicing as of 25 June 1940, however, was fifty-nine. Of these, twenty-four had been eliminated in the meantime by the ban on foreign-fathered doctors. According to the letter of the law, only seventeen Jews would be allowed, but if more than that number had military credentials, they could be retained up to a maximum of fifty-nine. Nineteen Jewish doctors qualified automatically as military veterans and were authorized. The Seine-et-Oise council was so vigilant in excluding foreigners and Jews that it was regularly reprimanded by the prefect for taking enforcement into its own hands.[149]

Outside the Paris region there were far fewer Jewish doctors. In the Puy-de-Dôme, nine Jewish doctors were retained out of about fifteen who were practicing there before the quota. The Eure-et-Loir counted nine Jews among its 146 doctors: 2 percent of the 137 non-Jewish doctors meant that only two of them would be allowed to remain. In the Pyrénées-Orientales, the three Jewish doctors were permitted to remain in practice since they numbered fewer than 2 percent of the non-Jewish doctors. The two Jewish doctors in the Aude might have been retained under the quota, since there were 210 non-Jewish doctors, if both of them had not already been eliminated by the foreign-father ban. Two Jewish candidates in the Lozère were not retained because there were no Jewish doctors in practice in the Lozère on 25 June 1940. The same was true in Aveyron. In the Nièvre, there were eight Jewish doctors to 146 non-Jewish doctors: six of them had to go. Thirty Jewish doctors were practicing in Marseille before the defeat, but given the city's location as a refuge and transit point for Jews in 1941, the number of declared Jewish doctors wishing to be included in the quota swelled to over ninety. The quota allowed for eighteen. Fourteen Jewish doctors qualified automatically; the department medical council chose the remaining four on its own.[150]

Procedures for calculating quotas were revised in early 1942. In departments with 76 to 125 non-Jewish doctors, two Jewish doctors would be allowed to practice; in departments with 126 to 175 non-Jewish doctors, three Jewish doctors were allowed; in departments with 176 to 225 non-Jews, four Jewish doctors were allowed, and so on.[151] The rationale behind liberalizing the calculation of the 2 percent quota, also done for lawyers, was likely due to the dawning recognition that a shortage of professionals was hurting the delivery of basic health care and judicial functioning.

Department medical councils were charged with issuing a favorable or unfavorable opinion on exemption cases and then forwarding the requests to the national medical council. In one case, the Haute-Vienne department medical council forwarded the exemption request of a Dr. T. but declined to add a favorable or unfavorable opinion, a telling absence given that issuing an opinion was one of the corporatist order's main prerogatives. T. was a graduate of the Paris Medical School, married to a Frenchwoman, and greatly esteemed by the local Sereilhac population in the Haute-Vienne. But T. was not naturalized (his two attempts to naturalize in the 1930s had been rejected by French authorities and his third attempt was pending), and he was Jewish. His December 1941 exemption dossier was filled with letters of attestation from the Sereilhac mayor, the parish priest, and other local figures. The consensus was that attracting and maintaining a doctor in such a modest-sized town was difficult, and Dr. T. had won everyone over with his devotion to providing care day and night, traveling on his bicycle, and without financial motive. His supporters pleaded to medical and government authorities that with the gasoline shortage, no other doctor from neighboring towns would be able to care for Sereilhac's residents if T. were kicked out of the profession. The CGQJ responded in January 1942 that T. would fail to meet conditions for an exemption based on eminent professional merit. Case closed.[152] Despite a desperate need for T.'s expertise and the strong support of Sereilhac's residents, the department medical council made only a limp effort to help him, and the CGQJ preempted a proper exemption request. The cyclist was shut out, and the small town of Sereilhac went without a doctor.

The department medical council in the Tarn-et-Garonne made more of an effort on behalf of a Dr. U., adding to his dossier not only proof of his veteran status but also attestations to his professional merits. This factor caused problems for U., however, because the CGQJ chose to classify his exemption request as based on eminent professional merit, which was not automatic, rather than on his military veteran status, which was. Accordingly, the CGQJ proceeded to determine that U. did not qualify for eminent merit and forced the department council to rescind his authorization. From January 1942 until May 1943, Dr. U.'s case was passed around among the decision makers—seventeen months of correspondence over whether the quota in the Tarn-et-Garonne allowed for three Jews or two. In rare defiance, the national council of the Medical Order repeatedly came to U.'s defense.[153] Nevertheless, once the state secretary for family and health seconded the CGQJ decision, U.'s application was conclusively denied.[154]

Even when there was local support for particular Jewish doctors, the CGQJ overruled nearly all proposals for exemption. In December 1941, Dr. A. U. appealed her removal from the medical profession by arguing that her family had been in France for over six generations, and that she had never sought a clientele-based private practice but had always worked in laboratories and in social services. U.'s argument about not seeking clients spoke directly to doctors' fears about competition for patients. The Dordogne medical council supported her request for an exemption, as did the regional representative of the Health Ministry and the regional CGQJ, who agreed that she seemed worthy of the "eminent merit" exception. Despite this support—unusual in itself—CGQJ chief Xavier Vallat refused to grant her an exemption.[155]

In other instances, overzealous attention to detail by department councils put local Jewish doctors in jeopardy. In one case, the president of the Basses-Pyrénées medical council in Pau requested permission from the CGQJ for two Jewish doctors to work for free in a clinic, even though it was unnecessary to query the CGQJ about charitable work by banned Jewish doctors. The regional CGQJ official in Toulouse, Captain Joseph Lécussan, rejected the request, declaring, "If these Jews are asking to work in a clinic without remuneration, it is because they are absolutely planning on getting a clientele out of it, and it would be highly naïve to believe in their disinterestedness."[156]

In another case, the Gers department council had included four Jews in its quota, but the CGQJ decided that only three were permitted. Furthermore, the CGQJ protested that all four were naturalized citizens, that one might even be a foreigner, and that none of them had military service credentials. Much correspondence was exchanged over this issue during the first half of 1942 among the CGQJ, the Gers prefect, and the president of the department medical council. In the meantime, local doctors in the Gers department had denounced a fifth doctor, a Romanian Jew, for practicing medicine illegally. The CGQJ ordered the Gers prefect to arrest and imprison him.[157]

Personal contacts proved important for doctors seeking to appeal their ejection. Even Dr. Victor Balthazard, the leader of the movement against naturalized citizens and dean of the Paris Medical School during the interwar years, was forced to ask Vallat in January 1942 for a favor for his niece's husband, Dr. G. R. A French-born Jewish doctor, R. was married to Balthazard's brother's daughter, who was considered "Aryan" according to the dossier. Apparently Balthazard had been too busy leading the campaign against *métèques* in French medicine to have made the acquaintance of his nephew at the Paris Medical School in the early 1930s. Although R. was technically not a *métèque* because he was French-born, Balthazard had regularly scapegoated medical students of "Romanian" origin, a circumlocution used in the 1930s by many anti-Semites who conflated naturalized and Jewish doctors. In May 1942 the CGQJ notified Balthazard that it could pull no strings since the decision rested with the Medical Order.[158] This was untrue because the CGQJ was solely responsible for approving exemptions for non-veterans beyond the quota limits. It was also uncharacteristic of the CGQJ to claim to be less powerful than the Medical Order. This refusal to grant a personal favor to Balthazard potentially stemmed from his corporatist crusade against state control of medicine: during the first half of the Vichy era, Balthazard had been an outspoken critic of statism. Leader of the largest interwar medical union, and excluded from Vichy's Medical Order councils, Balthazard also decried the dissolution of the medical unions. As for G. R.'s fate, corporatist-statist battles made little difference: both Balthazard's clan and the CGQJ were anti-Semitic.

Just as Ménétrel, Pétain's right-hand man, was solicited by individuals about the ban on foreign-fathered doctors, he was petitioned both by Jews appealing their expulsion and by anti-Semites denouncing their colleagues. Ménétrel's abundant correspondence proves that for doctors to receive an exemption, they had to endure a veritable "soldier's obstacle course."[159] The circumstances in which he chose to lift a finger for an acquaintance, or not, are also revelatory. Ménétrel, for example, readily helped his close Jewish friend André Meyer get his war citation ratified so he would be able to practice, but Ménétrel did nothing for Meyer's deported parents.[160]

In response to a request for help from his half-Jewish friend Dr. H. N. in August 1940, Ménétrel expounded: "I won't teach you anything new by saying that the current anti-Semitic movement is becoming more and more defined, and is impressive more for its indiscrimination and blindness than for its actual violence. You [*tu*] know me well enough to know that I do not subscribe to this type of sentiment. There is, however, one sentiment that I do have: that too many bad Jews have imprudently taken up too much space and too much importance in French public life and that they are among those who have hurled us into the catastrophe in which we find ourselves." Ménétrel went on to reveal the balance of power between Vichy and occupying authorities: "What will become of this [anti-Semitic] movement, what measures will we be obliged to take? It is impossible to foresee right now. Our enemies absolutely do not dictate our actions, and this is, I believe, a completely spontaneous movement of desperate people mortified to find themselves so low, who seek to assuage their rancor anywhere and on anyone." Putting his friend Dr. N. in the category of a "true and excellent Frenchman," Ménétrel nonetheless abstained from helping him find a job, and concluded his response to N.'s request for assistance with the words "Keep in touch."[161]

Dr. B. F.'s case reveals power plays between state and corporatist authorities. F. had served as a provisional hospital intern in Toulon under Dr. G. Laurès, who was the president of the Var medical department council. F. had been practicing medicine in the town of Sainte-Maxime as of March 1941 until colleagues informed the Var council that he had a Jewish grandparent. Even though no written denunciation was made, the Var medical council asked the CGQJ to open an investigation into F.'s Jewishness. His case was sent to the CGQJ along with those of five other Var doctors suspected of being Jewish. In August 1942 the CGQJ determined that F. was Jewish. After he produced baptismal certificates for himself and his parents but not for his grandparents, the Var medical council continued to petition the CGQJ for its input but in the meantime expelled him in September 1942. The national council rejected his appeal one month later.[162] Dr. F. subsequently produced baptismal certificates for his grandparents and contacted Ménétrel, with whom he was acquainted, to intercede on his behalf. When Ménétrel inquired about the case in November 1942, the CGQJ quickly reversed itself, claiming that in fact F. should *not* be considered Jewish. With his certificate of non-belonging in the Jewish race in hand, F. was readmitted to the Var Medical Order. Ex post facto, when Ménétrel inquired how this whole affair had come to pass, Laurès defended the Var council's conduct of "non-precipitation" and "our spirit of tact," and volubly blamed the CGQJ's "légèreté."[163] Three important conclusions emerge from this case. First, the entire matter originated with oral denunciations by local doctors. Second, the Var council behaved proactively to eliminate F. and others "suspected" of being Jewish. Once the process began, the national council had little influence over either the department council below it or the CGQJ above it. Third, F.'s ban from medical practice would not have been reversed without Ménétrel's intervention, thus indicating that other eligible individuals, if lacking in personal connections, were likely not authorized.

Dr. M. L.-K., one of the best-known lung specialists in France, also solicited Ménétrel's help, but he was not as lucky as Dr. F. Ménétrel wrote the Haute-Garonne department council in December 1941 to gather information about L.-K., noting, "I don't think there is a reason to undo anything, but I would still be grateful if you communicated any elements of a response for me, and confidentially." Department medical council president Dr. E. Roques responded that the quota had already been filled in the Haute-Garonne, and that L.-K. did not fulfill any conditions for exception. In addition, since the department council had already asked the CGQJ for an eminent merit exception for one Jewish doctor, it could not envision asking for another one. Roques also noted to Ménétrel that L.-K. had approached some doctors around Toulouse for work, and they in turn tattled to the council.[164] Dr. L.-K. was probably trying to be hired as a medical assistant in a doctor's office, but to no avail.

Ultimately, the terrifying policies of the Occupation authorities forced the few exempted Jewish doctors to abandon their profession as well. Even André Meyer, an elite former Paris intern and close friend of Ménétrel, was unable to escape the stranglehold. The desperation he expressed to Pétain's private secretary in November 1943 exemplifies the experience of close to a thousand Jewish doctors who were put out of work: "What will become of me? What will become of my wife and my children? What will become of my unfortunate parents? What should I do?"[165]

The department councils of the Medical Order were the front line of decision making over the fate of their Jewish colleagues: they ensured that Jewish doctors declared themselves as Jews, they evaluated the dossiers, they decided who fulfilled exemption criteria, they ranked them, and they notified Jews of their expulsion from the profession. Overall, historians have found evidence that the Saône-et-Loire and the Bouches-du-Rhône department medical councils were zealous in their application of the anti-Semitic quota, and that the Nord, Gironde, Haute-Garonne, Dordogne, and Aveyron department medical councils made some attempts to attenuate the application of the quota.[166] While departmental archives reveal a few examples of leniency toward Jewish doctors, in general the department medical councils, in their rush to eliminate Jews, regularly accused the national council of dragging its feet on deciding appeals and exemptions from the anti-Semitic quota, just as they had accused the Superior Inspection Commission of delaying with regard to appeals from doctors born of foreign fathers. On numerous occasions the national council reminded department councils that its workload was overwhelming. The national council noted in one instance that for the Seine department alone it had evaluated 250 exemption requests that had "not been able to be accepted" by the department council.[167] The use of such euphemistic language illustrates that even within closed medical circles, there was a certain denial about medical leaders' participation in anti-Semitic actions. No such guarded language was used in ejecting foreign-fathered doctors.

The national council admonished department councils for poorly vetting Jewish doctors' credentials, for adding unnecessary cases to the national council's docket, and for subjecting the Medical Order to potential accusations of denial of justice.[168] A dossier of 170 appeals decided by the Medical Order national council between July 1942 and December 1943 provides an indication of typical outcomes for Jewish doctors banned by their department medical councils.[169] Of the 170 appeals, the national council rejected 130 outright (thus confirming the department councils' decisions) and reauthorized eight Jewish doctors improperly expelled from their department medical orders. The national council sent another seven cases back to their department councils for reconsideration of their merits, regardless of a tardy declaration of Jewishness.[170] The national council proposed eight names to the CGQJ for exemption on the grounds of eminent professional merit.[171] It proposed another six Jewish doctors for exemption on the grounds of exceptional family service to France, and though it declined to recommend another six on the same grounds, it informed those doctors that they could apply for exemption directly to the CGQJ. The national council referred another six to the CGQJ to determine if they were Jewish; such action was unlikely to conclude positively for the candidates. A large majority of these appeals came from the Seine department. The national council ruled on 125 of these cases during one monthly meeting in July 1942, confirming concerns raised by national council members regarding their inability to process the overwhelming number of cases fairly. According to this appeals dossier, the CGQJ exempted three doctors for exceptional family service to France.[172]

Although the national council corrected some of the department councils' precipitous expulsions, it rejected three-quarters of the appeals in this sample.[173] Indeed, the national council claimed about itself that "upon demand" of persons filing an appeal, the council "has generally refused to favorably decide supplementary readmissions that would have the effect, because of the interplay of the 2 percent maximum, of an automatic elimination of an equal number of Jewish doctors already authorized [by the department councils], and whose merits we cannot judge."[174]

The national council went about the business of eliminating Jewish and foreign-fathered doctors from the profession without acknowledging the humanitarian consequences of its actions. For example, in the late July 1942 meeting of the national council, no mention was made of the recent Vélodrome d'Hiver roundup of Jews, which had, for the first time, awakened popular sympathy for Jews in French society. The absence of comment is especially noteworthy because doctors were called upon to care for the imprisoned Jews. Instead, the national council of the Medical Order proceeded with its regular monthly agenda of examining appeals from Jewish doctors, rejecting more than 75 percent of them.[175]

As for the law profession, the CGQJ always interpreted anti-Semitic legislation in the most restrictive way. It yielded rarely to the occasional pressure from other government officials such as Ménétrel and the health secretaries, and only after fierce resistance.[176] Often the CGQJ accused the Medical Order of laxity and pressured the department and national councils. In 1942, for example, the CGQJ claimed that the Tarn department medical council had kept three Jews in practice but the quota was for two: the council needed to expel one Jew. The Basses-Pyrénées council had kept two Jews in practice but the quota was for one: one of them needed to go.[177] The CGQJ's obsessive diligence was not attenuated by the small size of the task. Given the legislative dictates and the ultimate authority of the CGQJ, no medical leader refused to participate in the whole process. No doctor resigned from the department or national councils. None protested publicly. Although it was possible during Vichy for practicing doctors to manifest solidarity with Jews without reprisal, recorded cases of such behavior are rare.[178]

German occupying authorities pressed Vichy actors on a few occasions with regard to the quota against Jewish doctors. For example, a few weeks after the quota became law in August 1941, the commander of German military forces in France informed the French government delegate that any exemptions must be subject to his express agreement.[179] When CGQJ head Louis Darquier de Pellepoix requested in 1943 that Jewish doctors be exempt from the prohibition on telephone usage, SS Obersturmführer Heinz Roethke responded in the negative.[180] That the CGQJ head made this request of the Germans in favor of Jewish doctors was an aberration. In fact, the Medical Order had initiated the request. Claiming that "in all matters, the national council has tried to reconcile its duty of medical fraternity with the concern of correctly implementing the law," the national council publicized its gesture in the Medical Order bulletin.[181]

The CGQJ was much more likely to coordinate repression with the Nazis. Under pressure from German authorities, the CGQJ confronted the Seine department medical council in early 1943 about Jewish doctors whose figures surpassed the 2 percent quota.[182] Roethke sent a strongly worded missive to the CGQJ titled "Exercise of Important Professions by Jews," in which he warned, "I intend to take the most energetic measures in regard to the intolerable situation" of Jews holding influential positions. He demanded that the CGQJ provide lists of all Jews authorized as doctors, dentists, pharmacists, lawyers, notaries, judges, professors, teachers, and top civil servants.[183] Pledging his commitment to eliminate every possible Jew from the profession, CGQJ cabinet director Joseph Antignac assured Roethke that he would double-check the credentials of the authorized Jewish doctors in the Seine and added, "I may be mistaken but it seems to me very unlikely that 203 Jewish doctors hold the required military titles to benefit from the exemptions." Antignac went on to propose a more expedient solution: "As soon as I have the lists I will forward them to you. Not afraid to affirm my point of view to you on this topic, I am persuaded that total deportation would simplify all of these issues."[184]

One month later Antignac sent the Nazis a list of Jewish practitioners in the Seine: all of the 207 (not 203) doctors had valid authorizations for exemption.[185] One can only wonder what the Nazi commander did with the complete list of names and addresses. In any case, few of the authorized Jewish doctors were likely to be tranquilly peering down throats and writing prescriptions in 1943. It is far more probable that their situation resembled that of the other seven hundred or so banned Jewish doctors from the Seine department increasingly under life-threatening circumstances. As in the legal profession, Jews banned from their livelihood had good reason to join the Resistance movement; some were among the founders of groups such as the Front national des médecins and the Comité médical de la Résistance.[186]

Temporary Replacements for Absent Doctors

It has been suggested that one reason why methods for calculating the quota of authorized Jewish doctors were revised in 1942 was a growing awareness of the shortage of health care in certain areas of France. The issue of medical replacements, already a source of debate in the 1930s over naturalized citizens' rights, became even more pressing after 1940, when many French doctors were mobilized or taken as prisoners of war. In October 1941, nearly 1,300 doctors and medical students were in German prison camps.[187] Some people agreed that a logical solution would be to allow banned Jewish doctors, an able and available contingent, to replace mobilized doctors and serve in the many villages without health care. The CGQJ, however, was against it.[188]

One case illuminated the dire need for medical practitioners in many regions across France. In January 1942, a Madame G. wrote to the Haute-Vienne department medical council about Dr. R. L., who had been replacing her imprisoned husband since September 1940 and who was going to be banned from the profession as a Jew. She demanded that Dr. L. be allowed to remain in temporary charge of her husband's practice: "I would like to emphasize the fact that it is currently next to impossible to find a doctor who is not a Jew for long-term replacements such as those for prisoners, and that, if my husband's medical practice were to become vacant during his captivity, he would find his clientele completely dispersed upon his return, causing him great harm."[189] The regional CGQJ administrator, Guy Cadiou, however, dismissed G.'s assertion in early 1942 that replacements were hard to find: he suggested one doctor he knew of who had escaped from prison and who could take over.

Whether Jewish medical *students* could temporarily replace absent doctors, as non-Jewish students could, gave rise to prolonged disagreement among different authorities. The national council of the Medical Order published in its bulletin that Jewish students could serve as replacements; no law forbade it, and the Minister of Health explicitly informed the Order that it was permissible.[190] But the Vaucluse department council secretary-general, in a letter to the CGQJ, disagreed:

> Our council decided to raise an energetic protest against such an inter-
> pretation which follows the letter, but not the spirit, of the law....
> [A replacement] is assimilated to the status of a doctor, holds the same
> prerogatives, and can have the same opportunities for political activity.
> What becomes of the legally authorized quota in the department orders
> if several doctors replace themselves with Jews as they please? Do we
> want to give back to Jews the weapons for anti-national propaganda
> by allowing them to infiltrate French families with the social aura of a
> doctor?[191]

In this particular conflict, which lasted well into 1943, the CGQJ sided with the Vaucluse department medical council, and the Health Secretariat sided with the national council of the Medical Order.[192] On the one hand, the state secretary for health insisted that Jewish medical students (as long as they were authorized under the 3 percent student quota) could serve as temporary replacements for doctors, but banned Jewish doctors could not.[193] The CGQJ, on the other hand, insisted in May 1943 that both Jewish ex-doctors and current Jewish medical students should be barred from acting as replacements. The state secretary for health counterargued in June 1943, "Any measure tending to ban Jews [from serving as replacements] could only be taken, in my opinion and given the current state of the legislation, without any legal basis, and if brought before the Council of State, would risk subjecting *my department* to paying penalties and damages." He concluded, "I add that Jewish medical students are subject to a numerus clausus and that it is this numerus clausus that applies to them, as long as they have not graduated, no matter how long their studies last."[194]

Although the Health Secretariat won this battle for Jewish medical students on legalistic grounds, the discussions about replacements demonstrated that exclusionary doctors had no moral argument behind which they could hide their turf protectionism and their anti-Semitism. By resisting even temporary coverage by qualified Jewish doctors in their absence, the doctors in the Vaucluse department medical council were publicly advocating that their patients, friends, and neighbors be deprived of medical care. The obvious need for replacements in rural areas also gave the lie to long-standing claims that the medical profession was overcrowded. With local populations and even a few doctors calling for Jews to provide needed replacement medical care, complaints of a "plethora" should have been ignored.

★ ★ ★

Anti-Semitism in the late Third Republic and Vichy France cannot be easily ana-lyzed as distinct from xenophobia. For one thing, geopolitical events in Europe contributed to the increase in the percentage of Jews in the foreign-origin popu-lation in French universities and the liberal professions during the interwar years. This development served to stoke latent anti-Semitic sentiment among French doctors and medical students. Nonetheless, it was the legacy of the nationality-based exclusionary movement from the 1930s in French medicine that continued to predominate during Vichy. From foreigners to naturalized citizens to recently naturalized citizens—each targeted in turn as outsiders to the French medical "family"—Vichy took a further step by permanently banning doctors born of foreign fathers. There were, therefore, republican precedents for limiting rights for naturalized citizens. Taking away civil and professional rights from Jewish citizens, however, gave the national council of the Medical Order pause. Their proposal to apply the quota to medical students rather than practicing doctors revealed misgivings about participating in the anti-Semitic quota. (Medical leaders experi-enced no equivalent ethical hesitation in expelling foreign-fathered doctors.) Still, the medical leadership across all department and national levels went ahead and implemented the anti-Semitic legislation thoroughly and without public protest.

A few features of the Vichy-era exclusion from medicine of foreign-fathered and Jewish French citizens are distinct from the equivalent exclusions in the legal profession. By the late 1930s, two discursive patterns had emerged within the professions. First, doctors overwhelmingly used the term "foreigners" when they meant naturalized, foreign-born, or foreign-fathered citizens, with no distinction or recognition that any of them might possess French nationality. Lawyers hardly ever did this. Two explanations can be proffered. Legal train-ing made for a more careful and precise use of language, and since foreigners had been excluded from the law bars since 1864, Vichy era restrictions on foreign-fathered citizens were new and distinct for lawyers, making them less susceptible to mislabeling. Because French medicine had for decades during the Third Republic tried to limit professional access to "insiders," in the minds of many doctors, foreigners and naturalized citizens together inhabited a broad category of otherness. Doctors' systematic use of "foreigner" to refer to French citizens who were simply of foreign ancestry might have been verbal sloppiness but also suggests purposeful alarmism. The medical profession in the 1930s was already known for its indiscreet xenophobic discourse compared to the legal profession, for there were many more foreigners and recently naturalized citizens in medicine than in law. Second, doctors also used the term "foreign-ers" when they meant Jews. This euphemism disappeared, however, when state anti-Semitism opened the floodgates to a change in social mores.

One of the important lessons of this chapter is that Vichy's exclusionary legislation did not always exclude foreign-fathered and Jewish doctors in ways agreed upon by rank-and-file doctors. The concerns of the Indre medical department council, when told to exempt two foreign-fathered Jews with military credentials instead of Jewish doctors of old French stock without a military background, spoke volumes: "We, members of the Indre medical council, called to express our opinion on the prefect's nominations, cannot in our soul and conscience sacrifice a French doctor in favor of foreigners [*sic*], even if the latter served during the war, an honorable gesture certainly, but a gesture of acknowledgment toward a country where these foreigners benefited from hospitality that they judged to be to their advantage."[195] The CGQJ responded tersely to the Indre council that if "foreign" Jews' military credentials qualified them for exemptions and French Jews' credentials did not, then the former were to be retained and the latter were not. The law was the law. Military service trumped French origin.[196]

Although it was more socially acceptable to discriminate against doctors of foreign origin than against French Jews, Medical Order leaders, at the national council level of appeal and exemption, participated more directly in ousting Jews than foreign-fathered doctors. For the ban on foreign-fathered doctors, a Superior Inspection Commission was specially set up consisting of only one member of the national council of the Medical Order, as well as a member from the Ministry of Health and from the Council of State. For the anti-Semitic quota, it was the national council of the Medical Order as a whole, with no outside state influence, that ruled on appeal and exemption cases. Such a paradox is more symbolic than real, since the critical decision making to eliminate both foreign-fathered doctors and Jewish doctors originated at the level of the department councils of the Medical Order. It is also clear that Jews were more often the victims of persecution than foreign-fathered doctors because Jews were up against the CGQJ with the Nazis behind them. In the end, though, French doctors were responsible for excluding their colleagues.

Even after foreign-fathered doctors were banned and after Jewish students and doctors were limited by quotas, the medical profession was unsatisfied. The perception of overcrowding and the instinct to reduce competition— major characteristics of the interwar medical profession—persisted throughout Vichy and well after the professions were "purified" of undesirable elements.[197] Every initiative taken up by the medical corps between 1940 and 1944 can be understood in terms of the Malthusian outlook dating back to the nineteenth century, an outlook that had transformed into a battle cry in the 1930s. During Vichy, in addition to pursuing the exclusion of foreign-fathered and Jewish doctors, doctors also lobbied for longer training periods for medical school graduates, limitations on holding multiple posts (*cumul*), regulations on charity health clinics, and the reorganization of medical insurance. A commission nominated by the Ministry of National Education in 1941 proposed one solution for reducing the number of medical graduates: "It is also desirable that access to medical studies be forbidden, or if not, then at least very significantly restricted, for young women. They should be oriented elsewhere."[198] Doctors never argued for these efforts in frank economic terms but instead cloaked their arguments in a moralistic guise.

A major strategy was to use the hard-won corporatist structure to set a maximum number of doctors allowed to practice in each department.[199] The law of 2 April 1941 gave the Medical Order the power to set such limits.[200] The Order originally proposed to set the maximum at 20 percent above the number of doctors practicing in each department in 1939, but soon considered this too high. In consultation with department councils, the national council allowed for 700 doctors in the department of the Alpes-Maritimes, for example, 90 in Cantal, 260 in the Côtes-d'Or, 530 in the Haute-Garonne, 900 in Seine-et-Oise, and 190 in the Vaucluse. These limits were considered provisional; the department councils regularly pushed for lower limits throughout the war, and the national council repeatedly reprimanded department councils for using the proposed limits to illegally refuse new registrations of doctors.[201]

But the most important scheme for limiting the number of doctors during Vichy was a plan to institute a blanket quota on the number of medical school graduates in France every year. President Leriche of the Medical Order national council wrote to the state secretary for national education several times, at one point remarking, "To help place doctors seeking vacant posts, we cannot count very much on the departure of doctors who are sons [sic] of foreigners.... Those vacancies have been filled by now. As for spots freed by the quota on Jewish doctors, they will concern only Paris. Outside of Paris, the number of Jewish doctors is very low." Leriche argued for a maximum limit on medical students based on the year 1931.[202] State Secretary of Health Huard "fully seconded" the Medical Order's proposal.[203] Repeating the plethora mantra from the 1930s, Leriche lamented that "the number of medical students, whose constant growth, out of proportion with the real needs of the nation, is becoming a worrisome danger." He continued, "The detrimental transfer credits too easily granted to foreigners who then naturalize," among other factors, lead to "a lamentable medical proletariat which would be a danger for our nation."[204] In a formidable rallying of the medical leadership, thirty-nine of the unoccupied zone department councils of the Medical Order met in September 1941 to formulate a demand to the Ministry of National Education for a numerus clausus for admission to medical studies.[205] There was no hesitation about using the same term that was employed for Jews. The issue figured regularly in national council meetings and circulars throughout the Occupation years.[206] The law of 19 October 1942 was passed, setting a predetermined number of students to be admitted to medical schools each year, decided by the Ministry of Education with input from the Ministry of Health and the Medical Order.[207] It was a coup for the Medical Order to obtain an advisory role in determining the quantity of its future members. A dissent from the dean of the Montpellier Medical School in 1944 did not divert the medical profession from its general direction of narrowing the pipeline for educating medical doctors in the postwar era.[208]

Conclusion

*Postwar Continuities and the Rupture
of Public Apology*

           This book has analyzed a social movement
from genesis to crystallization. The mobilization against foreigners and naturalized citizens in the professions was initiated and led "from below." The
legislation restricting access to law and medicine was instigated by lawyers,
doctors, and students. They pressured parliament and government to satisfy
their demands, and their mobilization prospered in the near absence of correctives by state actors. While many doctors and lawyers held political mandates themselves, corporatist orders and professional associations regularly
engaged in double-edged tactics by making demands of state actors and simultaneously trying to seize authority for themselves. The rabidly xenophobic
Dr. Querrioux once railed, "It is not against foreign doctors that we fight…it
is against our laws and our legislators who do not know how to defend the
French."[1] Quite to the contrary, French political leaders during the interwar
and Vichy years granted an impressive amount of protection to French practitioners of medicine and law. The Bureau universitaire de statistique, whose job
was to assemble accurate statistical data for the development of labor policy,
rarely acknowledged that there was no danger of professional overcrowding,[2]
and instead actively worked to satisfy professional demands. Certain authorities
such as Victor Balthazard, dean of the Paris Medical School, used his influence
in all kinds of forums during years of agitation to proclaim the triple falsehood
that the medical profession was overcrowded, that overcrowding was harmful

to public health, and that overcrowding was due to the influx of foreigners. Deputies Armbruster and Aulois—a doctor and a lawyer by training—mediated as spokespersons for interest group lobbies, quite often at the expense of the public welfare. Their parliamentary colleagues readily accepted their arguments. Restrictions against foreigners and naturalized citizens in the professions formed the basis of three major pieces of legislation during the 1930s.

The protectionist movement in the liberal professions was marked by a fundamental distinction between French nationals and "others." Foreigners were the top priority targeted for exclusion, followed by naturalized citizens. Foreigners were an easy scapegoat because they had little social or political clout with which to fight back in an increasingly insular French society. The hierarchy of targets of exclusion was based more on professional accord and social acceptability than on numerical efficiency. Even though the greatest influx of new professionals came from the ranks of French men of the lower-middle classes, strategically it made sense to prioritize the exclusion of foreigners because xenophobia rallied a factious profession and silenced weak countervailing points of view.[3]

Exclusionary strategies were fueled by xenophobia and by economic self-defense, as well as by a third factor: concerns about professional image. The shift from a conservative, traditional professional identity to a modern, democratic one touched many nerves when new social categories began to seek access to the professions. The targeting of reputedly ill-prepared secondary students in strategies for raising the intellectual standards of the professions stemmed from conservatives' fear that democratization was diminishing their prestige. Likewise, proposals that questioned women's right to access stemmed from fear that the traditional professional identity based on masculine pride and honor was being undermined by women's inroads. In cultivating their image, French professionals did their best to portray foreign competitors as inferior and corrupt; the truth was that many refugee and immigrant professionals were extremely competent, spoke excellent French, and constituted real competition for French doctors and lawyers. It was not unheard of, for example, for a French doctor to hire an experienced but unauthorized foreign doctor to perform difficult surgical procedures secretly in his place,[4] as Erich Maria Remarque represented fictionally in his novel *Arc de Triomphe* about a German refugee doctor in France in the 1930s.[5]

As the Third Republic collapsed into the authoritarian regime of Vichy, corporatist defense, xenophobia, and anti-Semitism became more and more entangled. Jacques Charpentier, president of the Paris bar during most of the Vichy era, claimed unself-consciously in his postwar memoirs that "a 'Jewish problem' always existed in the Paris bar."[6] It was the depression combined with the Jewish refugee crisis in the mid-1930s, Vicki Caron has maintained, that heightened French professionals' prejudice against east European Jewish immi-grants and Jewish refugees from central Europe. She argues, "There is no doubt that [middle-class grievances against foreigners] were aimed almost exclusively at foreign Jews, since Jews, unlike the majority of other foreigners in France, were overwhelmingly middle class."[7]

Xenophobia and anti-Semitism evolved historically in separate ways, but they also influenced each other.[8] Anti-Semitic sentiment was frequently packaged as xenophobia before anti-Semitism became socially acceptable in France. For example, the insult *métèque* officially meant "outsider" but took on an anti-Semitic tone for most French people. "Romanian" in the medical profession was often a code word for "Jew." Apart from propagandists in the Action française, doctors (and even more rarely lawyers) dared to express anti-Semitism in the 1930s only by grounding it—or hiding it—in anti-foreigner sentiment. It is dif-ficult to determine, all the same, whether resentment toward Romanians arose because they were numerically dominant among foreign students in Parisian universities or because it was believed that most of them were Jewish. Once state anti-Semitism was instituted in Vichy France, the state made it permissible, in fact obligatory, to categorize Jews—French Jews—as outsiders to the nation.

Foreigners and Jews were not the same thing by Vichy standards. Why legislate anti-Semitic quotas if, as some have asserted, the laws banning foreign-fathered doctors and lawyers were meant for Jews?[9] The priority was to elimi-nate foreign-born lawyers and doctors: these bans were passed several months before the Statute on the Jews and up to a year before the anti-Semitic profes-sional quotas. Furthermore, in the eyes of some members of the Medical Order national council, the foreign-father ban obviated the need for an anti-Semitic quota. To legislate religious discrimination was an extraordinary step in 1940, whereas waiting periods and restrictions for French persons of foreign origin had become commonplace and were not generally even considered discrimina-tory.

Exclusion and Regime Change: From the Third Republic to the Fourth

Restrictions against foreigners instituted in the 1930s made it easier for Vichy to discriminate, since the Third Republic had already prepared the ground with a language and a technique of exclusion. Republican practices prepared the way for Vichy exclusionism through the protection of French labor and the creation in 1889 of a new category of citizenry (*les naturalisés*) with limited rights, which was reaffirmed legislatively in 1927, 1933, 1934, 1935, 1936, 1938, 1940, and 1941. Although the anti-Semitic turn during the Vichy regime was unprec-edented in that it consisted of lawyers' and doctors' participation in a racist, repressive state policy, it can also been understood as a logical continuation of prewar tendencies.[10] "I have the impression," wrote the historian Michael Marrus, "that public discourse at the end of the 1930s habituated members of the legal profession, as well as others, to think in terms of a 'Jewish problem' and not to blush at such expressions as 'Juif de race.'"[11]

And yet it was not inevitable that the xenophobic measures of the 1930s in the professions would lead to bans on foreign-fathered persons and anti-Semitic quotas during Vichy. Products of nationalism, the economic depression, and the refugee crisis in the climate of the hollow years of the 1930s, xenophobia and anti-Semitism flourished under an authoritarian regime promoting National Revolution and operating partly under pressure from Nazi Germany.[12] While an "ordinary" anti-Semitism had been part of the professional landscape long before Vichy, it had deadly consequences at Vichy. What was different during the war was that opposition to extreme anti-Semites such as Vallat and Alibert in law and Querrioux and Hollier in medicine was weaker. Their anti-Semitic virulence was no longer tempered by polite society, republican values, and a state that had frequently served in the 1930s as a buffer against extremist xenophobia. Catherine Fillon has asserted that the Vichy regime unleashed a surge of naked hostility: "In 1940, scruples, hesitations, and hypocrisy were no longer de rigueur."[13]

While the legal and medical professions officially welcomed the return of democracy after the Occupation, their platforms were not in favor of repealing all the exclusionary measures of the previous two decades. The transition from an authoritarian regime back to a republican one did little to extinguish lawyers' and doctors' prejudices, which flourished into the Fourth and Fifth Republics. In the immediate postwar period, some attempts at commemoration were made to provide closure to the recent tumultuous past, but they typically ignored Vichy's discriminatory measures. The Paris law bar held a ceremony in July 1946 to honor the lawyers who died for France during the Second World War. Bar president Marcel Poignard on this occasion whitewashed the bar's record of anti-Semitic and xenophobic regulations, claiming, "Nowhere else in all of France was the indignation as acute as it was within our Bar."[14] Poignard's remarks included a laudatory portrait of Lucien Vidal-Naquet, but mentioned nothing about Vidal-Naquet's eviction from the bar for being a Jew.[15] Nor was any mention of the anti-Semitic or anti-foreigner legislation made in the first postwar bulletin of the conference of departmental law bar presidents. This is a particularly salient absence, given that the issue was dedicated to a thorough inventory of Vichy legislation that was to be repealed by the Provisional Government, with special focus on laws pertaining to the legal profession. Nor did the question of the reintegration of lawyers who were Jewish or of foreign origin arise in the speech of conference president and law bar president Allaert during the first post-Liberation general assembly of this group of all French bar presidents.[16] The Vichy syndrome had truly begun.[17]

In French society, the postwar purge was meant to condemn the worst collaborators while prodding the nation to unify and move forward.[18] The purges in the legal and medical professions mirrored the rest of French society. Those conducting the investigations were the same leaders of the law and medical orders during Vichy, anti-Semitic behavior figured marginally in the charges, and anti-foreigner measures were not considered as unlawful. Few sanctions were meted out.[19]

At the same time, excluded persons were being reintegrated into their former places in French society. The ordinances of 9 August and 11 October 1944 reestablished the republican rule of law and declared all exclusionary legislation passed by the Vichy regime null and void. With this reversal, Jewish doctors and lawyers were permitted to reoccupy their medical and law practices, hospital positions, civil service functions, and university posts. In reality, of course, the number of Jews in a position to return to prewar normalcy had been vastly diminished by death and deportation. For the few who did return to reclaim their offices and clients, not all were warmly welcomed. Some doctors who had replaced banned Jews refused to relinquish equipment and patients. The medical orders were called upon to resolve many of these conflicts, mirroring the multitude of cases of restitution of "Aryanized" business property in French society at the time. The Paris law bar council, for its part, decided in September 1944 that Jewish lawyers would have to request reinstatement to the bar; there would be no blanket readmission for expelled Jewish lawyers. Moreover, the Paris law bar required Jewish lawyers to make up the premiums on their pensions that were missed during the period of their expulsion from the bar.[20]

There was little support for abrogating the Vichy laws against those born of a foreign father.[21] In a 10 October 1944 meeting the Paris bar council concurred that the legislation against foreign-fathered lawyers was useful and should be maintained, but not retroactively. Bar president Jacques Charpentier quickly wrote to the new minister of justice of the Provisional Government to protest the legislation's repeal. "The immigration which resulted from the troubles that have desolated Europe," he wrote, "and which will surely continue in the coming years, in fact populates the bar with recently naturalized French persons [*Français de fraîche date*] who possess neither our traditions nor our moral education, nor even knowledge of the French language.... The bar requests the reestablishment of the measures of the law [banning foreign-fathered doctors] in the near future, as long as they do not undo established rights."[22] The statement could have been lifted right out of 1934, when the law bars succeeded in creating a second-class category of French citizenry.[23] The Provisional Government's ordinances of 6 and 8 August 1945 eased—temporarily—the Vichy bans on foreign-fathered doctors and lawyers, allowing them to return to practice if they were French citizens, or even if they were in the middle of the naturalization process. In addition, the transformation of a *diplôme d'université* into a *diplôme d'état* was facilitated for those who had military or Resistance credentials. The Confédération des syndicats médicaux, newly reinstated, protested vigorously against these measures.[24]

While Vichy represents the twentieth-century apex of exclusion in the French professions, discriminatory legislation remained on the books for several decades after the war. The ordinance of 19 October 1945 created a new code of nationality, which replaced the 1927 nationality law. Notably the three-year residency requirement—the source of much outcry in the interwar years—was increased to five years. Several waiting periods or *incapacités* on naturalized citizens' rights from the 1927 law and 1938 decree-law were left intact: a ten-year delay before naturalized citizens could run for elected office and a five-year delay for voting. The 1945 ordinance also maintained the delay for naturalized citizens' access to the law bar and the civil service, as it was first instituted by the 1934 law, but it reduced the wait from ten years to five. This discrimination against naturalized citizens in the legal profession was not entirely removed, along with the delay on voting, until the law of 9 January 1973. As for naturalized doctors after the war, their situation was governed anew by the complicated regulations set by the series of laws passed in 1933, 1935, and 1936 described in chapter 2. Only in 1978 did the law of 17 July finally revoke the discriminations against naturalized doctors and remove the five-year waiting period before naturalized citizens could work in the French civil service. It was not until 1983, with the law of 8 December, that ineligibility for elected office was nullified for naturalized citizens, who, from that year forward, finally possessed equal rights with "native" French citizens.

Regarding the reestablishment of republican legislation after the war, the political scientist Patrick Weil has remarked: "One would imagine that a break with Vichy's racial policies would go without saying. But this would be to neglect the influence and the permanence of the ethnic approach—since the middle of the 1930s—in political debates over immigration and nationality." Drafters of the postwar republic's immigration policy and nationality law in fact reproduced many of the same exclusionary agendas that had prevailed during the late Third Republic and Vichy, and they also envisioned novel ways to discriminate. For example, a Comité français de la Libération nationale (CFLN) draft of a "Statut des minorités" contained provisions for defining a minority as someone who could not trace a direct paternal link to an ancestor who was a French citizen on 1 January 1800, for the purpose of putting a "minorité" stamp on persons' vital statistics documents (*état-civil*), and for a 1 percent numerus clausus on minorities in certain professions.[25] Moreover, the CFLN and the

Provisional Government initially based their postwar immigration policy on an American model, with naturalizations heavily determined by ethnic and professional criteria.[26] None of these projects were enacted, but their elaboration suggests that paradigms about "others"—even though the term "minority" was undefined in this document—had transferred intact from Vichy to the Fourth Republic.

Although the public display of anti-Semitism became taboo for most Frenchmen after the Liberation, doctors, lawyers, and students continued to exhibit anti-foreigner sentiment without compunction. Shortly after the war, professional grievances were again voiced about a chronic plethora in the medical profession.[27] In the Association of Paris Interns' first bulletin published after the war in 1947, the question of foreigners' access to medical internship programs appeared three times, most notably in the welcome-back message from the president on the first page. While in its postwar rhetoric the association was more careful to avoid blatant xenophobia, the distinction between foreign-born and French-born remained palpable.[28] Students in the Latin Quarter lashed out against "nègres" and "métèques" in 1947.[29] And in 1960, during the worldwide "year of the refugee," the Medical Order and the Association nationale des avocats successfully quashed Deputy Jean-Paul Palewski's bill that would have allowed refugees the right to practice law and medicine in France.[30] According to Palewski, who was from the Seine-et-Oise, refugees had the right to practice a liberal profession in Great Britain, Denmark, Ireland, Sweden, Norway, West Germany, and Belgium, but not in France.[31] These few examples demonstrate the persistence of discriminatory sentiment within the professional corps after the war, despite the demographic and economic expansion of the *trente glorieuses.*

Although important exceptions exist, as a general principle French nationality and French diplomas are still required to practice medicine and law in France today.[32] In itself this is not terribly striking since many Western countries demand similar qualifications of their doctors and lawyers. European integration has pushed the professions to allow European Union citizens access to these careers. In response to Europeanization, the French legal profession completely reinvented itself in 1990: all types of law practice outside the bar structure were abolished, and foreigners already practicing law in France as *conseils juridiques* (notably Americans at that point in history) were grandfathered into bar membership.[33] Seemingly a shift toward inclusiveness, the move actually restricted the freedom of foreign lawyers. By assimilating them into the corporatist structure and obliging them to adhere to bar regulations, the law orders regained control over the entire legal field for the first time since the French Revolution.[34] In the hope of ending once and for all the supposed *pléthore,* the medical profession and state authorities agreed in the 1970s to restrict the number of medical school graduates. Not long after, this policy was recognized as draconian and mistaken. Many hospitals were so understaffed by the 1990s that, ironically, France had to call on foreign doctors to maintain minimum coverage for emergency rooms and other hospital services. Six thousand or so non-European and non-European-trained foreign doctors were working in underpaid and temporary hospital positions in France at the turn of the twenty-first century, and they began to organize for equal pay and equal rights.[35] Although the Weil report in 1997 proposed an easing of restrictions for foreigners of the intellectual and scientific elite (to the chagrin of those favoring a more democratic approach), the criterion of nationality still remains at the core of determining professional insiders and outsiders in France.[36]

Legacies of Professional Prejudice

Despite the persistence of nationality-based bias in their professions, doctors and lawyers at the turn of the twenty-first century have begun to face their legacy of anti-Semitism from the Vichy era. Following President Jacques Chirac's official public apology in 1995 for the French state's role in the Holocaust, French lawyers and doctors joined in a wave of apology-making for their particular roles in applying anti-Semitic legislation during Vichy. Various French groups and institutions publicly addressed their pasts and took responsibility for the particular roles that their predecessors played in fostering wartime anti-Semitism. The apologies of the French state, the Paris law bar, the French Catholic Church, a Paris police unit, the Medical Order, and the Council of State coalesced in a memorial wave across French society.

Two months after his election to the presidency, on 16 July 1995, the fifty-third anniversary of the Vélodrome d'Hiver tragedy, President Chirac officially recognized the French state's role in the Final Solution. Chirac's statement of recognition radically departed from prevailing official attitudes toward the Vichy past. He admitted France's guilt and took responsibility for its "collective fault."[37] His predecessor, socialist François Mitterrand, had refused to make an official apology despite considerable pressure from public opinion. Chirac's apology became a point of departure leading from state recognition of official complicity in the Holocaust to a more extensive examination of collective responsibility within French civil society.[38]

In April 1997, former minister of justice Robert Badinter published a book documenting the French legal profession's role in the Holocaust. It told the story of how the French law bars carried out Vichy's exclusionary legislation establishing a 2 percent quota on Jewish lawyers. Badinter accused French lawyers of complacency toward the plight of the Jews: "Throughout it all, in the countryside as well as in Paris, not at any moment . . . was a single protest made against the exclusion of Jews from the bar."[39] A few weeks after Badinter's book appeared, the Paris bar issued a resolution recognizing the injustices committed toward Jewish and foreign-fathered lawyers during the war. Mentioning the historical evidence presented in Badinter's book, the Paris bar council admitted that contrary to its mission, bar members helped implement the laws of 1940 and 1941 excluding certain colleagues from practice. The statement concluded, "Conscious of its responsibilities to the history of the bar, the council bows its head before those who had been victims." The Paris bar also announced that it would open its archives.[40] As this book went to press, however, liberalization of archival access had not yet taken place.[41]

Although the apology was not representative of the entire French legal profession, the Paris bar was by far the largest and most important one in France, whose actions had affected the greatest number of Jews during the war. Even though the Paris law bar declaration did not provoke any discernable negative reaction among lawyers (as was the case for several apologies that were to follow from other civil groups), no other French law bar came forward to second the apology from Paris. Only one individual, a former president of the Bordeaux law bar, made a public plea to his colleagues to repeat the gesture, to no avail.[42] This attempt was made in the midst of the trial in Bordeaux of Maurice Papon, accused of committing crimes against humanity while serving in the Bordeaux prefecture during the war. With limited access to law bars' archives, it remains unknown if a public apology was debated in other law bar councils.[43]

Several factors explain why the legal profession was the first civil group to face its Vichy past and take responsibility for its predecessors' actions in the wake of Chirac's collective apology. Compared to scholars who had already begun to examine the wartime moral collapse of the French legal profession in preceding years,[44] Badinter had the gravitas to attract media coverage of his book, which may have served to nudge his law bar into action. A former president of the elite Constitutional Council and a prominent member of the Paris bar, he had earned fame for abolishing the death penalty in France in 1981 as minister of justice. Like Badinter himself, most members of the Paris bar in the 1990s had begun their legal careers after the war, and thus had not participated in or witnessed the implementation of anti-Semitic quotas, which made it easier for the institution to accept blame for its past. Looming on the legal horizon, furthermore, was the trial of Papon, which would raise new questions about the links between justice and history. Because, as one scholar of historical reconciliation has observed, institutions often apologize "in order to restore an institutional reputation . . . or to defuse a volatile situation,"[45] the lawyers' initiative was likely motivated in part by a desire to face the past on their own terms before being dragged into it by the media covering the Papon trial.

Lawyers' recognition of their past failings—their self-described mission is to serve the rights of man and to protect the oppressed—was matched by a more activist role in contemporary political issues. The Paris bar intervened several times in parliamentary debates over immigration since the late 1990s to protect the rights of foreigners.[46] After the urban riots of autumn 2005 that revealed the limits of French society's integration of second-, third-, and fourth-generation youth of Maghrebi origin, associations such as the Syndicat des avocats de France and the Conseil national des barreaux criticized the proposed expulsions of foreigners and the failure to integrate minorities into French society.[47] Providing legal support for immigrants and foreigners had been, in fact, one of the defining concerns of the Syndicat des avocats de France.[48] The bar's apology for anti-Semitism can therefore be understood as "an act of discourse that modifies a situation."[49] It signified an evolution of the legal profession toward an identity more steeped in post-1989 human rights culture.[50] At the same time, this strand of social activism can trace its ancestry in part to the participation of the legal profession in the Resistance, however diversified that resistance had been.[51]

After bishops representing the French Catholic Church offered an apology to the Jewish community in a solemn commemoration in September 1997, the penetration of apology into civil society reached the French medical profession. At an annual meeting on 11 October 1997, the Medical Order issued a declaration of regret for discrimination against Jewish doctors during the Vichy period. This took place during the first few days of the Papon trial, and the date was not lost on Jews: it fell on Yom Kippur, the Day of Atonement. In a "symbolic request for forgiveness in the name of the medical community" extended to Jewish doctors, president of the Order Bernard Glorion admitted: "Colleagues became guilty, voluntarily or not[,] . . . [and] had to participate in this sad and shameful operation of discrimination and exclusion. . . . We can only regret and repudiate with gravity and humility." He concluded, "It is up to us today in the name of the medical community to remind all those who succeed us that our duty, their duty, will be never to yield to the temptation of exclusion and never to accept, even by our silence, any discrimination or rejection of any group."[52]

The apology was complemented by a promise of transparency: the Order announced that it would open its archives to the public, something historians had been requesting for years. It was reputed that sacks filled with thousands of letters from French doctors denouncing colleagues as Jews, foreigners, and charlatans were found at the Medical Order's offices after the war and subsequently burned in an effort to rebuild the nation.[53] On orders from Pasteur Vallery-Radot, president of the Comité médical de la Résistance and Charles de Gaulle's nominee for minister of health, Dr. Paul Milliez entered the premises of the Health Ministry on 21 August 1944 in the midst of the liberation of

Paris, walked past the guard, and promptly found another such collection. In his memoirs he recounted:

> Upon entering the office of the cabinet director, which was going to be mine temporarily, I found a dossier containing a whole series of letters of denunciation placed prominently on the desk. All of them were written by well-known doctors and were probably the only existing copies. Some of the authors had joined the Resistance in the meantime. I knew all the denounced doctors well. They were either Jewish, married to Jews, or suspected of having Jewish or English friendships.... All the anonymous letters must have been thrown away. I did the same with this pile of garbage and I burned it.[54]

The Medical Order's apology contained several weaknesses. Ambivalent references to doctors who, "voluntarily or not," "had to participate" in anti-Semitic actions constituted a significant abdication of responsibility. The "duty to remember" invoked by Glorion, moreover, called for remembrance only of the "admirable and anonymous behavior of doctors who, risking their lives, obeyed their duty and assisted the sick and often their fellow colleagues" and not of excluded Jewish doctors. The apology was further undermined by an artificial distancing of the past from the present: the declaration asserted that the Medical Order was refounded after the Liberation and was therefore completely distinct as an institution from the wartime Order. In these ways the statement maintained an ambiguity and reiterated a pattern of denial, making it a classic non-apology. The tainted origins of the Order—created by the Vichy regime—had been a source of illegitimacy for the postwar medical profession. Many of the same doctors who had participated in discriminatory policies and collaborative activities during the war continued in leadership roles in the Order after the war.

The most serious problem was that the Medical Order—whether conceived as an institution, an ensemble of individuals, or their elected leadership council—did not support the apology. The representatives of the medical institution did not debate, approve, or publicize their president's initiative.[55] The Order's monthly journal made no mention of the apology in the months preceding or following it,[56] and no sign of it appeared on the institution's Web site.[57] If this medical "apology" was so half-hearted and instantaneously buried, what had engendered it in the first place? President Glorion was under pressure from outside to do it, records indicate, and he doubted that collective agreement could be achieved through internal debate.[58] The apology that the Paris law bar had already made subjected the Medical Order to institutional peer pressure in the 1990s climate of Vichy memorialization. There was a sense that some gesture, however perfunctory, had to be made. An editorial in *Le monde* had specifically called on the Medical Order to follow the conciliatory initiatives of the church and the Paris law bar.[59] And Minister of Health Bernard Kouchner had insisted publicly, "I am impatiently waiting for this declaration from the doctors."[60] Only through institutional cleansing performed through the work of memory, apology, and mourning, Kouchner provocatively argued, could the Order reclaim its dignity.

For many doctors, however, the apology felt neither cleansing nor dignified. Physicians' letters to the editors of medical journals provided evidence of acerbic dissent. One doctor from Versailles, for instance, had "had enough of these mediatized epileptic tremors over the Second World War. I was not there. I did not do anything. So leave me alone. . . . Collective responsibility does not exist."[61] The claim that some doctors assisted Jews figured prominently among physicians' reactions to the apology. For example, a seventy-six-year-old member of the Order's Seine department council, a former Resistant and current member of the National Front political party, rejected the apology because he claimed that many of his colleagues had protected Jewish doctors during the war.[62] Another doctor voiced his indignation: "What would all the big names in French medicine who fought against the invader and who constantly risked their lives to save Jewish lives think of this 'repentance'?"[63]

Nor were department order leaders fully cooperative in the national directive to open their archives.[64] The vice president of the Gironde department council proclaimed: "It's very late, too late. We should have opened the files in the 1950s. To do so today is to attack the memory of those who had taken on responsibilities and whom we are incapable of judging outside the context of the period." According to the president of the Nord department council, there was nothing of interest in the archives.[65] Paul Milliez's hasty decision at the Ministry of Health offices in August 1944 may cause heartbreak to historians, but the national council of the Medical Order, unlike the Paris law bar, kept its promise and deposited its remaining wartime records in the French National Archives. They have been consulted for this book; some of them are very damaging. The archives of the department orders, arguably the most important since they contain records of the original decision making about Jewish quotas and foreign-father bans, were as a general rule poorly conserved.[66]

Nonetheless, some positive reaction to the apology surfaced within the French medical profession. Despite disappointment over the hedged language, Jewish doctors expressed overall satisfaction.[67] Several medical journals followed up on the apology by investigating the history of the profession under Vichy, thus filling the informational and memorial void created by the Order's stunted declaration of regret.[68] As one medical journal put it: "Zealous and obedient creature of Pétain. . . the Order was subservient to the regime.

The department medical council leaders were the perfect implementers of the exclusionary laws."[69] For some, the apology came as a long-awaited reckoning: "Fifty-seven years! We had to wait fifty-seven years for the Order to ask forgiveness."[70]

Some doctors sought to link the apology to contemporary French debates about immigration and public memory. The Committee of Foreign-Diploma Doctors, for instance, drew a comparison between wartime exclusion and current discriminations against foreign doctors.[71] In a letter to the editor of a medical journal, one doctor expressed hope that a similar process of acknowledgment would be undertaken for acts of torture committed during the Algerian war.[72] With all its imperfections, the recognition of medical anti-Semitism during Vichy can nevertheless be viewed as part of the profession's evolution. One instance attests to doctors' renewed post-apology pledge of tolerance: doctors were among the more active professional groups to protest against Jean-Marie Le Pen, "a carrier of xenophobia and exclusion," during the second round of the 2002 presidential elections.[73] Collective recognition of past faltering has thus been matched by more activist agendas on broad questions of social justice in contemporary France by both medical and legal professionals.

A comparison of the apologies for Vichy anti-Semitism in the 1990s reveals that some were more successful than others. Ultimately, the Medical Order's apology proved to be abortive. Although it stimulated discussion of the Order's past ex post facto, the declaration was ambivalent and unrepresentative, and it conveyed the impression that it was reluctantly given. Conflicts were buried anew with no final sense of reconciliation.[74] One frustrated doctor summed it up: "This individual and timid 'repentance' is not enough. . . . The Order wants us to 'turn the page' that no one has read yet."[75] Dissent over apologies, in the case of the Medical Order, weakened their impact. The authority of the issuer of the apology counted for a lot. All of the apologies except for Chirac's state apology were criticized for not being representative enough: the Catholic Church apology was not signed by all the bishops; the lawyers' apology affected only Paris; the apology of the doctors had not been debated and voted on. Yet individuals played significant roles in making these apologies happen: Chirac and Badinter in quite daring fashion, Bishop Olivier de Berranger working quietly but instrumentally, and Dr. Glorion meekly so, perhaps because of the resistance of his colleagues. If an apology is a meaningful speech act, then language is a key element of comparison. Chirac spoke of "collective fault" and "immutable debt"; the Catholic bishops "confessed," "begged forgiveness," and made an act of "repentance"; the Paris law bar recognized its "responsibility" and "bowed its head" before victims; and the doctors expressed "regret." The safe term "recognition" was also used by most of these groups.

Apology has its limits. As in the case of the Medical Order, apology is often an imperfect means to clarify historical truths and heal wounds. In contrast to the church's statement of repentance, which forged a clear link of solidarity between past and present members of the religious institution, President Glorion of the Medical Order maintained the version that Vichy was a parenthesis in French medical history. Apologies never guarantee the dispersion of myths about the past. Bad apologies, if they re-solidify falsehoods, can be worse than none at all.

Apology obviously does not inoculate a society against future injustice and prejudice. But apology can reassure descendants of victimized groups that they are no longer vulnerable and can remind the rest of society of the need for wariness. As Elazar Barkan and Alexander Karn argue, apology can also be "an opportunity to reimagine identity, not to change the past, but to change the way groups and their members stand in relation to it."[76] In the civil cases studied here, apology coincided with renewed commitments to social activism in defense of human rights. Almost everyone would agree that post-apology behavior is an important measure of the sincerity of an apology. This is what makes apologies forward-looking.[77]

Such professional turns at the end of the twentieth century confirm the necessity of analyzing the *longue durée* of professionalization, identity formation, and exclusion together. Doctors' and lawyers' shift toward a more activist agenda in contemporary social debates over immigration and foreigners' rights, crystallized in the apology phenomenon of the late 1990s, constitutes an example of continuity across political regimes. The very act of taking responsibility for the Vichy past exemplified a widespread recognition by French society of the bonds between Vichy and contemporary France.[78] The apology turn can be viewed not as the birth of a new vision for French medicine and law but rather as the reemergence of one strand of professional identity that has always existed, a tolerant strand with roots in republicanism. It has always manifested itself, for instance, in lawyers' grand historical raison d'être: the defense of vulnerable widows and orphans. For some, this path led them during the war to the Resistance. More recently, French doctors' seminal role in humanitarian initiatives such as Médecins sans frontières and Médecins du monde, and French lawyers' participation in the Groupe d'information et de soutien des immigrés (GISTI), serve as instantiations of a potential redirection away from the professions' exclusionary pasts.

 **Notes**

The following abbreviations have been used in the notes:

AdP	Archives de Paris
AN	Archives nationales, Paris
AP	Archives du Rectorat de l'Académie de Paris
BMD	Bibliothèque Marguerite Durand
BOM	*Bulletin de l'Ordre des Médecins*
Bulletin de l'ANA	*Bulletin de l'Association nationale des avocats inscrits aux barreaux de France, des colonies, des pays de protectorat et de mandat*
Bulletin de l'UJA	*Bulletin de l'Union des jeunes avocats*
CAC	Archives nationales, Centre des Archives contemporaines, Fontainebleau
CDJC	Archives du Centre de documentation juive contemporaine
MAE	Archives du Ministère des Affaires étrangères
SM Aube	*Bulletin mensuel du Groupement des syndicats médicaux de l'Aube*
SM Nord	*Bulletin de la Fédération des syndicats médicaux du département du Nord*
SMP	*Bulletin officiel du Syndicat médical de Paris*
SM Seine, Banlieue Ouest et Nord	*Fédération des Syndicats médicaux de la Seine, Syndicat des médecins de la banlieue ouest et nord de Paris, bulletin officiel*
SM Seine-et-Oise	*Bulletin du Syndicat médical de Seine-et-Oise*

Introduction

1. Dossier "Concurrence des étrangers aux travailleurs intellectuels," Archives nationales [hereafter AN] F60 641. On engineers, see AN F17 17889; Louis Sarran, "À propos d'une loi récente, vétérinaires et maréchaux-experts," *La vie judiciaire* (10–11 July 1938): 1.

2. Vicki Caron, *Uneasy Asylum: France and the Jewish Refugee Crisis, 1933–1942* (Stanford, 1999); Steven Zdatny, *The Politics of Survival: Artisans in Twentieth-Century France* (Oxford, 1990); Philip Nord, *Paris Shopkeepers and the Politics of Resentment* (Princeton, 1986); Ralph Schor, *L'opinion française et les étrangers, 1919–1939* (Paris, 1985); Ezra Suleiman, *Private Power and Centralization in France: The Notaires and the State* (Princeton, 1987).

3. Many patterns of professional exclusion analyzed herein are universal, as the bodies of literature in the history and sociology of the professions elucidate. See Geoffrey Cocks and Konrad H. Jarausch, eds., *German Professions, 1800–1950* (New York, 1990); Magali Sarfatti Larson, *The Rise of Professionalism: A Sociological Analysis* (Berkeley, 1977); Andrew Abbott, *The System of Professions: An Essay on the Division of Expert Labor* (Chicago, 1988); Richard Abel and P. S. C. Lewis, eds., *Lawyers in Society* (Berkeley, 1988); Konrad Jarausch, *The Unfree Professions: German Lawyers, Teachers, and Engineers, 1900–1950* (Oxford, 1990); Catherine Fillon, *Histoire du barreau de Lyon sous la Troisième République* (Lyon, 1995); Lucien Karpik, *Les avocats: entre l'État, le public et le marché* (Paris, 1995); Karpik, "La profession libérale, un cas, le barreau," in *Les lieux de mémoire,* ed. Pierre Nora (Paris, 1992), 284–321; Bénédicte Vergez, "Internes et anciens internes des hôpitaux de Paris de 1918 à 1945" (Ph.D. diss., Institut d'Études Politiques, 1995); Vergez, *Le monde des médecins au XXe siècle* (Paris, 1996).

1. The Nineteenth-Century Origins of Exclusion in the Professions

1. The concept of nationality being relatively new at the time, "foreigner" meant a person born outside the French dominion and of foreign parents. See Patrick Weil, *Qu'est-ce qu'un Français? Histoire de la nationalité française depuis la Révolution* (Paris, 2002).

2. Surgeons, a different occupation altogether and considered to be not a profession but a skilled trade or *métier,* had to fulfill fewer educational and apprenticeship requirements. Edmond Goblot, *La barrière et le niveau: étude sociologique sur la bourgeoisie française moderne* (Paris, 1925), 27; George Weisz, "Les transformations de l'élite médicale en France," *Actes de la recherche en sciences sociales* 74 (Sept. 1988): 38.

3. Matthew Ramsey, "Medical Power and Popular Medicine: Illegal Healers in Nineteenth-Century France," in *The Medicine Show,* ed. Patricia Branca (New York, 1977), 191; Jean-Pierre Goubert, *Initiation à une nouvelle histoire de la médecine* (Paris, 1998), 49.

4. Jacques Léonard, "Les guérisseurs en France au XIXe siècle," *Revue d'histoire moderne et contemporaine* 27 (July–Sept. 1980): 507–515; Léonard, *La vie quotidienne du médecin de province au XIXe siècle* (Paris, 1977), 163; Léonard, "L'exemple d'une catégorie socio-professionnelle au XIXe siècle: les médecins français," in *Ordres et classes,* ed. Daniel Roche and Camille-Ernest Labrousse (Paris, 1973), 224.

5. Ramsey, "Medical Power and Popular Medicine," 186, 190–193.

6. Edna Hindie Lemay, "Thomas Hérier, A Country Surgeon outside Angoulême at the End of the XVIIIth Century: A Contribution to Social History," in Branca, *The Medicine Show,* 229–242.

7. See George Weisz, *The Medical Mandarins: The French Academy of Medicine in the Nineteenth and Early Twentieth Centuries* (New York, 1995).

8. Jean-Pierre Goubert, "L'art de guérir: médecine savante et médecine populaire dans la France de 1790," *Annales: Économies, sociétés, civilisations* [hereafter *Annales ESC]* 32, no. 5 (Sept.–Oct. 1977): 909; Goubert, *Initiation à une nouvelle histoire de la médecine,* 40–41.

9. Ramsey, "Medical Power and Popular Medicine," 204, 198.

10. Jacques Léonard, "Women, Religion, and Medicine," in *Medicine and Society in France: Selections from the Annales ESC,* ed. Robert Forster and Orest Ranum (Baltimore, 1980), 31.

11. Ibid., 41–42.

12. Léonard, "Les guérisseurs en France au XIXe siècle," 514; Léonard, *La vie quotidienne du médecin de province,* 162; Jacques Léonard, *La médecine entre les savoirs et les pouvoirs* (Paris, 1981), 79.

13. Eugen Weber, *Peasants into Frenchman* (Stanford, 1976).

14. Jacques Léonard, "Le corps médical au début de la IIIe République," in *Médecine et philosophie à la fin du XIXe siècle,* ed. Jacques Poirier and Jean-Louis Poirier, special issue of Cahiers de l'Institut de recherche universitaire d'histoire de la connaissance, des idées et des mentalités, Créteil, Université de Paris XII 2 (1981), 12.

15. Leonard Charles Groopman, "The Internat des Hôpitaux de Paris: The Shaping and Transformation of the French Medical Elite, 1802–1914" (Ph.D. diss., Harvard University, 1986), 234.

16. Léonard, *La médecine entre les savoirs et les pouvoirs,* 300. All translations from the French are my own.

17. "Note de M. Cazeneuve, directeur de l'École secondaire de médecine à Lille, à propos de la transformation de cette école en faculté," n.d., AN AJ 16 6685; Léonard, "Le corps médical au début de la IIIe République," 18.

18. George Weisz, "Reform and Conflict in French Medical Education, 1870–1914," in *The Organization of Science and Technology in France, 1808–1914,* ed. Robert Fox and George Weisz (Cambridge, 1980), 69–70.

19. Weisz, *The Medical Mandarins,* 13.

20. Martha Hildreth, "Medical Rivalries and Medical Politics in France: The Physicians' Union Movement and the Medical Assistance Law of 1893," *Journal of the History of Medicine and Allied Sciences* 42 (1987): 11.

21. Jack Ellis, *The Physician-Legislators of France: Medicine and Politics in the Early Third Republic, 1870–1914* (Cambridge, 1990), 141–142, 147–148; Martha Hildreth, *Doctors, Bureaucrats, and Public Health in France, 1888–1902* (New York, 1987), 177.

22. Léonard, *La médecine entre les savoirs et les pouvoirs,* 82, 294; Léonard, *La vie quotidienne du médecin de province,* 176; Weisz, "Reform and Conflict in French Medical Education, 1870–1914," 69, 88; Hildreth, *Doctors, Bureaucrats, and Public Health in France,* 55, 82–85; Hildreth, "Medical Rivalries and Medical Politics in France," 10–11.

23. Hildreth, *Doctors, Bureaucrats, and Public Health in France,* 272–273.

24. "Note de M. Cazeneuve, directeur de l'École secondaire de médecine à Lille"; Goubert, *Initiation à une nouvelle histoire de la médecine,* 59; Léonard, *La médecine entre les savoirs et les pouvoirs,* 292, 299–301; Groopman, "The Internat des Hôpitaux de Paris," 143–159.

25. Hildreth, *Doctors, Bureaucrats, and Public Health in France,* 60.

26. Ibid., 43, 54; Léonard, *La médecine entre les savoirs et les pouvoirs,* 236; Léonard, "Le corps médical au début de la IIIe République," 14.

27. Dominique Damamme, "La jeunesse des syndicats de médecins ou l'enchantement du syndicalisme," *Genèses* (March 1991): 31, 43–44; Evelyn Bernette Ackerman, *Health Care in the Parisian Countryside, 1800–1914* (New Brunswick, 1990), 56; Léonard, *La vie quotidienne du médecin de province,* 184.

28. Léonard, *La médecine entre les savoirs et les pouvoirs,* 277; Léonard, *La vie quotidienne du médecin de province,* 177–181.

29. Richard Weisberg, "The Representation of Doctors at Work in Salon Art of the Early Third Republic in France" (Ph.D. diss., New York University, 1995), 787; Alexander F. Dracobly, "Disciplining the Doctor: Medical Morality and Professionalism

in Nineteenth-Century France" (Ph.D. diss., University of Chicago, 1996), 39, 343; Jérôme Cucarull, "Les médecins et l'assistance médicale gratuite, 1893–1914: l'exemple de l'Îlle-et-Vilaine," *Le mouvement social* 161 (Oct.–Dec. 1992): 68; Hildreth, "Medical Rivalries and Medical Politics in France," 6; Hildreth, *Doctors, Bureaucrats, and Public Health in France,* chap. 1.

30. Léonard, "Le corps médical au début de la IIIe République," 13, 15; Bénédicte Vergez-Chaignon, "Le syndicalisme médical français de sa naissance à sa refondation: intérêts et morale au pays de l'individualisme (1892–1945)," *Revue d'histoire moderne et contemporaine* (Oct.–Dec. 1996): 711. Hildreth affirms that it is impossible to procure exact statistics of unionization, but she notes that membership rose when crucial issues were at stake in public debate. Hildreth, *Doctors, Bureaucrats, and Public Health in France,* 46.

31. Hildreth, *Doctors, Bureaucrats, and Public Health in France,* 215, 224, 274, 330–331.

32. Léonard, "Le corps médical au début de la IIIe République," 18.

33. Damamme, "La jeunesse des syndicats de médecins ou l'enchantement du syndicalisme," 34–35; Claudine Herzlich, "The Evolution of Relations between French Physicians and the State from 1880 to 1980," *Sociology of Health and Illness* 4, no. 3 (1982): 243–244.

34. Léonard, *La médecine entre les savoirs et les pouvoirs,* 299.

35. The term "lawyer" is used here to indicate only an *avocat à la cour,* and "the legal profession" is meant to refer only to this profession.

36. The terms *procureurs* and *avoués* are often translated in English as "attorneys," but since in American usage "attorney" is interchangeable with "lawyer," I will use the term *avoué* or solicitor throughout this book.

37. Jean-Louis Halpérin, ed., *Avocats et notaires en Europe: les professions judiciaires et juridiques dans l'histoire contemporaine* (Paris, 1996), 42.

38. See Michael Fitzsimmons, *The Parisian Order of Barristers and the French Revolution* (Cambridge, Mass., 1987); Lenard Berlanstein, *The Barristers of Toulouse in the Eighteenth Century* (Baltimore, 1972); David Bell, *Lawyers and Citizens: The Making of a Political Elite in Old Regime France* (New York, 1994).

39. The 1804 law permitted only lawyers and *avoués* who had a *licence en droit* (law degree) to plead in court. An 1812 decree reserved *cours d'appel* to lawyers only. An 1822 ordinance ended the right of *avoués* to plead in *tribunaux de première instance,* but not retroactively. Halpérin, *Avocats et notaires en Europe,* 45.

40. These terms became more current in the twentieth century, although *agent d'affaires* was commonly used up until the Second World War.

41. Halpérin, *Avocats et notaires en Europe,* 70.

42. Only in 1920, however, did fraudulent use of the title "lawyer" become illegal for anyone not registered with a law bar. Halpérin, *Avocats et notaires en Europe,* 128–129; Jean-Louis Halpérin, "Les sources statistiques de l'histoire des avocats en France au XVIIIe et au XIXe siècles," *Revue de la société internationale d'histoire de la profession d'avocat* 3 (1991): 57.

43. John Savage, "Advocates of the Republic: The Paris Bar and Legal Culture in the Early Third Republic" (Ph.D. diss., New York University, 1999), 113.

44. The Toulouse law bar, however, allowed its members to put their addresses on letterhead stationery, demonstrating some regional diversity in anticommercial discourse. Halpérin, *Avocats et notaires en Europe,* 237.

45. Lucien Karpik, "Que faire de la singularité?" *Revue trimestrielle de la Cour d'appel de Versailles* (1990): 13–28; Karpik, *Les avocats,* 167–168.

46. Anne Boigeol and Yves Dezalay, "De l'agent d'affaires au barreau: les conseils juridiques et la construction d'un espace professionnel," *Genèses* 27 (1997): 53; Halpérin, *Avocats et notaires en Europe,* 51.

47. John Savage, "La première Femme-Avocate: Gender, Bourgeois Culture, and the Legal Profession in Fin-de-Siècle France," New York University Institute of French Studies Luncheon Seminar, Spring 1999.

48. Christophe Charle, "Le recrutement des avocats parisiens, 1880–1914," in *Avocats et barreaux en France,* ed. Gilles Le Béguec (Nancy, 1994), 32–33.

49. Christophe Charle, "La bourgeoisie de robe en France au XIXe siècle," *Le mouvement social* 181 (Oct.–Dec. 1997): 64–65; Charle, "Le recrutement des avocats parisiens, 1880–1914," 23.

50. Charle, "La bourgeoisie de robe en France au XIXe siècle," 65; Halpérin, "Les sources statistiques de l'histoire des avocats en France," 64–67.

51. Savage, "Advocates of the Republic," 224–225.

52. Halpérin, *Avocats et notaires en Europe,* 125–145.

53. Ibid., 226.

54. Savage, "Advocates of the Republic," 76.

55. Boigeol and Dezalay, "De l'agent d'affaires au barreau"; Karpik, *Les avocats;* Halpérin, *Avocats et notaires en Europe.*

56. Savage, "Advocates of the Republic," 347–352.

57. Ibid., 369–376.

58. Yves Ozanam, "Les projets de suppression de l'Ordre des avocats et de réforme de la profession avant 1914: étude des propositions de loi soumises à la Chambre entre 1886 et 1910," *Revue de la société internationale d'histoire de la profession d'avocat* 6 (1994): 226–237.

59. Halpérin, *Avocats et notaires en Europe,* 245.

60. Ozanam, "Les projets de suppression de l'Ordre des avocats," 231, 219–242.

61. Yves-Henri Gaudemet, *Les juristes et la vie politique de la IIIe République* (Paris, 1970), 9.

62. Ibid., 15–27; François Lafarge, "Les avocats dans les cabinets ministériels à la veille de la guerre de 1914," in *Avocats et barreaux en France,* ed. Le Béguec, 92–94. On the myth of the "republic of lawyers," see Laurent Willemez, "La 'République des avocats,' 1848: le mythe, le modèle et son endossement," in *La profession politique, XIXe–XXe siècles,* ed. Michel Offerlé (Paris, 1999), 201–229. Cf. Gilles Le Béguec, *La République des avocats* (Paris, 2003).

63. Ellis, *The Physician-Legislators of France,* 3–4.

64. Of those elected between 1876 and 1914, 48.2 percent were moderate (opportunist) republican, 34.4 percent were radical or radical-socialist, and 11.3 percent were conservative republican, with 3.1 percent socialist and 2.8 percent monarchist or Bonapartist. Ellis, *The Physician-Legislators of France,* 93–94.

65. Léonard, *La vie quotidienne du médecin de province,* 232.

66. Ellis, *The Physician-Legislators of France,* 242–243; Gaudemet, *Les juristes et la vie politique de la IIIe République,* 15–16, 19.

67. See David Kimon, "Mission antisémitique du barreau," *Le peuple français,* 3 Aug. 1898. Thanks to Vicki Caron for this reference. Cf. Jean-Pierre Royer, *Histoire de la justice en France de la monarchie absolue à la République* (Paris, 1996), 659–677; Christophe Charle, "Le déclin de la République des avocats," in *La France de l'Affaire Dreyfus,* ed. Pierre Birnbaum (Paris, 1994), 56–87; Catherine Fillon, *Histoire du barreau de Lyon sous la Troisième République* (Lyon, 1995), 67–101.

68. Ellis, *The Physician-Legislators of France,* 141, 139–156.

69. Vergez-Chaignon, "Le syndicalisme médical français de sa naissance à sa refondation," 710. In contrast, Hildreth believes that the unions greatly influenced the AMG debate; see "Medical Rivalries and Medical Politics in France," and *Doctors, Bureaucrats, and Public Health in France,* 22 and chap. 4.

70. Savage, "Advocates of the Republic," 184–185; Savage, "La Première Femme-Avocate."

71. Françoise Mayeur, *L'enseignement secondaire des jeunes filles sous la Troisième République* (Paris, 1977), 388–438; Carole Lécuyer, "Une nouvelle figure de la jeune fille sous la IIIe République: l'étudiante," *CLIO* 4 (1996): 166–176; Karen Offen, "The Second Sex and the Baccalaureat in Republican France, 1880–1924," *French Historical Studies* 13, no. 2 (1983): 252–286.

72. See Vicki Caron, *Between France and Germany: The Jews of Alsace-Lorraine, 1870–1918* (Stanford, 1988), 175.

73. Jean Jacques Dreifuss, "Les premières étudiantes à la Faculté de médecine et leurs activités professionelles à Genève," *Gesnerus* 48, nos. 3–4 (1991): 429; Nancy Green, "L'émigration comme émancipation: les femmes juives d'Europe de l'est à Paris, 1881–1914," *Pluriel* 27 (1981): 58; Melina Lipinska, *Les femmes et le progrès des sciences médicales* (Paris, 1930), 169; Thomas Neville Bonner, *To the Ends of the Earth: Women's Search for Education in Medicine* (Cambridge, Mass., 1992), 26–27, 78, 155.

74. J. Poirier and R. Nahon, "L'accession des femmes à la carrière médicale (à la fin du XIXe siècle)," in *Médecine et philosophie à la fin du XIXe siécle,* ed. J. Poirier and J. L. Poirier, 25–26; Goubert, *Initiation à une nouvelle histoire de la médecine,* 117–118.

75. The Association amicale des internes des hôpitaux de Paris would represent about 50 percent of interns and former interns before the end of the century. Groopman, "The Internat des Hôpitaux de Paris," 134.

76. All of women's pioneering steps took place in Paris. Women's access to medicine came more slowly in the countryside, but every provincial medical school in France counted at least one woman graduate before 1900.

77. On masculine codes of behavior in medicine, see Robert A. Nye, "The Legacy of Masculine Codes of Honor and Admission of Women to the Medical Profession in the Nineteenth Century," in *Women Physicians and the Cultures of Medicine,* ed. Ellen S. More, Elizabeth Fee, and Manon Parry (Baltimore, 2009), 141–159.

78. Poirier and Nahon, "L'accession des femmes à la carrière médicale."

79. John Savage, "The Problems of Wealth and Virtue: The Paris Bar and the Generation of the *Fin-de-Siècle,*" in *Lawyers and Vampires: Cultural Histories of Legal Professions,* ed. W. Wesley Pue and David Sugarman (Oxford, 2003), 198–200.

80. Ibid., 200.

81. *Recueil des statistiques scolaires et professionnelles de 1936 à 1942,* Bureau universitaire de statistique [hereafter BUS], Secrétariat d'État à l'Éducation Nationale et à la Jeunesse (1942), 12.

82. For an account of Chauvin's thesis defense and fight for bar access, see Sara Kimble, "Justice Redressed: Women, Citizenship, and the Social Uses of the Law in Modern France, 1890–1939" (Ph.D. diss., University of Iowa, 2002), chap. 2. Cf. Savage, "Advocates of the Republic," 356–368.

83. James C. Albisetti, "Portia ante Portas: Women and the Legal Profession in Europe, ca. 1870–1925," *Journal of Social History* 33, no. 4 (2000): 841–844; Catherine

Fillon, "La profession d'avocat et son image pendant l'entre-deux-guerres" (Ph.D. diss., Université de Lyon III, 1995), 326–336.

84. Kimble, "Justice Redressed," 96.

85. Edmée Charrier, *L'évolution intellectuelle féminine* (Paris, 1937). The Paris bar admitted not Chauvin but another candidate as the first woman in its ranks, Olga Balachowsky-Petit, a Russian by birth, married to a Paris lawyer. Chauvin is nonetheless often cited as "the first woman lawyer in France." Geo London, "Le Palais de Justice nouveau: les avocats aux deux robes," *Le journal* (12 February 1931): 1, Bibliothèque Marguerite Durand [hereafter BMD] DOS 349 AVO.

86. See Kimble, "Justice Redressed," 89–99, for more detailed analysis of the political ideologies at work. She notes that supposedly progressive lawyers were not always very progressive when it came to gender.

87. Bonner, *To the Ends of the Earth,* 164. See also Bonner, *Becoming a Physician: Medical Education in Britain, France, Germany, and the United States, 1750–1945* (New York, 1995), 339.

88. Albisetti, "Portia ante Portas," 825–838, 846–847.

89. Robert A. Nye, "Medicine and Science as Masculine 'Fields of Honor,'" *Osiris* 12 (1997): 60–79; Nye, "Honor Codes and Medical Ethics in Modern France," *Bulletin of the History of Medicine* 69 (1995): 91–111; Nye, *Masculinity and Male Codes of Honor in Modern France* (Oxford, 1993); Nye, *Crime, Madness, and Politics in Modern France: The Medical Concept of National Decline* (Princeton, 1984).

90. Nye, "The Legacy of Masculine Codes of Honor," 148.

91. Julie Fette, "Pride and Prejudice in the Professions: Women Doctors and Lawyers in Third Republic France," *Journal of Women's History* 19, no. 3 (Fall 2007): 60–86.

92. Poirier and Nahon, "L'accession des femmes à la carrière médicale," 29. In all French medical schools in 1900, women constituted 22 percent of foreign students (178 foreign women; 639 foreign men). *Recueil des statistiques.*

93. See the Association générale des médecins de France and the journals *Le concours médical, La semaine médicale,* and *Le bulletin médical,* AN AJ16 6709. Cf. Pierre-Georges-Gaston Gervais de Lafond, "De l'étude et de l'exercice de la médecine en France par les étrangers" (medical diss., Université de Paris, 1934), 152–159.

94. In 1911 there were 541 foreigners practicing (2.6 percent of all doctors in France), of whom 355 practiced in the Seine (8.2 percent of all doctors in the Seine). Jacques Léonard has no doubt that the legislation was a response to a lobbying campaign from below, not a political initiative from above. Léonard, *La médecine entre les savoirs et les pouvoirs,* 341 note 40, 92–93, 297.

95. This section of the chapter is based on Jean Pécout, "L'étude et l'exercice de la médecine par les étrangers" (law diss., Faculté d'Aix, 1939); Gervais de Lafond, "De l'étude et de l'exercice de la médecine en France par les étrangers"; and Marie Waxin, "Statut de l'étudiant étranger dans son développement historique" (law diss., Université de Paris, 1939).

96. Poirier and Nahon, "L'accession des femmes à la carrière médicale," 29. The petition was sent during the heated debate over women's access to hospital internships.

97. "Faculté de Médecine de Lyon, Rapport adressé à M. le Ministre de l'Instruction Publique sur la question des étudiants et des médecins étrangers au nom du Conseil de la Faculté," from *Bulletin des travaux de l'Université de Lyon* (June 1896), AN AJ16 6496.

98. *Bulletin administratif de l'Instruction publique* 1222, no. 60 (1896): 187. The circular did not address doctors' complaints about foreigners in internships.

99. The Romanian exception dated from an 1857 agreement between France and Romania. A Romanian prince asked the French government to help him organize a health service in his country. France sent Dr. Charles Davila, who founded a medical school in Bucharest. Davila encouraged the Romanian students there to study partly in Paris in order to benefit from French science. In a spirit of international exchange, the French minister of education decreed in 1857 that students from the Bucharest school could earn a doctorate in medicine at the Paris Medical School with equivalencies for their secondary study and credits for their medical studies done abroad. Decrees in 1866 and 1880 extended this right to all Romanian students and to all French medical schools, and a ministerial circular of 1896 further institutionalized the notion of equivalency between the Romanian and French baccalaureates. The principle behind the accord was that Romanian medical students were to be granted exemptions for access to French education and diplomas, while France would augment its influence and prestige in the Balkans. The Mauritian exception was a favor extended to natives of Mauritius, considered "Français d'origine," whose British baccalaureate had long been considered equivalent to the French one. *Journal officiel* [hereafter *JO*], Débats Parlementaires, Sénat (6 Feb. 1930 session): 80–81; *JO*, Débats Parlementaires, Sénat (9 June 1931 session): 1024–33; Donna Evleth, "The 'Romanian Privilege' in French Medicine and Anti-Semitism," *Social History of Medicine* 11, no. 2 (1998): 213–232.

100. All faculties in Paris envisioned the *diplôme d'université* as in no way convertible into a *diplôme d'état*. "Les propositions faites par toutes les facultés... au sujet de l'organisation d'un doctorat universitaire," Conseil de l'Université de Paris, 8 and 29 March 1897, dossier "Institution d'un doctorat d'université," AN AJ16 8351.

101. "Rapport de M. P. Brouardel," Commission pour l'étude de l'institution d'un doctorat universitaire, au nom du Conseil de l'Université de Paris et du Conseil de la Faculté de Médecine, Assemblée de la Faculté de Médecine, 21 Jan. 1897, AN AJ16 8351.

102. "Question de MM. Astier et Dubois sur la tendance de la Faculté de Médecine de Paris à éloigner les étudiants étrangers," *Bulletin municipal officiel* (10 July 1897): 2239–40, AN AJ16 6496.

103. Letter from Professor Debove, *Le monde médical* (1 Aug. 1897), AN AJ16 6496; Rapport de la Commission chargée d'examiner la proposition de M. le Professeur Debove demandant l'admission des étrangers à la Faculté de Médecine de Paris (1897?), AN AJ16 8351.

104. *The Nation* (24 Oct. 1901), AN AJ16 8351.

105. Consular responses to the 3 Feb. 1912 survey by the minister of foreign affairs (Poincaré) about the rights of foreign *diplomés* to practice medicine in each country, as requested of him by the minister of education. Archives du Ministère des Affaires Étrangères [hereafter MAE] C 253.

106. Many countries had rules regulating foreigners practicing medicine, though they tended to be less strict than the late-nineteenth-century trends in France. Italy, Portugal, Denmark, Russia, Romania, Great Britain, Turkey, New Zealand, Chile, Venezuela, Canada, and the United States required proof of a foreign diploma, the final medical exam to be passed in the country of practice, and administrative formalities. Luxembourg and Belgium were almost entirely closed to foreigners, although both countries had diplomatic conventions with France allowing nationals of the countries to practice on either side of the border. Other countries also experienced popular mobilization against foreigners in medicine at this time. In both Germany and Switzerland, medical students accused foreigners of crowding their schools. In Germany, xenophobia was marked by

anti-Semitism toward Russian Jewish medical students, and yielded government restrictions on foreign students in 1912. Overall, French medicine was on the restrictive end of the international spectrum at the end of the nineteenth century, and would follow in the steps of Serbia and Germany toward a more extreme direction after the First World War. See consular responses to the 3 Feb. 1912 survey by the minister of foreign affairs about the rights of foreign doctors to practice medicine in each country, as requested of him by the minister of education, MAE C 253. In Belgium, it was commonplace for medical juries to approve foreign doctors' credentials but for the Gouvernement Royal not to approve the candidates as a "measure of protectionism to prevent foreign doctors from competing with Belgian doctors in their own country." French Consul General in Brussels to the Minister of Foreign Affairs (12 March 1912), MAE C 253. Cf. Bonner, *Becoming a Physician,* 315–316.

107. Two issues remained contentious, however: disputes with foreign doctors along France's borders and the right of foreign students to replace doctors during sick leave or vacation. Ministre de l'Intérieur to Ministre des Affaires Étrangères (27 April 1912), MAE C 253; Doyen de la Faculté de Médecine de Paris to Préfet de Police, Bureau de l'Hygiene (22 Sept. 1911), AN AJ16 8351; Ministre de l'Intérieur to Préfets (15 Nov. 1913), AN AJ16 8351.

108. Christophe Charle, "Méritocratie et profession juridique: les secrétaires de la Conférence du stage des avocats de Paris, une étude des promotions 1860–1870 et 1879–1889," *Paedogogica historica* 30, no. 1 (1994): 303–324.

109. *Recueil des statistiques,* 12; Charle, "Le recrutement des avocats parisiens, 1880–1914," 23.

110. In 1910 there were 1,143 foreigners out of 9,721 students in French medical schools, compared with 1,158 foreigners out of 16,915 students in French law schools.

111. Halpérin, *Avocats et notaires en Europe,* 174.

112. Savage, "Advocates of the Republic," 82–85, 189–191, 393.

113. Charle, "Le recrutement des avocats parisiens," 22.

114. Matthew Ramsey, "The Politics of Professional Monopoly in Nineteenth-Century Medicine: The French Model and Its Rivals," in *Professions and the French State, 1700–1900,* ed. Gerald Geison (Philadelphia, 1984), 240.

115. Ackerman, *Health Care in the Parisian Countryside,* 165–168; Ramsey, "Medical Power and Popular Medicine," 202. Ramsey's analysis, differing with Foucault's, emphasizes the limits of medical power.

116. Halpérin, *Avocats et notaires en Europe,* 66; see also 301.

117. Savage, "Advocates of the Republic," 106–113.

2. Defense of the Corps

1. Patrick Weil, "The History of French Nationality: A Lesson for Europe," in *Towards a European Nationality: Citizenship, Immigration, and Nationality Law in the EU,* ed. Randall Hansen and Patrick Weil (New York, 2001), 59.

2. Naturalized French citizens were first deprived of full citizenship rights by the 1889 Nationality Code, which instituted a waiting period of ten years for eligibility for election to parliamentary assemblies. The 1927 nationality law extended the principle of reduced citizenship rights for naturalized French by applying the ten-year delay to all elected functions. Gérard Noiriel, *Le creuset français* (Paris, 1988), 83–84, 93–95.

3. Weil, *Qu'est-ce qu'un Français?* 244–246.

4. Bernard Laguerre, "Les dénaturalisés de Vichy, 1940–1944," *Vingtième siècle* 20 (1988): 3–15.

5. Caron, *Uneasy Asylum*.

6. Pierre Guillaume, "Du bon usage des immigrés en temps de crise et de guerre, 1932–1940," *Vingtième siècle* 7 (July–Sept. 1985): 117–125; Mary Lewis, *The Boundaries of the Republic: Migrant Rights and the Limits of Universalism in France, 1918–1940* (Stanford, 2007); Schor, *L'opinion française et les étrangers*.

7. Zdatny, *The Politics of Survival*.

8. Claire Zalc, *Melting Shops: une histoire des commerçants étrangers en France* (Paris, 2010); Nord, *Paris Shopkeepers and the Politics of Resentment*.

9. Marie-Claire Laval-Reviglio, "Parlementaires xénophobes et antisémites sous la IIIe République: débats relatifs à la nationalité et à la 'protection du travail national,'" in *Le droit antisémite de Vichy* (Paris, 1996), 85–114.

10. Alain Chatriot, "La lutte contre le 'chômage intellectuel': l'action de la Confédération des travailleurs intellectuels (CTI) face à la crise des années trente," *Le mouvement social* 214 (Jan.–March 2006): 77–91.

11. "Statistique générale des étudiants français, coloniaux, étrangers, Université de Paris" and "Statistique des étudiants des Facultés de Médecine au 31 juillet 1939," Archives de l'Académie de Paris [hereafter AP] 226, 227, or 228 (original cartons have since been reclassified, see bibliography).

12. The only source from the period that makes these explicit distinctions is Pierre Babin, "Étude statistique sur la profession médicale: répartition des médecins dans les divers milieux" (medical diss., Université de Paris, 1939), 32.

13. Nicolas Manitakis, "Étudiants étrangers, universités françaises et marché du travail intellectuel," in *Construction des nationalités et immigration dans la France contemporaine*, ed. Eric Guichard and Gérard Noiriel (Paris, 1997), 135–137.

14. See Nicolas Manitakis, "L'essor de la mobilité étudiante internationale à l'âge des états-nations, une étude de cas: les étudiants grecs en France (1880–1940)" (Ph.D. diss., École des hautes études en sciences sociales, 2004).

15. "Statistique générale des étudiants français, coloniaux, étrangers, Université de Paris" and "Statistique des étudiants des Facultés de Médecine au 31 juillet 1939," AP 226, 227, or 228. The vast majority of foreign medical students in France studied in Paris.

16. See Ezra Mendelsohn, *The Jews of East Central Europe between the Wars* (Bloomington, 1983); Bonner, *To the Ends of the Earth*, 66, 94, 97; Maria M. Kovacs, "Luttes professionnelles et antisémitisme: chronique de la montée du fascisme dans le corps médical hongrois, 1920–1944," *Actes de la recherche en sciences sociales* 56 (March 1985): 31–44; Victor Karady and Istvan Kemeny, "Antisémitisme universitaire et concurrence de classe: la loi du numerus clausus en Hongrie entre les deux guerres," *Actes de la recherche en sciences sociales* 34 (Sept. 1980): 67–96.

17. Recueil des statistiques, 6, 67–71; Babin, "Étude statistique sur la profession médicale," 34–35.

18. Alfred Rosier, "Du chômage intellectuel: de l'encombrement des professions libérales," Bureau universitaire de statistique (BUS) report for Anatole de Monzie (31 March 1933), 45–46, AP 350.

19. Babin, "Étude statistique sur la profession médicale," 23–29.

20. Ibid., 6.

21. Total statistics include Algeria. "Rapport fait au nom de la Commission de l'Hygiène chargée d'examiner la proposition de loi de M. Cousin," Ministère de la

Santé Publique and BUS, cited in *JO*, Documents Parlementaires, Chambre des Députés, Annexe 5010 (18 March 1935): 630.

22. Babin, "Étude statistique sur la profession médicale," 18–22.

23. "Statistique des étudiants des Facultés de Médecine au 31 juillet 1939," AP 226, 227, or 228; Recueil des statistiques; "Université de Clermont-Ferrand, Rapports sur la situation et les travaux des établissements d'enseignement supérieur pendant l'année scolaire 1936–37, rentrée solennelle des Facultés" (2 Dec. 1937).

24. Gustave Roussy, "L'enseignement de la médecine en France," excerpts from *Bulletin trimestriel* of the Organisation d'Hygiène of the League of Nations 1, no. 3 (Sept. 1932). Roussy, a famous oncologist, was named to a chair as a professor in Paris in 1926, and became dean of the Paris Medical School in 1933 and rector of the Paris Academy in 1937. In the 1930s he resisted the anti-foreigner mobilization and became himself a victim of Vichy's anti-foreigner legislation, losing his job as rector because of his Swiss origins.

25. Schor, *L'opinion française et les étrangers*, 602. Schor does not cite his source.

26. On the statistical disappearance of naturalized citizens, see Eric Guichard, "Manières de voir, manières de compter dans les recensements de 1931 et 1936," in *Construction des nationalités et immigration*, ed. Guichard and Noiriel, 71–97.

27. Waxin, "Statut de l'étudiant étranger dans son développement historique," 258–259.

28. "Xénophobie?... Non, mais Francophilie," *La butte médicale: bulletin de la Société amicale des médecins du XVIII arrondissement* (Paris) [hereafter *La butte médicale*] 93 (July 1939): 7.

29. Victor Balthazard, "Réforme des études médicales," sub-commission report of the Comité consultatif de l'enseignement supérieur, sections de Médecine et Pharmacie (March 1931), AN AJ16 6498.

30. *JO*, Débats Parlementaires, Sénat (9 June 1931 session): 1024.

31. *JO*, Documents Parlementaires, Chambre des Députés, Annexe 6193, (22 Jan. 1932 session): 95 (citing Professeur Sergent).

32. Luxembourgeois doctors also hoping to benefit from this special favor were refused by the French government, which saw no need to go beyond the Belgian exception. Exchange of correspondence between the Direction des affaires administratives et techniques and the Direction des affaires politiques et commerciales of the Ministry of Foreign Affairs (3 and 5 March 1915), MAE C 253, page 12.

33. "Médecins étrangers," *Bulletin officiel du Syndicat médical de Paris* [hereafter *SMP*] 1 (Jan. 1925): 17.

34. "Conseil d'administration de la Fédération corporative des médecins de la région parisienne" (5 Oct. 1928 session), *SMP* 9 (Nov. 1928): 400. French women doctors had also found more opportunities to establish themselves professionnally during the mobilization, but they were equally targetted for dismissal upon male doctors' return from the front. Vergez, "Internes et anciens internes des Hopitaux de Paris," 38–41.

35. For example, Paris Medical School dean Henri Roger in 1919 ordered three thousand brochures to be printed and distributed to lure foreign students to register for studies at the school, albeit for the diplôme d'université. AN AJ16 6498.

36. "Rapport annuel sur le fonctionnement de la Faculté de Médecine de Paris," *La science médicale pratique* 8 (1 July 1928): 265.

37. Dr. Paul Guérin, "La médecine française devant l'invasion étrangère," *Candide* (8 Oct. 1934), republished in *Revue médicale de l'Office central de médecine de l'Union*

nationale des étudiants et de Clermont-Ferrand 9 (Dec. 1934): 7. Cf. "Le Front médical français," *Bulletin mensuel de l'Association amicale des étudiants en médecine de Paris* 1 (May 1935): 20; Eugen Weber, *The Hollow Years: France in the 1930s* (New York, 1994), 88.

38. Founded in 1883 in order to provide doctors for Syria and the Near East, the Beirut school did not require the French baccalaureate but only a simple entrance examination. The purpose of the school was to spread French influence in the region and not, it was argued, to allow its graduates to practice in France. Senateur Dentu, "Rapport fait au nom de la Commission de l'enseignement," *JO*, Documents Parlementaires, Sénat, Annexe 147 (3 March 1931): 81; "Pour la défense de la médecine française," *L'écho des étudiants* 488 (27 Dec. 1931): 2.

39. For complaints about the number of foreigners in Parisian high schools and initiatives to restrict them, particularly during the 1934 German refugee crisis, see correspondence among the director of the Lycée Pasteur, the rector of the Académie de Paris, and the minister of Public Instruction, April–May 1934, AN AJ16 8804.

40. Robert A. Nye and Anaïs Bokobza, "Médecins, éthique médicale et état en France, 1789–1947," *Le mouvement social* 214 (Jan.–March 2006): 32.

41. Jean Pécout, "L'étude et l'exercice de la médecine par les étrangers" (law diss., Université d'Aix-Marseille, 1939), 38.

42. "Le décret Herriot," *Bulletin de la Fédération des syndicats médicaux du département du Nord* [hereafter *SM Nord*] 20 (Dec. 1928): 338.

43. Timothy B. Smith, "The Social Transformation of Hospitals and the Rise of Medical Insurance in France, 1914–1943," *Historical Journal* 41, no. 4 (Dec. 1998): 1057, 1082.

44. "Chronique du provincial," *La science médicale pratique* 16 (15 Oct. 1930): 614.

45. H. Signoret, "Nous et eux (ou la véritable cause de la pléthore médicale)," *La butte médicale*, 38 (May 1930): 7.

46. Gervais de Lafond, "De l'étude et de l'exercice de la médecine en France par les étrangers," 174.

47. Paul Cibrie, secretary-general of the Confédération, to all member unions, published in *SM Nord* 2 (Feb. 1929): 27.

48. Senateur Armbruster, Proposition de loi, *JO*, Documents Parlementaires, Sénat, Annexe 229 (8 April 1930): 766.

49. Ibid., 765–767.

50. Some active union members wishing to take matters into their own hands occasionally accused the Confédération of inaction and incompetence regarding its antiforeigner agenda. See "Syndicat des médecins de la banlieue ouest et nord de Paris, Assemblée générale du 26 juin 1936," *Fédération des Syndicats médicaux de la Seine, Syndicat des médecins de la banlieue ouest et nord de Paris, bulletin officiel* [hereafter *SM Seine, Banlieue Ouest et Nord*] 111 (Nov. 1936): 39–51.

51. Dr. Vauzanges, "Impressions d'Assemblée générale," *Bulletin mensuel du Groupement des syndicats médicaux de l'Aube* [hereafter *SM Aube*] (Dec. 1932): 362.

52. On court cases of illegal medical practice, see AN BB18 60022, 60023, 6582, 6583, 6584.

53. "Les indésirables," *Bulletin du Syndicat médical de Seine-et-Oise* [hereafter *SM Seine-et-Oise*] 11 (Aug. 1931): 9.

54. "Association corporative des étudiants en médecine de Paris," *L'écho des étudiants* 477 (10 Oct. 1931): 3, reprinted in *La science médicale pratique* 15 (1 Oct. 1931):

726; "Pour la défense de la médecine française," *L'écho des étudiants* 488 (27 Dec. 1931): 2.

55. Dr. G. Jayles, "Le péril de la médecine française," *Revue médicale de la Section corporative de Montpellier et de l'Office central de médecine de l'Union nationale des étudiants* (Montpellier) 32 (Feb. 1932): 41–54.

56. "Office de médecine, communications du directeur: la loi Armbruster," *Revue médicale de la Section corporative de Montpellier et de l'Office central de médecine de l'Union nationale des étudiants* (Montpellier) 31 (Jan. 1932): 9.

57. "Un exemple à ne pas suivre," *AEMP, bulletin mensuel* 6 (April 1939): 11.

58. Signoret, "Nous et eux," 5–6.

59. *JO*, Débats Parlementaires, Sénat, (27 June 1935 session): 758.

60. Maurice Mordagne interviewing Dean Roger of Paris Medical School in *L'information universitaire*, excerpts reprinted in *L'écho des étudiants* 428 (30 July 1930): 3, discussed by Senateur Dentu, "Rapport fait au nom de la Commission de l'enseignement," *JO*, Documents Parlementaires, Sénat, Annexe 147 (3 March 1931): 81.

61. Created in 1820, the Académie de médecine was meant to advise the government on all issues of public health. The academy's long history, its close relationship with the ministry of public health, and its numerous well-known and well-connected members (dean of the Paris Medical School Victor Balthazard, for example), gave it great influence over parliament. See Weisz, *The Medical Mandarins*.

62. "Séance du 7 juillet 1931," *Bulletin de l'Académie de médecine* 26 (1931); "Pour la défense de la médecine française," *L'écho des étudiants* 471 (23 July 1931): 3.

63. Dr. Joseph Chalier, "La pléthore médicale: ses dangers," *Bulletin officiel du Syndicat des médecins de Marseille et d'arrondissement, de la Fédération des syndicats médicaux des Bouches-du-Rhône* 6 (June 1931): 524–532, quotation 530.

64. Gervais de Lafond, "De l'étude et de l'exercice de la médecine en France par les étrangers," 181, 190.

65. "Voeu adressé à tous les parlementaires du Lot-et-Garonne," *Bulletin de la Société des médecins et du Syndicat médical de Lot-et-Garonne* 38 (Dec. 1929): 38.

66. Senateur Dentu, "Rapport fait au nom de la Commission de l'enseignement," *JO*, Documents Parlementaires, Sénat, Annexe 147 (3 March 1931): 81.

67. Dr. Chauveau, Séance du 9 juin 1931, Sénat, excerpts from *JO* published in *SM Aube* (July 1931): 181.

68. Dr. Armbruster, Séance du 9 juin 1931, Sénat, excerpts from *JO* published in *SM Aube* (July 1931): 189.

69. Dr. Chauveau, *JO*, Débats Parlementaires, Sénat (9 June 1931 session): 1027.

70. Dr. Armbruster, Séance du 9 juin 1931, 189.

71. Dr. Deguignand, "La proposition de loi Armbruster au Sénat," *SM Aube* (July 1931): 176.

72. Henri Nahum, *La médecine française et les juifs, 1930–1945* (Paris, 2006), 70.

73. Dr. G. Dhers, "Nouvelles médicales," *La science médicale pratique* 17 (1 Nov. 1931): 835–836.

74. As defined by the 10 August 1927 law on nationality.

75. Correspondence, Ministry of Foreign Affairs, Documents no. 48, 49, 50, 51, MAE C 254.

76. Evleth, "The 'Romanian Privilege' in French Medicine and Anti-Semitism," 213–232.

77. Dr. Henry, "La question des étudiants en médecine étrangers," *L'Université de Paris, revue mensuelle de l'Association générale des étudiants* 245 (Oct. 1922): 7–8.

78. "Étudiants roumains" (handwritten document), and untitled document on Université de Paris, Faculté de Médecine letterhead (two drafts, one of which is dated October 1923), AN AJ16 6498.

79. Nahum, *La médecine française et les juifs*, 56–61.

80. *JO*, Débats Parlementaires, Sénat (6 Feb. 1930 session): 80–81; *JO*, Débats Parlementaires, Sénat (9 June 1931 session): 1024–33; *JO*, Documents Parlementaires, Sénat, Annexe 802 (26 Nov. 1931 session): 1176–77.

81. Senateur Dentu, Rapport fait au nom de la Commission de l'enseignement, *JO*, Documents Parlementaires, Sénat, Annexe 147 (3 March 1931): 81.

82. Balthazard, "Réforme des études médicales," cited in Chalier, "La pléthore médicale," 528.

83. Balthazard, "Réforme des études médicales." A Paris medical school dissertation of 1939 also asserted that Jewish medical students came to France not just because they were discriminated against but because their intellectual level was too low for them to gain acceptance in their native universities. Albin Faivre, "Aspect médical et social du problème des étrangers en France" (medical diss., Université de Paris, 1939), 75. Even though a numerus clausus, or quota, on Jews in Romanian universities did not officially exist until the mid- to late 1930s, Romanian students had agitated for it since 1922. Students and professors were key actors in Romanian anti-Semitic movements, and universities were the site of the most violent anti-Semitism. See Leon Volovici, *Nationalist Ideology and Antisemitism: The Case of Romanian Intellectuals in the 1930s* (Oxford, 1991); Mendelsohn, *The Jews of East Central Europe between the Wars*, chap. 4, "Romania"; Caron, *Uneasy Asylum*, 173–174.

84. Balthazard, "Réforme des études médicales."

85. "Chronique du provincial," *La science médicale pratique* 9 (1 May 1931): 422.

86. Caron, *Uneasy Asylum*, 29–32; Evleth, "The 'Romanian Privilege' in French Medicine."

87. Romanian Prime Minister Nicolae Iorga made no objection to the French renunciation of the privilege, although his minister of health expressed disagreement. Correspondence, Ministère des Affaires Étrangères, 1930–1931, MAE C 253; Ministre des Affaires Étrangères to Balthazard (1931 or 1932); Légation de Romanie en France to Balthazard, 28 April 1931, AN AJ16 6498. On Iorga's non-defense of Romanians in France, see Volovici, *Nationalist Ideology and Antisemitism*, and Iorga's own publications, which include *Histoire des Relations entre la France et les Roumains* (1918).

88. *JO*, Débats Parlementaires, Sénat (8 Dec. 1931 session): 1564. See also "Projet de loi Armbruster," *Bulletin officiel du Syndicat des médecins de Marseille et d'arrondissement, de la Fédération des syndicats médicaux des Bouches-du-Rhône* 7 (July 1931): 593.

89. Students were to apply directly to French medical schools, and the deans were to forward the applications to the Ministry of Education, where decision making would be centralized. Ministre de l'Instruction Publique circular, 22 July 1931, Arrêtés, 21 and 22 July 1931, *JO* (23 July 1931), published in *SM Aube* (Aug. 1931): 203–208.

90. M.V., "L'élimination des médecins juifs en Allemagne et leur apport à la science médicale allemande," *Races et racismes: bulletin du Groupement d'étude et d'information* 9, no. 10 (June–Sept. 1938): 14–16.

91. Caron, *Uneasy Asylum*, 80–86, 117–141. Cf. Ligue française pour la défense des droits de l'homme et du citoyen to Ministre des Affaires Étrangères, 8 June 1933, in favor of German refugee doctors, MAE C 254.

92. "Section syndicale du 18e, séance du 10 juin 1933," *La butte médicale* 57 (July 1933): 29–30; "Association corporative des étudiants en médecine de Paris," *L'écho des étudiants* 559 (21 July 1933): 4; "Malgré la loi Armbruster ... on ouvre largement les portes aux médecins étrangers," *SM Seine-et-Oise* 23 (Aug. 1933): 156–157; "La question des médecins israélites allemands," *SM Seine, Banlieue Ouest et Nord* 92 (Sept. 1933): 22; "Réunion du 28 juin 1933," *Le bouclier* 37 (Sept. 1933): 200; "Congrès d'Aix-Marseille, 3–10 avril 1934, Office central des études de médecine," *Revue médicale de l'Office central de l'Union nationale des étudiants et de Clermont-Ferrand* 6 (March–April 1934): 25; "À propos des étudiants en médecine et médecins israélites allemands réfugiés en France," *SMP* 8 (Oct. 1933): 400–403.

93. Ministry of Justice report, 1 Aug. 1933, regarding the Interministerial Commission of 27 May 1933 organized to examine the situation of German refugees, AN F7 16079; Caron, *Uneasy Asylum*, 142–170, 191.

94. Sous-Direction d'Europe, "Note pour la Sous-Direction d'Afrique-Levant," Ministère des Affaires Étrangères, 29 April 1933, and correspondence between Ministère des Affaires Étrangères and Consul de France in Berlin, May 1933, MAE C 254.

95. See the petition of the Syndicat des médecins de Colombes, *SM Seine, Banlieue Ouest et Nord* 105 (Nov. 1935): 57; Peyrouton, Ministère des Affaires Étrangères, Tunis, to Ministère des Affaires Étrangères, Paris, 24 Nov. 1934, MAE C 254 no. 62.

96. *JO*, Débats Parlementaires, Sénat (9 June 1931 session): 1032–33.

97. "Conseil d'administration de la Confédération, 3 juillet 1938," minutes reprinted in "La question des naturalisations des médecins étrangers," *Bulletin officiel du Syndicat des médecins du département d'Oran* 44 (1938): 13–14.

98. Togo and Cameroon were excepted. Ministère des Affaires Étrangères to Consul Général de France in Dresden, Sept. 1938, MAE C 254 no. 58.

99. Vergez, "Internes et anciens internes des hôpitaux de Paris," 211–217.

100. "Question écrite de M. le Général Stuhl, sénateur, à M. le Ministre d l'Éducation Nationale," *L'écho des étudiants* 624 (30 Jan. 1935): 2–5. Cf. "Note concernant les réfugiés juifs," Ministère de l'Intérieur, Direction de la sûreté générale, Service central des cartes d'identités des étrangers, 24 May 1933, AN F7 16079.

101. The medical school in Lwów subjected Jews to a numerus clausus and a physical exam. To discourage the return of Polish Jews who had studied medicine abroad, Poland passed regulations in the mid-1930s to disallow foreign medical diplomas for the practice of medicine in Poland. "L'Association des diplômés polonais de France à M. le Doyen et MM. les Professeurs de la Faculté de Médecine de Paris," 1935(?), AN AJ16 8374; Consulat de France, Warsaw, to M. le Ministre des Affaires Étrangères, 21 July 1939, MAE C 255 no. 113–114; "Assemblée générale du 25 novembre 1928," *SM Nord* 20 (Dec. 1928): 337–338; dossier "Circulaire du Ministre de l'Intérieur, D-4–1, du 31 août 1939," AN F7 16050.

102. M. P. Chastand, Consul de France, Lwów, to Ministre des Affaires Étrangères, 8 Feb. 1931, MAE Z 433 no. 30; Chastand, Consul de France, Lwów, to Ministre des Affaires Étrangères, 23 Jan. 1932, MAE Z 433 no. 102–103.

103. Le Chargé d'Affaires de France, Romania, to M. le Ministre des Affaires Étrangères Georges Bonnet, 8 Aug. 1938, forwarded to Ministre de la Santé Publique, 27 Aug. 1938, AN F17 17634.

104. Cf. "Statistique générale des étudiants français, coloniaux, étrangers, Université de Paris" and "Statistique des étudiants des facultés de médecine au 31 juillet 1939," AP 226, 227, or 228.

105. Guérin, "La médecine française devant l'invasion étrangère," 13.

106. Vergez, "Internes et anciens internes des hôpitaux de Paris," 60–62, 172–174, 196–217.

107. "Dr. d'Ayrenx intervention, Conseil d'administration de la Fédération corporative des médecins de la région parisienne, séance du 5 décembre 1930," *SMP* 1 (Jan. 1931): 45–46; Dr. d'Ayrenx, "Rapport sur les médecins étrangers," *SMP* 4 (April 1935): 103.

108. "La vie corporative," *Revue médicale de la Section corporative de Montpellier* 51 (March 1934): 357; "Congrès d'Aix-Marseille, 3–10 avril 1934, Office central des études de médecine," *Revue médicale de l'Office central de l'Union nationale des étudiants et de Clermont-Ferrand* 6 (March–April 1934): 25; Maurice Mordagne, "La situation des étudiants en médecine juifs allemands dans nos facultés: Dans quelles conditions pourront-ils exercer la médecine en France?" *SMP* 7 (July 1934): 263.

109. D'Ayrenx "Rapport sur les médecins étrangers," 104–105.

110. "Historique de l'Association des étudiants en médecine de Paris," ca. 1937, AP 214.

111. "Question parlementaire de Senateur Achille Naudin au Ministre de la Santé Publique," 16 June 1933, *JO*, 18 Oct. 1933, published in *SM Aube* (Dec. 1933): 369–370.

112. "Conseil d'état, demande d'avis sur l'interprétation à donner à l'article unique de la loi du 19 juillet 1934," *SM Seine-et-Oise* 38 (July 1935): 299–306. An official at the Ministry of Public Health, however, signaled to doctors a different, more restrictive interpretation. Dr. Aublant, Médecin Chef des services de l'hygiène, Directeur de l'Office départemental d'hygiène social, letter, 16 May 1935, *SM Seine-et-Oise* 38 (July 1935): 297–98.

113. Guérin, "La médecine française devant l'invasion étrangère," 13.

114. Dr. F. Querrioux, "Rapport sur l'application aux médecins étrangers naturalisés de la loi du 29 juillet 1934 visant les avocats étrangers naturalisés," *SM Seine, Banlieue Ouest et Nord* 101 (March 1935): 126, also published in *SMP* 1 (Jan. 1935): 18.

115. Proposition de loi Dommange, *JO*, Documents Parlementaires, Chambre des Députés, Annexe 4425 (10 Jan. 1935): 17–18; Rapport de M. le Député Louis Rolland, *JO*, Documents Parlementaires, Chambre des Députés, Annexe 4811 (26 Feb. 1935): 369.

116. "Réponse à la 'Conférence sur l'Ordre des médecins' faite par le Dr. Paul Cibrie le 22 mars 1935," *La science médicale pratique* 8 (15 April 1935): 249. The reference is to Alexandre Stavisky, a Russian Jewish swindler at the heart of a financial scandal in 1930s France that had major political ramifications.

117. Proposition de loi Dommange, 17–18.

118. Querrioux, "Rapport sur l'application aux médecins étrangers naturalisés de la loi du 29 juillet 1934 visant les avocats étrangers naturalisés," 131–134.

119. D'Ayrenx, "Rapport sur les médecins étrangers," 104–105.

120. Doyen de la Faculté de Droit (Allix) to the Recteur de l'Académie de Paris, 2 Feb. 1935, and Recteur de l'Académie de Paris to the Ministre de l'Education Nationale, 2 Feb. 1935, AP 269.

121. "Après la grève," *L'écho des étudiants* 626 (13 Feb. 1935): 2–3.

122. Roger Coujard, "L'externat aux Français," *Le front médical, bulletin mensuel de l'Association amicale des étudiants en médecine de Paris* 2 (June 1935): 3.

123. "Après la grève," 3–4; "La grève des étudiants s'est poursuivie hier," *Action française* (3 Feb. 1935): 2.

124. See "Les étudiants contre l'invasion des métèques," *Action française* (1 Feb. 1935): 1; "Les étrangers dans la médecine française," *Action française* 193 (15 Feb. 1935): 1.

125. Pierre Péan, *Une jeunesse française* (Paris, 1994), 33–39, and photo section.

126. On the right-wing agitation of students in the first half of the twentieth century, see Jean-François Sirinelli, "Action française: main basse sur le quartier latin!" *L'histoire* 51 (Dec. 1982): 6–15.

127. On 1 March, medical student members of the Action française organized an anti-foreigner meeting in Paris. Some notable non-students present included Dr. Querrioux and Léon Daudet. "Les revendications des étudiants en médecine," *L'écho des étudiants* 630 (13 March 1935): 2.

128. Recteur de l'Académie de Paris to the Ministre de l'Education Nationale, 2 Feb. 1935, AP 269.

129. "La grève des étudiants s'est poursuivie hier," 2.

130. AP 269.

131. "Après la grève," 4–5.

132. "L'Association corporative des étudiants en médecine de Paris chez M. Mallarmé," *L'oeuvre* (6 April 1935), AP 213.

133. *JO*, Débats Parlementaires, Chambre des Députés, 22 Feb. 1935 session (23 Feb. 1935): 630.

134. Proposition de loi Cousin, *JO*, Documents Parlementaires, Chambre des Députés, Annexe 4256 (10 Dec. 1934): 209.

135. Proposition de loi Dommange, 17–18; Rapport de Député Louis Rolland, 368–369.

136. "Après la grève," 4–5.

137. "Les revendications des étudiants en médecine," *L'écho des étudiants* 627 (20 Feb. 1935): 2, 4. Laffitte had ties to the Action française.

138. Henri Queuille, Ministre de la Santé Publique, circular, 4 Feb. 1935, published in "Les premiers résultats des manifestations des étudiants en médecine," *Le siècle médical* 194 (1 March 1935): 5.

139. "Après la grève," 3.

140. "Remplacements médicaux," *SM Aube* (March 1935): 70.

141. "Congrès annuel du Groupement des syndicats médicaux de Lorraine du 27 septembre 1931," *Le médecin de Lorraine* 6 (Nov. 1931): 10.

142. "Remplacements médicaux," 70–74.

143. "À propos des médecins étrangers et des troubles du Quartier latin," *L'UMFIA [l'Union médicale franco-ibéro-américaine], revue mensuelle* 98 (June 1935), AP 269.

144. "Le docteur Dartigues est nommé Commandeur du grand ordre de l'Étoile de Roumanie," *L'UMFIA, revue mensuelle* 98 (June 1935), AP 269.

145. Letter from the director of *L'information universitaire*, 9 April 1937, AP 213.

146. "Les revendications des étudiants," *L'écho des étudiants* 631 (20 March 1935): 2.

147. Paul Vivien, "L'association des externes et les étudiants étrangers," *La science médicale pratique* 8 (15 April 1935): 255–257; "Assemblée générale de l'A.E" (Association des externes et anciens externes des hôpitaux de Paris), 8 June 1935, *La science médicale pratique* 13–14 (1–15 July 1935): 413–416. Roussy's participation here is presumably perfunctory, since he was against the anti-foreigner mobilization.

148. Vergez, "Internes et anciens internes des hôpitaux de Paris," 252–266; Nahum, *La médecine française et les juifs*, 74–77.

149. "La grève des étudiants s'est poursuivie hier," 2.

150. Recteur de l'Académie de Nancy to the Ministre de l'Éducation Nationale, 6 Feb. 1935, AP 269.

151. Maurice Mordagne, "Exercice de la médecine en France par les étrangers," excerpt from the session of 7 June 1935 of the Fédération corporative des médecins de la région parisienne, published in *SMP* 6 (June 1935): 22.

152. "Bravo les jeunes," *SM Seine-et-Oise* 32 (Jan. 1935); "Les médecins étrangers," *Bulletin de l'Internat des hôpitaux de Paris* 86 (Jan. 1935): 8; "À propos de la protestation des étudiants," *Syndicats médicaux picards, bulletin officiel de la Fédération des syndicats médicaux de la Somme* 31 (April 1935): 6; "La grève des étudiants en médecine," *Bulletin officiel de l'Association professionnelle des internes et anciens internes des hôpitaux de Marseille* 2 (Feb. 1935): 10–11.

153. D'Ayrenx, "Rapport sur les médecins étrangers," 104.

154. "Après la grève," 5.

155. Dr. L. Vaslin, "Syndicat des médecins de la banlieue ouest et nord de Paris, Conseil d'administration, réunion du 8 mars 1935," *SM Seine, Banlieue Ouest et Nord* 103 (July 1935): 83.

156. Dr. Hilaire, "Les médecins étrangers," *SM Seine, Banlieue Ouest et Nord* 102 (May 1935): 107–108.

157. "Conseil d'administration du Syndicat des médecins de la banlieue ouest et nord de Paris, du 8 février 1935," *SM Seine, Banlieue Ouest et Nord* 102 (May 1935): 38.

158. Rapport fait au nom de la Commission de l'Hygiène chargée d'examiner la proposition de loi de M. Cousin, *JO*, Documents Parlementaires, Chambre des Députés, Annexe 5010 (18 March 1935): 629–635.

159. Archer blamed the monetary policy of the Bank of France, not foreigners, as the cause of the overall crisis in French society; *JO*, Débats Parlementaires, Chambre des Députés (20 June 1935 session): 1861.

160. *JO*, Débats Parlementaires, Sénat (27 June 1935 session): 759; *JO*, Débats Parlementaires, Chambre des Députés (20 June 1935 session): 1866.

161. *JO*, Débats Parlementaires, Sénat (27 June 1935 session): 749–760; *JO*, Débats Parlementaires, Chambre des Députés (20 June 1935 session): 1859–97.

162. "Loi relative à l'exercice de la médecine et de l'art dentaire," *JO* (27 July 1935).

163. One complicated exception was allowed: naturalized doctors who had not performed their military service were exempt from the delay if "les naturalisés en cours d'études médicales le 21 avril 1933 et qui, avant la promulgation de la loi ont demandé leur naturalisation et se sont mariés à des Françaises ayant conservé leur nationalité." Senator Sari presented this amendment. *JO*, Débats Parlementaires, Sénat (27 June 1935 session): 760.

164. Pécout, "L'étude et l'exercice de la médecine par les étrangers," 63.

165. On debates over the scope of civil service positions to be addressed by the law, see *JO*, Débats Parlementaires, Sénat (27 June 1935 session): 751–755.

166. Rapport supplémentaire fait au nom de la Commission de l'hygiène chargée d'examiner la proposition de loi de M. Cousin, *JO*, Documents Parlementaires, Chambre des Députés, Annexe 5356 (30 May 1935): 876.

167. Caron, *Uneasy Asylum*, 51–57.

168. Correspondence among the Commission du Gouvernement du Territoire de la Sarre and Ministrères des Affaires Étrangères, Santé Publique, and Éducation Nationale, 1932–1935, MAE C 253; MAE C 254 no. 52, 72–73, 166–167, among others. Cf. *JO*, Débats Parlementaires, Chambre des Députés (20 June 1935 session): 1861–62.

169. Proposition de loi, *JO*, Documents Parlementaires, Chambre des Députés, Annexe 5261 (28 May 1935): 814; Rapport supplémentaire fait au nom de la Commission de l'hygiène chargée d'examiner la proposition de loi de M. Cousin, *JO*, Documents Parlementaires, Chambre des Députés, Annexe 5356 (30 May 1935): 875–876; Rapport, *JO*, Documents Parlementaires, Chambre des Députés, Annexe 5439 (18 June 1935): 933.

170. *JO*, Débats Parlementaires, Sénat (27 June 1935 session): 749–757.

171. Ibid., 749–751.

172. Deputy Dommange in particular fought persistently for a ten-year waiting period for private practice. His colleagues in parliament would not go that far. *JO*, Débats Parlementaires, Chambre des Députés (20 June 1935 session): 1864–67. Cf. Gervais de Lafond, "De l'étude et de l'exercice de la médecine en France par les étrangers," 181, 190.

173. *JO*, Débats Parlementaires, Sénat (27 June 1935 session): 752.

174. "Rapports du Syndicat avec la Préfecture, Assemblée générale du Syndicat médical de Loir-et-Cher du 4 juin 1936," *Le bouclier* 72 (Aug. 1936): 172.

175. "En Seine-et-Oise," *Syndicats médicaux de la Seine-et-Oise et de l'Aube, mensuel* 69 (Aug.–Sept. 1938): 357–61.

176. Those naturalized doctors already exercising a public service medical function at the time of the law's passage also retained their right to remain in public service. Naturalized doctors practicing privately could continue to do so but would have to wait five years from the date of their graduation before obtaining a public sector position.

177. "Clinicat à titre étranger," *Bulletin de l'Internat des hôpitaux de Paris* 91 (Jan.–July 1937): 50–55. Cf. "Questions corporatives," *AEMP, bulletin mensuel* 7 (May 1939): 10; "Allocution du Dr. Georges Labey, Président, Assemblée générale de l'Assocation amicale des internes et anciens internes, 30 avril 1938," *Bulletin de l'Internat des hôpitaux de Paris* 93 (April–June 1938): 25–26; "Comité de l'Association, séance du 12 décembre 1938," *Bulletin de l'Internat des hôpitaux de Paris* 95 (Oct.–Dec. 1938): 145.

178. Abadie's letter went unanswered for one week until someone took up her cause before the hospital authorities, with no known result. Dossier "Concours de Clinicat, 1937"; documents "Lettre de Mlle. Abadie à M. le Professeur Bezançon, Président du Jury, Hôpital Laennec," 22 Oct. 1937; and "Note concernant Melle Abadie, docteur en médecine," 29 Oct. 1937, AN AJ16 8352. Abadie's name appears on an untitled, undated, handwritten alphabetical list of 261 Jewish doctors appealing their expulsion from medicine as a result of Vichy's 1941 anti-Semitic quota, suggesting that Abadie managed to carry on a career in medicine up until then. The list notes that the national council of the Medical Order nominated Abadie for an exemption based on eminent professional merit, but the result of the nomination, decided by the Commissariat général aux questions juives (CGQ J), is not known. Centre des Archives contemporaines, Fontainebleau [hereafter CAC] 20000243 2.

179. "Allocution du Dr. Georges Labey, président, Assemblée générale de l'Assocation amicale des internes et anciens internes, 30 avril 1938," *Bulletin de l'Internat des hôpitaux de Paris* 93 (April–June 1938): 25.

180. Letter and petition from Dr. E. Davidovici, "Pour les étudiants et médecins roumains diplômés d'état, victimes de la loi Nast-Armbruster 1935," to Monsieur le Président du Conseil, June 1936, AN F60 602.

181. "Réunion de l'arrondissement de Villeneuve, 24 juillet 1936," *Bulletin de la Société des médecins et du Syndicat médical de Lot-et-Garonne* 78 (Aug. 1936): 11–12; "Les naturalisations," *Le médecin de Lorraine* 2 (Feb. 1938): 7. See calls for a halt in "Réunion de l'arrondissement d'Agen, 28 juillet 1936," *Le médecin de Lorraine* 79 (Oct. 1936): 7; "Fédération des syndicats médicaux de Maine-et-Loire, conseil d'administration du 30 juin 1937," *Le bouclier* 84 (Aug. 1937): 177; "Syndicat médical des arrondissements de Vannes-Ploërmel, réunion du 13 novembre 1937," *Le bouclier* 89 (Jan. 1938): 24; "Syndicat des médecins de la banlieue ouest et nord de Paris, réunion du Conseil d'administration du 10 décembre 1937," *SM Seine, Banlieue Ouest et Nord* 119 (March 1938): 88. Regarding doctors' complaints about naturalizations, see correspondence among Conseil général, Département de la Sarthe, Préfet de la Sarthe, and Ministre de l'Intérieur, Nov.–Dec. 1938, AN F7 15166; and "Syndicat médical de Dunkerque et de l'arrondissement, réunion du 23 novembre 1938," *SM Nord* 2 (Feb. 1939): 60.

182. Dr. d'Ayrenx, "Naturalisation des médecins et étudiants étrangers," *SMP* 9 (Nov. 1936): 18.

183. Dr. Querrioux, "Loi sur l'exercice de la médecine pour les étrangers, Syndicat des médecins de la banlieue ouest et nord de Paris, Conseil d'administration du 10 janvier 1936," *SM Seine, Banlieue Ouest et Nord* 108 (May 1936): 134. Cf. "Conseil d'administration du 13 décembre 1935," *SM Seine, Banlieue Ouest et Nord* 107 (March 1936): 122–125.

184. Dr. Armbruster, *JO*, Débats Parlementaires, Sénat (9 June 1931 session): 1029.

185. "Chronique du provincial," *La science médicale pratique* 16 (15 Oct. 1930): 614.

186. "Naturalisations," *La science médicale pratique* 10 (Dec. 1938): 246. Cf. Querrioux, "Rapport sur les dangers de l'exercice de la médecine par les étrangers: les remèdes," *SM Seine, Banlieue Ouest et Nord* 111 (Nov. 1936): 38.

187. Signoret, "Nous et eux," 6.

188. Rémy Estournet, "De la pratique de la naturalisation depuis la loi du 10 août 1927" (law diss., Université de Montpellier, 1937), 84–86.

189. "Syndicat des médecins de la Somme, séance du Conseil du 21 juin 1937," *Syndicat médical picard, bulletin officiel du Syndicat des médecins de la Somme* 40 (July 1937): 32; "Association syndicale des médecins de Meurthe-et-Moselle, Assemblée générale du 15 mars 1938," *Le médecin de Lorraine* 3 (March 1938): 12. Cf. Caron, *Uneasy Asylum*, 137.

190. "La naturalisation des médecins et étudiants en médecine étrangers dans la Seine en 1936 et 1937," Rapport adopté par le Conseil d'administration du Syndicat médical de la Seine, le 18 mai 1938, *SMP* 7 (July 1938): 22–27; also published in *SM Seine, Banlieue Ouest et Nord* 122 (Sept. 1938): 86–91.

191. "Syndicat médical de Lille et de la région, Assemblée générale du 18 novembre 1938," *SM Nord* 10 (Dec. 1938): 419.

192. D'Ayrenx, "Naturalisation des médecins et étudiants étrangers," 19–21.

193. "La naturalisation des médecins et étudiants en médecine étrangers dans la Seine en 1936 et 1937," 90.

194. Dr. A. Giry, "Allocution du Président," *Le médecin de Lorraine* 10 (Dec. 1938): 29.

195. "La naturalisation des médecins et étudiants en médecine étrangers dans la Seine en 1936 et 1937," 91.

196. Proposed by Dr. d'Ayrenx and passed unanimously by General Assembly, D'Ayrenx, "Naturalisation des médecins et étudiants étrangers:" 20.

197. Correspondence between André Marie, deputy of the Seine-Inférieure, and M. Loriot, conseiller d'état au Ministère de la Justice, July–Aug. 1934, regarding the naturalization candidacy of M. Gocalki (Gottschalk), AN BB30 1605.

198. Papers of M. Loriet, Conseiller d'État en service extraordinaire, Directeur des Affaires civiles et du Sceau, Ministère de la Justice, 1934, AN BB30 1605. Mary Lewis describes how family and residence criteria became more important than labor contracts for foreigners wishing to obtain privileged rights to remain in France; *The Boundaries of the Republic*, 120, 220–221, 247–248.

199. See also correspondence among Ministères de la Justice, de l'Éducation Nationale, and de la Santé Publique regarding naturalization criteria, 1935–1959, AN F17 17634.

200. Caron, *Uneasy Asylum*, 41.

201. Many deputies proposed a global revision of the 1927 nationality law, notably two conservatives, Louis Marin and Fernand Laurent, who wanted to limit "inadmissable competition" from newly naturalized citizens in commerce and the liberal professions; see "Proposition de loi tendant à modifier l'article 6 de la loi du 10 août 1927 sur la nationalité," *JO*, Documents Parlementaires, Chambre des Députés, Annexe 4422 (8 Dec. 1938 session): 58.

202. In 1938 the Seine Medical Union urged that all naturalization candidates be legally subjected to an "examen sanitaire complet demandé par l'Académie de médecine." "La naturalisation des médecins et étudiants en médecine étrangers dans la Seine en 1936 et 1937," Rapport adopté par le Conseil d'administration du Syndicat médical de la Seine, le 18 mai 1938, *SM Seine, Banlieue Ouest et Nord* 122 (Sept. 1938): 90.

203. "Contrôle sanitaire," AN F7 16101. Cf. Amy Lauren Fairchild, *Science at the Borders: Immigrant Medical Inspection and the Shaping of the Modern Industrial Labor Force* (Baltimore, 2003).

204. In *L'index médical*, and reprinted in Dr. Charles Grimbert, "L'invasion," *SMP* 3 (March 1935), 81.

205. "Les revendications des étudiants en médecine," *L'écho des étudiants* 627 (20 Feb. 1935): 3–4.

206. Dr. Dentu, séance du 9 juin 1931, Sénat, excerpts from *JO* published in *SM Aube* (July 1931): 179.

207. "Syndicat médical de Paris, Assemblée générale du 29 mars 1939," *SMP* 5 (May 1939): 20–21.

208. Caron, *Uneasy Asylum*, esp. 13–42.

209. René Senès, "Les conditions d'exercice de la médecine en France en temps de paix et en temps de guerre" (law diss., Université de Paris, 1939); Henri Beaudot, "L'exercice illégal de la médecine et le charlatanisme: ressemblances et différences dans leurs éléments et dans leurs répressions" (law diss., Université de Lyon, 1939). The former dissertation was rigorous and objective; the latter was not.

210. Faivre, "Aspect médical et social du problème des étrangers en France," 77.

211. Jacques Boudard, "De l'envahissement du corps médical français par certains éléments 'nés' en Pologne et Roumanie" (medical diss., Université de Paris, 1939).

212. Cf. Nahum, *La médecine française et les juifs*, 81–85.

213. "Question des médecins frontaliers," *Le médecin de Lorraine* 5 (Sept. 1935): 4.

214. M. de Marcilly, Ambassadeur de France, Bern to the Ministre des Affaires Étrangères, 5 Dec. 1931, MAE C 253.

215. L'Ambassadeur de France, Bern, to the Ministre des Affaires Étrangères, 17 March 1933, MAE C 254. Cf. Président du Conseil, Ministre des Affaires Étrangères, to the Ambassadeur de France, Bern, 12 Feb. 1932, MAE C 253.

216. "Réunion des médecins de la partie est de la frontière franco-belge, 25 mars 1932," *SM Nord* 14 (April 1932): 410–414; "Convention franco-belge," *Le médecin de Lorraine* 2 (March 1935): 22; "Liste des médecins belges pouvant venir exercer la médecine en France," *SM Nord* 7 (July 1937): 200.

217. MAE C 254 no. 162–165, 278, 283–288; MAE C 255 no. 4–5, 10–13, 24–25, 68–71.

218. Dr. Nouviale, "Syndicat des médecins de la Banlieue Ouest et Nord de Paris, réunion du 5 juillet 1935," *SM Seine, Banlieue Ouest et Nord* 105 (Nov. 1935): 122.

219. Dr. Dauby to the Ministre de l'Intérieur, 28 April 1940, AN F7 16050.

220. Some deputies used this argument to favor obligatory naturalization of doctors. *JO*, Débats Parlementaires, Sénat (27 June 1935 session): 751.

221. Correspondence between the Présidence du Conseil and Senateur Armbruster, 9 Feb. 1940, AN F60 602.

222. "Fédération des Syndicats médicaux de la Seine, séance du 22 septembre 1938," *SMP* 9 (Nov. 1938): 14–15. Many local medical unions had urged the Confédération to take this position. See, for example, "Association syndicale des médecins de Meurthe-et-Moselle, Assemblée générale du 11 décembre 1938," *Le médecin de Lorraine* 10 (Dec. 1938): 30, 34.

223. Circular no. 95 of the Confédération to its member unions, 10 Nov. 1939, "Recensement des médecins étrangers exerçant pendant la guerre," *SM Nord* 1 (Jan. 1940): 27–28.

224. "Fédération des syndicats médicaux de la Seine, séance du 22 septembre 1938," *SMP* 9 (Nov. 1938): 14–15.

225. The assembly warmly applauded a report given on the topic, as well as an anti-Semitic remark uttered during the meeting. "Syndicat médical de Paris, Conseil d'administration, Assemblée générale du 30 Nov. 1938," *SMP* 10 (Dec. 1938): 18–20.

226. Dr. Mackiewicz, "Après l'alerte," *Syndicats médicaux de la Seine-et-Oise et de l'Aube, mensuel* 71 (Dec. 1938): 447–448.

227. "Les médecins mobilisés sur place," *SM Nord* 1 (Jan. 1940): 7–8.

228. "L'insuffisance du nombre des médecins dans le Nord," *SM Nord* 5 (May 1940).

229. "L'exercice de la médecine dans le Nord pendant les hostilités," *SM Nord* 9 (Nov. 1939): 346–350.

230. "La pénurie de médecins dans le Nord," *SM Nord* 1 (Jan. 1940): 4–7.

231. "Note pour la Direction des Affaires Politiques (Défense Nationale)," Ministère des Affaires Étrangères, 24 May 1940, MAE C 255 no. 128–131.

232. Ibid.

233. "Syndicat médical de Paris, Conseil d'administration, Assemblée générale du 30 novembre 1938," *SMP* 10 (Dec. 1938): 17. Cf. Dr. Chambonas, *Le temps médical* (May 1937), republished in "Métèques, mouzabis et cie," *Bulletin officiel de l'Association professionnelle des internes et anciens internes des hôpitaux de Marseille* 6 (June 1937): 17.

234. Dr. Paul Blondel, "Contingentement," *Syndicats médicaux picards, bulletin officiel de la Fédération des syndicats médicaux de la Somme* 38 (Jan. 1937): 6.

235. Caron, *Uneasy Asylum*, 11, 15, 22.

236. Proposition de loi Dommange, *JO*, Documents Parlementaires, Chambre des Députés, Annexe 4425 (10 Jan. 1935): 17.

237. *JO*, Débats Parlementaires, Sénat (9 June 1931 session): 1026.

238. Giry, "Allocution du Président," 26–29.

3. The Art of Medicine

1. The Confédération des syndicats médicaux français claimed that a ratio of 1,400 to 1,500 inhabitants per doctor was appropriate. Dr. Fernand Decourt, "Notre enquête sur la réforme des études médicales," *Le médecin de France* (1932[?]): 388, AN AJ16 6357.

2. Louis Gourichon, "Rapport de la Commission d'initiative et de propagande sur la doctrine syndicale et les desiderata du corps médical," *SMP* 6 (Oct. 1922): 324.

3. *Étudiants, mensuel des étudiants de Paris* [Section de Paris de l'UFE] 2 (Jan. 1937): 2, AP 222.

4. *Recueil des statistiques*, 213–215.

5. Ibid., 68.

6. "Note de M. Cazeneuve, directeur de l'École secondaire de médecine à Lille, à propos de la transformation de cette école en faculté," n.d., AN AJ 16 6685.

7. Much of the BUS propaganda encouraging French youth to venture out into rural areas of France in the late 1930s stemmed from practical concerns about national employment and regional equilibrium. But one can also detect an ideological rejection of modern urbanism growing in France at the time, a precursor to the Vichy regime's call to go back to the land. In 1936 the BUS proposed that "il serait désirable d'aider au retour dans les provinces françaises d'une jeunesse intellectuelle qui constitue l'armature nécessaire à leur renaissance." "L'activité du Bureau universitaire de statistique en 1937," *Le musée social* 10 (Oct. 1938): 278, AP 350. The BUS remained very active throughout the Occupation period; its director Alfred Rosier worked under Pétain's orders. In 1941 the BUS argued, "Le 'retour à la terre' tant préconisé, n'est pas, croyez le bien, le mythe d'un pays vaincu qui veut revivre, mais une véritable nécessité sociale." A. Rosier, conférence "Tour d'horizon," Spring 1941, AP 350.

8. One such announcement read: "Monsieur Desoncles, secrétaire de la Mairie de Villefranche du Périgord, nous informe que ce chef-lieu de canton est sans médecin depuis plusieurs mois. En plus des 910 habitants résidant dans la commune, le praticien qui s'y installerait pourrait visiter la population des agglomérations avoisinantes totalisant environ 2.900 habitants. Le médecin le plus proche de Villefranche est à 9 km." "Liste des postes médicaux," sent from the BUS to the rector of the Académie de Paris, 26 Nov. 1935, AP 350.

9. "Proposition de loi déposée sur le bureau de la Chambre par M. Pomaret, le 5 juin 1936," *Bulletin mensuel du Syndicat médical de Seine-et-Oise* 48 (July 1936): 211.

10. BUS, "Contre le chômage intellectuel," *L'écho des étudiants* 642 (12 June 1935): 7.

11. Rosier, "Du chômage intellectuel: de l'encombrement des professions libérales," 46–52.

12. Babin, "Étude statistique sur la profession médicale," 38.

13. J. Leroy, "Le chômage des diplômés," *Étudiants, mensuel des étudiants de Paris* (15 Feb. 1936): 3.

14. Decourt, "Notre enquête sur la réforme des études médicales," 388.

15. Motion adoptée le dimanche 20 novembre 1938 au cours de la réunion du Bureau de l'UNEF, AP 221.

16. H. Signoret, "Xénophobie?... Non, mais francophilie," *La butte médicale* 93 (July 1939): 11.

17. Dossier "Union fédérale des étudiants," AN AJ16 8374. Cf. "Une lettre ouverte de l'Union fédérale des étudiants: l'agitation xénophobe et antisémite dans les facultés," *L'humanité* (13 March 1930), AN AJ16 8362.

18. AP 325; Charles Ayoub, "La nouvelle législation de la naturalisation en France" (law diss., Université de Paris, 1937), 121, 136–137.

19. Tract of Union générale des étudiants pour l'enseignement, adhérente à l'UFE, Section Sorbonne, Nov. 1932, plus various other tracts, AP 222.

20. "Sur la question des médecins étrangers," *SMP* 4 (June–July 1922): 220–222.

21. Daniel had been named a Paris intern in 1901. His 1936 banquet speech directly addressed the question of foreigners in the Paris internat. He affirmed that "ce qui a fait la gloire de l'internat, c'est que furent admis à concourir les étrangers," making explicit that the number of foreigners in the Paris internat was nevertheless minimal, and that most Romanian interns returned to their native country afterwards. "Banquet de l'Internat," *Bulletin de l'Internat des hôpitaux de Paris* 89 (Jan. 1936): 22–27.

22. Waxin, "Statut de l'étudiant étranger dans son développement historique," 248.

23. Professeur Hartmann, "Les étudiants étrangers à la Faculté de médecine: des lois et des réglements existent, que les syndicats et les tribunaux les fassent fonctionner," *Le siècle médical* 194 (1 March 1935): 1.

24. "Les médecins étrangers," *Le bouclier: bulletin mensuel du Groupement des syndicats médicaux de la Loire-Inférieure, du Maine-et-Loire, et du Loir-et-Cher* [hereafter *Le bouclier*] 61 (Sept. 1935): 191.

25. Léonard, *La médecine entre les savoirs et les pouvoirs*, 301.

26. Sociologists have long studied the links among educational qualifications, professionalization, and monopolization of market share. See Sarfatti-Larson, *The Rise of Professionalism*; Abbott, *The System of Professions*; Abel and Lewis, *Lawyers in Society*; as well as the work of Talcott Parsons and Eliot Freidson. Cf. Patrick Hassenteufel, "Vers le déclin du 'pouvoir médical'? Un éclairage européen, France, Allemagne, Grande-Bretagne," *Pouvoir* 89 (1999): 51–64.

27. Rosier, "Du chômage intellectuel: de l'encombrement des professions libérales," 38–39.

28. Gourichon, "Rapport de la Commission d'initiative et de propagande," 323–324.

29. F. Bertillon, "À propos de l'enseignement secondaire," *L'Université de Paris, revue mensuelle illustrée de l'Association générale des étudiants* 225 (Dec. 1920): 22–23.

30. Marc Schittly, "Essai sur les médecins parlementaires en France de 1920 à 1940" (law diss., Université de Strasbourg, 1982), 245, 299.

31. *JO*, Débats Parlementaires, Sénat (8 Dec. 1931 session): 1562.

32. Raymond Armbruster, Séance du 9 février 1933 au Sénat, published in "La loi Armbruster," *SM Aube* (Feb. 1933): 40–41.

33. *JO*, Débats Parlementaires, Sénat (6 Feb. 1930 session): 81; *JO*, Débats Parlementaires, Sénat (9 June 1931 session): 1029–30; Rapport supplémentaire, *JO*, Documents Parlementaires, Sénat, Annexe 598 (23 June 1931): 991.

34. M. Hervey, *JO*, Débats Parlementaires, Sénat (8 Dec. 1931 session): 1562.

35. The student campaign was led by Maurice Mordagne, who had led the anti-foreigner movement. "Pour la défense de la médecine française," *L'écho des étudiants* 492 (30 Jan. 1932), 2; "Association corporative des étudiants en médecine de Paris," *L'écho des étudiants* 496 (27 Feb. 1932): 3; "Le grec en médecine," *L'écho des étudiants* 505 (7 May 1932), 3–4; "Chronique du provincial: la loi sur l'exercice de la profession médicale," *La science médicale pratique* (1932): 321–322; "Baccalauréat latin-grec et études médicales," *Syndicats médicaux, banlieue ouest et nord, banlieue est et sud de Paris et Fédération des syndicats médicaux de la Seine, bulletin officiel* 85 (July–Sept. 1932): 52–53.

36. *JO*, Documents Parlementaires, Sénat, Annexe 800 (1 Dec. 1933 session): 1128.

37. M. Séjournet, in discussion of report by Dr. Tissier-Guy, "Le corps médical de la Seine et la CTI," *SM Seine, Banlieue Ouest et Nord* 87 (Nov.–Dec. 1932): 132; "Fédération corporative et confédération des travailleurs intellectuels (CTI)," *SM Seine, Banlieue Ouest et Nord* 90 (May 1933): 196–197.

38. *JO*, Débats Parlementaires, Sénat (8 Dec. 1931 session): 1561.

39. Séance du 9 février 1933 au Sénat, published in "La loi Armbruster," *SM Aube* (Feb. 1933): 39–42. After the Armbruster law was passed, some medical unions continued to push for the revision of the baccalaureate requirement, to no avail in the interwar years. "Réforme des études médicales," *SM Seine, Banlieue Ouest et Nord* 93 (Nov. 1933): 29.

40. "Proposition de loi," *L'écho des étudiants* 617 (5 Dec. 1934): 3.

41. "Tribune corporative," *Revue médicale de la Corporative des étudiants en médecine* (Montpellier) 29 (May 1931); "L'examen écrit et les étudiants de seconde année de médecine," *Revue médicale de l'Office central de médecine de l'Union nationale des étudiants, Clermont-Ferrand* 2 (July–Sept. 1933): 47–48.

42. "Congrès de Nice, mars–avril 1932: compte rendu," *Revue médicale de la Section corporative de Montpellier et de l'Office central de médecine de l'Union nationale des étudiants* (Montpellier) 34 (April 1932): 137; Robert Ghnassia, "Où va la jeunesse universitaire?" *La voix dentaire, revue mensuelle, organe de l'Association générale des étudiants en chirurgie dentaire de France* 22 (April 1936): 20–23.

43. Voeux de l'Association des étudiants en médecine de Strasbourg, in "Congrès de Nice, mars–avril 1932, compte rendu," *Revue médicale de la Section corporative de Montpellier et de l'Office central de médecine de l'Union nationale des étudiants* (Montpellier) 34 (April 1932): 138.

44. Ch. Flandin, "Réglementation de l'entrée des étudiants dans les Facultés de Médecine: la proposition Portmann et le syndicalisme médical," *Le bouclier* 51 (Nov. 1934): 245.

45. Dr. Vauzanges, "À propos du projet de loi Portmann sur la limitation du nombre des étudiants en médecine," *SM Aube* (Oct. 1934): 321–322, 325.

46. Flandin, "Réglementation de l'entrée des étudiants," 245.

47. "Pléthore médicale: projet de loi Portmann," *Le bouclier* 54 (Feb. 1935): 42; M. Tissier-Guy, "La réforme des études médicales (projet de loi Portmann)," *SMP* 9 (Nov. 1934): 20; intervention of M. Bourguignon, *SMP* 9 (Nov. 1934): 25.

48. Intervention of Dr. Barre-Rat, Syndicat des médecins de la banlieue ouest et nord de Paris, Conseil d'administration du 11 janvier 1935, *SM Seine, Banlieue Ouest et Nord* 102 (May 1935): 50–51; Flandin, "Réglementation de l'entrée des étudiants," 246.

49. "Un exemple à ne pas suivre," *AEMP, bulletin mensuel* 6 (April 1939): 10–11; "Questions corporatives," *AEMP, bulletin mensuel* 7 (May 1939): 12; "Questions

corporatives," *AEMP, bulletin mensuel* 8 (June 1939): 8–10; *Le front médical français, bulletin mensuel de l'Association amicale des étudiants en médecine de Paris* 1 (May 1935): 4; Leroy, "Le chômage des diplômés," 3.

50. Tissier-Guy, "La réforme des études médicales (projet de loi Portmann)," 20.

51. Flandin, "Réglementation de l'entrée des étudiants," 243–249; Vauzanges, "À propos du projet de loi Portmann:" 321–322, 325.

52. Balthazard, "Réforme des études médicales."

53. Dr. Paul Cibrie, secrétaire-général de la Confédération, to the professeurs des Facultés et Écoles de médecine françaises, 26 April 1932, AN AJ16 6357. Cf. "Tribune corporative," *Revue médicale de la Corporative des étudiants en médecine* (Montpellier) 29 (May 1931); "L'examen écrit et les étudiants de seconde année de médecine," *Revue médicale de l'Office central de médecine de l'Union nationale des étudiants, Clermont-Ferrand* 2 (July–Sept. 1933): 47–48.

54. Rapport supplémentaire, *JO*, Documents Parlementaires, Sénat, Annexe 598 (23 June 1931): 991; Balthazard, "Réforme des études médicales"; Mallarmé's declarations in "La situation des jeunes diplômés," *L'écho des étudiants* 628 (27 Feb. 1935): 2; Rosier, "Du chômage intellectuel," 51.

55. Babin, "Étude statistique sur la profession médicale."

56. AN AJ16 8374.

57. Leroy, "Le chômage des diplômés," 3.

58. BUS, "Contre le chômage intellectuel," *L'écho des étudiants* 642 (12 June 1935): 3. On identification procedures, see also Gérard Noiriel, *La tyrannie du national* (Paris, 1991), and *Les origines républicaines de Vichy* (Paris, 1999).

59. See, for example, Proposition de loi, *JO*, Documents Parlementaires, Chambre des Députés, Annexe 3573 (1 Feb. 1938): 150–152.

60. "Exercice illégal de la médecine," *Le bouclier* 67 (March. 1936): 73.

61. "Résultats obtenus au cours de l'année 1927 par l'Office de répression de l'exercice illégal de la médecine," *La science médicale pratique* 11 (15 Oct. 1928): 376.

62. The doctors' campaign was so widespread that the definition of "usurper" in the *Robert and Collins French-English Dictionary* (2nd ed., 1987) gives "usurper le titre de docteur en médecine" as its example.

63. Vergez, "Internes et anciens internes des hôpitaux de Paris de 1918 à 1945," 170–172.

64. For example, Cass. Cr. 24 avril 1929 (*Gazette du Palais*, 1929–2-57), against an American doctor for hanging a plaque with the term *docteur* in bold, followed by his foreign qualifications in small print. Brochin and Tissier-Guy, "Protection des droits et prérogatives attachés au titre de docteur en médecine," *SMP* 4 (April 1932): 201.

65. A. Herpin, "Le titre de docteur," *SMP* 9 (Nov. 1932): 403–411.

66. Tissier-Guy, "Le corps médical de la Seine et la CTI," 124–137; "Protection du titre de 'docteur en médecine' et Confédération des travailleurs intellectuels (CTI)," *SM Seine, Banlieue Ouest et Nord* 88 (Jan. 1933): 132–141; "Fédération corporative et Confédération des travailleurs intellectuels (CTI)," *SM Seine, Banlieue Ouest et Nord* 90 (May 1933): 185–206.

67. H. Vachette, "À propos du titre de docteur," *Bulletin officiel du Syndicat des médecins de Marseille et d'arrondissement, de la Fédération des syndicats médicaux des Bouches-du-Rhône* 8 (Aug.–Sept. 1936): 625–629.

68. Michel Charpentier, "La protection des titres professionnels" (law diss., Université de Paris, 1939), 7–11, 80–84.

69. Dr. Vauzanges, "Bolchevisme," *SM Aube* (May 1934): 147.

70. Non-doctor dentists held a monopoly over dental care at this time. It was admitted that if non-doctors were forbidden to practice dentistry, there would not be enough stomatology specialists to fill the demand in the short run. "Le vote de l'Académie de Médecine sur la loi Milan-Rio," *Syndicats médicaux, banlieue ouest et nord, banlieue est et sud de Paris et Fédération des syndicats médicaux de la Seine, bulletin officiel* 83 (Jan.–March 1932): 52–57.

71. Vauzanges, "Bolchevisme," 143–147; Dr. Vauzanges, "Encore la dent!" *SM Aube* (July 1934): 220–222.

72. Dentists were seeking "doctoral" recognition for their scholarly qualifications. "Le vote de l'Académie de Médecine sur la loi Milan-Rio," 52–57; Vauzanges, "Bolchevisme," 143–147.

73. There was much debate among French doctors over whether American dental training was superior to French training. "Protection du titre de 'docteur en médecine' et Confédération des travailleurs intellectuels (CTI)," *SM Seine, Banlieue Ouest et Nord* 88 (Jan. 1933): 132–141; Herpin, "Le titre de Docteur," 410; Charpentier, "La protection des titres professionnels," 47–53, 89–95.

74. George Weisz, "Regulating Specialties in France during the First Half of the Twentieth Century," *Social History of Medicine* 15, no. 3 (2002): 457–480; Weisz, *Divide and Conquer: A Comparative History of Medical Specialization* (New York, 2006).

75. "Médecins! Faites attention à votre diplôme! Défendez-le," *SM Aube* (Oct. 1934): 338.

76. Gustave Roussy, "La réforme des études médicales," *La presse médicale* (8 April 1933): 571–574, AN AJ16 6357; BUS, "Chômage intellectuel" (1938), AN 63AJ 59.

77. Schittly, "Essai sur les médecins parlementaires en France de 1920 à 1940," 247.

78. For example, "Exercice illégal, séance de la Butte médicale du 12 novembre 1929," *La butte médicale* 36 (Jan. 1930): 26.

79. "Le diplôme devant la vie," *L'écho des étudiants* 607 (18 Aug. 1934): 5.

80. "Ordre du jour en faveur des propharmaciens, Fédération des syndicats médicaux de la Seine, séance du 6 février 1936," *SM Seine, Banlieue Ouest et Nord* 108 (May 1936): 33; "Exercice par les médecins de la profession de pharmacien, Fédération des syndicats médicaux de la Seine, séance du 14 mai 1936," *SM Seine, Banlieue Ouest et Nord* 109 (July 1936): 29. Cf. "La grève des étudiants en pharmacie," *L'écho des étudiants* 509 (4 June 1932): 1; Roger Bruel, "Une nouvelle offensive des herboristes," *L'Université de Paris, revue mensuelle de l'Association générale des étudiants* (May 1933).

81. "Exercice illégal de la médecine," *Bulletin de la Fédération des syndicats médicaux du département du Nord* 7 (July 1938): 279.

82. "Fédération des syndicats médicaux de la Seine, séance du 16 mai 1935," *SM Seine, Banlieue Ouest et Nord* 103 (July 1935): 27.

83. "À propos du programme des cours aux infirmières," *SM Aube* 11 (Nov. 1936): 290–292.

84. Schittly, "Essai sur les médecins parlementaires en France de 1920 à 1940," 248.

85. Pierre Bourdieu, *La distinction: critique sociale du jugement* (Paris, 1979).

86. "La pléthore médicale," *La science médicale pratique* 15 (31 July–1 Oct. 1930): 579; "La vie syndicaliste," *Bulletin de la Société des médecins et du Syndicat médical de Lot-et-Garonne* 40 (April 1930): 29–31.

87. See Table 2.1. "Pléthore médicale: projet de loi Portmann," *Le bouclier* 54 (Feb. 1935): 42; Vauzanges, "À propos du projet de loi Portmann," 325.

88. Vauzanges, "À propos du projet de loi Portmann," 326.

89. BUS, "Chômage intellectuel" (1938). Two pieces of legislation were passed limiting *cumul* for civil service positions and retirement plans: a decree-law of 1934 and a law of 29 October 1936.

90. "Compte rendu des séances de l'Office central de médecine, séance du 9 avril 1934," *Revue médicale de l'Office central de médecine de l'Union nationale des étudiants et de Clermont-Ferrand* 6 (March–April 1934): 31; Leroy, "Le chômage des diplômés," 3.

91. "À propos du projet de loi sur les cumuls," *SM Seine, Banlieue Ouest et Nord* 112 (Jan. 1937): 104; "La loi sur les cumuls s'est trouvée...," *SM Seine, Banlieue Ouest et Nord* 114 (May 1937): 33–34.

92. "Démission," *SM Seine-et-Oise* 21 (April 1933): 52; "Jurisprudence," *SM Seine, Banlieue Ouest et Nord* 89 (March 1933): 22.

93. James C. Albisetti claims that in nearly every European country, women gained professional access to medicine before law. He argues that "few viewed admission of women to medicine as leading so directly [as law] to other rights, especially not to suffrage." Albisetti, "Portia ante Portas," 825, 844.

94. Of these, 56 percent resided in the Seine department. Mme. le Dr. Darcanne-Mouroux, "Évolution du féminisme médical en France," report given at the April 1929 Congress of the Association internationale des femmes-médecins, 4, BMD DOS 610 MED; Lipinska, *Les femmes et le progrès*, 175.

95. To compute the percentage of women, I arrived at an approximate figure for the total number of practicing doctors in 1928 (24,700) by averaging the statistics for 1925 and 1931, available from the BUS report "Chômage intellectuel" (1938), 45–46.

96. Lipinska, *Les femmes et le progrès*, 169; Bonner, *To the Ends of the Earth*, 78, 155.

97. Green, "L'émigration comme émancipation," 58.

98. Not all members responded to the survey, and association members may not be representative of women doctors as a whole. "Liste des membres," *Association française des femmes-médecins* 4 (Jan.–March 1931): 14–24; "France," *Association internationale des femmes-médecins* 4 (June 1931): 16–17.

99. Darcanne-Mouroux, "Évolution du féminisme médical en France"; Josette Dall'Ava Santucci, *Des sorcières aux mandarines: histoire des femmes médecins* (Paris, 1989), 212.

100. "Concours de l'Internat," *Bulletin du comité de l'Association amicale des internes et anciens internes en médecine des hôpitaux et hospices civils de Paris* (May 1921, March–June 1922, March–June 1923, Sept. 1925–June 1926, March 1928, March 1929, March 1930). Mlle. Dreyfus-Sée was the first woman to earn first place in the Paris internship competition, in 1924. Marguerite Dauban was the first woman to earn first place in the Paris externship competition, in 1929. *L'écho des étudiants* 357 (8 Jan. 1929): 1.

101. Dr. Labey, discours du président, banquet de l'Internat du 17 avril 1937, published in *Bulletin de l'Internat des hôpitaux de Paris* 91 (Jan.–July 1937): 31. Labey was a virulent anti-foreigner. See the episode related in chapter 2 in which he violently intimidated a naturalized woman intern out of taking the *clinicat* exam.

102. Vergez, "Internes et anciens internes des hôpitaux de Paris," 298.

103. *Association internationale des femmes-médecins* 4 (June 1931): 16; *Association internationale des femmes-médecins* 8 (Dec. 1933): 24–25; Mme. Darcanne-Mouroux, "Role des femmes médecins aux colonies," *Association française des femmes-médecins* 6 (July–Sept. 1931): 8–13.

104. *Association internationale des femmes-médecins* 5 (Dec. 1931): 52.

105. "Les possibilités d'exercice de la médecine dans les différents pays," *Association internationale des femmes-médecins* 8 (Dec. 1933): 26–32; "Les possibilités d'exercice de la médecine dans les différents pays," *Association internationale des femmes-médecins* 9 (Dec. 1934): 4–5, 14–15; "Les possibilités d'exercice de la médecine dans les différents pays," *Association internationale des femmes-médecins* 11 (Dec. 1936): 23.

106. Christine Bard, *Les filles de Marianne: histoire des féminismes, 1914–1940* (Paris, 1995), 178–186; Bard, ed., *Madeleine Pelletier (1874–1939): logiques et infortunes d'un combat pour l'égalité* (Paris, 1992).

107. Correspondence between H. Bonnet, Institut international de coopération intellectuelle, League of Nations, and A. Rosier, BUS, 31 Dec. 1934 and 19 Jan. 1935, AN 63AJ 59; "Médecin assistant des établissements de l'Office public d'hygiène sociale du département de la Seine," *La science médicale pratique* (1929): 528. One position of *médecin assistant* in a hospital in the Var was offered only to women; see *La science médicale pratique* (1929): 202. Cf. Linda L. Clark, *The Rise of Professional Women in France: Gender and Public Administration since 1830* (Cambridge, 2000), chap. 6.

108. Husbands' legal authority over wives was only fully abolished in France in 1965. Marc Ancel, ed., *La condition de la femme dans la société contemporaine* (Paris, 1938); Aline Roux, *Contribution à l'étude de la feminisation de la profession médicale: quelques réflexions sur l'image du médecin au travers de l'évolution historique et psycho-sociologique de la condition de la femme* (Paris, 1974). It remains unknown whether this authorization was commonly required in practice. Christine Bard says it was rarely requested by employers; *Les femmes dans la société française au 20e siècle* (Paris, 2001), 43. Since there was no Medical Order, women doctors would not have anyone to show such an authorization to, although their husband could legally stop them from working. For women doctors in civil service positions, the state would be the authority.

109. See, for example, Professor Nobécourt, "La dénatalité française et l'opinion médicale," *Gazette des hôpitaux* (24 June 1939), reprinted in *SMP* 7 (July 1939), 26–28. See also Elinor A. Accampo, Rachel G. Fuchs, and Mary Lynn Stewart, *Gender and the Politics of Social Reform in France, 1870–1914* (Baltimore, 1995), 15–16, 180–181; Marie-Monique Huss, "Pronatalism in the Inter-war Period in France," *Journal of Contemporary History* 25 (1990): 39–68; Francine Muel-Dreyfus, *Vichy et l'éternel féminin: contribution à une sociologie politique de l'ordre des corps* (Paris, 1996); Françoise Thébaud, "Le mouvement nataliste dans la France de l'entre-deux-guerres: l'alliance nationale pour l'accroissement de la population française," *Revue d'histoire moderne et contemporaine* (April–June 1985): 276–301.

110. "Les destinées de la jeunesse universitaire de France," *La voix dentaire, revue mensuelle: organe de l'Association générale des étudiants en chirurgie dentaire de France* 22 (April 1936): 7.

111. Antoine Prost, *Histoire de l'enseignement en France, 1800–1967* (Paris, 1968), 328–335.

112. "Le diplôme devant la vie," *L'écho des étudiants* 607 (18 Aug. 1934): 3–4; "La pléthore médicale," *SM Nord* 10 (Dec. 1938): 393.

113. "La grève des étudiants en médecine," *Bulletin officiel de l'Association professionnelle des internes et anciens internes des hôpitaux de Marseille* 2 (Feb. 1935): 11.

114. Nobécourt, "La dénatalité française et l'opinion médicale," 28.

115. Dr. Willette, "L'égalité des sexes," *La butte médicale* 34 (Sept. 1929): 11–12.

116. H. Signoret, "Voteront… Voteront pas!" *La butte médicale* 53 (Nov. 1932): 4–8.

117. Ibid., 9–10.

118. Émile Sergent, "Le médecin dans la société moderne," *La science médicale pratique* 9 (1 May 1931): 415.

119. See Nye, "The Legacy of Masculine Codes of Honor and Admission of Women to the Medical Profession."

120. Even before this the BUS had quietly advocated the concept of obligatory retirement in the liberal professions as one initiative in its program to alleviate "intellectual unemployment." But the idea went unnoticed until Pomaret's proposed law in 1936. BUS, "Contre le chômage intellectuel," *L'écho des étudiants* 642 (12 June 1935): 5–6; "Le Bureau universitaire de statistique et la 'limite d'âge,'" *Le bouclier* 73 (Sept. 1936): 200. See also Chatriot, "La lutte contre le 'chômage intellectuel.'"

121. Charles Pomaret, "La loi Pomaret permettra-t-elle de donner du travail aux jeunes," *L'Europe médicale* (Nov. 1936), republished in *Étudiants, mensuelle des étudiants de Paris* 3 (Feb.–March 1937): 2, AP 222.

122. "Proposition de loi déposée sur le bureau de la Chambre par M. Pomaret, le 5 juin 1936," *SM Seine-et-Oise* 48 (July 1936): 206.

123. AP 214.

124. Leroy, "Le chômage des diplômés," 3.

125. Maurice Mordagne, the leader of the Association des étudiants en médecine de Paris, asserted that "toutes les Associations d'étudiants consultés par nous y sont farouchement opposées," in "Projet de loi et contre propositions sur la retraite du médecin," *SMP* 7 (July 1939): 10–14. Cf. "Un exemple à ne pas suivre," *AEMP, bulletin mensuel* 6 (April 1939): 10; Mordagne, *Gazette des hôpitaux* 54 (4 July 1936), AP 214; Mordagne, "Une contre-proposition au projet de loi Pomaret sur la retraite des médecins," *Le médecin corporatif: organe de la Fédération corporative des médecins de la région parisienne* 4 (April 1939): 96–99.

126. "Proposition de loi Pomaret," *Bulletin de la Société des médecins et du Syndicat médical de Lot-et-Garonne* 78 (Aug. 1936): 7–10; "Ordre du jour voté par le Conseil d'administration de la Fédération des S.M.S. dans sa séance du 9 juillet 1936 au sujet de la proposition de loi Pomaret," *SM Seine, Banlieue Ouest et Nord* 110 (Sept. 1936): 111–112.

127. Pochon, "Le projet de loi Pomaret," speech given at CTI and reiterated at Assemblée générale du Syndicat médical de Paris, 18 Nov. 1936, *SMP* 9 (Nov. 1936): 10–11.

128. Dr. Dournel, "Projet de loi Pomaret," *SM Seine, Banlieue Ouest et Nord* 110 (Sept. 1936): 117; "Ordre du jour voté par le Conseil d'administration de la Fédération des S.M.S.," 111–112.

129. "Conseil d'administration de la Confédération des Syndicats médicaux français, le 19 juillet 1936," *Bulletin de la Société des médecins et du Syndicat médical de Lot-et-Garonne* 78 (Aug. 1936): 10–12.

130. "Loi Pomaret," *Le bouclier* 78 (Feb. 1937): 47; "Proposition de loi Pomaret," *Bulletin de la Société des médecins et du Syndicat médical de Lot-et-Garonne* 79 (Oct. 1936): 6–7; "Ordre du jour voté par le Conseil d'administration de la Fédération des S.M.S. dans sa séance du 9 juillet 1936 au sujet de la proposition de loi Pomaret," 111–112; Mordagne, "Projet de loi et contre propositions sur la retraite du médecin," 10–14.

131. Pochon, "Le projet de loi Pomaret," 11; Pochon, "Le projet de loi Pomaret, 2e édition," *SMP* 1 (Jan. 1937): 7–10.

132. "Voeu X: institution de retraites dans les professions libérales," in BUS report "Chômage intellectuel" (1938).

4. The Barrier of the Law Bar

1. Robert-Martin, "Tableaux indiquant le nombre des avocats dans les barreaux français de 1912 à 1931," *Bulletin de l'Association nationale des avocats (ANA)* [hereafter *Bulletin de l'ANA*] 45 (Oct.–Nov.–Dec. 1932): 18–37; Halpérin, *Avocats et notaires en Europe*, 73.

2. See Waxin, "Statut de l'étudiant étranger dans son développement historique," 254–256.

3. "Statistique générale des étudiants français, coloniaux, étrangers, Université de Paris," 1928–1940, AP 226, 227, or 228.

4. *Recueil des statistiques*, 13.

5. Ibid., 6.

6. Ibid., 19–23.

7. Rosier, "Du chômage intellectuel: de l'encombrement des professions libérales," 39–44.

8. Ibid., 42.

9. Robert-Martin, "Tableaux indiquant le nombre des avocats," 18–37; Robert-Martin, *Bulletin de l'ANA* 58 (Jan.–Feb.–March 1936); Rosier, "Du chômage intellectuel: de l'encombrement des professions libérales," 45–46; *Recueil des statistiques*, 237–240. These statistics are for metropolitan France.

10. Rosier, "Du chômage intellectuel: de l'encombrement des professions libérales," 40–41.

11. Robert-Martin, "Tableaux indiquant le nombre des avocats," 18–37; *Recueil des statistiques*, 237–240.

12. Robert Planty, "Les barreaux à créer: un peu de courage et beaucoup de géographie," *Bulletin de l'ANA* 52 (July–Aug.–Sept. 1934); Planty, "Comment aider le barreau?" *Bulletin de l'ANA* 49 (Oct.–Nov.–Dec. 1933).

13. Planty, "Comment aider le barreau?"

14. Fillon, *Histoire du barreau de Lyon sous la Troisième République*, 201–216.

15. Yves Ozanam, "L'U.J.A. de Paris dans les archives," *Bulletin de l'Union des jeunes avocats de Paris (UJA), 75e anniversaire, 1922–1997* (March 1997): 28–29.

16. The group was also a member of the Union internationale des avocats. *Conférence des bâtonniers des départements, bulletin trimestriel* 2 (July 1934). See also the October 1936 issue, nos. 1–2.

17. Le Comité, "La Conférence des bâtonniers des départements et l'ANA," *Bulletin de l'ANA* 28 (July 1928): 242–244.

18. Fernand Payen, "Le palais et le parlement, Me. Paul Marchandeau," *La vie judiciaire* (20–21 Feb. 1938): 1.

19. "Union des jeunes avocats," *La vie judiciaire* (29 Feb. 1936): 3.

20. Gaudemet, *Les juristes et la vie politique de la IIIe République*, 53–81.

21. Ibid., 81.

22. Ibid., 53–81. Cf. Le Béguec, *La République des avocats*, chap. 3.

23. Some lawyers in parliament were reputed to be failed legal practitioners, "*des ratés du barreau*." Savage, "Advocates of the Republic," 195.

24. Gilles Le Béguec, "L'aristocratie du barreau, vivier pour la République: les secrétaires de la Conférence du stage," *Vingtième siècle* 30 (April–June 1991): 24; Chris-

tophe Charle, "Méritocratie et profession juridique: les secrétaires de la Conférence du stage des avocats de Paris, une étude des promotions, 1860–1870 et 1879–1889," *Paedogogica historica* (1994): 305.

25. Gilles Le Béguec, "Un conservatoire parlementaire: la conférence Molé-Tocqueville à la fin de la IIIe République," *Bulletin de la Société d'histoire moderne* (1984): 16.

26. See, for example, Payen, "Le palais et le parlement," *La vie judiciaire* (20 May 1932): 4; "Le palais et le parlement," *La vie judiciaire* (20 June 1932); "Tablettes parlementaires," *La vie judiciaire* (30 Dec. 1932): 2; "Tablettes parlementaires: le 100e cabinet de la 3e République," *La vie judiciaire* (30 Jan. 1936): 4; "Tablettes parlementaires: rentrée parlementaire et présentation ministerielle," *La vie judiciaire* (10 June 1936): 4.

27. The right-wing demonstration on 6 February 1934 developed into a riot under the influence of extreme right political leagues and led to the downfall of the government. The riot symbolized mounting anti-parliamentarian sentiment and the radicalization of left and right in France. See the dossier "Avocats impliqués dans l'affaire Stavisky," AN BB 18 6772, dossier 86 BL 1464, nos. 10 and 4.

28. Discussed in the general assembly of the Conférence des bâtonniers, 26 May 1934, published in *Conférence des bâtonniers des départements, bulletin trimestriel* 2 (July 1934): 20–60.

29. Decree of 10 March 1934 amending the decree of 20 June 1920 regulating the legal profession, in Louis Crémieu, *Traité de la profession d'avocat* (Aix-Marseille, 1939), 423–424.

30. "Les débouchés ouverts aux bacheliers," in "Les guides des carrières," brochure published by the Secretariat d'État à l'Éducation Nationale et à la Jeunesse, Centre national de documentation professionnelle, BUS (1 Oct. 1943), AN 78AJ 14.

31. Faculté de Médecine and Faculté de Droit, Université de Paris, 1938–39, AP 226, 227, and 228. The parents of 431 students declared "no occupation."

32. John Savage, "The Social Function of the Law Faculty: Demographics, Republican Reform, and Professional Training at the Paris Law Faculty, 1870–1914," *History of Education Quarterly* 48, no. 2 (May 2008): 221–243.

33. Charpentier, "La protection des titres professionnels," 15–21.

34. *Conseils juridiques* tried to distinguish themselves from *agents d'affaires* by creating imitation "law bars" of their own. Boigeol and Dezalay, "De l'agent d'affaires au barreau," 53–57; Halpérin, *Avocats et notaires en Europe,* 49, 94.

35. André Barthélemy, report of the Congrès annuel de l'ANA, Morocco, 23–26 April 1935, *Bulletin de l'ANA* 55 (April–May–June 1935).

36. Marcel Bloch, *Bulletin de l'UJA à la cour de Paris* (1930–31): 18–20.

37. Jean Appleton, *Traité de la profession d'avocat* (Paris, 1923), 223–226.

38. Marcel Fournier, response to Barthélemy, report of the Congrès annuel de l'ANA, Morocco, 23–26 April 1935.

39. See Lucien Karpik, "La profession libérale, un cas, le barreau," in *Les lieux de mémoire,* ed. Pierre Nora (Paris, 1992), 284–321.

40. Crémieu, *Traité de la profession d'avocat,* 11–15.

41. Appleton, *Traité de la profession d'avocat,* 217–249; Fernand Payen and Gaston Duveau, *Les règles de la profession d'avocat et les usages du barreau de Paris* (Paris, 1926), 126–152. Opinions differed on whether practicing lawyers should be allowed to double as law professors.

42. Appleton, *Traité de la profession d'avocat,* 226–228.

43. Payen and Duveau, *Les règles de la profession d'avocat,* 139–147; Halpérin, *Avocats et notaires en Europe,* 77.

44. Payen and Duveau, *Les règles de la profession d'avocat,* 139–147; Appleton, *Traité de la profession d'avocat,* 223–226, 247–249.

45. Charpentier, "La protection des titres professionnels," 24–35, 72–79; Fillon, *Histoire du barreau de Lyon sous la Troisième République,* 241–246. In another example of distinction through entitlement, lawyers were fond of calling one another and themselves *maître.* Often abbreviated, as in "Me. Marius Moutet," this practice was similar to doctors' use of *docteur* in spoken and written French.

46. Pascal Plas, "La professionnalisation des avocats au début des années vingt," in *Avocats et barreaux en France,* ed. Le Béguec, 59–76.

47. André Barthélemy, report of the Congrès annuel de l'ANA, Morocco, 23–26 April 1935.

48. Rosier, "Du chômage intellectuel: de l'encombrement des professions libérales," 44; BUS, "Chômage intellectuel" (1938).

49. Halpérin, *Avocats et notaires en Europe,* 51.

50. *Recueil des statistiques,* 12, 60.

51. Fillon, "La profession d'avocat et son image pendant l'entre-deux-guerres," 336–347.

52. Appleton, *Traité de la profession d'avocat,* 195–203.

53. Payen and Duveau, *Les règles de la profession d'avocat,* 112.

54. Anne-Laure Catinat, "Les premières avocates du barreau de Paris," *Mil neuf cent* 16 (1998): 48–52.

55. Charles d'Avron, "Il y a eu hier 25 ans que les femmes sont inscrites au barreau," *Excelsior* (2 Oct. 1925), 2, BMD DOS 349 AVO.

56. Kimble, "Justice Redressed," 177–179.

57. Joseph Python, "Mme. Nanine Morin-Blum, avocat à la Cour d'appel, secrétaire de la Conférence," *La vie judiciaire* (20 Dec. 1933): 1; Georges Claretie, "Les secrétaires de la Conférence," *Figaro,* 13 July 1934, BMD DOS 349 AVO.

58. "La première 'bâtonnière,'" *Conférence des bâtonniers des départements* 2 (Oct. 1933): 25; Jean Appleton, "Mme. Paule René Pignet, du barreau de la Roche-sur-Yon, la première femme élue bâtonnier," *La vie judiciaire* (20 Oct. 1933): 1.

59. "Dans les ministères," *La vie judiciaire* (20 July 1936): 5; Agathe Dyvrande-Thévenin, "Mme. Marcelle Kraemer-Bach, avocat à la cour, chargée de mission au cabinet de M. Herriot, président du Conseil," *La vie judiciaire* (10 Oct. 1932): 1.

60. Auguste Vigne, "Tablettes parlementaires: les femmes au palais et au parlement," *La vie judiciaire* (28 Feb.–1 March 1937): 2; Imbrecq, "Tribune libre: les femmes et la magistrature," *La vie judiciaire* (30 Jan. 1933): 2.

61. See, for example, Jean Appleton, "Mme. Camille Ballofy, avocat à la Cour d'appel de Lyon," *La vie judiciaire* (30–31 July 1933): 1.

62. "La Fédération internationale des femmes magistrates et avocats," *La vie judiciaire* (30 Oct. 1930): 4; Juliette Gunsbert, "Le Congrès internationale des femmes magistrates et avocats," *La vie judiciaire* (20 Jan. 1937): 1; Agathe Dyvrande-Thévenin, "Les femmes ne sont-elles pas à leur place au palais?" *L'oeuvre* (2 July 193?), BMD DOS 349 AVO.

63. Société des femmes qui se vouent aux professions libérales (ca. 1880s), pamphlet, AN AJ16 6707.

64. Kimble, "Justice Redressed," 190–192.

65. Bard, *Les filles de Marianne,* 178–186.

66. Catinat, "Les premières avocates du barreau de Paris," 52–55.

67. Bard, *Les femmes dans la société française au 20e siècle,* 114.

68. Frances I. Clark, *The Position of Women in Contemporary France* (Westport, Conn., 1937), 59.

69. Anne Boigeol, "Les femmes et les cours: la difficile mise en oeuvre de l'égalité des sexes dans l'accès à la magistrature," *Genèses* 22 (March 1996): 107–129.

70. Ancel, *La condition de la femme dans la société contemporaine;* Roux, *Contribution à l'étude de la feminisation de la profession médicale.*

71. Fillon, *Histoire du barreau de Lyon sous la Troisième République,* 164–188.

72. Guy Péron, "Bachelièr … e!" *L'Université de Paris* 247 (Dec. 1922): 15; François Le Roy, "Les problèmes du chômage dans les professions intellectuelles," *Musée social* 9 (Sept. 1937): 237–258; Dyvrande-Thévenin, "Les femmes ne sont-elles pas à leur place au palais?"

73. "Jeunes filles 1932 à la conquête des diplômes," *L'écho des étudiants* 517 (6 Aug. 1932): 10.

74. Louis Sarran, "Rapport sur l'organisation des professions intellectuelles et les mésures à prendre pour le relèvement de leur dignité morale et de leur situation économique," *Bulletin de l'ANA* 39 (April 1931): 131–135.

75. "Au sujet de la proposition Pomaret," *Bulletin de l'ANA* 61 (Oct.–Nov.–Dec. 1936): 39.

76. See Pierre Véron, "À propos de la proposition de loi Pomaret," *Bulletin de l'Union des jeunes avocats à la cour de Paris* (1935–1936); and Véron, report, *Bulletin de l'ANA* 62 (Jan.–Feb.–Mar. 1937): 85.

5. Citizens into Lawyers

1. Jean Appleton admitted that jurisprudence supporting the requirement of French nationality for the practice of law was based on weak argumentation, but he reasoned that because the practice of law should be considered a public service, it ought to be reserved for French nationals. For case history references, see Appleton, *Traité de la profession d'avocat.*

2. Crémieu, *Traité de la profession d'avocat,* 21–25; Payen and Duveau, *Les règles de la profession d'avocat,* 107–109; Waxin, "Statut de l'étudiant étranger dans son développement historique," 254–256; Halpérin, *Avocats et notaires en Europe,* 174.

3. Décret du 20 juin 1920 portant règlement d'administration publique sur l'exercice de la profession d'avocat et la discipline du barreau, in Crémieu, *Traité de la profession d'avocat,* 414–415.

4. "Académie de Paris, Conseil de l'Université de Paris - Conseil académique, Rapports sur les travaux et les actes des établissements d'enseignement supérieur pendant l'année scolaire 1920–1921," AN AJ16 2640.

5. "La Faculté de droit doit être agrandie," *L'écho des étudiants* 571 (19 Nov. 1933): 3.

6. "Avis aux étudiants étrangers," *Les études de droit à l'Université de Paris: guide pratique pour les études de droit,* brochure published by Librairie Receuil Sirey for the University of Paris Law School, 1939–40.

7. Association corporative des étudiants en droit, tract, ca. April 1935, AP 269.

8. Gustave-M. Rémond, "Les naturalisés et l'admission au stage" (Assemblée générale de l'UJA, 19 March 1934), *Bulletin de l'ANA* 51 (April–May–June 1934): 312.

9. Marcel Vigo, "Les équivalences du baccalauréat de l'enseignement secondaire et de la licence en droit" (Assemblée générale du Jeune barreau français, 27 March 1935), *La vie judiciaire* (30 March 1935): 4.

10. The minister of education chided the Ministry of Justice throughout the late 1920s for not having heeded his warning about specifying only certain university diplomas that could confer the right to a one-year waiting period. According to the law, all university diplomas counted, and this remained true throughout the interwar years. AN F17 17634.

11. See "Procès-verbal de l'assemblée générale de l'UJA du 19 mars 1934," *Bulletin de l'ANA* (April–May–June 1934): 309–313; tract of the Association corporative des étudiants en droit. April 1935, AN F7 13320.

12. AN F17 17634.

13. Noiriel, *Le creuset français,* 84.

14. Ibid., 93.

15. "Rapport de M. Louis Rolland, fait au nom de la Commission de législation civile et criminelle," *JO,* Documents Parlementaires, Chambre de Députés, Annexe 3737 (30 June 1934 session): 1117.

16. "Rapport sur l'organisation des professions intellectuelles et les mésures à prendre pour le relèvement de leur dignité morale et de leur situation économique" (Congrès de la Confédération des travailleurs intellectuels de 1931), *Bulletin de l'ANA* 39 (April 1931): 131–135.

17. Albert Rodanet, "Le Barreau et les naturalisés, une importante question d'actualité," *La vie judiciaire* (10 March 1934): 1. Cf. Rodanet, "Un grave péril pour le Barreau," *La vie judiciaire* (20 Nov. 1933): 6; Rodanet, "Le Barreau et les naturalisés," *La vie judiciaire* (30 Nov. 1933): 3; Rodanet, "Le Barreau et les naturalisés," *La vie judiciaire* (10 July 1934): 3.

18. "Séance solonelle d'ouverture, le 21 mai 1934, Congrès de Caen," *Bulletin de l'ANA* 52 (July–Aug.–Sept. 1934).

19. Appleton, *Traité de la profession d'avocat,* 191–193.

20. Rémond, "Les naturalisés et l'admission au stage," 310.

21. Rodanet, "Un grave péril pour le Barreau," 6.

22. Rodanet, "Le Barreau et les naturalisés" (30 Nov. 1933), 3.

23. Ibid.

24. Appleton, *Traité de la profession d'avocat,* 191–193.

25. Ibid., 207–210.

26. Rémond, "Les naturalisés et l'admission au stage," 310.

27. Rodanet, "Un grave péril pour le Barreau," 6.

28. "Rapport sur l'organisation des professions intellectuelles et les mésures à prendre."

29. Rodanet, "Le Barreau et les naturalisés" (10 July 1934), 3.

30. Marcel Fournier, "L'œuvre de l'Union des jeunes avocats à la Cour de Paris," *Bulletin de l'ANA* 57 (Oct.–Nov.–Dec. 1935).

31. Séance du Conseil de l'Ordre du 5 avril 1927, cited in Yves Ozanam, "L'Ordre des avocats à la Cour de Paris de 1910 à 1930," in *Avocats et barreaux en France,* ed. Le Béguec, 45.

32. Rodanet, "Le Barreau et les naturalisés" (30 Nov. 1933), 3.

33. "Voeu rélatif à l'admission des avocats d'origine étrangère," *Bulletin de l'ANA* 50 (Jan.–Feb.–Mar. 1934).

34. "Extrait de la discussion au Sénat le 12 mai 1933," *JO* (13 May 1933): 1006, reprinted in "Documentation parlementaire et legislative," *Bulletin de l'ANA* 48 (July–Aug.–Sept. 1933): 411–413.

35. "Procès-verbal de l'assemblée générale de l'UJA, 19 March 1934," *Bulletin de l'ANA* (April–May–June 1934): 313.

36. "L'Association nationale des avocats," *La vie judiciaire* (20 April 1934); "Naturalisés," *Bulletin de l'ANA* 51 (April–May–June 1934).

37. Rodanet, "Le Barreau et les naturalisés, une importante question d'actualité," 1.

38. Ibid.

39. Rémond, "Les naturalisés et l'admission au stage," 312.

40. Caron, *Uneasy Asylum,* 14.

41. Caron argues this point in *Uneasy Asylum,* 28–31.

42. "Loi sur l'exercice de la médecine pour les étrangers: Syndicat des médecins de la banlieue ouest et nord de Paris, Conseil d'administration du 10 janvier 1936," *SM Seine, Banlieue Ouest et Nord* 108 (May 1936): 135; Dr. F. Querrioux, "Rapport sur l'application aux médecins étrangers naturalisés de la loi du 29 juillet 1934 visant les avocats étrangers naturalisés," *SMP* 1 (Jan. 1935): 17–22.

43. Rémond, "Les naturalisés et l'admission au stage," 312.

44. Marc Knobel, "L'élimination des juristes juifs en Europe à partir de 1933," *Cahiers Bernard Lazare* 125–126 (1990): 145–146.

45. Raymond Hesse, *Quarante ans de Palais* (Paris, 1950), 53.

46. Jacques Isorni, *Mémoires, 1911–1945* (Paris, 1984), 115–117.

47. Lucienne Scheid was one of fourteen lawyers recommended by the Paris bar council for the "eminent professional merit" exemption to the anti-Semitic quota in 1941. All were rejected by the CGQJ. See chapter 6.

48. Laurent Joly, *Xavier Vallat: du nationalisme chrétien à l'antisémitisme d'état* (Paris, 2001), 148–158; Caron, *Uneasy Asylum,* 270.

49. Robert Badinter, *Un antisémitisme ordinaire: Vichy et les avocats juifs (1940–1944)* (Paris, 1997), 22.

50. Joly, *Xavier Vallat,* 163–165.

51. Talk by Robert Badinter, 23 June 1997, Maison du Barreau, place Dauphine, Paris, on the occasion of the publication of his book *Un antisémitisme ordinaire.*

52. Discussion following talk by Badinter, ibid.

53. Pierre Masse, "Me. Raoul Péret," *La vie judiciaire* (30 April 1930): 1.

54. *La vie judiciaire* (20 June 1934).

55. *La vie judiciaire* (28 Feb. 1930); *La vie judiciaire* (30 Nov.–1 Dec. 1930): 8.

56. M. Henri-Robert, "Me. Marcel Bloch, avocat à la Cour, président de l'UJA," *La vie judiciaire* (20 Feb. 1930): 1.

57. *La vie judiciaire* (20 Jan. 1933): 1. Idzkowski was a supporter of the ten-year waiting period for naturalized citizens. Rémond, "Les naturalisés et l'admission au stage," 313.

58. *La vie judiciaire* (10 May 1933): 1.

59. *La vie judiciaire* (30 March 1939): 3. Crémieu favored the restrictions on naturalized citizens joining the bar. Crémieu, *Traité de la profession d'avocat,* 25–27.

60. V. de Moro-Giafferri, avocat à la Cour d'appel to the Ministre de l'Intérieur, 26 Jan. 1934, AN F7 16080.

61. "Réunion du comité du 4 juin 1933" and "Congrès de l'ANA à Grenoble, 5 juin 1933," *Bulletin de l'ANA* 48 (July–Aug.–Sept. 1933): 177, 218–219.

62. See Caron, *Uneasy Asylum,* 142–170.

63. Ministre des Affaires Étrangères to M. Binet, Consul de France à Berlin, 18 May 1933, and additional documents, MAE C 254.

64. "Communications du comité: naturalisations," *Bulletin de l'ANA* 52 (July–Aug.–Sept. 1934).

65. *JO*, Documents Parlementaires, Chambre des Députés, Annexe 3177 (6 March 1934 session): 276–279.

66. Aulois, "Proposition de loi sur l'accession des naturalisés à certaines fonctions," *JO*, Documents Parlementaires, Chambre de Députés, Annexe 3655 (22 June 1934 session): 1075.

67. "Rapport de M. Louis Rolland, fait au nom de la Commission de législation civile et criminelle," 1117–18.

68. *JO*, Débats Parlementaires, Chambre de Députés (3 July 1934 session): 1993.

69. *JO*, Documents Parlementaires, Sénat, Annexe 504 (3 July 1934 session): 843.

70. *JO*, Sénat (5 July 1934 session): 1067–68.

71. *JO* (20 July 1934): 7347.

72. See Schor, *L'opinion française et les étrangers,* 600–602; and Noiriel, *Le creuset français,* 284–285.

73. Schor, *L'opinion française et les étrangers,* 601. For similar analyses, see Ayoub, "La nouvelle législation de la naturalisation en France," 121, 136–137; Caron, *Uneasy Asylum,* 28.

74. Dr. F. Querrioux, "Rapport sur l'application aux médecins étrangers naturalisés de la loi du 29 juillet 1934 visant les avocats étrangers naturalisés," *SM Seine, Banlieue Ouest et Nord* 101 (March 1935): 131–134.

75. *JO*, Débats Parlementaires, Chambre des Députés (20 June 1935 session): 1866.

76. Association corporative des étudiants en droit, tract, ca. April 1935, AP 269.

77. Pamphlet of the Association corporative des étudiants en droit, 1941, 3–4, AP 269.

78. "Le Jeune barreau français," *La vie judiciaire* (10–11 March 1935): 4; Vigo, "Les équivalences du baccalauréat de l'enseignement secondaire et de la licence en droit," 4.

79. In accordance with French archival regulations, the names of private persons will be protected. First (when available) and last initials will be used.

80. Arrêté du Conseil de l'Ordre des avocats de Paris, 29 Oct. 1935, Archives de Paris [hereafter AdP] 1319 W 1.

81. Thorp may be the same William Thorp who was elected deputy of the Gironde in 1936 with the Popular Front and who was later an opponent of the Algerian war. His political career demonstrates that men of the left shared the nationalistic conception of bar membership in the 1930s.

82. AdP 1319 W 1.

83. Arrêté du 10 décembre 1933 du Conseil de l'Ordre, quoted in Payen and Duveau, *Les règles de la profession d'avocat,* 111–112.

84. See Guérin, "La médecine française devant l'invasion étrangère," 13.

85. Péan, *Une jeunesse française,* 33–39 and photo section.

86. Sirinelli, "Action française," 8.

87. See Marc Milet, *La Faculté de droit de Paris face à la vie politique, de l'affaire Scelle à l'affaire Jèze, 1925–1936* (Paris, 1996). In 1935, Gaston Jèze acted as legal adviser to Ethiopia before the League of Nations in the matter of the Italian invasion. At the Archives de l'Académie de Paris, there is a trove of documentation about the Jèze affair.

88. Untitled report of 3 April 1935, Dossier 1934–1936, AN F7 13320.

89. "Conseil d'État, demande d'avis sur l'interprétation à donner à l'article unique de la loi du 19 juillet 1934," 299–306. The Council of State, looking at broader nationality law, determined that categories of persons who attained French nationality through means other than naturalization were also exempt from the provisions of the 1934 law: first, individuals born in France to a foreign parent, and second, French women who had married a foreigner (thus losing their French nationality) but then divorced (thus regaining it, but not through naturalization).

90. Crémieu, *Traité de la profession d'avocat,* 21–25. Cf. Appleton, *Traité de la profession d'avocat,* 210.

91. "Réunion de l'assemblée générale de l'UJA du 19 mars 1934," *Bulletin de l'ANA* (April–May–June 1934): 311; Appleton, *Traité de la profession d'avocat,* 210; Payen and Duveau, *Les règles de la profession d'avocat,* 107–113; Crémieu, *Traité de la profession d'avocat,* 21–25.

92. Louis Gardenat, *Traité de la profession d'avocat* (Paris, 1932), 88; Payen and Duveau, *Les règles de la profession d'avocat,* 107–113; Jean-Philippe Dedieu, "L'intégration des avocats africains dans les barreaux français," *Droit et société* 56–57, no. 1 (2004): 209–229.

93. Payen and Duveau, *Les règles de la profession d'avocat,* 111–112. Payen cited the *Gazette du Palais,* 9 February 1935, for the decision of the court.

94. "Arrêtés du Conseil de l'Ordre de Paris le 6 novembre 1934 et le 18 décembre 1934, confirmés par la Cour d'Appel de Paris du 24 janvier 1935," *Gazette du Palais* (9 Feb. 1935); "Arrêté du Conseil de l'Ordre de [X], confirmé par la Cour d'Appel de Colmar du 30 octobre 1935," *Sirey* 2, no. 21 (1936). Cf. Ayoub, "La nouvelle législation de la naturalisation en France," 151–152; and Payen and Duveau, *Les règles de la profession d'avocat,* 111–112.

95. Rapport de M. le Député Louis Rolland, *JO,* Documents Parlementaires, Chambre des Députés, Annexe 4811 (26 Feb. 1935): 368–369.

96. Maurice Lansac, "L'évolution générale de la profession d'avocat depuis le rétablissement de cette profession en 1804 jusqu'à 1935," *La vie judiciaire* (20 March 1935): 1.

97. Rapport de M. le Député Louis Rolland, *JO,* Documents Parlementaires, Chambre des Députés, Annexe 4811 (26 Feb. 1935): 369; *JO,* Débats Parlementaires, Chambre des Députés (20 June 1935 session): 1865.

98. *JO,* Débats Parlementaires, Chambre des Députés (20 June 1935 session): 1865.

99. *JO,* Débats Parlementaires, Sénat (27 June 1935 session): 756.

100. Untitled report of 3 April 1935, Dossier 1934–1936, AN F7 13320.

101. Crémieu, *Traité de la profession d'avocat,* 430–431.

102. Quoted in Liora Israël, *Robes noires, années sombres: avocats et magistrats en résistance pendant la Seconde guerre mondiale* (Paris, 2005), 456 note 64. Cf. Ayoub, "La nouvelle législation de la naturalisation en France," 160.

103. E. Meaux, président du Jeune barreau français, "Banquet du 26 Jan. 1937," *La vie judiciaire* (30 Jan. 1937): 6.

104. "ANA Congrès de Besançon, 18 mai 1937," *Bulletin de l'ANA* 64 (July–Aug.–Sept. 1937); "ANA Congrès de Lyon, mai 1939," *Bulletin de l'ANA* 72 (July–Aug.–Sept. 1939).

105. André Touleman, *Bulletin de l'ANA* 56 (July–Aug.–Sept. 1935).

106. "Tablettes parlementaires: les obligations militaires des étrangers en France," *La vie judiciaire* (10 April 1939): 1.

107. "Tablettes parlementaires: une nouvelle législation sur le changement de noms des étangers naturalisés," *La vie judiciaire* (10 Feb. 1939): 3.

108. Georges Delavente, "Les avocats roumains à l'honneur," *La vie judiciaire* (10 Jan. 1935): 2–3. See also laudatory remarks about Ionesco at the UJA general assembly of 30 May 1934, published in *La vie judiciaire* (10–11 June 1934), and (10 May 1935): 1.

109. Personal interview with Yves Ozanam, 28 Nov. 1997, L'Ordre des avocats, Palais de justice, Paris. Cf. Fernand Payen, *Le barreau et la langue française* (Paris, 1939).

110. "Une lettre ouverte de l'Union fédérale des étudiants: l'agitation xénophobe et antisémite dans les facultés," *L'humanité* (13 March 1930). Cf. "L'élimination des étudiants minoritaires," *UFE: les étudiants nouveaux* (March–April 1930): 2–3, both in "Dossier: Blanchetière," AN AJ16 8362.

111. "14e Congrès annuel de l'ANA au Maroc, le 23–26 avril 1935: textes de voeux" *Bulletin de l'ANA* 55 (April–May–June 1935).

112. Lewis, *The Boundaries of the Republic,* 146–148.

113. Senator Lémery to Loriot, 16 May 1934, AN BB30 1605.

114. "Compte rendu de la réunion du comité, 25 Oct. 1936," *Bulletin de l'ANA* 61 (Oct.–Nov–Dec. 1936).

115. "Aide aux avocats espagnols," *Bulletin de l'ANA* 71 (April–May–June 1939).

116. Israël, *Robes noires,* 97.

117. Ibid., 98–99.

118. *Guide de l'étudiant,* Université de Poitiers, année scolaire 1932–33.

119. Rémond, "Les naturalisés et l'admission au stage," 310.

120. Note de la Direction politique et commerciale, Ministère des Affaires Étrangères, 15 Dec. 1936, Documents 290–291, MAE C 254; ANA president Robert-Martin to the Ministre de la Justice, 5 July 1938, CAC 19950407 492.

121. Rapport de M. le Député Louis Rolland, *JO,* Documents Parlementaires, Chambre des Députés, Annexe 4811 (26 Feb. 1935): 369.

122. Rémond, "Les naturalisés et l'admission au stage," 311.

123. See Catherine Nicault, "Yvonne Netter, avocate, militante féministe et sioniste," *Archives juives* 30, no. 1 (1997): 117.

6. Lawyers during the Vichy Regime

1. Denis Peschanski, "Vichy 1940–1944," in *21 historiens expliquent la France contemporaine,* (Paris, 2005), 184.

2. Peter Sahlins, *Unnaturally French: Foreign Citizens in the Old Regime and After* (Ithaca, 2004).

3. AN BB30 1711.

4. Bernard Laguerre, "Les dénaturalisés de Vichy, 1940–1944," *Vingtième siècle* 20 (1988): 3–15.

5. Jean-Marc Béraud, "Le juif interdit de travail," in *Le droit antisémite de Vichy,* 220; Catherine Kessedjian, "Le juif déchu da la nationalité française," ibid., 232.

6. Kessedjian, "Le juif déchu da la nationalité française," 231.

7. A previous legislative project to bar from public service any French citizen with fewer than three generations of French parentage had failed in 1895. Dominique Rémy, *Les lois de Vichy* (Paris, 1992), 52–53. Cf. Laurent Joly, "L'entrée de l'antisémitisme sur la scène parlementaire française: le débat sur l' 'infiltration juive' à la Chambre en mai 1895," *Archives juives* 38, no. 1 (2005): 114–128.

8. Linda L. Clark, "Higher-Ranking Women Civil Servants and the Vichy Regime: Firings and Hirings, Collaboration and Resistance," *French History* 13, no. 3 (1999): 332–359.

9. France deported 75,721 Jews from its territory on trains bound for Nazi death camps; only 2,500 returned after the war. Several thousand more Jews were killed on French territory. In all, nearly 25 percent of Jews in France died in the Holocaust. Foreign Jews in France had worse survival rates: 41 percent of foreign Jews died, compared to 12 percent of French Jews. Of the 330,000 Jews living in France at the end of 1940, about 195,000 of them, or 59 percent, were French and 135,000 or 41 percent, were foreigners. Susan Zuccotti, *The Holocaust, the French, and the Jews* (New York: 1993), 207, 284 (citing Klarsfeld); Laurent Joly, *Vichy dans la "solution finale": histoire du Commissariat général aux questions juives, 1941–1944* (Paris, 2006), 845–848.

10. Laurent Joly claims that five hundred Jewish lawyers were expelled from French bars but does not cite a source. Joly, *Vichy dans la "solution finale,"* 588. Unfortunately, no definitive list for all French bars has yet been found.

11. Catherine Fillon, *Le barreau de Lyon dans la tourmente: de l'Occupation à la Libération* (Lyon, 2003), 54.

12. Ministère de la Justice, press release, 26–27 July 1941, AN BB30 1707; Dossier "Oeuvre legislative de Vichy," AN BB30 1711.

13. Israël, *Robes noires,* 104–105.

14. Fillon, *Le barreau de Lyon dans la tourmente,* 56–61; on the draft of the text debated between the Ministry of Justice and Charpentier, see 61–66.

15. Talk by Robert Badinter, 23 June 1997, Maison du Barreau, Paris, on the occasion of the publication of his book *Un antisémitisme ordinaire.*

16. Caron, *Between France and Germany.*

17. Badinter, *Un antisémitisme ordinaire,* 36.

18. Richard Weisberg, *Vichy Law and the Holocaust in France* (New York, 1996).

19. Yves Ozanam, "De Vichy à la Résistance: le bâtonnier Jacques Charpentier," in *La justice de l'épuration, à la fin de la Seconde Guerre mondiale* (Paris, 2008), 157.

20. Charpentier is wrong to use "sons" here because the law excluded children—daughters and sons alike—of fathers who were not French at the time of their birth.

21. Jacques Charpentier, *Au service de la liberté* (Paris, 1949), 127.

22. Fillon, *Le barreau de Lyon dans la tourmente,* 61.

23. Noël Verney to Lyon law bar president, 14 Oct. 1940. Thanks to Catherine Fillon for sharing this document and the attestations of other Lyon lawyers, including Louis Montrochet and Louis Laval.

24. Procureur général près la Cour d'appel de Paris to the Ministre de la Justice, 21 May 1937, CAC 19950407 492.

25. Badinter, *Un antisémitisme ordinaire,* 61–62; Yves Ozanam, "Le barreau de Paris pendant la Seconde Guerre mondiale, 1940–1945," in *La justice des années sombres, 1940–1945* (Paris, 2001), 146. Cf. Jean-Louis Halpérin, "La législation de Vichy relative aux avocats et aux droits de la défense," *Revue historique* 597 (July–Sept. 1991): 151.

26. Weisberg, *Vichy Law and the Holocaust,* 299–300.

27. "Note sur maître Rosenmark, avocat à la Cour de Paris," AN F1a 3687–3688.

28. Fillon, *Le barreau de Lyon dans la tourmente,* 66, 67–69.

29. Antoine Navarro to Lyon law bar president, 16 Dec. 1940; Lyon law bar president to the procureur général 13 and 14 Feb. 1941; Lyon law bar president to Ministre

de la Justice, 13 and 14 Feb. 1941; Ministère de la Justice arrêté, 10 July 1941. Thanks to Catherine Fillon for sharing these documents.

30. Caron, *Uneasy Asylum,* 74–78; Weil, *Qu'est-ce qu'un Français?* 81–87.

31. Lyon law bar president to the Ministre de la Justice, 11 Oct. 1940; Ministère de la Justice, arrêté, 7 Feb. 1941. Thanks to Catherine Fillon for sharing these documents.

32. Ugo Iannucci, "L'attitude du barreau de Lyon pendant l'Occupation," in *La justice des années sombres,* 169.

33. "Extrait du registre des déliberations de la Cour d'Appel de Lyon," 1 Dec. 1941; Lyon *procureur général* to Lyon law bar president, 17 Dec. 1941; Lyon law bar president to Mlle. Benaroya, 17 Dec. 1941. Thanks to Catherine Fillon for sharing these documents.

34. Iannucci, "L'attitude du barreau de Lyon pendant l'Occupation," 169.

35. Liora Israël, "L'épuration des barreaux français après la Seconde Guerre mondiale: une socio-histoire fragmentaire," report submitted to the Groupe d'Intérêt Public - Mission de recherche Droit et Justice, Ministère de la Justice (Jan. 2004), www.gip-recherche-justice.fr/recherches/syntheses/110-epuration-barreaux.pdf, 109–111. (Full unpublished report available upon request from the GIP.)

36. Isorni, *Mémoires,* 211.

37. Ibid., 214. The senior lawyer on Pétain's defense team was Fernand Payen, former president of the Aix bar and a leader of the interwar exclusionary movement.

38. AN BB30 1711.

39. Badinter, *Un antisémitisme ordinaire,* 63–64; Weisberg, *Vichy Law and the Holocaust,* 298.

40. Israël, *Robes noires,* 161.

41. Badinter, *Un antisémitisme ordinaire,* 61–3; Ozanam, "Le barreau de Paris pendant la Seconde Guerre mondiale, 1940–1945," 146 and note 7; Fillon, *Le barreau de Lyon dans la tourmente,* 71–72.

42. In Aix, two lawyers, sons of foreign fathers and also Jewish, were removed from the bar under the 10 September 1940 law. Badinter, *Un antisémitisme ordinaire,* 185.

43. Published in *Bulletin de l'ANA* 75 (Dec. 1941): 7–8.

44. Ozanam, "Le barreau de Paris pendant la Seconde Guerre mondiale," 163 note 7.

45. Quoted in Israël, *Robes noires,* 107. Cf. Jeune barreau français in "Epuration: dossiers d'avocats A–Z (1945–1949)," AdP 1320 W 134.

46. Dossier Jeune barreau français, CAC 19950407 453.

47. Cited in Badinter, *Un antisémitisme ordinaire,* 137.

48. Renée Poznanski, *Les juifs en France pendant la Seconde Guerre mondiale* (Paris, 1997), 262.

49. Badinter, *Un antisémitisme ordinaire,* 62.

50. Ibid., 64. Freemasons were also banned from bar councils. Halpérin, "La législation de Vichy relative aux avocats et aux droits de la défense," 152.

51. "Loi du 21 juin 1941," *JO* (24 June 1941): 2628. Cf. Claude Singer, *Vichy, l'université et les juifs* (Paris, 1992); Claude Singer, *L'université libérée, l'université épurée (1943–1947)* (Paris, 1997).

52. "Extrait des minutes du greffe de la Cour d'Appel de Paris, Arrêté concernant les avocats juifs," 13 Feb. 1942, AdP 1320 W 148.

53. Ministère de la Justice to Ambassadeur Brinon, 15 June 1942, AN F60 1485; President of the Paris Court of Appeals to CGQJ, 5 Oct. 1942, AN AJ38 14.

54. Béraud, "Le juif interdit de travail," 216.

55. Ibid., 217, 224; Rémy, *Les lois de Vichy,* 126.

56. Rapport de réunion de l'Assemblée générale du Conseil d'État, 30 Jan. 1941, AN AJ38 1146; Garde des Sceaux to Secrétaire général des Anciens combattants, 11 Feb. 1941, Archives du Centre de documentation juive contemporaine [hereafter CDJC] CCCLXXIX 9; CGQJ to Conseil d'État, 15 May 1941, AN AJ38 1146; Joseph Billig, *Le Commissariat général aux questions juives (1941–1944),* 3 vols. (Paris, 1955), 3:23; Joly, *Vichy dans la "solution finale,"* 201–205; Badinter, *Un antisémitisme ordinaire,* 68–95.

57. *JO* (17 July 1941): 2999.

58. For debate over basing the quota only on non-Jews, see AN AJ38 1146.

59. In North Africa, anti-Semitic quotas were also established in the law bars in 1941. "Le Statut des avocats juifs au Maroc," AN 72 AJ 1837; CGQJ, "Note sur le projet de décret portant application à l'Algérie du décret du 16 juillet 1941, réglementant, en ce qui concerne les juifs, la profession d'avocat," AN F60 490; "Arrêté résidentiel réglementant en ce qui concerne les juifs la profession d'avocat en Tunisie," 30 March 1942, CDJC CVIII 108:9; Sétif bar president letter to Vallat, CGQJ, 16 May 1941, CDJC LXXX 80:2; "Note sur le conflit qui divise la Cour d'Appel de Rabat et le Conseil de l'Ordre des avocats de Casablanca," CGQJ in Casablanca, 3 March 1942, AN AJ38 58; Moroccan Resident General Noguès to CGQJ, 11 Feb. 1942, AN AJ38 150; Claude Nataf, "L'exclusion des avocats juifs en Tunisie pendant la Seconde Guerre mondiale," *Archives juives* 41, no. 1 (2008): 90–107; Badinter, *Un antisémitisme ordinaire,* 211–214; Israël, *Robes noires,* 387–388; Israël, "L'épuration des barreaux français après la Seconde Guerre mondiale," 135–136.

60. Badinter, *Un antisémitisme ordinaire,* 181.

61. Joseph Barthélemy to CGQJ and to Conseil d'État, 4 June 1941, AN AJ38 1146.

62. Ibid.

63. CGQJ minutes of the Conférence interministerielle, Vichy, 7 June 1941, AN AJ38 1146.

64. Joly, *Xavier Vallat,* 235.

65. Badinter, *Un antisémitisme ordinaire,* 68–95.

66. CGQJ to the Aix-en-Provence procureur général, April 1942, CDJC CXI 28.

67. Badinter, *Un antisémitisme ordinaire,* 109.

68. "Résultats des délibérations des colonnes réunies les 23, 24, 25 octobre 1940," minutes of the Lyon bar council, 6 Nov. 1940. Thanks to Catherine Fillon for sharing this document.

69. Fillon, *Le barreau de Lyon dans la tourmente,* 75–76.

70. Badinter, *Un antisémitisme ordinaire,* 117.

71. Weisberg, *Vichy Law and the Holocaust,* 399.

72. CGQJ to the Garde des Sceaux and to the Lyon procureur général, 9 Oct. 1941, CDJC CXCV 156; Fillon, *Le barreau de Lyon dans la tourmente,* 87–88.

73. Badinter, *Un antisémitisme ordinaire,* 181–183; Weisberg, *Vichy Law and the Holocaust,* 304.

74. Some figures are available in "États des avocats non juifs," July 1941, AN AJ38 58.

75. Aix procureur général to CGQJ, 12 June 1942, AN AJ38 58.

76. Badinter, *Un antisémitisme ordinaire,* 183–187.

77. "Nombre des avocats juifs," CGQJ, 23 April. 1941, AN AJ38 58; Ryan, *The Holocaust and the Jews of Marseille,* 47.

78. Israël, *Robes noires,* 108. Cf. Ryan, *The Holocaust and the Jews of Marseille,* 46–48.

79. Cf. untitled handwritten note regarding attempts to find exceptions for Crémieu in AN AJ38 1146.

80. Official Web site of the Ordre des avocats à la Cour d'appel d'Aix en Provence, "Chronique no. 9: le bâtonnier Louis Crémieu; sa lettre au Conseil de l'Ordre, le 29 octobre 1940," http://www.barreau-aixenprovence.avocat.fr/fr/barreau/historique/id-11-le-batonnier-louis-cremieu-sa-lettre-au-conseil-de-l-ordre-le-29-octobre-1940 (accessed 1 April 2010).

81. Israël, *Robes noires,* 165.

82. Véronique Girard, "Le barreau de Grenoble de l'Occupation à la Libération," in *La justice de l'épuration, à la fin de la Seconde Guerre mondiale,* 185–186.

83. In the Bordeaux bar, five lawyers declared themselves Jewish out of a bar membership of over three hundred; therefore all five were maintained under the 2 percent quota. In Besançon, one Jewish lawyer was eliminated from bar membership. The Lille bar eliminated two. Badinter, *Un antisémitisme ordinaire,* 181–183; Weisberg, *Vichy Law and the Holocaust,* 304; Israël, "L'épuration des barreaux français après la Seconde Guerre mondiale," 110.

84. Fillon, *Le barreau de Lyon dans la tourmente,* 83–89; Badinter, *Un antisémitisme ordinaire,* 187–88.

85. "Note sur le barreau de Lyon," CGQJ Lyon regional office, 18 July 1941, AN AJ38 58.

86. Iannucci, "L'attitude du barreau de Lyon pendant l'Occupation," 167.

87. "Nombre des avocats juifs," CGQJ, 23 April 1941, AN AJ38 58; Badinter, *Un antisémitisme ordinaire,* 25, 150–151; Joly, *Xavier Vallat,* 236.

88. "État des avocats juifs du barreau de Paris ayant souscrit la déclaration prévue par le décret du 16 juillet 1941," 6 Sept. 1941, AdP 1320 W 148.

89. Procureur général to the directeur de la Police judiciaire, 8 Oct. 1941, AdP 1320 W 148.

90. "Avocats juifs reconnus comme tels et n'ayant pas fait la déclaration," Préfecture de Police, Direction de la Police Judiciaire, Cabinet de M. Permilleux, Affaires Juives, Oct.–Nov. 1941, AdP 1320 W 148.

91. Robert Badinter, "Peut-on être avocat lorsqu'on est juif en 1940–1944?" in *Le droit antisémite de Vichy,* 147.

92. Agence française d'informations de presse (AFIP) release, "50 avocats juifs vont rester au barreau de Paris," 29 Dec. 1941, AN 72 AJ 1825 and AN 72 AJ 1837; AFIP release "La situation des avocats juifs du barreau parisien," 6 Jan. 1942, AN 72 AJ 1825 and AN 72 AJ 1837; "À Paris, 246 avocats juifs cessent de plaider aujourd'hui…et voici quelques rescapés," *Paris soir,* 7 Jan. 1942, AN 72 AJ 1837. As propaganda organs, these sources are not reliable.

93. K. C. was born in Poland and naturalized as French as a result of his military service in World War I; he must have survived the foreign-father ban as well. He shared Zionist opinions with Xavier Vallat, his acquaintance and colleague at the Paris bar, throughout the interwar and Vichy periods. C. was ultimately deported to Auschwitz and never returned. Joly, *Xavier Vallat,* 347–348; Michael Marrus and Robert Paxton, *Vichy France and the Jews* (New York, 1981), 311–315. Cf. Richard I. Cohen, *The Burden of Conscience: French Jewish Leadership during the Holocaust* (Bloomington, 1987), 20–21.

94. "Extrait des originaux du greffe de la Cour d'Appel de Paris, Affaire Disciplinaire," 2 Jan. 1942, CDJC CVIII 7; "Liste des avocats juifs maintenus à Paris par arrêté de la Cour d'Appel en date du 2 janvier 1942," CDJC CVIII 6; "Avocats

israélites autorisés par décisions de la Cour d'Appel de Paris à exercer leur profession," Ordre des avocats à la Cour de Paris, AN AJ38 146; Premier président de la Cour d'Appel de Paris to CGQJ, 5 Oct. 1942, AN AJ38 69; Badinter, *Un antisémitisme ordinaire,* 152–153.

95. "Extrait des minutes du greffe de la Cour d'Appel de Paris, arrêté concernant les avocats juifs," 13 Feb. 1942, AdP 1320 W 148.

96. CGQJ to Dr. Schneider, Militarbefehlshaber in frankreich verwaltungsstab, 16 Jan. 1942, CDJC CVIII 7.

97. Nevertheless, the president of the Béthune bar in northern France, Charles de l'Estoile, accused the CGQJ and the Paris bar council of protecting Jewish lawyers and dragging their feet on carrying out the anti-Semitic quotas. Correspondence between Béthune bar president de l'Estoile and CGQJ, 26 and 29 Jan. 1942, CDJC XXIII 2.

98. Badinter, *Un antisémitisme ordinaire,* 166.

99. Fourteen decisions rendered by the Paris bar council, 6 and 27 Jan. 1942, AN AJ38 146; "Extrait des minutes du greffe de la Cour d'Appel de Paris," 13 Feb. 1942, CDJC CVIII 8.

100. Badinter, *Un antisémitisme ordinaire,* 156–158.

101. Garde des Sceaux to CGQJ, 27 March 1942, AN AJ38 58.

102. "Extrait des minutes du greffe de la Cour d'Appel de Paris, arrêté concernant les avocats juifs," 13 Feb. 1942, AdP 1320 W 148; Badinter, *Un antisémitisme ordinaire,* 160, 169.

103. "Liste des avocats détenus auprès des autorités allemandes, 22 Feb. and 5 May 1942, CDJC CVIII 10.

104. Pierre Vidal-Naquet, *Mémoires: la brisure et l'attente, 1930–1955* (Paris, 1995), 80–81, 120–121, 132–138, 174–176.

105. Billig, *Le Commissariat général aux questions juives,* 1:327.

106. CGQJ to Garde des Sceaux, 4 April 1942, AN AJ38 146; correspondence between CGQJ and Garde des Sceaux, 28 March and 4 April 1942, CDJC CXI 25, and 8 and 18 June 1942, CDJC CXI 35.

107. Badinter, *Un antisémitisme ordinaire,* 169–171.

108. Handwritten note by Garde des Sceaux Joseph Barthélemy, 8 July 1942, AN F60 518; Badinter, *Un antisémitisme ordinaire,* 174–175. In his postwar memoirs, Barthélemy claimed to have done his best to attenuate Vichy anti-Semitism. Joseph Barthélemy, *Ministre de la Justice: Vichy, 1941–1943* (Paris, 1989).

109. CGQJ to Chief of Service for Secret Societies, 4 April 1942, and response 25 April 1942, AN AJ38 146. Only one of the lawyers was found to be associated with such a society.

110. CGQJ to Garde des Sceaux, 24 Aug. 1942, CDJC CXI 25; Badinter, *Un antisémitisme ordinaire,* 176.

111. Minutes of the Paris bar council meeting, 27 Oct. 1942, cited in Badinter, *Un antisémitisme ordinaire,* 199.

112. Badinter, *Un antisémitisme ordinaire,* 155–156.

113. Because the law did not clearly specify whether these conditions were cumulative, the Council of State was consulted and determined that only one condition had to be met for a person to benefit from the exception. Weisberg notes that out of well over a hundred applications for exemption for exceptional service to the French state from Jewish career government attorneys in the civil service, only seven were granted. Weisberg, *Vichy Law and the Holocaust,* 98.

114. Badinter, *Un antisémitisme ordinaire,* 178. This exception applied to other professions as well.

115. Badinter, *Un antisémitisme ordinaire,* 179.

116. Weisberg reports that the Court of Appeals rejected almost all of the Paris bar's petitions for exceptions, whereas Badinter claims that of thirty-five "other" dossiers examined for this exemption, nine received very favorable recommendations from the Paris bar council, seven favorable, nine honorable professional practice, nine without objection, and only one unfavorable. The procureur général and the Ministry of Justice supported these recommendations, but CGQJ chief Darquier accepted not a single lawyer for this exemption. Weisberg, *Vichy Law and the Holocaust,* 307–308; Badinter, *Un antisémitisme ordinaire,* 179–180.

117. Ozanam, "Le barreau de Paris pendant la Seconde Guerre mondiale, 1940–1945," 148 and note 20. Ozanam repeatedly refused my requests for access to bar council records.

118. Ministère de la Justice to Ambassadeur Brinon, 15 June 1942, AN F60 1485; "État nominatif des avocats de race juive des barreaux du ressort de la Cour d'Appel de Paris bénéficiaires des dispositions de l'article 3 de la loi du 2 juin 1941," AN AJ38 150; Badinter, *Un antisémitisme ordinaire,* 160. Figures vary between forty-eight and fifty-three.

119. Correspondence between Charpentier and CGQJ, 17 March and 7 April 1943, CDJC CVIII 15; Badinter, *Un antisémitisme ordinaire,* 154, 201.

120. President of the Paris Court of Appeals to CGQJ, 5 Oct. 1942, AN AJ38 14.

121. "Liste des avocats détenus auprès des autorités allemandes," 22 Feb. and 5 May 1942, CDJC CVIII 10.

122. Garde des Sceaux to CGQJ, 27 March 1942, AN AJ38 58. Figures vary between 203 and 210.

123. "Encore 50 avocats juifs au barreau de Paris!" *Le matin* (31 Dec. 1941), AN 72 AJ 1837.

124. "Les avocats juifs au barreau parisien," *Le petit parisien* (30 Dec. 1941), AN 72 AJ 1837; R. Loffet, "Les professions libérales: situation légale des juifs de France, III," *Les nouveaux temps* (14 Nov. 1941), AN 72 AJ 1837.

125. "Comment les avocats juifs ont trouvé le moyen de continuer à plaider," *Le cri du peuple* (4 June 1941), AN 72 AJ 1837.

126. CAC 19950407 444.

127. Fillon, *Le barreau de Lyon dans la tourmente,* 27, 39–41.

128. "Extrait des minutes du registre des délibérations," Cour d'Appel de Limoges, 14 Nov. 1941, AN AJ38 1045. Cf. Weisberg, *Vichy Law and the Holocaust,* 109.

129. CGQJ to CGQJ Limoges regional office, 16 Dec. 1941, AN AJ38 1045.

130. Limoges procureur général to CGQJ, 20 April 1942, CDJC XXIII 5; CGQJ to Ministre de la Justice, 1 May 1942, CDJC XXIII 5a; Limoges procureur général to CGQJ, 31 Oct. 1942, CDJC XXIII 5c; Limoges procureur général to CGQJ, 14 Dec. 1942, CDJC XXIII 5d.

131. Ministre de la Justice to CGQJ, 8 July 1942, CDJC XXIII 5b.

132. Limoges bar president to CGQJ Limoges regional office, 10 Aug. 1944, AN AJ38 258.

133. Badinter, *Un antisémitisme ordinaire,* 189–190; "Note sur la situation des avocats juifs dépendant du barreau de Marseille," CDJC CVIII 11/12.

134. Israël, *Robes noires,* 109.

135. Ryan, *The Holocaust and the Jews of Marseille,* 13, 46–48.

136. Girard, "Le barreau de Grenoble de l'Occupation à la Libération," 183–185.

137. Badinter, *Un antisémitisme ordinaire,* 190.

138. Correspondence among Paris bar president Jacques Charpentier, procureur général Raoul Cavarroc près la Cour d'Appel de Paris and his substitute Dardot, and CGQ J, Oct. 1942, CDJC CVIII 13; correspondence between Charpentier and CGQ J, 17 March and 7 April 1943, CDJC CVIII 15; Badinter, *Un antisémitisme ordinaire,* 199–201; correspondence between CGQ J and Befehlshaber der Sicherheitspolizei und des SD im Bereich des Militarbefehlshabers in Frankreich, AN AJ38 14.

139. Correspondence between CGQ J and Befehlshaber der Sicherheitspolizei und des SD im Bereich des Militarbefehlshabers in Frankreich, AN AJ38 14.

140. Weisberg, *Vichy Law and the Holocaust,* 313–315; Badinter, "Peut-on être avocat lorsqu'on est juif en 1940–1944?" 149.

141. Alexis de Tocqueville, *Democracy in America* (New York, 2004), 305.

142. Martine Fabre, "La doctrine sous Vichy," in *Le droit sous Vichy,* ed. Bernard Durand, Jean-Pierre Le Crom, and Alessandro Somma (Frankfurt am Main, 2006), 375–401.

143. Danièle Lochak, "Écrire, se taire . . . Réflexions sur l'attitude de la doctrine française," in *Le droit antisémite de Vichy,* 434–436.

144. Weisberg, *Vichy Law and the Holocaust,* xv, 41–45, 68, chap. 7; Bernard-Michel Bloch, "Le regard des juristes sur les lois raciales de Vichy," *Les temps modernes* 547 (Feb. 1992): 161–174.

145. Maurice Duverger, "La situation des fonctionnaires depuis la Révolution de 1940," *Revue de droit public et de science politique* (1940–41): 277–539. Cf. Grégoire Bigot, "Vichy dans l'oeil de la Revue de droit public," in *Le droit sous Vichy,* 415–435.

146. Dominique Gros, "Peut-on parler d'un 'droit antisémite'?" in *Le droit antisémite de Vichy,* 17, 23. Cf. Gros, "Le droit antisémite de Vichy contre la tradition républicaine," in *Juger sous Vichy,* 21; Gros, "Le 'statut des juifs' et les manuels en usage dans les facultés de droit," *Cultures & conflits* 9–10 (1993): 154–171.

147. Danièle Lochak, "La doctrine sous Vichy ou les mésaventures du positivisme," in *Les usages sociaux du droit* (Paris, 1989), 252–285.

148. M. Troper, "La doctrine et le positivisme (à propos d'un article de Danièle Lochak)," ibid., 286–292.

149. Lochak, "Écrire, se taire," 455, 458.

150. Catherine Fillon, "Le Tribunal d'État, Section de Lyon (1941–1944): contribution à l'histoire des juridictions d'exception," *Histoire de la justice* 10 (1997): 193–222; Marc du Pouget, "Les juridictions d'exception de la période de l'occupation et de la libération à Lyon," *Cahiers d'histoire* 39, nos. 3–4 (1994): 221–229; Michèle Cointet, "Les juristes sous l'occupation," in *Les facs sous Vichy: étudiants, universitaires et universités de France pendant la Seconde Guerre mondiale,* ed. André Gueslin (Clermont-Ferrand, 1994), 51–64; *Juger sous Vichy; Le droit antisémite de Vichy;* Marc Olivier Baruch, *Servir l'État français: l'administration en France de 1940 à 1944* (Paris, 1997).

151. Israël, *Robes noires,* 132, 182.

152. Joë Nordmann and Anne Brunel, *Aux vents de l'histoire* (Arles, 1996), 109.

153. Nathalie Sarraute, *Enfance* (Paris, 1983), 220.

154. Badinter, *Un antisémitisme ordinaire,* 62. Cf. "Liste des avocats du barreau de Paris qui ont été arrêtés le 21 août 1941 par ordre des autorités allemandes," AN AJ38 7.

155. See http://www.leseditionsdeminuit.eu/f/index.php?sp=livAut&auteur_id= 1449# (accessed 25 February 2009).

156. Badinter, *Un antisémitisme ordinaire,* 165.

157. Correspondence between la Compagnie des conseils juridiques de la Seine and CGQJ, 17 and 30 March 1943, CDJC CVIII 14; Dossiers on experts-comptables and conseils juridiques, AN AJ38 120; Béraud, "Le juif interdit de travail," 217.

158. Badinter, *Un antisémitisme ordinaire,* 162; Ozanam, "Le barreau de Paris pendant la Seconde Guerre mondiale, 1940–1945," 148–149.

159. CGQJ to Ministère de la Justice, 14 March 1942, CDJC XXIII 4; "Octroi d'indemnité aux avocats juifs ayant dû cesser l'exercice de leur profession," CGQJ, 6 June 1942, CDJC LIII 48.

160. Badinter, *Un antisémitisme ordinaire,* 163–165.

161. Weisberg, *Vichy Law and the Holocaust,* 99.

162. "Liste des avocats du barreau de Paris qui ont été arrêtés le 21 août 1941 par ordre des autorités allemandes," AN AJ38 7.

163. Poznanski, *Les juifs en France pendant la Seconde Guerre mondiale,* 257–258. In the Vélodrome d'Hiver roundup on 16–17 July 1942, French authorities arrested over thirteen thousand Jews, interned them in this former bicycle racing stadium in Paris, and subsequently transferred them to French concentration camps or deported them.

164. "50 avocats du barreau de Paris se sont rencontrés au camps de concentration juif de Drancy," *Le petit parisien,* 12 Sept. 1941, CDJC DLXXV 13b; Badinter, *Un antisémitisme ordinaire,* 128–144.

165. CDJC VI 138 and 139; "Les autorités allemandes d'occupation ont fait procéder, il y a une huitaine de jours, à l'arrestation de tous les avocats juifs résidant à Paris et dans les environs," Ministère de l'Intérieur, Direction générale de la Police nationale, 4 Sept. 1941, CDJC CII 8a and 8b.

166. Comment by Yves Jouffa in Centre de documentation juive contemporaine, *Il y a 50 ans: le Statut des Juifs de Vichy, Actes du colloque du 1er octobre 1990* (Paris, 1991), 45; Badinter, *Un antisémitisme ordinaire,* 134, 161 and Appendix 10, 227.

167. Badinter, *Un antisémitisme ordinaire,* 143. Cf. Bernard Mélamède to Prof. R. Cassin on behalf of Pierre Masse, London, 12 Sept. 1941, AN F60 1678; on Maurice Ribet's efforts in Masse's favor, see Israël, *Robes noires,* 110–111.

168. Badinter, *Un antisémitisme ordinaire,* 129, 149.

169. Ibid., 130–133, 140; Weisberg, *Vichy Law and the Holocaust,* 86–100.

170. Eric Loquin, "Le juif 'incapable,'" in *Le droit antisémite de Vichy,* 184–185.

171. Billig, *Le Commissariat général aux questions juives,* 1:79.

172. Badinter, *Un antisémitisme ordinaire,* 92; Fillon, *Le barreau de Lyon dans la tourmente,* 181; Ryan, *The Holocaust and the Jews of Marseille,* 48.

173. On resistance to Legrand as well as the related issue of bar council elections, see Fillon, *Le barreau de Lyon dans la tourmente,* 155–172.

174. Israël, *Robes noires,* 141, 140–142, 146, 260, 289–290. Cf. Israël, "L'épuration des barreaux français après la Seconde Guerre mondiale," 23.

175. ANA to Garde des Sceaux, 9 July 1943, republished in *Bulletin de l'ANA* 79 (June [*sic*] 1943).

176. Letter to General von Falkenhausen, Commandant militaire pour la Belgique et le nord de la France, 19 Nov. 1940, CDJC IV 203.

177. Nordmann, *Aux vents de l'histoire,* 110; cf. 133.

178. Ozanam, "Le barreau de Paris pendant la Seconde Guerre mondiale," 161.

179. Badinter, *Un antisémitisme ordinaire,* 40–43, 111.

180. Gilles Martinez, "Joseph Barthélemy et la crise de la démocratie libérale," *Vingtième siècle* 59 (July–Sept. 1998): 41, 47; Weisberg, *Vichy Law and the Holocaust,* 9, 147, chap. 4.

181. Joly, *Vichy dans la "solution finale,"* 525–526.

182. Charpentier once wrote an irritated letter to the CGQJ in 1941 asking that Jewish lawyers be at least allowed to conclude their ongoing legal business before being kicked out of the bar and having their cases transferred (which was the prerogative of the CGQJ) to a replacement lawyer. Paris bar president to CGQJ, 1 Aug. 1941, CDJC CVIII 4.

183. Weisberg, *Vichy Law and the Holocaust,* 21–22, 85.

184. Ibid., 390.

185. Vicki Caron, "French Public Opinion and the 'Jewish Question,' 1930–1942: The Role of Middle-Class Professional Associations," in *Nazi Europe and the Final Solution,* ed. David Bankier and Israel Gutman (Jerusalem, 2003): 378.

186. On the topic of resistance and the law professions, see AN 490 AP 1, AN BB30 1707, AN 72 AJ 1895, and AN 72 AJ 73.

187. Israël, *Robes noires,* 295.

188. Noiriel, *Le creuset français,* 287.

189. Auguste Vigne, "Tablettes parlementaires: une nouvelle législation sur le séjour des étrangers en France et leur expulsion éventuelle," *La vie judiciaire* (10 Jan. 1938): 4.

190. Joly, *Xavier Vallat,* 148–158.

191. "Le Conseil de l'Ordre doit-il être maître de son tableau?" undated memorandum, AN BB30 1711.

192. Badinter, *Un antisémitisme ordinaire,* 60–61.

7. L'Ordre des Médecins

1. Bénédicte Vergez-Chaignon, *Le docteur Ménétrel, éminence grise et confident du maréchal Pétain* (Paris, 2001); Vergez, "Internes et anciens internes des hôpitaux de Paris de 1918 à 1945," 316–320.

2. Already in October 1940 Ménétrel had obliged a request by Dr. Albin Faivre to pass a copy of his Paris Medical School dissertation on to Pétain. Faivre's dissertation blamed foreigners, women, and Jews for degrading French medicine. Faivre to Ménétrel, 10 Oct. 1940, AN 3W 291; Faivre, "Aspect médical et social du problème des étrangers en France."

3. Francine Muel-Dreyfus, *Vichy et l'éternel féminin: contribution à une sociologie politique de l'ordre des corps* (Paris, 1996), 293.

4. Maurice Mordagne to Ministre de l'Instruction publique Ripert, 10 Oct. 1940, AN F17 17512.

5. Maurice Mordagne to Ministre de l'Instruction publique Ripert, 30 Sep. 1940, AN F17 17512.

6. "Loi instituant l'Ordre des médecins," *JO* (26 Oct. 1940): 5430–31; A. Oudin, *L'Ordre des médecins* (Paris, 1941).

7. Cited in Vergez, "Internes et anciens internes des hôpitaux de Paris," 341.

8. Bénédicte Vergez, *Le monde des médecins au XXe siècle* (Paris, 1996), 70.

9. Doctors probably totaled thirty thousand if French overseas territories are included. Over one thousand doctors were imprisoned in 1941, thereby reducing the

actual number of health care providers for French people. Vergez, "Internes et anciens internes des hôpitaux de Paris," 405, 410–413.

10. Ibid., 206.

11. Minutes, Syndicat médical de Seine-et-Oise, 9 July 1940, AN 2AG 78.

12. Report from Dr. Hollier to the Maréchal Chef de l'État français, 8 July 1940, AN 2AG 78. Cf AN 2AG 77.

13. Against regulations, he was also nominated to be a founding member of the Seine-et-Oise department medical council.

14. For a socio-medical history of Clichy, see chap. 5 in Nicholas Hewitt, *The Life of Céline: A Critical Biography* (Oxford, 1999). Cf. dossier Céline, AN 72 AJ 598.

15. Bruno Halioua, *Blouses blanches, étoiles jaunes* (Paris, 2000), 65–66. Dr. Fernand Querrioux referred to "mon ami Céline" in correspondence with Vichy officials to bolster his arguments for eliminating Jews from medicine. Querrioux to Ambassadeur Brinon, Délégué du Gouvernement français pour les territoires occupés, ca. Nov. 1941, AN F60 1485.

16. Louis-Ferdinand Céline, *L'école des cadavres* (Paris, 1938), 208–210.

17. *JO* (19 Aug. 1940): 4735–36. A 16 January 1941 decree applied similar measures in Algeria against doctors born of a non-French father.

18. As I noted in chapter 6, for the sake of accuracy, I use the awkward term "foreign-fathered doctors" to refer to the persons targeted by this legislation; as with lawyers, nearly all documentation from the period uses the incorrect term "foreigner" to describe those excluded by the law.

19. The decree for the legal profession, which was signed one month later, added an additional exemption for direct descendants of war veterans. In the second version of both laws, these exemptions were expanded.

20. Mary Lewis documents the impact of ministerial circulars on the implementation of the residency rights of foreigners. As a way to bypass legislative debate and respond quickly to public pressure, such "circular reasoning," as she puts it, was not always bad for foreigners, as my examples later in this chapter also illustrate. Lewis, *The Boundaries of the Republic,* 123–126.

21. Vergez, "Internes et anciens internes des hôpitaux de Paris," 330.

22. Minutes, Conseil supérieur de l'Ordre national des Médecins, 21–25 June 1941, p. 7, CAC 20000243 1.

23. *JO* (29 Oct. 1940): 5466.

24. Secrétaire-général à la Famille et à la Santé, note for the directeur-général de la Sûreté nationale, 7 Dec. 1940, AN F7 16050. Cf. Ministère de l'Intérieur to prefects, "Circulaire sur l'application de la loi du 16 août 1940 concernant l'exercice de la médecine, No. 186," 1 Nov. 1940, AN 2AG 606.

25. Weil, *Qu'est-ce qu'un Français?* 218–224.

26. Minutes, Conseil supérieur de l'Ordre national des Médecins, 21–25 May 1941, p. 33, CAC 20000243 1.

27. Ministère de l'Intérieur to prefects, "Circulaire complémentaire à la circulaire du 1er novembre sur l'application de la loi du 16 août 1940 concernant l'exercice de la médecine, No. 92," 27 Nov. 1940, AN 2AG 606 (also in AN 72AJ 1859).

28. Nahum, *La médecine française et les juifs,* 153, 156.

29. "M. le Professeur Lemierre ignore les médecins prisonniers," *Le cri du peuple,* 11 April 1942, AN 72AJ 1859. In a medical forum a few days after the liberation of Paris,

Lemierre publicly lamented the treatment of Jewish doctors during the Occupation. Halioua, *Blouses blanches, étoiles jaunes,* 221–222.

30. Indre department council of the Medical Order to Secrétaire d'État à la Santé, 16 March 1942, AN 2AG 78.

31. See, for example, the case of Dr. A. in the Seine-et-Oise, CAC 20000243 4.

32. Minutes, Conseil supérieur de l'Ordre national des Médecins, 21–25 May 1941, pp. 202–203, CAC 20000243 1; "La question des médecins étrangers," *Bulletin de l'Ordre des Médecins* [hereafter *BOM*] (June 1941): 102, AN 3W 185.

33. Minutes, Conseil supérieur de l'Ordre national des Médecins, 19–22 April 1941, CAC 2000243 1. Medical journals such as *Le concours médical* (with a circulation of eleven thousand) and *La presse médicale* nonetheless obtained and published names of doctors ejected from the profession. Halioua, *Blouses blanches, étoiles jaunes,* 80–81.

34. Minutes, Conseil supérieur de l'Ordre national des Médecins, 15–21 March 1941, p. 102, CAC 20000243 1.

35. Minutes, Conseil supérieur de l'Ordre national des Médecins, 1–5 Nov. 1941, pp. 138–139, CAC 20000243 1; Circular no. 11, from the Conseil supérieur de l'Ordre national des Médecins to the Conseils départementaux, 8 Nov. 1941, p. 17, AdP 3099 W 1.

36. Minutes, Conseil supérieur de l'Ordre national des Médecins, 21–25 May 1941, pp. 143–144, CAC 20000243 1. Cf. Minutes, Conseil supérieur de l'Ordre national des Médecins, 21–25 June 1941, p. 3, CAC 20000243 1.

37. Minutes, Conseil supérieur de l'Ordre national des Médecins, 21–25 May 1941, p. 194, CAC 20000243 1.

38. Secrétaire d'État à la Famille et à la Santé Huard to the president of the Conseil supérieur de l'Ordre national des Médecins, 30 Aug. 1941, published in "Convention avec le gouvernement monégasque," *BOM* (Oct. 1941): 209–210, AN 3W 185; Circular no. 10 from the Conseil supérieur de l'Ordre national des Médecins to the Conseils départementaux, 3 Oct. 1941, CAC 20000243 2.

39. Circular no. 6 from the Conseil supérieur de l'Ordre national des Médecins to the Conseils départementaux, 28 April 1941, p. 20, AdP 3099 W 1; Minutes, Conseil supérieur de l'Ordre national des Médecins, 21–25 May 1941, pp. 194–195, CAC 20000243 1; "Application de la loi du 6 [*sic*] août 1940 sur les étrangers [*sic*]," *BOM* (June 1941): 88–89, AN 3W 185; Minutes, Conseil supérieur de l'Ordre national des Médecins, 27 Sept.–1 Oct. 1941, pp. 105–106, CAC 20000243 1.

40. Minutes, Conseil supérieur de l'Ordre national des Médecins, 19–22 April 1941, CAC 20000243 1.

41. The national council's vow ignored the situation of foreign-fathered women doctors and their French husbands and children. Minutes, Conseil supérieur de l'Ordre national des Médecins, 15–21 March 1941, pp. 102–103, CAC 20000243 1; Circular no. 6 from the Conseil supérieur de l'Ordre national des Médecins to the Conseils départementaux, 28 April 1941, pp. 12, 20–21, AdP 3099 W 1; "Application de la loi du 6 [*sic*] août 1940 sur les étrangers [*sic*]," *BOM* (June 1941): 88–89, AN 3W 185; Minutes, Conseil supérieur de l'Ordre national des Médecins, 1–5 Nov. 1941, pp. 139–140, CAC 20000243 1.

42. "Inscription au tableau de l'Ordre - Installations - Remplacements," *BOM* (Nov. 1941): 222–223, AN 3W 185; emphasis added.

43. Secrétaire d'État à la Famille et à la Santé to the president of the Commission supérieure de contrôle, 25 March 1942, published in "Application de la législation sur les médecins d'origine étrangère," *BOM* (March 1942): 72–73, AN 3W 185.

44. "Conseils départementaux et les commissions régionales," *BOM* (Aug. 1941): 124, AN 3W 185.

45. Circular from the Secrétaire d'État à la Famille et à la Santé to prefects, 3 Dec. 1941, published in *BOM* (Dec. 1941): 266, AN 3W 185.

46. See, for example, Minutes, Conseil supérieur de l'Ordre national des Médecins, 2–8 Aug. 1941, p. 67, CAC 20000243 1.

47. Vergez, "Internes et anciens internes des hôpitaux de Paris," 429.

48. Minutes, Conseil supérieur de l'Ordre national des Médecins, 19–22 April 1941, CAC 20000243 1.

49. Patrick Weil, "Georges Mauco: un itinéraire camouflé; ethnoracisme pratique et antisémitisme fielleux," in *L'antisémitisme de plume, 1940–1944,* ed. Pierre-André Taguieff (Paris, 1999), 268.

50. Department councils were asked to alert the national council about all newly vacant posts so that the opportunities could be brought to the attention of doctors seeking employment. "Inscription au tableau de l'Ordre - Installations - Remplacements," *BOM* (Nov. 1941): 222–223, AN 3W 185; Circular no. 10 from the Conseil supérieur de l'Ordre national des Médecins to the Conseils départementaux, 3 Oct. 1941, CAC 20000243 2.

51. *JO* (29 Nov. 1941): 5142.

52. Minutes, Conseil supérieur de l'Ordre national des Médecins, 1–5 Nov. 1941, p. 140, CAC 20000243 1.

53. No equivalent possibility was made for foreigners in the law bars. Cf. Decree of 20 Dec. 1941, *JO* (31 Dec. 1941): 5597.

54. Secrétaire d'État à la Famille et à la Santé to the president of the Commission supérieure de contrôle, 25 March 1942, published in "Application de la législation sur les médecins d'origine étrangère," *BOM* (March 1942): 72–73, AN 3W 185; Circular, Secrétaire d'État à la Famille et à la Santé to the prefects, 5 Feb. 1942, regarding the application of the 22 Nov. 1941 law, CAC 20000243 2.

55. French authorities were indeed solicited by foreign diplomats on this topic. See, for example, Vice-Président du Conseil to Secrétaire d'État à la Santé about a request from the Organization for Armenian Refugees, Oct. 1941, AN F60 602.

56. "Au Congrès des conseils de l'Ordre de la zone non occupée à Aurillac le 23 août 1942: un important exposé du Secrétaire d'État à la Santé," *Le concours médical* (20 Sept. 1942): 764–771.

57. Donna Evleth, "Vichy France and the Continuity of Medical Nationalism," *Social History of Medicine* 8, no. 1 (April 1995): 104–107. Nahum claimed that about 915 foreign-fathered doctors out of about 6,000 in the Seine department were affected by the ban. Of the 915 doctors, he said, 567 requested exemptions and 348 accepted their immediate ban. Nahum, *La médecine française et les juifs,* 153.

58. *BOM* (March 1942): 83; *BOM* (June 1942): 112–115; *BOM* (Aug. 1942): 146–147, AN 3W 185; "Listes des arrêtés parus à l'Officiel relatifs aux dérogations intervenus en faveur des médecins d'origine étrangère et aux interdictions définitives…," *BOM* (Jan. 1943): 19–20, AN 3W 185; "Médecins étrangers," *BOM* (Oct. 1942): 175, AN 3W 185; Circular no. 8 from the Conseil supérieur de l'Ordre national des Médecins to the Conseils départementaux, 30 June 1941, AdP 3099 1; Circular no. 10 from the Conseil supérieur de l'Ordre national des Médecins to the Conseils départementaux, 3 Oct. 1941, CAC 20000243 2 (also in AdP 3099 1); Circular no. 12 from the Conseil supérieur de l'Ordre national des Médecins to the Conseils départementaux, 20 Dec. 1941, AdP 3099 W 1.

59. "Au Congrès des conseils de l'Ordre de la zone non occupée à Aurillac le 23 août 1942: un important exposé du Secrétaire d'État à la Santé": 764–771.

60. Nahum and Halioua reproduce Grasset's figures. Nahum, *La médecine française et les juifs,* 179–180; Halioua, "La xénophobie et l'antisémitisme dans le milieu médical sous l'Occupation vus au travers du *Concours médical," Médecine/Sciences* 19, no. 1 (Jan. 2003): 111. Cf. Vergez, *Le monde des médecins,* 183–184.

61. Note pour la Commission supérieure de contrôle, 27 April 1942, AN 2AG 77.

62. Circular no. 10 from the Conseil supérieur de l'Ordre national des Médecins to the Conseils départementaux, 3 Oct. 1941 (Appendix 1, 10th list, *arrêté* 16 Aug. 1941), p. 14, CAC 20000243 2 (also in AdP 3099 1).

63. Dr. Pierre Masquin, president of the Vaucluse department council, to the Inspecteur de la Santé, Avignon, 15 May 1942, AN 2AG 77.

64. Dr. Madon, mayor of Orange, to Ménétrel, 10 Oct. 1942; Ménétrel to Madon, 14 Oct. 1942, AN 2AG 77.

65. Vice-président du Conseil, Secrétaire-général auprès du Chef du Gouvernement to the Secrétaire d'État à la Famille et à la Santé, for the Commission supérieure de contrôle, 1 June 1942, AN F60 602.

66. His mother had lost her French nationality by marrying a Greek subject, but once the 1927 law undid this discrimination, she reapplied and was "reintegrated" into French nationality in 1937.

67. Ménétrel to the president of the Commission supérieure de contrôle, Ministère de la Santé, 9 Oct. 1942, AN 2AG 77. The archives do not reveal how F's case was resolved.

68. No known result of his case is found in the archives. Lutomsky dossier, AN F1a 3692; and AN F1a 3694.

69. Dr. F. to Ménétrel, 6 Jan. and 2 March 1941, AN 2AG 77.

70. See AN F60 602 for an instance of a Vichy official attempting to gain exemption for his family doctor, born of a foreign father.

71. Dr. W. S. to Ménétrel, 16 April 1942, and Ménétrel to S., 22 April 1942, AN 2AG 77.

72. JO (7, 20, and 23 June, 25 and 26 July 1942), AN 72 AJ 1837 and AN 72 AJ 1859.

73. Vergez, "Internes et anciens internes des hôpitaux de Paris," 406–407.

74. Published in "Ordre national des Médecins, Cahiers de doléances et de voeux présentés à la réunion des conseils départementaux, le 25 janvier 1942, à Paris," *Journal de médecine de Bordeaux,* 15 March 1942, AN 2AG 78.

75. The delegates who declined to sign did so because they disagreed with Mauriac's retirement fund proposal, according to Émile Aubertin, author of a report of the conference in *Journal de médecine de Bordeaux,* 30 Jan. 1942, AN 2AG 77.

76. Fernand Querrioux, *La médecine et les juifs* (Paris, 1940), 33.

77. Ibid., 51. Cf. Querrioux, IEQ J (Institut d'étude des questions juives), to CGQ J, 17 June 1941, AN AJ38 1146.

78. Le Général d'Armée, Secretaire-général du Chef d'État, Président du Conseil to CGQ J, 31 Jan. 1942, AN AJ38 1146.

79. Querrioux, IEQ J Service médical, to Ambassador Brinon, Délégué du Gouvernement français pour les territoires occupés, n.d., AN F60 1485.

80. "Note pour le ministre," CGQ J, 10 March 1942, AN AJ38 1146.

81. See Billig, *Le Commissariat général aux questions juives,* 2:271–297.

82. Nahum, *La médecine française et les juifs,* 190.

83. "Groupement corporatif sanitaire français, Ordre du jour, 22 février 1942," report forwarded from Ambassadeur de Brinon to Ménétrel, 12 March 1942, AN 2AG 78.

84. "Groupement corporatif sanitaire français, Fédération nationale des groupements corporatifs français, section sanitaire," undated brochure, AN 2AG 78.

85. Vergez, "Internes et anciens internes des hôpitaux de Paris," 358, 389.

86. Dr. Raymond Tournay, secretary-general of the Fédération des associations amicales de médecins du front, to the Secrétaire d'État de la Santé publique and to the councils of the Medical Order, 29 Jan. 1941, AN AJ38 1146.

87. Dr. Ch.-E. Boursat, speech at 14 Nov. 1940 meeting of Union médicale française, groupement des praticiens de race française résolus à collaborer à l'oeuvre de renovation nationale, and sent to Ménétrel 2 Jan. 1941, AN 2AG 77; Union médicale française, brochure in Ménétrel Papers, AN 2AG 77; Dr. Gringoire, Union médicale française, to Xavier Vallat, CGQJ, 23 June 1941, AN AJ38 1146.

88. Communiqué, Fédération des associations amicales de médecins du front, 1 March 1941, AN AJ38 1146.

89. Minutes, Conseil supérieur de l'Ordre national des Médecins, 15–21 March 1941, p. 101, CAC 20000243 1.

90. Billig, *Le Commissariat général aux questions juives,* 3:28–29.

91. Dr. O. to Ménétrel, 30 Aug. 1940, AN 3W 291.

92. See Caron, "French Public Opinion and the 'Jewish Question,' 1930–1942: The Role of Middle-Class Professional Associations," 400–401.

93. Ménétrel to Secrétaire-général à la Santé publique, 10 Sept. 1940, AN 3W 291.

94. Halioua, *Blouses blanches, étoile jaunes,* 18–22.

95. Vergez, "Internes et anciens internes des hôpitaux de Paris," 415.

96. Student tract and report on student response to creation of the history of Judaism course at the Paris School of Letters inaugurated 15 Dec. 1942, "La France libre, Commissariat national à l'Intérieur, Service de documentation," 21 March 1943, AN F60 1678. Cf. "Dossier Labroue," AN AJ16 7142; Claude Singer, "Henri Labroue, ou l'apprentissage de l'antisémitisme," in *L'antisémitisme de plume,* 233–244.

97. Marc Knobel, "George Montandon et l'ethno-racisme," in *L'antisémitisme de plume,* 277–293; Joly, *Vichy dans la "solution finale,"* 550–555. Cf. Alice L. Conklin, *In the Museum of Man: Ethnography, Racial Science, and Empire in France 1850–1950* (Ithaca, forthcoming).

98. Carole Reynaud Paligot, *Races, racisme et antiracisme dans les années 1930* (Paris, 2007); Pierre-André Taguieff, "La 'science' du docteur Martial, ou l'antisémitisme saisi par l''anthropo-biologie des races,'" in *L'antisémitisme de plume,* 295–332; Weil, "Georges Mauco," 267–276; Claude Singer, *Vichy, l'université et les juifs* (Paris, 1992), 198–206.

99. Andrés Horacio Reggiani, *God's Eugenicist: Alexis Carrel and the Sociobiology of Decline* (New York, 2007), 183. Cf. Muel-Dreyfus, *Vichy et l'éternel féminin,* 339–356; Alain Drouard, *Alexis Carrel (1873–1944): de la mémoire à l'histoire* (Paris, 1995); R. Pfefferkorn, "Alexis Carrel: vulgarisateur de l'eugénisme et promoteur de 'l'aristocratie biologique,'" *L'information psychiatrique* 73, no. 2 (Feb. 1997): 123–128.

100. See, for example, Admiral de la Flotte, Ministre Secrétaire d'État aux Affaires Étrangères, to the Garde des Sceaux, 8 March 1942, AN BB30 1711. Cf. Anne Carol, *Histoire de l'eugénisme en France: les médecins et la procréation, XIXe-XXe siècle* (Paris, 1995).

On Germany, see Robert Proctor, *Racial Hygiene: Medicine under the Nazis* (Cambridge, Mass., 1988).

101. William Schneider, *Quality and Quantity: The Quest for Biological Regeneration in Twentieth-Century France* (Cambridge, 1990); Muel-Dreyfus, *Vichy et l'éternel féminin,* chap. 8, "Le contrôle des corps."

102. Gérard Noiriel, *Les origines républicaines de Vichy* (Paris, 1999), 211–272. Cf. Muel-Dreyfus, *Vichy et l'éternel féminin.*

103. "Conversation avec le Dr. Aublanc," 16 May 1941, CGQJ, AN AJ38 1146.

104. Secrétaire d'État à la Famille et à la Santé to CGQJ, 23 July 1941, AN AJ38 1146.

105. Military exemptions applied. Note that Vichy banned women—with French citizenship and of all religious backgrounds—from medical positions in the civil service. Linda L. Clark, "Higher-Ranking Women Civil Servants and the Vichy Regime: Firings and Hirings, Collaboration and Resistance," *French History* 13, no. 3 (1999): 332–59.

106. Secrétaire-Général à la Santé Huard to the Secrétaire d'État à la Famille et à la Santé, 31 March 1941, AN AJ38 1146. Cf. Baruch, *Servir l'État français,* chap. 5, "Les Réprouvés."

107. See dossier on the medical profession in AN AJ38 1099.

108. Secrétaire d'État à la Famille et à la Santé to CGQJ, 23 July 1941, AN AJ38 1146.

109. Secrétaire d'État à la Famille et à la Santé circular to regional directors, 9 Sept. 1941, AN AJ38 1144.

110. Captain Corvette de Lécussan, directeur régional du CGQJ, Toulouse-Montpellier, to the president of the Commission administrative des hospices, Hôtel Dieu, Toulouse, 10 June 1942, AN AJ38 1099 and CDJC XVIIa 40, Document 188; Vallat, CGQJ, to Secrétaire d'État à la Famille et à la Santé, 31 Dec. 1941, AN AJ38 119.

111. Alexandre Minkowski, *Mémoires turbulents* (Paris, 1990).

112. Vergez, "Internes et anciens internes des hôpitaux de Paris," 422–423.

113. Rapport général sur la situation en France, CFLN Commissariat à l'Intérieur, service courrier, 24 May 1944, AN F1a 3743; Nahum, *La médecine française et les juifs,* 283–290; Halioua, *Blouses blanches, étoiles jaunes,* 197–218.

114. Vice-Président du Conseil and Secrétaire d'État à l'Éducation nationale et à la Jeunesse to Monsieur le Maréchal, draft, June 1941, AN AJ38 1144. Cf. Jérôme Carcopino, Secrétaire d'État à l'Éducation nationale et à la Jeunesse, to CGQJ, 24 May 1941, AN AJ38 1144; Stéphanie Corcy-Debray, "Jérôme Carcopino et les lois d'exception," *Revue d'histoire moderne et contemporaine* 49, no. 4 (Oct.–Dec. 2002): 91–100.

115. Beginning in the 1941 academic year, the number of Jewish students was limited to 3 percent of non-Jewish students. Jews were required to self-declare and to request inclusion based on military credentials and family background. *JO* (24 June 1941): 2628. Cf. "Effectif des étudiants—non juifs et juifs, 1941–1942," Ministre de l'Éducation nationale et de la Jeunesse, Direction de l'Enseignement supérieur, AN F17 13361.

116. "Conversation avec M. Ourliac, Chef du cabinet de M. le Ministre de l'Éducation nationale, au sujet du numérus clausus dans les facultés," CGQJ, 17 May 1941, AN AJ38 1144.

117. Vergez, "Internes et anciens internes des hôpitaux de Paris," 421–422.

118. Minutes, Conférence interministerielle du 25 novembre 1941, réunie au CGQJ pour examiner l'application de la loi du 21 juin 1941 aux établissements d'enseignement supérieur, AN AJ38 1144.

119. Was Hungary's defense of its Jewish nationals in French universities more strategic than paradoxical? With its own anti-Semitic quota at home, perhaps Hungarian

diplomats thought it better for Hungarian Jews to study in Paris than in Budapest. Légation royale de Hongrie, France, to the Secrétaire d'État à l'Éducation nationale, 24 Sept. 1941, AN AJ38 1144; Dossier 5, "Enseignement," Subdossier 5, "Étudiants étrangers," CGQJ communication to the Secrétaire d'État à l'Éducation nationale, AN AJ38 119.

120. Minutes, Conférence interministerielle du 25 novembre 1941, réunie au CGQJ pour examiner l'application de la loi du 21 juin 1941 aux établissements d'enseignement supérieur, AN AJ38 1144. Cf. minutes, Conférence interministerielle du 29 août 1941, réunie au CGQJ pour examiner l'application de la loi du 21 juin 1941 aux établissements d'enseignement supérieur, AN AJ38 1144.

121. Secrétaire d'État à l'Éducation nationale to CGQJ, 23 Oct. 1941; CGQJ to the Secrétaire d'État à l'Éducation nationale, 15 Nov. 1941, AN AJ38 1144.

122. CGQJ to the Secrétaire d'État à l'Éducation nationale, 10 Oct. 1941, AN AJ38 1144.

123. Minutes, Conseil supérieur de l'Ordre national des Médecins, 21–25 May 1941, pp. 145–146, CAC 20000243 1.

124. Minutes, Conseil supérieur de l'Ordre national des Médecins, 21–25 June 1941, pp. 3–4, CAC 20000243 1.

125. Declaration transmitted from the Conseil supérieur to the Secrétaire-Général à la Santé, 5 June 1941, noted in the minutes, Conseil supérieur de l'Ordre national des Médecins, 21–25 May 1941, p. 146, CAC 20000243 1.

126. Secrétaire-Général à la Santé Huard to CGQJ, 24 May 1941, AN AJ38 1146.

127. Cited in Nahum, *La médecine française et les juifs,* 182.

128. Minutes, Conseil supérieur de l'Ordre national des Médecins, 21–25 May 1941, p. 146, CAC 20000243 1.

129. Secrétaire-Général à la Santé Huard to CGQJ, 24 May 1941, AN AJ38 1146; emphasis added.

130. *JO* (6 Sept. 1941): 3787.

131. An anti-Semitic quota for doctors was legislated in Algeria, Tunisia, and Morocco in late 1941 and early 1942. Dr. Perrot, president of the Oran Department Medical Union, to CGQJ, 19 Feb. 1942, AN AJ38 1146; Claude Singer, "Les études médicales et la concurrence juive en France et en Algérie (1931–1941)," in *Les juifs et l'économique: miroirs et mirages,* ed. Chantal Benayoun, Alain Médam, and Pierre-Jacques Rojtman (Toulouse, 1992), 197–212.

132. Note sur le project de décret réglementant, en ce qui concerne les juifs, la profession de médecin, n.d., AN AJ38 1146.

133. Nahum, *La médecine française et les juifs,* 177.

134. In comparison, eminently meritorious lawyers were to be proposed by the law bar, seconded by the Court of Appeals, approved by the CGQJ, and their exemptions enacted by the minister of justice. The quota on Jewish lawyers did not provide for an appeals process at all. The state representative who shuffled dossiers among the different parties was the public prosecutor (*procureur général*) for lawyers and the medical health inspector (*médecin inspecteur de la santé*) for doctors.

135. Minutes, Conseil supérieur de l'Ordre national des Médecins, 13–17 Dec. 1941, pp. 45–48, 62, CAC 20000243 1.

136. Minutes, Conseil supérieur de l'Ordre national des Médecins, 24–28 Jan. 1942, pp. 25–27, CAC 20000243 1.

137. "Questions relatives aux médecins juifs," *BOM* (Aug. 1942): 129–131, AN 3W 185.

138. Ibid. The Medical Order calculated the figure as 16 percent.

139. Vergez, "Internes et anciens internes des hôpitaux de Paris," 413.

140. Ibid., 420–422.

141. Documents show that there were 206 Jewish doctors, but the Seine council reported 203 to the CGQJ. "Liste des médecins juifs retenus par le Conseil départemental de la Seine de l'Ordre des Médecins (titres militaires)," 1 Jan. 1943; Dr. Regaud, secretary-general of the Seine department council, to CGQJ, 2 March 1943, AN AJ38 150.

142. "Liste récapitulative des médecins israélites interdits, Département de la Seine," 1 Dec. 1942, AN AJ38 150.

143. CGQJ to Befehlshaber der Sicherheitspolizei, 16 April 1943, AN AJ38 14. See also three typed, undated lists of names and address of Jewish doctors in the Seine: "Liste des médecins juifs retenus par le Conseil départemental de la Seine de l'Ordre des médecins (Titres Militaires)" (178 names), "Liste des médecins juifs non retenus par le Conseil départemental de la Seine de l'Ordre des médecins" (290 names), and "Liste des médecins israélites du département de la Seine retenus par l'Ordre des médecins pour être admis à titre exceptionnel à jouir des droits et prérogatives des médecins aryens" (34 names), CAC 20000243 2. In these titles, note the use of the term *israélite* instead of *juif* only for the doctors nominated for exceptional exemption. Note also the term *aryen:* this is the only time the term was found in Medical Order archives. Note finally the use of the euphemistic term *non retenu* to indicate expelled doctors.

144. Vergez, "Internes et anciens internes des hôpitaux de Paris," 421.

145. Bernard Laguerre, "Les dénaturalisés de Vichy, 1940–1944," *Vingtième siècle* 20 (1988): 3–15.

146. "Au Conseil supérieur," *BOM* (June 1942): 91, AN 3W 185.

147. "Médecins juifs relevés d'interdiction d'exercer," undated dossier, CAC 20000243 2.

148. Nahum, *La médecine française et les juifs,* 225, 224–229.

149. Ibid., 212, 217, 219–220.

150. Ryan, *The Holocaust and the Jews of Marseille,* 42–45.

151. CGQJ to Ravier, directeur régional adjoint, Pau, "Exercice de la médecine par les juifs du départment de Gers," 12 Feb. 1942, AN AJ38 1099.

152. T. dossier, AN AJ38 1045.

153. Conseil supérieur de l'Ordre national des Médecins, Section disciplinaire, Recueil I Case 166, CAC 20000243 2.

154. U. dossier, AN F60 602.

155. A. U. dossier, AN AJ38 1045.

156. Captain Lécussan, directeur régional du CGQJ, Toulouse, to the president of the Basses-Pyrénées department medical council, Pau, 10 Oct. 1942, AN AJ38 1099.

157. Ravier, directeur régional adjoint, CGQJ Toulouse, Pau subdivision, to Dr. Lestrade, president of the Gers department medical council, 12 Jan. 1943, AN AJ38 1099.

158. R. dossier, AN AJ38 150.

159. Vergez, "Internes et anciens internes des hôpitaux de Paris," 446.

160. Ibid., 320–321.

161. Ménétrel to Médecin-Lieutenant Henry Netter, 22 Aug. 1940, AN 3W 291.

162. Conseil supérieur de l'Ordre national des Médecins, Section disciplinaire, Recueil I Case 150, CAC 20000243 2.

163. Dr. G. Laurès, president of the Var department medical council, to Dr. Ménétrel, Chef du Secrétariat particulier du Maréchal Pétain, 18 Dec. 1942, AN 2AG 77.

164. Correspondence between L.-K. and Ménétrel and between Ménétrel and Roques, Nov.–Dec. 1941, AN 2AG 77.

165. Cited in Vergez, "Internes et anciens internes des hôpitaux de Paris," 456.

166. Ibid., 409, 420; Nahum, *La médecine française et les juifs,* 231; Halioua, *Blouses blanches, étoiles jaunes,* 132–133.

167. "Au Conseil supérieur," *BOM* (June 1942): 91, AN 3W 185.

168. "Affaires disciplinaires," *BOM* (June 1942): 111, AN 3W 185; "Questions relatives aux médecins juifs," 129–131.

169. Conseil supérieur de l'Ordre national des Médecins, Section disciplinaire, Recueil I Cases 1–166, 174–182, 193–196, 210, July 1942–Dec. 1943, CAC 20000243 2.

170. See Affaire Dr. Rouff, in Minutes, Conseil supérieur de l'Ordre national des Médecins, 18 Dec. 1943, AdP Perotin/5221/56/1/27.

171. Dr. Marie Spitzer, for example, was rejected by the Seine department medical council, but the national council overruled and proposed her exemption to the CGQJ for eminent professional merit. She had written a number of scientific works, worked charitably without remuneration in medicine for many years, and was also the mother of two French children.

172. Jacques Weill on 3 Dec. 1943, Roger Moline on 2 Feb. 1944, and Madeleine Hirsch on 2 Feb. 1944, CAC 20000243 2.

173. Two alternate sources offer statistics on national council decisions on appeals to the anti-Semitic quota: though the numbers are different in all three sources, the decisions are proportionately similar, and several cases most certainly are counted in more than one of the three sources. One of the alternate sources, the published bulletin of the Medical Order, stated that by August 1942, the national council had rendered judgments on 310 appeal cases by Jewish doctors from both zones. Of these, the national council rejected 195 for not meeting exemption criteria, nine were reintegrated because of military veteran or non-Jewish status, fifteen cases were pending further investigation, forty-seven doctors were to be reintegrated into the medical profession as soon as their receipt of the Croix de guerre was ratified, twenty-eight were proposed to the CGQJ on the grounds of eminent professional merit, and sixteen were proposed to the CGQJ for exceptional service rendered to the state by their families. "Questions relatives aux médecins juifs." The second alternate source of statistics—also incomplete—comes from a handwritten, untitled, undated alphabetical list of 261 Jewish doctors who appealed their department council expulsion. Of these, the national council rejected approximately two hundred and proposed thirty-four for an exemption. Only twenty-six of the 261 appeals came from departments outside the Île-de France region. CAC 20000243 2.

174. "Questions relatives aux médecins juifs," 129–131.

175. Nahum, *La médecine française et les juifs,* 279–280.

176. Joly, *Vichy dans la "solution finale,"* 491–495.

177. Capitaine de Corvette Lécussan, directeur régional CGQJ, Toulouse, to the directeur régional à la Famille et à la Santé, Toulouse, 5 May 1942, AN AJ38 1099.

178. E. to Ménétrel, 27 Dec. 1941, AN 2AG 77.

179. Storz, signing for le Commandant des forces militaires en France, État-Major administratif, to the Délégué général du Gouvernement français près le Commandant des forces militaires en France, Paris, 26 Aug. 1941, AN AJ38 120.

180. Roethke, Befehlshaber der Sicherheitspolizei to Darquier de Pellepoix, CGQJ, 9 Feb. 1943, AN AJ38 14.

181. "Questions relatives aux médecins juifs."

182. Roethke, Befehlshaber der Sicherheitspolizei to CGQJ, 17 Feb. 1943; and CGQJ to Roethke, 23 Feb. 1943, AN AJ38 14.

183. Roethke to CGQJ, 8 March 1943, CDJC XXIII 21.

184. Antignac, directeur de cabinet, CGQJ, to Roethke, Befehlshaber der Sicherheitspolizei, 15 March 1943, AN AJ38 14.

185. CGQJ to Befehlshaber der Sicherheitspolizei, 16 April 1943, AN AJ38 14.

186. AN 78AJ 6; Vergez, "Internes et anciens internes des hôpitaux de Paris," 455; Singer, *Vichy, l'université et les juifs,* 316–319; Anne Simonin, "Le Comité médical de la Résistance: un succès différé," in *La Résistance, une histoire sociale,* ed. Antoine Prost (Paris, 1997), 159–178. See also the memoirs of a Hungarian-born Jewish doctor in France, Albert Haas, *The Doctor and the Damned* (New York, 1984).

187. Vergez, "Internes et anciens internes des hôpitaux de Paris," 393–95; Henri Hermon, "À propos du remplacement médical en général et du remplacement à la campagne en particulier" (medical diss., Université de Paris, 1942).

188. Directeur régional de Toulouse, CGQJ, Service de l'Aryanisation économique, to Ravier, directeur régional adjoint, Pau, 18 May 1942; and Captain Corvette de Lécussan, CGQJ Toulouse, to Dr. Corcelle, secretary-general of a department medical council (unspecified), 20 July 1942, AN AJ38 1099.

189. Madame G. to the president of the Haute-Vienne department medical council, circa 5 Jan. 1942, AN AJ38 1045.

190. "Correspondence de l'Ordre avec les ministères et les services: remplacements par des étudiants en médecine israélites," *BOM* (August 1942): 138, AN 3W 185; Circular no. 17 from the Conseil supérieur de l'Ordre national des Médecins to the Conseils départementaux, 30 July 1942, CAC 20000243 2.

191. Dr. Pierre Masquin, secretary-general of the Vaucluse department medical council, to CGQJ, 15 Sept. 1942, AN AJ38 1146.

192. AN AJ38 120.

193. Secrétaire d'État à la Famille et à la Santé to CGQJ, 29 April 1943, AN AJ38 1146.

194. Secrétaire d'État à la Famille et à la Santé to CGQJ, 25 June 1943, AN AJ38 1146.

195. Indre departmental medical council to the Secrétaire d'État à la Famille et à la Santé, 2 Dec. 1941, AN AJ38 120.

196. CGQJ to the Secrétaire d'État à la Famille et à la Santé, 29 Jan. 1942, AN AJ38 120.

197. "Sur la pléthore médicale," *BOM* (Aug. 1941): 114–116, AN 3W 185.

198. "Note au sujet de la réforme des études médicales," Ministre de l'Éducation nationale et de la Jeunesse, Direction de l'Enseignement supérieur, AN F17 17512. Cf. Commission interministerielle de réforme des études médicales, report of president Leriche, AN F17 13361; Dossier "Réforme des études médicales," AN 2AG 78.

199. Annex to Circular no. 1 from the Conseil supérieur de l'Ordre national des Médecins to the Conseils départementaux, 30 Dec. 1940, AdP 3099 W 1; Minutes, Conseil supérieur de l'Ordre national des Médecins, 15–21 March 1941, p. 90 bis, CAC 20000243 1; Minutes, Conseil supérieur de l'Ordre national des Médecins, 21–25 May

1941, p. 208, CAC 20000243 1; Minutes, Conseil supérieur de l'Ordre national des Médecins, 21–25 June 1941, pp. 8–25, CAC 20000243 1; Circular no. 8 from the Conseil supérieur de l'Ordre national des Médecins to the Conseils départementaux, 30 June 1941, CAC 20000243 2 (also in AdP 3099 W 1); Minutes, Conseil supérieur de l'Ordre national des Médecins, 2–8 Aug. 1941, pp. 2–6, CAC 20000243 1; Circular no. 9 from the Conseil supérieur de l'Ordre national des Médecins to the Conseils départementaux, 8 Aug. 1941, AdP 3099 W 1; Minutes, Conseil supérieur de l'Ordre national des Médecins, 1–5 Nov. 1941, pp. 123–124, CAC 20000243 1.

200. "Maître de son tableau," *BOM* (Aug. 1941): 145–147, AN 3W 185.

201. "Application de la loi instituant l'ordre des médecins," Secrétaire d'État à la Santé to the prefects and the directeurs régionaux de la Famille et de la Santé, 3 June 1941, AN 72AJ 1859.

202. Président du Conseil supérieur de l'Ordre des Médecins to the Secrétaire d'État à l'Éducation nationale, 23 June 1941, AN F17 17512. Cf. Leriche to Ménétrel, 18 Aug. 1940, AN 3W 291.

203. Secrétaire d'État à la Santé Huard to the Secrétaire d'État à l'Éducation nationale, 28 June 1941, AN F17 17512.

204. "Limitation du nombre des étudiants en médecine," President of the Conseil supérieur de l'Ordre national des Médecins, report to the Secrétaire d'État à l'Éducation nationale, n.d., AN F17 17512.

205. "Voeu émis par les présidents des conseils départementaux de l'Ordre des Médecins, à la réunion d'Aix les Bains," 14 Sept. 1941, forwarded from the Conseil supérieur de l'Ordre national des Médecins to the Secrétaire d'État à l'Éducation nationale, 23 Sept. 1941, AN F17 17512; Circular no. 11 from the Conseil supérieur de l'Ordre national des Médecins to the Conseils départementaux, 8 Nov. 1941, CAC 20000243 2.

206. Minutes, Conseil supérieur de l'Ordre national des Médecins, 15–21 March 1941, p. 87, CAC 20000243 1; Circular no. 11 from the Conseil supérieur de l'Ordre national des Médecins to the Conseils départementaux, 8 Nov. 1941, AdP 3099 W 1; Circular no. 3 bis f from the Conseil national de l'Ordre national des Médecins to the conseils des Collèges départementaux, 28 Jan. 1944, AdP 3099 W 1.

207. *JO* (27 Oct. 1942), no. 939. Cf. Decree of 4 Feb. 1943, *JO* (16 Feb. 1943), no. 128.

208. Dean of the Montpellier Medical School to the president of the Commission de réforme des études médicales, 14 Jan. 1944, AN F17 17512.

Conclusion

1. "Syndicat des médecins de la banlieue ouest et nord de Paris, réunion de l'Assemblée générale du 14 juin 1935," *SM Seine, Banlieue Ouest et Nord* 105 (Nov. 1935): 55.

2. See untitled BUS document [1935 or 1936?], pp. 84–92, AN 63AJ 59.

3. "Avant de vouloir limiter le nombre des médecins français, il est normal d'arrêter le recrutement des médecins étrangers," *AEMP, bulletin mensuel* 7 (May 1939): 12.

4. Schor, *L'oopinion française et les étrangers,* 604.

5. Erich Maria Remarque, *Arch of Triumph* (New York, 1945).

6. Charpentier, *Au service de la liberté,* 152.

7. Caron, *Uneasy Asylum,* 41.

8. There is no question that xenophobia and anti-Semitism are related, but Ralph Schor does not go far enough to distinguish between the two. He uses identical examples of popular French sentiment toward foreigners and attributes them to xenophobia in one of his books and to anti-Semitism in another. Schor, *L'opinion française et les étrangers,* 600–611; Schor, *L'antisémitisme en France pendant les années trente* (Paris, 1992), 148–152.

9. Nahum, *La médecine française et les juifs,* 120.

10. Noiriel, *Les origines républicaines de Vichy.*

11. Michael Marrus, "Les juristes de Vichy dans 'l'engrenage de la destruction,'" in *Le droit antisémite de Vichy,* 52.

12. Caron, *Uneasy Asylum.* See Weber, *The Hollow Years.*

13. Fillon, *Le barreau de Lyon dans la tourmente,* 51.

14. Cited in Badinter, *Un antisémitisme ordinaire,* 208.

15. Vidal-Naquet, *Mémoires: la brisure et l'attente,* 177.

16. *Conférence des bâtonniers des départements, bulletin trimestriel* (1945).

17. Henry Rousso, *Le syndrome de Vichy* (Paris, 1987).

18. Marc Olivier Baruch, ed., *Une poignée de misérables: l'épuration de la société française après la Seconde Guerre mondiale* (Paris, 2003), 43, 48–49, 196; Henry Rousso, *Vichy: l'événement, la mémoire, l'histoire* (Paris, 2001), 613, 621.

19. "Épuration: dossiers d'avocats A–Z (1945–1949)," AdP 1320 W 134; "Conseils juridiques et avocats poursuivis pour faits de collaboration," AdP, 1320 W 74; Yves Ozanam, "L'épuration professionnelle au barreau de Paris (1944–1951)," *Gazette du Palais* 72–73 (13–14 March 2002): 3–23; Israël, *Robes noires, années sombres,* 42, 384; Israël, "La défense accusée: l'épuration professionelle des avocats," in *Une poignée de misérables,* 204–228; Israël, "L'épuration des barreaux français après la Seconde Guerre mondiale: une socio-histoire fragmentaire," 10–15; Céline Lesourd, "L'épuration des médecins," in *Une poignée de misérables,* 336–367.

20. Jewish lawyers who had been imprisoned or deported were exempted from paying the missed premiums. In 1945, however, the Paris bar established a charitable fund for former prisoners and "deportees." Ozanam, "Le barreau de Paris pendant la Seconde Guerre mondiale, 1940–1945," 149; Badinter, *Un antisémitisme ordinaire,* 204–205.

21. See Evleth, "Vichy France and the Continuity of Medical Nationalism," 110–115.

22. Cited in Israël, "L'épuration des barreaux français après la Seconde Guerre mondiale," 47.

23. Ibid., 47–48.

24. Nahum, *La médecine française et les juifs,* 372–380; Halioua, *Blouses blanches, étoiles jaunes,* 227.

25. Statut des minorités, 21 March 1943, AN F1a 3743.

26. "Note à M. le Commissaire à la Justice sur les principes fondamentaux d'une politique des naturalisations," CFLN, Algeria, 194[?], AN BB30 1731; "Communication du Garde des Sceaux, Ministre de la Justice, relative aux travaux de la Commission interministerielle des naturalisations," GPRF, 27 June 1945, AN F60 492. On the postwar debates among governmental officials, see Patrick Weil, *La France et ses étrangers: l'aventure d'une politique de l'immigration, 1938–1991* (Paris, 1991), 77–90; Weil, *Qu'est-ce qu'un Français?* chapter 5; and Ralph Schor, *Histoire de l'immigration: de la fin du XIXe siècle à nos jours* (Paris, 1996), 194–196.

27. Jean-Georges Rozoy, "Le malthusianisme médical, mesure de regression sociale" (medical diss., Université de Paris, 1950); Jean-Maurice Hermann, "La presse française

envahie par les racistes," *Immigration: revue mensuelle du Comité français pour la défense de l'immigration* 2 (April 1949).

28. "Bonjour chers collègues," "Assemblée générale du 11 mai 1946," and "Séance du Comité du 4 novembre 1946," *Bulletin de l'Internat des hôpitaux de Paris* 98 (Feb. 1947): 2–3, 6–9, and 24. Cf. "Séance du Comité du 6 janvier 1948," *Bulletin de l'Internat des hôpitaux de Paris* 100 (March 1948): 40–41.

29. "Au quartier latin les étudiants luttent contre la mouise . . . un appartement qu'ils demandent et avec des 'garanties de moralité' ne pas être nègre ou métèque," *Franc tireur* (2 Nov. [Feb.?] 1947), AN 72AJ 598.

30. "Le protectionnisme des intellectuels," *La revue du Gisti, plein droit* 29–30 (Nov. 1995): 15.

31. Palewski proposed his bill again in 1969. "Proposition de loi no. 849 tendant à faciliter l'exercice des professions libérales aux réfugiés et apatrides," 8 Oct. 1969, CAC 19950407 4.

32. Franck Johannes, "Sept millions d'emplois franco-français," *Libération,* 11–12 March 2000; "Pour l'égalité de l'exercice de la médecine en France," *Publication des Ligues des droits de l'homme* 39, Actes du colloque, 26 Nov. 1998.

33. CAC 19950407 200; CAC 19950407 201.

34. John Grimes, "'Une et indivisibile'—The Reform of the Legal Profession in France: The Effect on U.S. Attorneys," *New York University Journal of International Law and Politics* 24 (1992): 1757–93.

35. Cyril Wolmark, "La situation des médecins à diplôme étranger: entre fonctions et statut, le hiatus," *La revue du Gisti, plein droit* 36–37 (December 1997): 80–83; Laurence Folléa, "La sélection draconienne des médecins titulaires d'un diplôme étranger," *Le monde,* 8 February 1997; Carlos Parada, "Les médecins ne sont pas tous égaux," *Libération,* 27–28 June 1998; Claire Hatzfeld and Jean Michel Lestang, "Les médecins refugiés et exilés, une élite déclassé," *ProAsile: la revue de France terre d'asile* 1 (March 1999), 11–13; Cécile Prieur, "Les médecins étrangers réclament un statut officiel," *Le monde,* 30 Jan. 2006; Sandrine Cabut, "Les médecins étrangers en grève contre la précarité," *Libération,* 14 July 2006.

36. Patrick Weil, "Pour une politique de l'immigration juste et efficace," Rapport au Premier Ministre français Lionel Jospin, Paris, July 1997.

37. "Pour la première fois, un président français reconnaît la responsabilité de la France dans la déportation et l'extermination de juifs pendant la Seconde Guerre mondiale," *Agence France presse,* 16 July 1995.

38. Julie Fette, "Apology and the Past in Contemporary France," *French Politics, Culture, and Society* 26, no. 2 (Summer 2008): 78–113.

39. Badinter, *Un antisémitisme ordinaire,* 190. Cf. Josyane Savigneau, "La douleur de Robert Badinter; soumission ou complaisance?" *Le monde des livres,* 25 April 1997.

40. "France-justice-juifs," *Agence France presse,* 13 May 1997; "Occupation: le barreau de Paris bat sa coulpe," *Les échos,* 14 May 1997; "Antisémitisme: le conseil de l'ordre du barreau de Paris . . ." *Le monde,* 15 May 1997.

41. This researcher was denied access. For another account of denied access to Paris law bar and other law bar archives in France, see Israël, "L'épuration des barreaux français après la Seconde Guerre mondiale," 10–15.

42. Dominique Simonnot, "'Moi si je vole, je vais au gnouf tout de suite,'" *Libération,* 14 Oct. 1997.

43. Former Lyon bar president Ugo Iannucci published an article in 2001 in which he harshly judged the record of his wartime predecessor Claude Valansio and regretted the lack of protest against discriminatory measures during the war. He claimed that the city of Lyon—the supposed capital of the Resistance—was between 1940 and 1944 the home of "if not an inglorious law bar, then an absolutely disgraceful one." Iannucci, "L'attitude du barreau de Lyon pendant l'Occupation," 178.

44. See Weisberg, *Vichy Law and the Holocaust in France; Juger sous Vichy; Le droit antisémite de Vichy.*

45. Robert R. Weyeneth, "The Power of Apology and the Process of Historical Reconciliation," *Public Historian* 23, no. 3 (Summer 2001): 22.

46. "Avocats," *Les annonces de la Seine* 19 (10 March 1997).

47. Jean-Pierre Mignard interviewed by Flore de Bodman, "Faire taire les rumeurs et les soupcons," *Le nouvel observateur,* 31 Oct. 2005; Sylvia Zappi, "À gauche, un début de mobilisation," *Le monde,* 14 Nov. 2005; "Le projet d'expulser les étrangers impliqués dans les violences urbaines suscite un tollé," *Le monde,* 10 Nov. 2005; Fodé Sylla and Francis Terquem, "La République blanche, c'est fini!" *Le monde,* 9 Dec. 2005.

48. See www.lesaf.org.

49. Olivier Abel, "Le pardon ou comment revenir au monde ordinaire," *Esprit* 8–9 (Aug.–Sept. 2000): 76.

50. See Le Béguec, *La République des avocats,* 208.

51. See Israël, *Robes noires, années sombres.*

52. Bruno Keller, "Le Pr. Glorion: 'un sentiment de regret, un souci de vérité, un devoir de mémoire,'" *Le quotidien du médecin,* 14 Oct. 1997.

53. Philippe Roy, "Vichy: après la repentance, l'ouverture des archives," *Le quotidien du médecin,* 15 Oct. 1997.

54. Paul Milliez, *Médecin de la liberté* (Paris, 1980), 71–72.

55. Jean-Yves Nau, "Le président de l'ordre des médecins fait acte de 'repentance,'" *Le monde,* 12 Oct. 1997; H.R., "Le mea culpa de l'Ordre," *Impact médecin hebdo,* 17 Oct. 1997.

56. Search undertaken in the *Bulletin de l'Ordre des Médecins* from September 1997 to January 1998.

57. See *Conseil national de l'Ordre des Médecins,* http://www.conseil-national.mede-cin.fr (accessed 14 Feb. 2003 and 1 June 2006). Note, however, that a 2004 presentation by the vice president of the Order, Dr. Jean Poullard, titled "Historique de l'Ordre national des Médecins, 1845–1945," which was presented at the Société française d'histoire de la médecine on 15 May 2004, appeared on the Order's Web site. In a single paragraph on the anti-Semitic exclusions under Vichy, the report reiterates several common postwar myths: that the exclusion of Jews from medicine was imposed by the state, that the Order implemented the exclusions "without overzealousness," and that the council of the Order did not protest the anti-Semitic laws because it was "caught in the stranglehold of Vichy."

58. Nau, "Le président de l'ordre des médecins fait acte de 'repentance.'"

59. Patrice Muller, "Le silence de l'ordre des médecins," *Le monde,* 27 Sept. 1997.

60. Cited in Annette Lévy-Willard, "L'examen de conscience de l'ordre des méde-cins," *Libération,* 11 Oct. 1997.

61. "Le quotidien des lecteurs," *Le quotidien du médecin,* 20 Oct. 1997.

62. Roy, "Vichy: après la repentance, l'ouverture des archives."

63. "Le quotidien des lecteurs," *Le quotidien du médecin,* 23 Oct. 1997.

64. Philippe Roy, "Vichy: l'Ordre des médecins entre en repentance," *Le quotidien du médecin,* 10 Oct. 1997.

65. Roy, "Vichy: après la repentance, l'ouverture des archives."

66. Henri Nahum consulted some Medical Order departmental archives for his book, *La médecine française et les juifs.*

67. Philippe Roy, "L'Ordre sous Vichy: le Pr. Kahn critique les conseils départementaux," *Le quotidien du médecin,* 13 Oct. 1997.

68. For example, see the dossier "Les médecins de Vichy," *Impact médecin hebdo,* 10 Oct. 1997.

69. "Pétain impose ses lois," *Impact médecin hebdo,* 10 Oct. 1997.

70. Roy, "Vichy: l'Ordre des médecins entre en repentance."

71. Keller, "Le Pr. Glorion."

72. "Le quotidien des lecteurs," *Le quotidien du médecin,* 20 Oct. 1997.

73. CMH (Coordination of Hospital Doctors) quoted in Paul Benkimoun and Claire Guélaud, "Le patronat sort de son silence, les médecins appellent à voter 'contre Le Pen,'" *Le monde,* 26 April 2002. Gérard Noiriel has pointed to a "radical evolution" of doctors who today refuse to embrace the National Front's propaganda of "immigré = sida" (Immigrant = AIDS). See "La République, l'extrême droite et nous," *Le monde,* 12 March 1997. Such an evolution was not complete, however, at the end of the twentieth century. See Jean-Michel Bezat, "Les dérapages xénophobes de M. Maudrux, patron de la Caisse de retraite des médecins," *Le monde,* 19 Dec. 1997.

74. See Mark Gibney and Erik Roxstrom, "The Status of State Apologies," *Human Rights Quarterly* 23, no. 4 (2001): 929–939.

75. "Le quotidien des lecteurs," *Le quotidien du médecin,* 20 Oct. 1997.

76. Elazar Barkan and Alexander Karn, "Group Apology as an Ethical Imperative," in *Taking Wrongs Seriously: Apologies and Reconciliation,* ed. Elazar Barkan and Alexander Karn (Stanford, 2006): 27.

77. Kathleen Gill, "The Moral Functions of an Apology," *Philosophical Forum* 31, no. 1 (Spring 2000): 14, 17.

78. Pascal Ory, "Why Be So Cruel? Some Modest Proposals to Cure the Vichy Syndrome," in *France at War: Vichy and the Historians,* ed. Sarah Fishman et al. (Oxford, 2000), 283.

# BIBLIOGRAPHY

Primary Sources

Archives

ARCHIVES DE PARIS (AdP)

1319W: 1–17
1320W: 74, 134, 135, 148
3099 W: 1
Perotin 5221 56 1: 27, 34, 40, 41, 45

ARCHIVES DU CENTRE DE DOCUMENTATION
JUIVE CONTEMPORAINE (CDJC)

"Professions": IIIa, IV, VI, XIa, XIb, XIc, XVIIa, XXIII, XXVII, LIII, LXXX, CII, CVIII,
    CX, CXI, CXCV, CCCLXXIX, DLXXV

ARCHIVES DU MINISTÈRE DES AFFAIRES ÉTRANGÈRES (MAE)

Series C: 85, 125, 253–256, 266, 433, 434, 710, 711

ARCHIVES DU RECTORAT DE L'ACADÉMIE DE PARIS (AP)

This material has since been transferred to the Archives nationales, Centre des Archives
contemporaines, Fontainebleau (CAC), where they have been assigned new classifica-
tion numbers, noted in square brackets next to the original AP carton numbers.
213 and 214 [CAC 20020476 343], 221 [CAC 20020476 341], 222 [CAC 20020476 345],
    226 [CAC 20020476 304], 227 [CAC 20020476 305], 228 [CAC 20020476 306],
    269 [CAC 20020476 295], 325 [CAC 20020476 349], 350 [CAC 20020476 308]

ARCHIVES NATIONALES, CENTRE DES ARCHIVES
CONTEMPORAINES, FONTAINEBLEAU (CAC)

19950407: 4, 14, 16, 17, 200, 201, 439, 442, 444, 448, 449, 453, 492, 493

19960096: 1
20000243: 1, 2, 3, 4

ARCHIVES NATIONALES, PARIS (AN)

Académie de Paris, Series AJ16

6496–6498, 6696, 6963, 6965, 6967, 6974, 6983, 6987, 6990, 7117–7119, 7122–7132,
    7135, 7140–7142, 7147–7149, 7154–7155, 8351, 8352, 8362, 8363, 8374, 8804

Bureau universitaire de statistique, Series 63AJ

4, 51, 59, 70

Cabinet du Chef de l'État, Series 2AG

74–78, 497, 521, 606, 607, 613, 659

Collection de tracts, journaux et imprimés divers, Series 78AJ

6, 7, 14, 17

Commissariat général aux questions juives, Series AJ38

7, 14, 19, 58, 69, 118–121, 123, 146, 150, 244, 258, 281, 297, 539, 540, 1045, 1075, 1099,
    1142, 1144–1150, 1158

Fonds Maurice Rolland, Series 490 AP

1

Haute Cour de Justice, Series 3W

185, 291, 323

Ministère de la Justice, Series BB

BB11: 1604–1605
BB18: 6002/2–6002/4, 6196, 6390, 6407, 6582–6584, 6772
BB30: 1707, 1711, 1714, 1729, 1731

Ministère de l'Instruction publique, Series F17

13361, 13381, 13384, 13386, 16572, 17501, 17512, 17516, 17549, 17590, 17634

Ministère de l'Intérieur, Series F1a

3655–3657, 3660, 3661, 3687, 3688, 3690–3692, 3694, 3706, 3743–3745, 3784

Police générale, Series F7

13518, 13955, 14654, 14658, 14659, 14661, 14662, 14711, 14759, 14774–14776, 14823, 14848, 15148, 15166, 15167, 16029, 16030, 16050, 16079, 16080, 16101, 16104

Présidence/vice-présidence du Conseil, Series F60

490, 492, 497, 499, 518, 600, 602, 641, 1035, 1038, 1384, 1406, 1424, 1485, 1678

Seconde Guerre mondiale, Series 72AJ

5, 73, 78, 251, 263, 266, 411–413, 546, 574, 598–606, 1825, 1837, 1859, 1895, 2033

Bibliothèque Marguerite Durand (BMD)

DOS 349 AVO, DOS 610 MED

Government Sources

Journal officiel de la République française. Documents parlementaires. Sénat.
Journal officiel de la République française. Débats parlementaires. Sénat.
Journal officiel de la République française. Documents parlementaires. Chambre des Députés.
Journal officiel de la République française. Débats parlementaires. Chambre des Députés.

Student Publications

AEMP, bulletin mensuel de l'Association des étudiants en médecine de Paris, 1930–1939.
Bulletin du comité de l'Association amicale des internes et anciens internes en médecine des hôpitaux et hospices civils de Paris (name changed to *Bulletin de l'Internat des hôpitaux de Paris* in 1931), 1920–1948.
L'écho des étudiants, 1926–1935.
Étudiants, mensuel des étudiants de Paris, Section de Paris de l'Union fédérale des étudiants, 1930–1939.
L'étudiant catholique, revue mensuelle de la Fédération française des étudiants catholiques, 1930–1938.
Le front médical français, bulletin mensuel de l'Association amicale des étudiants en médecine de Paris, 1930–1939.
L'indicateur de l'étudiant en droit, Paris, 1923–1938.
Revue médicale de la Corporative des étudiants en médecine, Montpellier, 1930–1939.
Revue médicale de l'Office central de médecine de l'Union nationale des étudiants, Clermont-Ferrand, 1930–1939.

Revue médicale de la Section corporative de Montpellier et de l'Office central de médecine de l'Union nationale des étudiants, 1930–1939.

La science médicale pratique, bulletin de l'Association professionnelle des externes et anciens externes des hôpitaux de Paris, 1926–1939.

L'Université de Paris, revue mensuelle de l'Association générale des étudiants, 1920–1926, 1932–1933.

La voix dentaire, revue mensuelle, organe de l'Association générale des étudiants en chirurgie dentaire de France, 1930–1939.

Medical Publications

Association française des femmes-médecins, 1930–1933.

Association internationale des femmes-médecins, 1930–1936.

Le bouclier, bulletin mensuel du Groupement des syndicats médicaux de la Loire-Inférieure, du Maine-et-Loire et du Loir-et-Cher, 1933–1938.

Bulletin de l'Académie de médecine, 1930–1935.

Bulletin de la Fédération des syndicats médicaux du département du Nord [SM Nord], 1925–1941.

Bulletin mensuel du Groupement des syndicats médicaux de l'Aube [SM Aube], 1930–1936.

Bulletin officiel du Syndicat des médecins du département d'Oran, 1938.

Bulletin officiel de l'Association professionnelle des internes et anciens internes des hôpitaux de Marseille, 1933–1938.

Bulletin officiel du Syndicat médical de Paris [SMP], 1920–1939.

Bulletin officiel du Syndicat des médecins de Marseille et d'arrondissement, de la Fédération des syndicats médicaux des Bouches-du-Rhône, 1928, 1931–1938.

Bulletin de l'Ordre des Médecins [BOM], 1941–1945.

Bulletin de la Société des médecins et du Syndicat médical de Lot-et-Garonne, 1928–1938.

Bulletin du Syndicat médical de Seine-et-Oise [SM Seine-et-Oise], 1930–1938.

Bulletin du Syndicat professionnel des médecins de colonisation d'Algérie, 1928–1932, 1934–1938.

Fédération des Syndicats médicaux de la Seine, Syndicat des médecins de la banlieue ouest et nord de Paris, bulletin officiel [SM Seine, Banlieue Ouest et Nord], 1932–1933, 1935–1938.

La butte médicale, bulletin de la Société amicale des médecins du XVIIIe arrondissement, 1925–1940.

Le concours médical, passim.

Le médecin corporatif, organe de la Fédération corporative des médecins de la région parisienne, 1939.

Le médecin de France, journal officiel de la Confédération des syndicats médicaux français, 1930–1933.

Le médecin de Lorraine, bulletin du Groupement des syndicats médicaux de Meurthe-et-Moselle, Meuse, Moselle, Vosges, 1931–1938.

Le siècle médical, passim.

Syndicats médicaux, banlieue ouest et nord, banlieue est et sud de Paris et Fédération des syndicats médicaux de la Seine, bulletin officiel, 1932.

Syndicats médicaux picards, bulletin official de la Fédération des syndicates médicaux de la Somme, 1931–1938.

Union medicale du nord-est, organe médical et scientifique du nord-est de la France, bulletin des syndicats médicaux de la région, 1931–1932, 1937.

Law Publications

Bulletin de l'Association nationale des avocats inscrits aux barreaux de France, des colonies, des pays de protectorat et de mandat [Bulletin de l'ANA], 1927–1944.
Bulletin de l'Union des jeunes avocats [Bulletin de l'UJA], 1930–1936.
Conférence des bâtonniers des départements, Ordre des Avocats, bulletin trimestriel, 1929–1947.
La vie judiciaire, 1930–1938.

Published Sources

Abbott, Andrew. *The System of Professions: An Essay on the Division of Expert Labor.* Chicago: University of Chicago Press, 1988.

Abel, Richard L., and P. S. C. Lewis, eds. *Lawyers in Society.* Berkeley: University of California Press, 1988.

Abel, Olivier. "Le pardon ou comment revenir au monde ordinaire." *Esprit* 8–9 (August–September 2000): 72–87.

Accampo, Elinor A., Rachel G. Fuchs, and Mary Lynn Stewart. *Gender and the Politics of Social Reform in France, 1870–1914.* Baltimore: Johns Hopkins University Press, 1995.

Ackerman, Evelyn Bernette. *Health Care in the Parisian Countryside, 1800–1914.* New Brunswick: Rutgers University Press, 1990.

Albisetti, James C. "Portia ante Portas: Women and the Legal Profession in Europe, ca. 1870–1925." *Journal of Social History* 33, no. 4 (2000): 825–857.

Ancel, Marc, ed. *La condition de la femme dans la société contemporaine: état actuel des législations concernant les droits politiques, l'activité professionnelle, la capacité civile, la situation de la femme dans la famille et la condition de la femme au regard du droit pénal.* Travaux et recherches de l'Institut de droit comparé de l'Université de Paris. Paris: Receuil Sirey, 1938.

Ancel, Pascal. "La jurisprudence civile et commerciale." In *Le droit antisémite de Vichy,* 363–383.

Appleton, Jean. *Traité de la profession d'avocat.* Paris: Dalloz, 1923.

Association française pour l'histoire de la justice. *La justice de l'épuration, à la fin de la Seconde Guerre mondiale.* Collection Histoire de la justice, no. 18. Paris: Documentation française, 2008.

———. *La justice des années sombres, 1940–1944.* Collection Histoire de la justice, no. 14. Paris: Documentation française, 2001.

Ayoub, Charles. "La nouvelle législation de la naturalisation en France." Law diss., Université de Paris, 1937.

Babin, Pierre. "Étude statistique sur la profession médicale: répartition des médecins dans les divers milieux." Medical diss., Université de Paris, 1939.

Badinter, Robert. *Un antisémitisme ordinaire: Vichy et les avocats juifs (1940–1944).* Paris: Fayard, 1997.

———. "Peut-on être avocat lorsqu'on est juif en 1940–1944?" In *Le droit antisémite de Vichy,* 143–151.

Bancoud, Alain. "La haute magistrature sous Vichy." *Vingtième siècle* 49 (January–March 1996).

Bard, Christine. *Les femmes dans la société française au 20e siècle.* Paris: Armand Colin, 2001.

———. *Les filles de Marianne: histoire des féminismes, 1914–1940.* Paris: Fayard, 1995.

———, ed. *Madeleine Pelletier (1874–1939): logiques et infortunes d'un combat pour l'égalité.* Paris: Côté-femmes, 1992.

Barkan, Elazar, and Alexander Karn. "Group Apology as an Ethical Imperative." In *Taking Wrongs Seriously: Apologies and Reconciliation,* edited by Elazar Barkan and Alexander Karn, 3–30. Stanford: Stanford University Press, 2006.

Barthélemy, André. *Les avocats devant les tribunaux de commerce: les huissiers et la profession d'avocat.* Toulouse, 1934.

Barthélemy, Joseph. *Ministre de la Justice: Vichy, 1941–1943.* Paris: Pygmalion-Watelet, 1989.

Baruch, Marc Olivier. *Servir l'État français: l'administration en France de 1940 à 1944.* Paris: Fayard, 1997.

———, ed. *Une poignée de misérables: l'épuration de la société française après la Seconde Guerre mondiale.* Paris: Fayard, 2003.

Beaudot, Henri. "L'exercice illégal de la médecine et le charlatanisme: ressemblances et différences dans leurs éléments et dans leurs répression." Law diss., Université de Lyon, 1939.

Bell, David. *Lawyers and Citizens: The Making of a Political Elite in Old Regime France.* New York: Oxford University Press, 1994.

Béraud, Jean-Marc. "Le juif interdit de travail." In *Le droit antisémite de Vichy,* 209–229.

Berlanstein, L. R. *The Barristers of Toulouse in the Eighteenth Century (1740–1793).* Baltimore: Johns Hopkins University Press, 1975.

Berthélemy, Henri. *L'École de droit.* Paris: Librairie générale de droit et de jurisprudence, 1932.

Bezat, Jean-Michel. *Les toubibs, radioscopie du corps medical: le quotidien du médecin.* Paris: Jean-Claude Lattès, 1987.

Bigot, Grégoire. "Vichy dans l'oeil de la *Revue de droit public.*" In Durand, Le Crom, and Somma, *Le droit sous Vichy,* 415–435.

Billig, Joseph. *Le Commissariat général aux questions juives (1941–1944).* 3 vols. Paris: Éditions du Centre, 1955.

Bloch, Bernard-Michel. "Le regard des juristes sur les lois raciales de Vichy." *Les temps modernes* 547 (February 1992): 161–174.

Boigeol, Anne. "Les femmes et les cours: la difficile mise en œuvre de l'égalité des sexes dans l'accès à la magistrature." *Genèses* 22 (March 1996): 107–129.

Boigeol, Anne, and Yves Dezalay. "De l'agent d'affaires au barreau: les conseils juridiques et la construction d'un espace professionnel." *Genèses* 27 (June 1997): 49–68.

Bonner, Thomas Neville. *Becoming a Physician: Medical Education in Britain, France, Germany, and the United States, 1750–1945.* New York: Oxford University Press, 1995.

———. *To the Ends of the Earth: Women's Search for Education in Medicine.* Cambridge: Harvard University Press, 1992.

Bonnet, Jean-Charles. *Les pouvoirs publics français et l'immigration dans l'entre-deux-guerres.* Lyon: Presses de l'Université de Lyon II, 1976.

Boudard, Jacques. "De l'envahissement du corps médical français par certains éléments 'nés' en Pologne et Roumanie." Medical diss., Université de Paris, 1939.

Boulègue-Camilleri, Valda. "Étude comparée du contrôle légal de l'exercice de la médecine dans les pays d'Europe." Medical diss., Université de Paris, 1935.

Bourdieu, Pierre. *La distinction: critique sociale du jugement.* Paris: Minuit, 1979.

Braun, André. *L'Ordre des médecins.* Paris: Recueil Sirey, 1941.

Branca, Patricia, ed. *The Medicine Show: Patients, Physicians, and the Perplexities of the Health Revolution in Modern Society.* New York: Science History Publications, 1977.

Broc, André. "La qualité de juif, une notion juridique nouvelle." Law diss., Université de Paris, 1943.

Brouardel, Paul. *L'exercice de la médecine et le charlatanisme.* Paris: Baillière, 1899.

———. *La profession médicale au commencement du XXe siècle.* Paris: Librairie J.-B. Baillière et Fils, 1903.

Broussolle, Denis. "L'élaboration du statut des juifs de 1940." In *Le droit antisémite de Vichy,* 115–139.

Bui Dang Ha Doan, Jean. "Les femmes dans la médecine libérale." *Cahiers de sociologie et démographie médicale* 4 (October–December 1964): 123–136.

Bungener, Martine. "Une eternelle pléthore médicale?" *Sciences sociales et santé* 11, no. 1 (1984): 77–110.

Burdeau, Georges. *Cours de droit constitutionnel.* Paris: *Librarie générale de droit et de jurisprudence,* 1942.

Carcopino, Jerome. *Souvenirs de sept ans, 1937–1944.* Paris: Flammarion, 1953.

Carol, Anne. *Histoire de l'eugénisme en France: les médecins et la procréation, XIXe-XXe siècle.* Paris: Seuil, 1995.

Caron, Vicki. "The Antisemitic Revival of the 1930s: The Socioeconomic Dimension Reconsidered." *Journal of Modern History* 70 (March 1998): 24–73.

———. *Between France and Germany: The Jews of Alsace-Lorraine, 1870–1918.* Stanford: Stanford University Press, 1988.

———. "French Public Opinion and the 'Jewish Question,' 1930–1942: The Role of Middle-Class Professional Associations." In *Nazi Europe and the Final Solution,* edited by David Bankier and Israel Gutman, 374–410. Jerusalem: Yad Vashem, 2003.

———. "The Politics of Frustration: French Jewry and the Refugee Crisis in the 1930s." *Journal of Modern History* 65, no. 2 (June 1993): 311–356.

———. "Prelude to Vichy: France and the Jewish Refugees in the Era of Appeasement." *Journal of Contemporary History* 20, no. 1 (January 1985): 157–176.

———. *Uneasy Asylum: France and the Jewish Refugee Crisis, 1933–1942.* Stanford: Stanford University Press, 1999.

Carrère, Gilbert-Antoine. "La Corporation médicale." Medical diss., Université de Bordeaux, 1939.

Carron, R. *Histoire de l'Ordre des médecins.* Lyon: Collection Fondation Marcel Mérieux, 1991.

Catinat, Anne-Laure. "Les premières avocates du barreau de Paris." *Mil neuf cent* 16 (1998): 48–52.

Céline, Louis-Ferdinand. *L'école des cadavres.* Paris: Denoël, 1938.

Centre de documentation juive contemporaine. *Il y a 50 ans: le Statut des Juifs de Vichy, Actes du colloque du 1er octobre 1990.* Paris: Éditions CDJC, 1991.

Centre universitaire de recherches administratives et politiques de Picardie (CURAPP). *Les usages sociaux du droit.* Paris: Presses universitaires de France, 1989.

Cérez, Jane. "La condition sociale de la femme de 1804 à l'heure présente: le problème féministe et la guerre." Étude de sociologie juridique. Paris: Librairie générale de droit et de jurisprudence, 1940.

Cerf, Joseph. *Le conseil juridique, son rôle, ses méthodes.* Paris: Librairie générale de droit et de jurisprudence, 1935.

Chadefaux, M. "De la séparation des fonctions d'avocat et d'avoué." Law diss., Université de Paris, 1912.

Charle, Christophe. "La bourgeoisie de robe en France au XIXe siècle." *Le mouvement social* 181 (October–December 1997): 53–72.

——. "Le déclin de la République des avocats." In *La France de l'Affaire Dreyfus,* edited by Pierre Birnbaum, 56–86. Paris: Gallimard, 1994.

——. *Les élites de la République, 1880–1900.* Paris: Fayard, 1987.

——. *Histoire sociale de la France au XIXe siècle.* Paris: Seuil, 1991.

——. "Méritocratie et profession juridique: les secrétaires de la Conférence du Stage des avocats de Paris, une étude des promotions 1860–1870 et 1879–1889." *Paedogogica historica* 30, no. 1 (1994): 303–324.

——. "Pour une histoire sociale des professions juridiques à l'époque contemporaine." *Actes de la recherche en sciences sociales* (1989): 117–119.

——. "Le recrutement des avocats parisiens, 1880–1914." In Le Béguec, *Avocats et barreaux en France, 1910–1930,* 21–34.

——. *La république des universitaires, 1870–1940.* Paris: Seuil, 1994.

——. "La toge ou la robe? Les professeurs de la Faculté de droit de Paris à la Belle Époque." *Revue d'histoire des Facultés de droit et de la science juridique* 7 (1988): 167–175.

Charpentier, Jacques. *Au service de la liberté.* Paris: Fayard, 1949.

Charpentier, Michel. "La protection des titres professionnels." Law diss., Université de Paris, 1939.

Charrier, Edmée. *L'évolution intellectuelle féminine (Le développement intellectuel de la femme, la femme dans les professions intellectuelles, la femme étudiante).* Paris: Receuil Sirey, 1937.

Chatriot, Alain. "La lutte contre le 'chômage intellectual': l'action de la Confédération des travailleurs intellectuels (CTI) face à la crise des années trente." *Le mouvement social* 214 (January–March 2006): 77–91.

Chinard, Gilbert. "The Life of a Parisian Medical Student in the Eighteenth Century." *Bulletin of the History of Medicine* 7 (1939): 374–380.

Chomienne, Christian. "Juger les juges?" In *Juger sous Vichy,* 9–16.

Clark, Frances I. *The Position of Women in Contemporary France.* Westport, Conn.: Hyperion, 1937.

Clark, Linda L. "Higher-Ranking Women Civil Servants and the Vichy Regime: Firings and Hirings, Collaboration and Resistance." *French History* 13, no. 3 (1999): 332–359.

——. *The Rise of Professional Women in France: Gender and Public Administration since 1830.* Cambridge: Cambridge University Press, 2000.

Cocks, Geoffrey, and Konrad H. Jarausch, eds. *German Professions, 1800–1950,* New York: Oxford University Press, 1990.

Cohen, Richard I. *The Burden of Conscience: French Jewish Leadership during the Holocaust.* Bloomington: Indiana University Press, 1987.

Cointet, Michèle. "Les juristes sous l'occupation: la tentation du Pétainisme et le choix de la résistance." In *Les facs sous Vichy: étudiants, universitaires et universités de France pendant la Seconde Guerre mondiale,* edited by André Gueslin, 51–64. Clermont-Ferrand: Presses universitaires Blaise Pascal, 1994.

———. "Les universités sous l'occupation." *Vingtième siècle* 43 (July–September 1994): 128–131.

Conklin, Alice L. *In the Museum of Man: Ethnography, Racial Science, and Empire in France, 1850–1950.* Ithaca: Cornell University Press, forthcoming.

Corcos, Fernand. *Les avocates.* Paris: Éditions Montaigne, 1931.

Corcy-Debray, Stéphanie. "Jérôme Carcopino, du triomphe à la roche tarpéienne." *Vingtième siècle* 58 (April–June 1998): 70–82.

———. "Jérôme Carcopino et les lois d'exception." *Revue d'histoire moderne et contemporaine* 49, no. 4 (October–December 2002): 91–100.

Cot, Pierre. "Les avocats et les universitaires dans la politique." *Revue politique et parlementaire* 10 (August 1925): 202–222.

Crémieu, Louis. *Traité de la profession d'avocat.* Aix-Marseille: Bibliothèque de l'Université d'Aix-Marseille, 1939.

Cucarull, Jérôme. "Les médecins et l'Assistance médicale gratuite, 1893–1914: l'exemple de l'Ille-et-Vilaine." *Le mouvement social* 161 (October–December 1992): 67–82.

Dall'Ava-Santucci, Josette. *Des sorcières aux mandarins: histoire des femmes médecins.* Paris: Calmann-Lévy, 1989.

Damamme, Dominique. "La jeunesse des syndicats de médecins ou l'enchantement du syndicalisme." *Genèses* 3 (March 1991): 31–54.

Dauvergne, Bertrand. "Les éléments du délit d'exercice illégal de la médecine." Law diss., Université de Rennes, 1935.

Dedieu, Jean-Philippe. "L'intégration des avocats africains dans les barreaux français." *Droit et société* 56–57, no. 1 (2004): 209–229.

De La Pradelle, Albert. "La nouvelle condition du naturalisé d'après la loi et la jurisprudence." *Nouvelle revue de droit international privé* 2 and 3 (1935): 161–208.

de Monzie, Anatole. *La saison des juges.* Paris: Flammarion, 1943.

Dezalay, Yves, ed. *Batailles territoriales et querelles de cousinage: juristes et comptables européens sur le marché du droit des affaires.* Paris: Librairie générale de droit et de jurisprudence, 1993.

d'Hugues, Philippe. *Les professions en France: évolution et perspectives.* Paris: Presses universitaires de France, 1969.

Dictionnaire des parlementaires français: notices biographiques sur les ministres députés et sénateurs français de 1889 à 1940. 7 vols. Paris: Presses universitaires de France, 1960–1977.

Dingwall, Robert, and Philip Lewis, eds. *The Sociology of the Professions: Lawyers, Doctors and Others.* London: Macmillan, 1983.

Dracobly, Alexander F. "Disciplining the Doctor: Medical Morality and Professionalism in Nineteenth-Century France." Ph.D. diss., University of Chicago, 1996.

Dreifuss, Jean Jacques. "Les premières étudiantes à la Faculté de médecine et leurs activités professionnelles à Génève." *Gesnerus* 48, nos. 3–4 (1991): 429–438.

Le droit antisémite de Vichy, Paris: Seuil (Le genre humain), 1996.

Drouard, Alain. *Alexis Carrel (1873–1944): de la mémoire à l'histoire.* Paris: L'Harmattan, 1995.

Dubois, Marc. *Que deviendront les étudiants? Étude sur le chômage des jeunes diplômés.* Edited by Comité d'entente des grandes associations internationales. Paris: Receuil Sirey, 1937.

Duhamel, Pierre. *Histoire des médecins français.* Paris: Plon, 1993.

du Pouget, Marc. "Les juridictions d'exception de la période de l'occupation et de la libération à Lyon." *Cahiers d'histoire* 39, nos. 3–4 (1994): 221–229.

Dupuy, Paul. "Du charlatanisme médical et de sa répression." Medical diss., Université de Bordeaux, 1929.

Durand, Bernard, Jean-Pierre Le Crom, and Alessandro Somma, eds. *Le droit sous Vichy.* Frankfurt am Main: Vittorio Klostermann, 2006.

Durand, Isabelle. "Les médecins ministres dans les gouvernements français de 1871 à 1958." Medical diss., Université de Paris René Descartes, 1985.

Durand Lepine, Gaetane. "La liberté d'établissement et de prestation de services des avocats étrangers en France." Law diss., Université de Paris 2, 1993.

Duveau, Gaston. "De la protection du titre d'avocat." Law diss., Université de Paris, 1913.

Duverger, Maurice. "La situation des fonctionnaires depuis la Révolution de 1940." *Revue de droit public et de science politique* (1940–41): 277–539.

Ellis, Jack D. *The Physician-Legislators of France: Medicine and Politics in the Early Third Republic, 1870–1914.* Cambridge: Cambridge University Press, 1990.

Estournet, Rémy. "De la pratique de la naturalisation depuis la loi du 10 août 1927." Law diss., Université de Montpellier, 1937.

Evleth, Donna. "The 'Romanian Privilege' in French Medicine and Anti-Semitism." *Journal of the Society for the Social History of Medicine* 11, no. 2 (1998): 213–232.

——. "Vichy France and the Continuity of Medical Nationalism." *Journal of the Society for the Social History of Medicine* 8, no. 1 (April 1995): 95–116.

Fabre, Martine. "La doctrine sous Vichy." In Durand, Le Crom, and Somma, *Le droit sous Vichy,* 375–401.

Fairchild, Amy Lauren. *Science at the Borders: Immigrant Medical Inspection and the Shaping of the Modern Industrial Labor Force.* Baltimore: Johns Hopkins University Press, 2003.

Faivre, Albin. "Aspect médical et social du problème des étrangers en France." Medical diss., Université de Paris, 1939.

Fauré, Christine. "Femmes et citoyenneté en France." In *Citoyenneté et nationalité: perspectives en France et au Québec,* edited by Dominique Colas, Claude Emeri, and Jacques Zylberberg, 111–121. Paris: Presses universitaires de France, 1991.

Fette, Julie. "Apology and the Past in Contemporary France." *French Politics, Culture, and Society* 26, no. 2 (Summer 2008): 78–113.

——. "Pride and Prejudice in the Professions: Women Doctors and Lawyers in Third Republic France." *Journal of Women's History* 19, no. 3 (Fall 2007): 60–86.

Filippi, M. F. "Les interdictions professionnelles sous le régime de Vichy." Mémoire de DEA, Université de Lyon 2, 1994.

Fillon, Catherine. *Le barreau de Lyon dans la tourmente: de l'occupation à la libération.* Lyon: Aléas, 2003.

——. *Histoire du barreau de Lyon sous la Troisième République.* Lyon: Aléas, 1995.

——. "La profession d'avocat et son image pendant l'entre-deux-guerres." Ph.D. diss., Université de Lyon 3, 1995.

——. "Le Tribunal d'État, Section de Lyon (1941–1944): contribution à l'histoire des juridictions d'exception." *Histoire de la justice* 10 (1997): 193–222.

Fitzsimmons, Michael P. *The Parisian Order of Barristers and the French Revolution.* Cambridge: Harvard University Press, 1987.

Flexner, Abraham. *Medical Education: A Comparative Study.* New York: Macmillan, 1925.

Friteau, F. *Pages d'histoire vécue: l'exercice de la médecine et de l'art dentaire en France par des étrangers.* Paris: Dormann, 1935.

Garçon, Maurice. *Histoire de la justice sous la IIIe République.* 3 vols. Paris: Fayard, 1957.

Gardenat, Louis. *Traité de la profession d'avocat.* Paris: Éditions Godde, 1931.

Garnal, Paul. *Les excès de l'étatisme, les responsabilités de la médecine et les moyens d'y remédier.* Cahors: Coueslant, 1935.

Gaudemet, Yves-Henri. *Les juristes et la vie politique de la IIIe République.* Paris: Presses universitaires de France, 1970.

Gazier, François. "L'Ordre des médecins, 1940–1945." In *L'exercice médical dans la société hier, aujourd'hui, demain,* edited by L'Ordre national des médecins, 285–297. Paris: Masson, 1995.

Gazzaniga, J.-L., ed. *Histoire des avocats et du barreau de Toulouse du XVIIIe siècle à nos jours.* Toulouse: Privat, 1992.

Gervais de Lafond, Pierre-Georges-Gaston. "De l'étude et de l'exercice de la médecine en France par les étrangers." Medical diss., Université de Paris, 1934.

Gibney, Mark, and Erik Roxstrom, "The Status of State Apologies." *Human Rights Quarterly* 23, no. 4 (2001): 911–939.

Gill, Kathleen. "The Moral Functions of an Apology." *Philosophical Forum* 31, no. 1 (Spring 2000): 11–27.

Girard, Véronique. "Le barreau de Grenoble de l'occupation à la libération." In Association française pour l'histoire de la justice, *La justice de l'épuration, à la fin de la Seconde Guerre mondiale,* 183–200.

Gleizal, J. J. "La formation des juristes dans l'État français." *Procès: cahiers d'analyse politique et juridique* 3 (1979): 50–78.

Goblot, Edmond. *La barrière et le niveau: étude sociologique sur la bourgeoisie française moderne.* Paris: Armand Colin, 1925.

Godt, Paul J. "Confrontation, Consent, and Corporatism: State Strategies and the Medical Profession in France, Great Britain, and West Germany." *Journal of Health Politics, Policy, and Law* 12, no. 3 (Fall 1987): 459–479.

Goubert, Jean-Pierre. "L'art de guérir: médecine savante et médecine populaire dans la France de 1790." *Annales: économies, sociétés, civilisations* 32, no. 5 (September–October 1977): 908–926.

——. "The Extent of Medical Practice in France around 1780." In Branca, *Medicine Show,* 211–228.

——. *Initiation à une nouvelle histoire de la médecine.* Paris: Ellipses, 1998.

Green, Nancy. "L'émigration comme émancipation: les femmes juives d'Europe de l'est à Paris, 1881–1914." *Pluriel* 27 (1981): 51–59.

Grélon, André, ed. *Les ingénieurs de la crise: titre et profession entre les deux guerres.* Paris: Éditions de l'Ecole des hautes études en sciences sociales, 1986.

Grimes, John M. "'Une et Indivisible'—The Reform of the Legal Profession in France: The Effect on U.S. Attorneys." *New York University Journal of International Law and Politics* 24 (1992): 1757–93.

Groopman, Leonard Charles. "The Internat des Hôpitaux de Paris: The Shaping and the Transformation of the French Medical Elite, 1802–1914." Ph.D. diss., Harvard University, 1986.

Gros, Dominique. "Le droit antisémite de Vichy contre la tradition républicaine." In *Juger sous Vichy,* 17–27.

——. "Peut-on parler d'un 'droit antisémite'?" In *Le droit antisémite de Vichy,* 13–44.

——. "Le 'statut des juifs' et les manuels en usage dans les facultés de droit." *Cultures & Conflits* 9–10 (1993): 154–171.

Guérin, Paul. "Contribution à la défense de la profession médicale: l'État contre le médecin; vers une renaissance corporative." Medical diss., Université de Paris, 1928.

Guichard, Eric. "Manières de voir, manières de compter dans les recensements de 1931 et 1936." In Guichard and Noiriel, *Construction des nationalités et immigration,* 71–98.

Guichard, Eric, and Gérard Noiriel, eds. *Construction des nationalités et immigration dans la France contemporaine.* Paris: Presses de l'École normale supérieure, 1997.

Guillaume, Pierre. "Du bon usage des immigrés en temps de crise et de guerre, 1932–1940." *Vingtième siècle* 7 (July–September 1985): 117–26.

——. "Modalités et enjeux de la professionnalisation." In *La professionnalisation des classes moyennes,* edited by Pierre Guillaume, 9–15. Bordeaux: Éditions de la Maison des sciences de l'homme d'Aquitaine, 1996.

——. "La préhistoire de l'Ordre des médecins." In *L'exercice médical dans la société hier, aujourd'hui, demain,* edited by L'Ordre national des médecins. Paris: Masson, 1995.

Haas, Albert. *The Doctor and the Damned.* New York: St. Martin's Press, 1984.

Hakki Eldem, Sadi. "Le statut des magistrats: recrutement." Law diss., Université de Paris, 1940.

Halioua, Bruno. *Blouses blanches, étoiles jaunes.* Paris: Liana Levi, 2000.

——. "La xénophobie et l'antisémitisme dans le milieu médical sous l'Occupation vus au travers du *Concours Médical.*" *Médecine/Sciences* 19, no. 1 (January 2003): 107–15.

Halpérin, Jean-Louis, ed. *Avocats et notaires en Europe: les professions judiciaires et juridiques dans l'histoire contemporaine.* Droit et société. Paris: Librairie générale de droit et de jurisprudence, 1996.

——. "La législation de Vichy relative aux avocats et aux droits de la défense." *Revue historique* 579 (July–September 1991): 143–56.

——. "Les sources statistiques de l'histoire des avocats en France au XVIIIe et au XIXe siècles." *Revue de la société internationale d'histoire de la profession d'avocat* 3 (1991): 55–74.

Hamburger, Maurice. *La robe noir, ou la tradition libérale de l'Ordre des avocats.* Paris: Presses Modernes, 1937.

Harari, Aby. "Situation de l'apatride et du réfugié dans la législation française actuelle." Law diss., Université de Paris, 1940.

Hassenteufel, Patrick. *Les médecins face à l'État: une comparaison européenne.* Paris: Presses de Sciences Po, 1997.

——. "Vers le déclin du 'pouvoir médical'? Un éclairage européen, France, Allemagne, Grande-Bretagne." *Pouvoir* 89 (1999): 51–64.

Hatzfeld, Henri. *Le grand tournant de la médecine libérale.* Paris: Éditions Ouvrières, 1963.

Hellery, Louis. "Des rapports entre l'Ordre des médecins et l'État." Medical diss., Université de Paris, 1941.

Heraud, M. *Pierre Masse.* Paris: Calmann-Lévy, 1947.

Hermon, Henri. "À propos du remplacement médical en général et du remplacement à la campagne en particulier." Medical diss., Université de Paris, 1942.

Herscovici, S. "De l'influence médicale française en Roumanie." Medical diss., Université de Paris, 1933.

Herzlich, Claudine. "The Evolution of Relations between French Physicians and the State from 1880 to 1980." *Sociology of Health and Illness* 4, no. 3 (1982): 241–253.

Herzlich, Claudine, Martine Bungener, and Geneviève Paicheler, eds. *Cinquante ans d'exercice de la médecine en France: carrières et pratiques des médecins français, 1930–1980.* Paris: Éditions INSERM, 1993.

Hesse, Raymond. *Quarante ans de palais.* Paris: Peyronnet, 1950.

Hewitt, Nicholas. *The Life of Céline: A Critical Biography.* Oxford: Blackwell, 1999.

Hildreth, Martha. *Doctors, Bureaucrats, and Public Health in France, 1888–1902.* New York: Garland, 1987.

———. "Medical Rivalries and Medical Politics in France: The Physicians' Union Movement and the Medical Assistance Law of 1893." *Journal of the History of Medicine and Allied Sciences* 42 (1987): 5–29.

Hubscher, Ronald. "L'invention d'une profession: les vétérinaires au XIXe siècle." *Revue d'histoire moderne et contemporaine* 43–44 (October–December 1996): 686–708.

Huerkamp, Claudia. "The Making of the Modern Medical Profession, 1800–1914: Prussian Doctors in the Nineteenth Century." In Cocks and Jarausch, *German Professions, 1800–1950,* 66–84.

Huss, Marie-Monique. "Pronatalism in the Inter-war Period in France." *Journal of Contemporary History* 25 (1990): 39–68

Iancu, C. *Les juifs en Roumanie (1919–1938): de l'émancipation à la marginalisation.* Paris: E. Peters, 1996.

Iannucci, Ugo. "L'attitude du barreau de Lyon pendant l'occupation." In Association française pour l'histoire de la justice, *La justice des années sombres, 1940–1945,* 167–178.

Isorni, Jacques. *Mémoires, 1911–1945.* Paris: Robert Laffont, 1984.

Israël, Liora. "La défense accusée: l'épuration professionelle des avocats." In Baruch, *Une poignée de misérables,* 204–228.

———. "L'épuration des barreaux français après la Seconde Guerre mondiale: une socio-histoire fragmentaire." Report submitted to the Groupe d'intérêt public—Mission de recherche droit et justice (Ministère de la Justice), January 2004. www.gip-recherche-justice.fr/recherches/syntheses/110-epuration- barreaux.pdf.

———. *Robes noires, années sombres: avocats et magistrats en résistance pendant la Seconde Guerre mondiale.* Paris: Fayard, 2005.

Jarausch, Konrad. *The Unfree Professions: German Lawyers, Teachers, and Engineers, 1900–1950.* New York: Oxford University Press, 1990.

Joly, Laurent. "L'entrée de l'antisémitisme sur la scène parlementaire française: le débat sur 'l'infiltration juive' à la Chambre en mai 1895." *Archives juives* 38, no. 1 (2005): 114–128.

———. *Vichy dans la "solution finale": histoire du Commissariat général aux questions juives, 1941–1944.* Paris: Grasset, 2006

———. *Xavier Vallat: du nationalisme chrétien à l'antisémitisme d'État.* Paris: Grasset, 2001.

Jonas, S. *Cent portraits de médecins illustrés.* Paris: Masson, 1961.

Jones, Colin. "Montpellier Medical Students and the Medicalisation of 18th-Century France." In *Problems and Methods in the History of Medicine,* edited by Roy Porter and Andrew Wear, 57–80. London: Croom Helm, 1987.

Juger sous Vichy, Paris: Seuil (Le genre humain), 1994.

Julia, Dominique, and Jacques Revel, eds. *Histoire sociale des populations étudiantes.* Vol. 2. Paris: Éditions de l'École des hautes études en sciences sociales, 1989.

Karady, Victor. "Les universités de la Troisième République." In *Histoire des universités en France,* edited by Jacques Verger, 323–366. Paris: Privat, 1986.

Karady, Victor, and Istvan Kemeny. "Antisémitisme universitaire et concurrence de classe: la loi du *numerus clausus* en Hongrie entre les deux guerres." *Actes de la recherche en sciences sociales* 34, no. 34 (September 1980): 67–96.

Karpik, Lucien. *Les avocats: entre l'État, le public et le marché, XIIIe–XXe siècle.* Paris: Gallimard, 1995.

——. "Démocratie et pouvoir au barreau de Paris: la question du gouvernement privé." *Revue française de science politique* 4 (August 1986): 496–518.

——. "La profession libérale, un cas, le barreau." In *Les lieux de mémoire,* edited by Pierre Nora, vol. 3, 284–321. Paris: Gallimard, 1992.

——. "Que faire de la singularité?" *Revue trimestrielle du ressort de la Cour d'appel de Versailles* 16–17 (January–July 1990): 13–28.

——. "Technical and Political Knowledge: The Relationship of Lawyers and Other Legal Professions to the Market and the State." In *The Formation of the Professions: Knowledge, State and Strategy,* edited by Rolf Torstendahl and Michael Burrage, 186–197. London: Sage, 1990.

Kater, Michael H. *Doctors under Hitler.* Chapel Hill: University of North Carolina Press, 1989.

Katz, Jacob. "Misreadings of Antisemitism." *Commentary* 76 (July 1983): 39–44.

Kessedjian, Catherine. "Le juif déchu de la nationalité française." In *Le droit antisémite de Vichy,* 231–242.

Kimble, Sara. "Justice Redressed: Women, Citizenship, and the Social Uses of the Law in Modern France, 1890–1939." Ph.D. diss., University of Iowa, 2002.

——. "No Right to Judge: Feminism and the Judiciary in Third Republic France." *French Historical Studies* 31, no. 4 (Fall 2008): 609–641.

Kingston, Paul J. *Antisemitism in France during the 1930s: Organization, Personalities and Propaganda.* Hull: University of Hull Press, 1983.

Knibiehler, Yvonne, and Catherine Fouquet. *La femme et les médecins: analyse historique.* Paris: Hachette, 1983.

Knobel, Marc. "L'élimination des juristes juifs en Europe à partir de 1933." *Cahiers Bernard Lazare* 125–126 (1990): 139–151.

——. "George Montandon et l'ethno-racisme." In Taguieff, *L'antisémitisme de plume, 1940–1944,* 277–293.

Koos, Cheryl A. "Gender, Anti-Individualism, and Nationalism: The Alliance Nationale and the Pronatalist Backlash against the *Femme Moderne,* 1933–1940." *French Historical Studies* 19, no. 3 (Spring 1996): 699–723.

Kovacs, Maria M. "Luttes professionnelles et antisémitisme: chronique de la montée du fascisme dans le corps médical hongrois, 1920–1944." *Actes de la recherche en sciences sociales* 56 (March 1985): 31–44.

Kraemer-Bach, Marcelle. *Les inégalités légales entre l'homme et la femme.* Paris: Presses universitaires de France, 1927.

——. *La longue route.* Paris: Pensée Universelle, 1988.

Laborie, Pierre. *L'opinion française sous Vichy.* Paris: Seuil, 1990.

Lafarge, François. "Les avocats dans les cabinets ministériels à la veille de la guerre de 1914." In Le Béguec, *Avocats et barreaux en France, 1910–1930,* 91–102.

Lagrave, Rose-Marie. "Une émancipation sous tutelle: éducation et travail des femmes au XXe siècle; Travail ou famille, quelle patrie pour les femmes? (1918–1945)." In *Histoire des femmes,* edited by Georges Duby and Michèle Perrot, 431–443. Paris: Plon, 1992.

Lagrée, Michel, and François Lebrun, eds. *Pour l'histoire de la médecine: autour de l'oeuvre de Jacques Léonard.* Paris: Presses universitaires de Rennes, 1994.

Laguerre, Bernard. "Les dénaturalisés de Vichy, 1940–1944." *Vingtième siècle* 20 (1988): 3–15.

Larson, Magali Sarfatti. *The Rise of Professionalism: A Sociological Analysis.* Berkeley: University of California Press, 1977.

Laval-Reviglio, Marie-Claire. "Parlementaires xénophobes et antisémites sous la IIIe République: débats relatifs à la nationalité et à la 'protection du travail national.'" In *Le droit antisémite de Vichy,* 85–114.

Le Béguec, Gilles. "L'aristocratie du barreau, vivier pour la République: les secrétaires de la Conférence du stage." *Vingtième siècle* 30, no. 30 (April–June 1991): 22–31.

———, ed. *Avocats et barreaux en France, 1910–1930.* Nancy: Presses universitaires de Nancy, 1994.

———. "Les avocats et la naissance des parties politiques organisés (1888–1903)." *Histoire de la justice* 5 (1992): 171–188.

———. "Un conservatoire parlementaire: la conférence Molé-Tocqueville à la fin de la IIIe République." *Bulletin de la Société d'histoire moderne* 2 (1984): 16–23.

———. "L'entrée au Palais Bourbon: les filières privilégiées d'accès à la fonction parlementaire, 1919–1939." Ph.D. diss., Université de Paris X, 1989.

———. *La République des avocats.* Paris: Armand Colin, 2003.

Leca, Jean. "Individualisme et citoyenneté." In *Sur l'individualisme,* edited by Pierre Birnbaum and Jean Leca, 159–209. Paris: Presses universitaires de France, 1986.

Lécuyer, Carole. "Une nouvelle figure de la jeune fille sous la IIIe République: l'étudiante," *CLIO* 4 (1996): 166–176.

Lemay, Edna Hindie. "Thomas Hérier, A Country Surgeon outside Angoulême at the End of the XVIIIth Century: A Contribution to Social History." In Branca, *Medicine Show,* 229–242.

Léonard, Jacques. "Le corps médical au début de la IIIe République." In Poirier and Poirier, *Médecine et philosophie à la fin du XIXe siècle,* 9–21.

———. "L'exemple d'une catégorie socio-professionnelle au XIXe siècle: les médecins français." In *Ordres et classes,* edited by Daniel Roche and Camille-Ernest Labrousse, 221–234. Paris: École pratique des hautes études, 1967.

———. "Les guérisseurs en France au XIXe siècle." *Revue d'histoire moderne et contemporaine* 27 (July–September 1980): 501–516.

———. *La médecine entre les savoirs et les pouvoirs.* Paris: Aubier-Montaigne, 1981.

———. *La vie quotidienne du médecin de province au XIXe siècle.* Paris: Hachette, 1977.

———. "Women, Religion, and Medicine." In *Medicine and Society in France: Selections from the Annales ESC,* edited by Robert Forster and Orest Ranum, 24–47. Baltimore: Johns Hopkins University Press, 1980.

Leroux-Hugon, Véronique. "L'infirmière au début du XXe siècle: nouveau métier et tâches traditionelles." *Le mouvement social* 140 (July–September 1987): 55–68.

Lesourd, Céline. "L'épuration des médecins." In Baruch, *Une poignée de misérables,* 336–367.

Le Van, Kim. "Féminisme et travail féminin dans les doctrines et dans les faits." Ph.D. diss., Université de Paris, 1926.

Lewis, Mary Dewhurst. *The Boundaries of the Republic: Migrant Rights and the Limits of Universalism in France, 1918–1940*. Stanford: Stanford University Press, 2007.

"L'exclusion des juifs de la magistrature et du barreau." *Juger* 6–7, special issue, *Justice et barbarie, 1940–1944* (1994): 36–41.

Lipinska, Mélina. *Les femmes et le progrès des sciences médicales*. Paris: Masson, 1930.

———. *Histoire des femmes médecins depuis l'antiquité jusqu'à nos jours*. Paris: G. Jacques, 1900.

Livian, Marcel. *Le regime juridique des étrangers en France*. Paris: Pichon et Durand-Auzias, 1936.

Lobin, Yvette. "Les tendances nationalistes de notre système français de droit international privé." Law diss., Université d'Aix, 1937.

Lochak, Danièle. "La doctrine sous Vichy ou les mésaventures du positivisme." In Centre universitaire de recherches administratives et politiques de Picardie, *Les usages sociaux du droit*, 252–285.

———. "Écrire, se taire…Réflexions sur l'attitude de la doctrine française." In *Le droit antisémite de Vichy*, 433–462.

———. "Le juge doit-il appliquer une loi inique?" In *Juger sous Vichy*, 29–39.

Longuet, Robert-Jean. *L'avocat: Comment on le devient? Avantages et inconvenient*. Collection choisissez votre profession. Paris: Éditions Bernardin Béchet, 1932.

Loquin, Eric. "Le juif 'incapable.'" In *Le droit antisémite de Vichy*, 173–188.

Lubetzki, J. *La condition des juifs en France sous l'occupation allemande, 1940–1944*. Paris: Centre de documentation juive contemporaine, 1945.

Maga, Timothy P. "Closing the Door: The French Government and Refugee Policy, 1933–1939." *French Historical Studies* 12, no. 3 (1982): 424–442.

Malatesta, Maria, ed. *Society and the Professions in Italy, 1860–1914*. Cambridge: Cambridge University Press, 1995.

Malino, Frances, and Bernard Wasserstein, eds. *The Jews in Modern France*. Hanover, NH: University Press of New England for Brandeis University Press, 1985.

Manitakis, Nicholas. "L'essor de la mobilité étudiante internationale à l'âge des États-Nations, une étude de cas: les étudiants grecs en France (1880–1940)." Ph.D. diss., École des hautes études en sciences sociales, 2004.

———. "Étudiants étrangers, universités françaises et marché du travail intellectuel (fin du XIXe-années 1930)." In Guichard and Noiriel, *Construction des nationalités et immigration*, 123–154.

Marcou, Jean. "Le Conseil d'État: juge administratif sous Vichy." In *Juger sous Vichy*, 83–96.

Marquiset, Jean. *Les gens de justice dans la littérature*. Paris: Librairie générale de droit et de jurisprudence, 1967.

Marrus, Michael. "Les juristes de Vichy dans 'l'engrenage de la destruction.'" In *Le droit antisémite de Vichy*, 47–54.

———. *The Unwanted: European Refugees in the Twentieth Century*. New York: Oxford University Press, 1985.

———. "Vichy before Vichy: Antisemitic Currents in France during the 1930s." *Wiener Library Bulletin* 33, n.s., nos. 51 and 52 (1980): 13–20.

Marrus, Michael, and Robert Paxton. *Vichy France and the Jews*. New York: Schocken Books, 1981.

Martin, Benjamin. "The Courts, the Magistrature, and Promotions in Third Republic France, 1871–1914." *American Historical Review* 87, no. 4 (1982): 977–1009.

——. *Crime and Criminal Justice under the Third Republic*. Baton Rouge: Louisiana State University Press, 1990.

Martinez, Gilles. "Joseph Barthélemy et la crise de la démocratie libérale." *Vingtième siècle* 59 (July–September 1998): 28–47.

Massot, Jean. "Le Conseil d'État et le régime de Vichy." *Vingtième siècle* 58 (April–June 1998): 83–99.

Maupas, Jacques. *La nouvelle législation française sur la nationalité (déchéances, révision des naturalisations, accès aux fonctions publiques et carrières libérales, femmes mariées)*. Issoudun: Éditions Internationales, 1941.

Mayeur, Françoise. *L'enseignement secondaire des jeunes filles sous la Troisième République*. Paris: Presses de la Fondation nationale des sciences politiques, 1977.

——. "Women and Elites from the Nineteenth to the Twentieth Century." In *Elites in France: Origins, Reproduction, and Power*, edited by Jolyon Howorth and Philip G. Cerny. New York: St. Martin's Press, 1981.

McClelland, Charles E. *The German Experience of Professionalizaton: Modern Learned Professions and Their Organization from the Early Nineteenth Century to the Hitler Era*. Cambridge: Cambridge University Press, 1991.

Mendelsohn, Ezra. *The Jews of East Central Europe between the Wars*. Bloomington: Indiana University Press, 1983.

Mestre, Achille. "*Études et étudiants (chroniques du Figaro)*. Paris: Dalloz, 1928.

Miaille, Michel. "Sur l'enseignement des Facultés de droit en France: les réformes de 1905, 1922, et 1954." *Procès: cahiers d'analyse politique et juridique* 3 (1979): 78–107.

Milet, Marc. *La Faculté de droit de Paris face à la vie politique: de l'affaire Scelle à l'affaire Jèze, 1925–1936*. Paris: Librairie générale de droit et de jurisprudence, 1996.

Milliez, Paul. *Médecin de la liberté*. Paris: Seuil, 1980.

Millman, Richard. *La question juive entre les deux guerres: ligues de droite et antisémitisme en France*. Paris: Armand Colin, 1992.

Minkowski, Alexandre. *Mémoires turbulents*. Paris: Plon, 1990.

Morand, René. "Considérations sur l'exercice illégal de la médecine par les magnétiseurs et les somnambules." Medical diss., Université de Paris, 1927.

Muel-Dreyfus, Francine. *Vichy et l'éternel féminin: contribution à une sociologie politique de l'ordre des corps*. Paris: Seuil, 1996.

Nahum, Henri. *La médecine française et les juifs, 1930–1945*. Paris: L'Harmattan, 2006.

Nataf, Claude. "L'exclusion des avocats juifs en Tunisie pendant la Seconde Guerre mondiale." *Archives juives* 41, no. 1 (2008): 90–107.

Noiriel, Gérard. *Le creuset français: histoire de l'immigration XIXe–XX siècles*. Paris: Seuil, 1988.

——. *État, nation et immigration*. Paris: Belin, 2001.

——. *Les origines républicaines de Vichy*. Paris: Hachette, 1999.

——. *La tyrannie du national: le droit d'asile en Europe, 1793–1993*. Paris: Calmann-Lévy, 1991.

Nord, Philip. *Paris Shopkeepers and the Politics of Resentment*. Princeton: Princeton University Press, 1986.

Nordmann, Joë, and Anne Brunel. *Aux vents de l'histoire*. Arles: Actes Sud, 1996.

Nye, Mary Jo. *Sciences in the Provinces: Scientific Communities and Provincial Leadership in France, 1860–1930*. Berkeley: University of California Press, 1986.

Nye, Robert A. *Crime, Madness, and Politics in Modern France: The Medical Concept of National Decline.* Princeton: Princeton University Press, 1984.

———. "Honor Codes and Medical Ethics in Modern France." *Bulletin of the History of Medicine* 69 (1995): 91–111.

———. "The Legacy of Masculine Codes of Honor and Admission of Women to the Medical Profession in the Nineteenth Century." In *Women Physicians and the Cultures of Medicine,* edited by Ellen S. More, Elizabeth Fee, and Manon Parry, 141–159. Baltimore: Johns Hopkins University Press.

———. *Masculinity and Male Codes of Honor in Modern France.* Oxford: Oxford University Press, 1993.

———. "Medicine and Science as Masculine 'Fields of Honor.'" *Osiris* 12 (1997): 60–79.

Nye, Robert A., and Anaïs Bokobza. "Médecins, éthique médicale et État en France, 1789–1947." *Le mouvement social* 214 (January–March 2006): 19–36.

Offen, Karen. "The Second Sex and the Baccalaureat in Republican France, 1880–1924." *French Historical Studies* 13, no. 2 (1983): 252–286.

Ory, Pascal. "L'université française face à la persécution antisémite." In *La France et la question juive, 1940–1944: actes du colloque du Centre de documentation juive contemporaine,* edited by CDJC. Paris: Sylvie Messinger, 1981.

———. "Why Be So Cruel? Some Modest Proposals to Cure the Vichy Syndrome." In *France at War: Vichy and the Historians,* edited by Sarah Fishman, Laura Lee Downs, Ioannis Sinanoglou, Leonard V. Smith, and Robert Zaretsky, 275–284. Oxford: Berg, 2000.

Oudin, A. *L'Ordre des médecins.* Paris: Éditions de la Nouvelle France, 1941.

Ozanam, Yves. "Le barreau de Paris pendant la Seconde Guerre mondiale, 1940–1945." In Association française pour l'histoire de la justice, *La justice des années sombres, 1940–1945,* 145–165.

———. "De Vichy à la Résistance: le bâtonnier Jacques Charpentier." In Association française pour l'histoire de la justice, *La justice de l'épuration,* 153–69.

———. "L'épuration professionnelle au Barreau de Paris (1944–1951)," *Gazette du Palais* 72–73 (13–14 March 2002): 3–23.

———. "L'Ordre des avocats à la Cour de Paris de 1910 à 1930." In Le Béguec, *Avocats et barreaux en France 1910–1930,* 35–57.

———. "Les projets de suppression de l'Ordre des avocats et de réforme de la profession avant 1914: étude des propositions de loi soumises à la Chambre entre 1886 et 1910." *Revue de la société internationale d'histoire de la profession d'avocat* 6 (1994): 219–242.

———. "L'U.J.A. de Paris dans les archives." *Bulletin de l'Union des jeunes avocats de Paris (UJA), 75e anniversaire, 1922–1997* (March 1997): 24–33.

Paxton, Robert. *Vichy France: Old Guard and New Order, 1940–1944.* New York: Columbia University Press, 1982.

Payen, Fernand. *Le barreau et la langue française.* Paris: Grasset, 1939.

———. *La justice en danger.* Paris: Plon, 1937.

Payen, Fernand, and Gaston Duveau. *Les règles de la profession d'avocat et les usages du barreau de Paris.* Paris: A. Pedone, 1926.

Péan, Pierre. *Une jeunesse française: François Mitterrand, 1934–1947.* Paris: Fayard, 1994.

Pécout, Jean. "L'étude et l'exercice de la médecine par les étrangers." Law diss., Université d'Aix-Marseille, 1939.

Pelisse, J. M. "Les origines du syndicalisme médical en France, 1850–1900." Medical diss., Université de Paris, 1971.

Pellinghelli Steiche, Sylvie. "L'évolution de la profession libérale: l'exemple des professions juridiques et médicales." Ph.D. diss., Université de Nice, 1995.

Péraud, Jeanne. "La femme médecin en Afrique du Nord et son rôle d'éducatrice." Medical diss., Université de Bordeaux, 1932.

Peschanski, Denis. "Exclusion, persécution, répression." In *Le régime de Vichy et les Français,* edited by Jean-Pierre Azéma and François Bédarida, 209–234. Paris: Fayard, 1992.

———. "Vichy 1940–1944." In *21 historiens expliquent la France contemporaine,* edited by Dominique Borne and Maurice Agulhon, 181–196. Paris: Documentation française, 2005.

Peter, Jean-Pierre, and Jacques Revel. "Le corps: l'homme malade et son histoire." In *Faire de l'histoire,* edited by Jacques Le Goff and Pierre Nora, 169–191. Paris: Gallimard, 1974.

Peters, Dolores. "Vichy, the Ordre des Médecins, and French Medical Men's Return to Republicanism, 1940–1944." Paper presented at the Society for French Historical Studies, Wilmington, DE, March 24–26, 1994.

Pfefferkorn, R. "Alexis Carrel: vulgarisateur de l'eugénisme et promoteur de 'l'aristocratie biologique.'" *L'Information psychiatrique* 73, no. 2 (February 1997): 123–128.

Pinon, Louis. "Les problèmes médicaux de l'immigration." Medical diss., Université de Paris, 1938.

Plas, Pascal. "La professionnalisation des avocats au début des années vingt: enjeux, ruptures et nouveaux modèles." In Le Béguec, *Avocats et Barreaux en France, 1910–1930,* 59–76.

Poirier, Jacques, and R. Nahon. "L'accession des femmes à la carrière médicale (à la fin du XIXe siècle)." In Poirier and Poirier, *Médecine et philosophie à la fin du XIXe siècle,* 23–46.

Poirier, Jacques, and Jean-Louis Poirier, eds. *Médecine et philosophie á la fin du XIXe siècle.* Special issue of Cahier de l'Institut de recherche universitaire d'histoire de la connaissance, des idées et des mentalités, Créteil, Université de Paris XII 2 (1981).

Poliakov, Léon. *Histoire de l'antisémitisme.* Paris: Hachette, 1981.

Portmann, Georges. *Georges Portmann, son action parlementaire, scientifique, sociale.* Bordeaux: Delmas, 1955.

Poznanski, Renée. *Les juifs en France pendant la Seconde Guerre mondiale.* Paris: Hachette, 1997.

Proctor, Robert. *Racial Hygiene: Medicine under the Nazis.* Cambridge: Harvard University Press, 1988.

Prost, Antoine. *Histoire de l'enseignement en France, 1800–1967.* Paris: Armand Colin, 1968.

———. "Jeunesse et société dans la France de l'entre-deux-guerres." *Vingtième siècle* 13 (January–March 1987): 35–43.

"Le protectionnisme des intellectuels." *Plein droit: la revue du Gisti* 29–30 (November 1995): 15.

Quemin, Alain. "Un diplôme, pour quoi faire? Coûts et bénéfices des examens comme instruments de fermeture des groupes professionnels: l'exemple des commissaires-priseurs." *Droit et société* 36–37 (1997): 345–362.

Querrioux, Fernand. *La médecine et les juifs.* Paris: Nouvelles Éditions Françaises, 1940.

Ramsey, Matthew. "Medical Power and Popular Medicine: Illegal Healers in Nineteenth-Century France." In Branca, *Medicine Show*, 183–210.

———. "The Politics of Professional Monopoly in Nineteenth-Century Medicine: The French Model and Its Rivals." In *Professions and the French State, 1700–1900,* edited by Gerald Geison, 225–305. Philadelphia: University of Pennsylvania Press, 1984.

———. *Professional and Popular Medicine in France, 1770–1830: The Social World of Medical Practice.* New York: Cambridge University Press, 1988.

———. "Sous le régime de la législation de 1803: trois enquêtes sur les charlatans au XIXe siècle." *Revue d'histoire moderne et contemporaine* 27 (July–September 1980): 485–500.

Reggiani, Andrés Horacio. *God's Eugenicist: Alexis Carrel and the Sociobiology of Decline.* New York: Berghahn, 2007.

Remarque, Erich Maria. *Arch of Triumph.* New York: D. Appleton-Century Company, 1945.

Rémy, Dominique. *Les lois de Vichy.* Paris: Romillat, 1992.

Revel, Jacques. "Les corps et communautés." In *The French Revolution and the Creation of Modern Political Culture,* edited by Keith Michael Baker, 225–242. Oxford: Pergamon Press, 1987.

Reynaud Paligot, Carole. *Races, racisme et antiracisme dans les années 1930.* Paris: Presses universitaires de France, 2007.

Rieutort, Elie. "Le charlatanisme danger social." Medical diss., Université de Paris, 1928.

Ropert-Précloux, Anne-Françoise. "Qu'enseignait-on à la Faculté de droit de Paris? Corporatisme et antisémitisme dans les cours et ouvrages (1940–1944)." In *Le droit antisémite de Vichy,* 413–432.

Rousso, Henry. *Le syndrome de Vichy.* Paris: Seuil, 1987.

———. *Vichy: l'événement, la mémoire, l'histoire.* Paris: Gallimard, 2001.

Roux, Aline. *Contribution à l'étude de la feminisation de la profession médicale: quelques réflexions sur l'image du médecin au travers de l'évolution historique et psycho-sociologique de la condition de la femme.* Paris: Masson, 1974.

Royer, Jean-Pierre. *Histoire de la justice en France de la monarchie absolue à la République.* Paris: Presses universitaires de France, 1996.

Royer, Jean-Pierre, Renée Martinage, and Pierre Lecocq. *Juges et notables au 19e siècle.* Paris: Presses universitaires de France, 1983.

Rozoy, Jean-Georges. "Le malthusianisme médical, mésure de regression sociale." Medical diss., Université de Paris, 1950.

Ryan, Donna F. *The Holocaust and the Jews of Marseille.* Urbana: University of Illinois Press, 1996.

Sahlins, Peter. *Unnaturally French: Foreign Citizens in the Old Regime and After.* Ithaca: Cornell University Press, 2004.

Sarraute, Nathalie. *Enfance.* Paris: Gallimard, 1983.

Savage, John. "Advocates of the Republic: The Paris Bar and Legal Culture in Early Third Republic France, 1870–1914." Ph.D. diss., New York University, 1999.

———. "La Première Femme-Avocate: Gender, Bourgeois Culture, and the Legal Profession in Fin-de-Siècle France." Paper presented at the Luncheon Seminar, Institute of French Studies, New York University, 1999.

——. "The Problems of Wealth and Virtue: The Paris Bar and the Generation of the *Fin-de-Siècle*." In *Lawyers and Vampires: Cultural Histories of Legal Professions,* edited by W. Wesley Pue and David Sugarman, 171–210. Oxford: Hart Publishing, 2003.

——. "Profession libérale, libéralisme républicain: le barreau et la République, 1871–1904." In *Justice et république(s),* edited by Jacques Lorgnier, Renée Martinage, and Jean-Pierre Royer, 43–50. L'espace juridique. Hellemmes: ESTER, 1993.

——. "The Social Function of the Law Faculty: Demographics, Republican Reform, and Professional Training at the Paris Law Faculty, 1870–1914." *History of Education Quarterly* 48, no. 2 (May 2008): 221–243.

Sayad, Abdelmalek. "Naturels et naturalisés." *Actes de la recherche en sciences sociales* 99 (September 1993): 26–35.

Schittly, Marc. "Essai sur les médecins parlementaires en France de 1920 à 1940." Law diss., Université de Strasbourg, 1982.

Schneider, William. *Quality and Quantity: The Quest for Biological Regeneration in Twentieth-Century France.* Cambridge: Cambridge University Press, 1990.

Schor, Ralph. *L'antisémitisme en France pendant les années trente.* Paris: Éditions Complexe, 1992.

——. *Histoire de l'immigration: de la fin du XIXe siècle à nos jours.* Paris: Armand Colin, 1996.

——. *L'opinion française et les étrangers, 1919–1939.* Paris: Publications de la Sorbonne, 1985.

Schucker, Stephen A. "Origins of the 'Jewish Problem' in the Later Third Republic." In Malino and Wasserstein, *The Jews in Modern France,* 135–180.

Schultheiss, Katrin. "The Republican Nurse: Church, State, and Women's Work in France, 1880–1922." Ph.D. diss., Harvard University, 1994.

Senès, René. "Les conditions d'exercice de la médecine en France en temps de paix et en temps de guerre." Law diss., Université de Paris, 1939.

Shepard, Alexandra. "Seeking a Sense of Place: Jewish Students in the Dartmouth Community, 1920–1940." Senior honors thesis, Dartmouth College, 1992.

Sialleli, Jean-Baptiste. *Les avocats de 1920 à 1987, A.N.A.—R.N.A.F.—C.S.A.* Paris: Litec, 1987.

Siegrist, Hannes. "Public Office or Free Profession? German Attorneys in the Nineteenth and Early Twentieth Centuries." In Cocks and Jarausch, *German Professions, 1800–1950,* 46–65.

Simonin, Anne. "Le Comité médical de la Résistance: un succès différé." In *La Résistance, une histoire sociale,* edited by Antoine Prost, 159–178. Paris: Atelier, 1997.

Singer, Claude. "Les études médicales et la concurrence juive en France et en Algérie (1931–1941)." In *Les juifs et l'économique: miroirs et mirages,* edited by Chantal Benayoun, Alain Médam, and Pierre-Jacques Rojtman, 197–212. Toulouse: Presses universitaires du Mirail, 1992.

——. "Henri Labroue, ou l'apprentissage de l'antisémitisme." In Taguieff, *L'antisémitisme de plume, 1940–1944,* 233–244.

——. *L'université libérée, l'université épurée (1943–1947).* Paris: Belles Lettres, 1997.

——. *Vichy, l'université et les juifs.* Paris: Belles Lettres, 1992.

Sirinelli, Jean-François. "Action française: main basse sur le Quartier latin!" *Histoire* 51 (December 1982): 5–15.

Smet, Catherine. "Secularization and Syndicalization: The Rise of Professional Nursing in France, 1870–1914." Ph.D. diss., University of California, San Diego, 1997.

Smith, Timothy B. "The Social Transformation of Hospitals and the Rise of Medical Insurance in France, 1914–1943." *Historical Journal* 41, no. 4 (December 1998): 1055–87.

Starobinski, J. "La chaire, la tribune, le barreau." In *Les lieux de mémoire,* edited by Pierre Nora, vol. 2, 425–485. Paris: Gallimard, 1986.

Stephenson, Jill. "Women and the Professions in Germany, 1900–1945." In Cocks and Jarausch, *German Professions, 1800–1950,* 270–288.

Sternhell, Zeev. "The Roots of Popular Anti-Semitism in the Third Republic." In Malino and Wasserstein, *The Jews in Modern France,* 103–134.

Stone, Deborah. *The Limits of Professional Power: National Health Care in the Federal Republic of Germany.* Chicago: University of Chicago Press, 1980.

Suleiman, Ezra. *Private Power and Centralization in France: The Notaires and the State.* Princeton: Princeton University Press, 1987.

Sussman, George D. "The Glut of Doctors in Mid-Nineteenth-Century France." *Comparative Studies in Society and History* 19, no. 3 (1977): 287–304.

Taguieff, Pierre-André. *L'antisémitisme de plume, 1940–1944.* Paris: Berg, 1999.

———, ed. *Face au racisme.* Paris: La Découverte, 1991.

———. "La 'science' du docteur Martial, ou l'antisémitisme saisi par l''anthropo-biologie des races.'" In Taguieff, *L'antisémitisme de plume,* 295–332.

Tenenbaum, Joseph. "Nazi Rule in Poland and the Jewish Medical Profession." In *The Martyrdom of Jewish Physicians in Poland,* edited by Louis Falstein, 124–300. New York: Exposition Press, 1963.

Thalmann, Rita. "L'immigration allemande et l'opinion publique en France de 1933 à 1936." In *La France et l'Allemagne, 1932–1936,* 149–172. Paris: Éditions du CNRS, 1980.

Thébaud, Françoise. "Maternité et famille entre les deux guerres: idéologies et politique familiale." In *Femmes et fascismes,* edited by Rita Thalmann, 85–97. Paris: Tierce, 1986.

———. "Le mouvement nataliste dans la France de l'entre-deux-guerres: l'alliance nationale pour l'accroissement de la population française." *Revue d'histoire moderne et contemporaine* (April–June 1985): 276–301.

Tocqueville, Alexis de. *Democracy in America.* New York: Library of America, 2004.

Troper, Michel. "La doctrine et le positivisme." In Centre universitaire de recherches administratives et politiques de Picardie, *Les usages sociaux du droit,* 286–292.

Valeur, Robert. "Deux conceptions de l'enseignement juridique: les facultés françaises de sciences sociales; les écoles professionnelles de droit aux États-Unis; leur influence respective sur le système juridique national." Law diss., Université de Lyon, 1928.

Vallat, Xavier. *Le nez de Cléopâtre: souvenirs d'un homme de droite.* Paris: Éditions Les Quatre Fils Aymon, 1957.

Valvidia, Moisès N. "La défense des titres médicaux." Medical diss., Université de Paris, 1928.

Vergez, Bénédicte. "Internes et anciens internes des hôpitaux de Paris de 1918 à 1945." Ph.D. diss., Institut d'études politiques, 1995.

———. *Le monde des médecins au XXe siècle.* Paris: Éditions Complexe, 1996.

Vergez-Chaignon, Bénédicte. *Le docteur Ménétrel, éminence grise et confident du maréchal Pétain.* Paris: Perrin, 2001.

——. "Le syndicalisme médical français de sa naissance à sa refondation: intérêts et morale au pays de l'individualisme (1892–1945)." *Revue d'histoire moderne et contemporaine* 43–44 (October–December 1996): 709–734.

Verpeaux, Michel. "Le juif 'non citoyen.'" In *Le droit antisémite de Vichy,* 189–207.

Vidal-Naquet, Pierre. "Journal de Me Lucien Vidal-Naquet." *Annales: économies, sociétés, civilisations* (May–June 1993): 501–543.

——. *Mémoires: la brisure et l'attente, 1930–1955.* Paris: Seuil, 1995.

Voldman, Danièle. "Étude de cas: les architectes." In *Le régime de Vichy et les Français,* edited by Jean-Pierre Azéma and François Bédarida, 613–20. Paris: Fayard, 1992.

Volovici, Leon. *Nationalist Ideology and Antisemitism: The Case of Romanian Intellectuals in the 1930s.* Oxford: Pergamon, 1991.

Vormeier, Barbara. "La République française et les réfugiés et immigrés d'Europe centrale." In *De l'exil à la Résistance,* edited by Karol Bartosek, René Gallissot, and Denis Peschanski, 13–26. Paris: Arcantère, 1989.

Waxin, Marie. "Statut de l'étudiant étranger dans son développement historique." Law diss., Université de Paris, 1939.

Weber, Eugen. *The Hollow Years: France in the 1930s.* New York: Norton, 1994.

——. *Peasants into Frenchman.* Stanford: Stanford University Press, 1976.

Weil, Patrick. *La France et ses étrangers: l'aventure d'une politique de l'immigration, 1938–1991.* Paris: Calmann-Lévy, 1991.

——. "Georges Mauco: un itinéraire camouflé: ethnoracisme pratique et antisémitisme fielleux." In Taguieff, *L'antisémitisme de plume, 1940–1944,* 267–276.

——. "The History of French Nationality: A Lesson for Europe." In *Towards a European Nationality: Citizenship, Immigration, and Nationality Law in the EU,* edited by Randall Hansen and Patrick Weil. New York: Palgrave, 2001.

——. "Pour une politique de l'immigration juste et efficace," Rapport au Premier Ministre français Lionel Jospin, Paris, July 1997.

——. *Qu'est-ce qu'un Français? Histoire de la nationalité française depuis la Révolution.* Paris: Grasset, 2002. In English: *How to Be French: Nationality in the Making since 1789,* translated by Catherine Porter. Durham: Duke University Press, 2008.

Weil, Roland. "Le chômage de la jeunesse intellectuelle diplômée." Law diss., Université de Paris, 1937.

Weisberg, Richard. "Les avocats français face au statut des juifs de Vichy." *Archives juives* 30, no. 1 (January–June 1997): 85–95.

——. "Les maîtres du barreau: réflexions à partir des achives de Maurice Garçon." In *Le droit antisémite de Vichy,* 401–412.

——. "The Representation of Doctors at Work in Salon Art of the Early Third Republic in France." Ph.D. diss., New York University, 1995.

——. *Vichy Law and the Holocaust in France.* New York: New York University Press, 1996.

Weisz, George. "The Anatomy of the University Reform, 1863–1914." In *The Making of Frenchmen,* edited by Donald Baker and Patrick Harrigan, 363–79: Waterloo, Ont.: Historical Reflections, 1980.

——. *Divide and Conquer: A Comparative History of Medical Specialization.* New York: Oxford University Press, 2006.

——. *The Emergence of Modern Universities in France, 1863–1914.* Princeton: Princeton University Press, 1983.

———. *The Medical Mandarins: The French Academy of Medicine in the Nineteenth and Early Twentieth Centuries.* New York: Oxford University Press, 1995.

———. "Reform and Conflict in French Medical Education, 1870–1914." In *The Organization of Science and Technology in France, 1808–1914,* edited by Robert Fox and George Weisz, 61–94. Cambridge: Cambridge University Press, 1980.

———. "Regulating Specialties in France during the First Half of the Twentieth Century." *Social History of Medicine* 15, no. 3 (2002): 457–480.

———. "Les transformations de l'élite médicale en France." *Actes de la recherche en sciences sociales* 74 (September 1988): 33–47.

Weyeneth, Robert R. "The Power of Apology and the Process of Historical Reconciliation." *Public Historian* 23, no. 3 (Summer 2001): 9–38.

Wibault, Stanislas. "La vie économique de l'avocat." Law diss., Université de Paris, 1941.

Willemez, Laurent. "La 'République des avocats,' 1848: le mythe, le modèle et son endossement." In *La profession politique, XIXe–XXe siècles,* edited by Michel Offerlé, 201–229. Paris: Belin, 1999.

Wilsford, David. "The Cohesion and Fragmentation of Organized Medicine in France and the United States." *Journal of Health Politics, Policy, and Law* 12, no. 3 (Fall 1987): 481–503.

———. *Doctors and the State: The Politics of Health Care in France and in the United States.* Durham: Duke University Press, 1991.

Witz, Anne. *Professions and Patriarchy.* London: Routledge, 1992.

Yarkony, Lisa. "The Discourse of Public Health in Lyon, 1848–1914." Ph.D. diss., University of Maryland, College Park, 1997.

Yver, Colette. *Femmes d'aujourd'hui, enquête sur les nouvelles carrières féminines.* Collection nouvelles. Paris: Calmann-Lévy, 1929.

Zalc Claire. *Melting Shops: une histoire des commerçants étrangers en France.* Paris: Perrin, 2010.

Zdatny, Steven. *The Politics of Survival: Artisans in Twentieth-Century France.* New York: Oxford University Press, 1990.

Zuccotti, Susan. *The Holocaust, the French, and the Jews.* New York: BasicBooks, 1993.

Index

Note: Page numbers with a *t* indicate tables.